THE
ESSENTIAL
BENNIS

FOREWORD BY CHARLES HANDY

THE ESSENTIAL BENNIS

WARREN BENNIS

WITH PATRICIA WARD BIEDERMAN

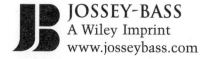

JOSSEY-BASS
A Wiley Imprint
www.josseybass.com

Published by Jossey-Bass
A Wiley Imprint
989 Market Street, San Francisco, CA 94103-1741—www.josseybass.com

Library of Congress Cataloging-in-Publication Data

Bennis, Warren G.
  The essential Bennis / Warren Bennis, with Patricia Ward Biederman ; foreword by
Charles Handy.—1st ed.
    p. cm.
  Includes bibliographical references and index.
  ISBN 978-0-470-43239-6 (cloth)
  1. Leadership. 2. Management. I. Biederman, Patricia Ward. II. Title.
  HD57.7.B4577 2009
  658.4'092—dc22

                                                          2009019775

Printed in the United States of America
FIRST EDITION
HB Printing   10 9 8 7 6 5 4 3 2

CONTENTS

To my true colleagues
who have responded so thoughtfully
to my discursionary essays

FOREWORD

By Charles Handy

I HAVE KNOWN WARREN BENNIS for more than forty years, after first meeting him in a corridor in the Sloan School of Management at MIT. I have been taught by him, have sat at his feet and listened to him, and, as important, have had him listen to me many a time down the years. We have worked together, visited often, and shared our hopes for the world and occasionally our despair. Meeting him that day at MIT changed the direction of my life, for he introduced me to the mysteries and the lure of organizations—things that until then I had just taken for granted as one of the regrettable necessities of life—and which, from that day on, became the focus of my own work. Now I have the enviable privilege of introducing this collection, this splendid retrospective of his lifetime's work.

Like all retrospectives, this one is a mixture of both life and work, particularly so in this case because Warren has the beguiling habit of mining the rich strata of his own experience for his insights and lessons. Nor is he shy of using the personal pronoun. Warren, the person, is present in all his work. It makes the work both immediately accessible and tempting to engage with. As with any retrospective exhibition, one should feel free to wander from room to room of this collection, to make a quick circuit and return for a closer study of the pieces that engaged your interest. But this retrospective has no closing date. You can visit again and again. It will be there for as long as you may need it, a vade mecum for life.

Moreover, rather like those audio guides that you find in art galleries, the curators of this retrospective, his publishers, have provided an accompanying series of commentaries on the works. The list of the authors of these commentaries reads like a roll call of the giants in the field. Here are outstanding leaders of businesses and charitable organizations, university deans and presidents, world-famous academics, political commentators, journalists, stars of screen and television. The list itself is evidence of the broad scope of Warren's work and of the esteem in which he is held.

The retrospective is divided into six rooms or sections. The unifying theme is that of leadership. It is a subject that Warren has made his own and one with which his name will, rightly, be forever twinned. The first section, however, is a personal history of his intellectual beginnings. He describes how he found his own first exemplars of leadership and then courageously sought to apply his own teaching by taking on major leadership roles in two great universities. After these two rather bruising episodes, which he discusses with almost painful honesty, he was, perhaps providentially, struck down by a near-fatal heart attack while on a visit to England.

He spent the next three months in enforced convalescence. It was a time for rethinking. In fact, he stayed during this period in our house, a thirteenth-century building, once part of the residence of King Henry III in the walls of Windsor Castle, where I happened to be working at that time. A place more removed from his accustomed habitats one can't imagine, but perhaps that very fact may have helped him as he pondered what use he should make of this new lease on life that he had been granted, and how and even where. Fate, then, in the shape of his friend, Jim O'Toole, led him to the University of Southern California, which welcomed into its midst this battle-hardened and pleasingly iconoclastic professor. He has been a distinguished and increasingly revered presence there for the last thirty years.

Those three decades have amounted to another lifetime, one that he has dedicated to the study and the elucidation of leadership, in all its varieties in a range of arenas. It was also one in which he has found his own distinctive voice, directing his words far beyond the confines of academia, often using op-ed pieces in major newspapers, articles in popular journals such as *Esquire,* or interviews on television to reach the wider fields where leaders play. Some of these pieces are included here. Many of them commanded wide attention. His article in the *Wall Street Journal* in 2007 (with Noel Tichy), just before the start of the Democratic primaries, emphasizing that judgment mattered more than experience in a leader, elicited an immediate and appreciative phone call from Barack Obama.

His writing sparkles with analogies, is enriched by historical or literary vignettes, and is studded with telling tales from real lives. He is, quite simply, great fun to read. His work is, however, always based on his interviews and meetings with current leaders. His Rolodex is star-studded with names that most people could only dream of meeting. His is no empty theorizing but the encapsulated experiences of a huge range of influential people in all spheres of life. That is his huge gift, his ability to transform experience into wisdom, and then to make it accessible to all, of every age.

Leadership, as he writes of it, is not some set of tricks to be studied and practiced, a how-to manual for the ambitious. Rather is it the all-encompassing study of the human condition. The five sections that follow the first autobiographical room show what a full curriculum that study involves. Some vision of what-might-be is essential, and Warren's essay on democracy is a perfect example of how to discern the seeds of the future in the present, even though they took over two decades to sprout. But imagination, other pieces emphasize, needs to be married to empathy if there are to be any fellow travelers on the journey to that future. Knowing oneself was held to be a precondition of success in Ancient Greece, and so it is today, but often, Warren points out, it is only fully realized in some crucible of experience.

One of my favorite essays in the collection was never published. "Leadership as a Performing Art" draws important lessons from the world of the theater. I once asked Declan Donnellan, one of Britain's leading directors, to tell me the secret of great acting. He thought for a long moment and then said "paying attention." It is, I believe, what gives an actor, or a leader, that elusive "presence," that ability to focus in on the person, the point, the audience, and all at the same time. Howard Gardner, in his piece here, makes the same point. It is a quality that Warren has in abundance, as anyone who has ever sat with him will testify.

There are more gems, more insights, and more truths to unearth as you roam through the rooms of this collection. The importance of candor and transparency in public life, the blindness and insensitivity that can accompany arrogance, the danger of drowning in other people's agendas, the proper education—or "formation" as the French call it—of leaders in business, or elsewhere for that matter, how or when to resign, all enlivened by telling insights into contemporary history. Leadership, the Bennis way, is nothing less than a full and proper preparation for life, if we want to leave even the lightest of footprints in the sands of time.

It is, therefore, hardly surprising that the undergraduate course on leadership that he still teaches annually at USC, together with Steve Sample, the university's president, is always ten times oversubscribed. Fortunate young people, to have this man so up-close and present. But Warren's warm personality comes through so clearly in his writings that, as we read, we can easily imagine ourselves sitting with him on his Santa Monica terrace, the object of his full attention, the recipient of his gathered wisdom and warm positive regard. I urge you, therefore, to wander through these virtual rooms, to read, savor, and enjoy.

THE
ESSENTIAL
BENNIS

INTRODUCTION

by Warren Bennis

FOR MOST OF MY PROFESSIONAL LIFE I have been thinking about the next essay, not the last one. So it felt a bit odd to sit down and read decades' worth of past work in putting together this collection. I was happily surprised to find that many of the essays were as evocative for me as old photos. As I reread each one, I was transported back to the era that produced it—the issues of the day, the people who filled my life, the whole rich human context was palpable again. Rereading "Learning Some Basic Truisms About Leadership," I was back in the 1970s, once again the neophyte president of the University of Cincinnati, at my desk night after night, desperately trying to learn how to lead a campus at a politically explosive moment in its history. The position was as demanding as any I have had. I learned the meaning of crisis management in Cincinnati, as I juggled problems as dissimilar as a faculty member's surprisingly controversial decision to tend his baby in his campus office and a whole-body radiation scandal in the medical school. I learned that media scrutiny makes any decision making more complicated. More important, I discovered the cost a young family pays when a parent is in a leadership role. And I learned, without wasting too many years, that I wanted to think and write about leadership far more than I wanted to run an organization.

In returning to these essays, I was reminded how much of my work has been in collaboration with others. I first learned to depend on others and how to become a worthy collaborator in the Army. We had to collaborate to survive. Later my thinking was shaped by a series of kind and brilliant mentors, beginning with Doug McGregor, whose extravagantly generous letter of recommendation smoothed my way into MIT. As a young academic in

Boston and Cambridge in the 1950s and 1960s I was part of a thrilling community in which ideas were the only currency, a world of creative collaboration that Margaret Mead dubbed a "sapiential circle." In such extraordinary communities every chance encounter triggers a tsunami of new ideas, each new colleague spurs, expands, and refines your own thinking. Since then, I have been fortunate to live the charmed life of an academic, constantly invigorated and inspired by people with fertile minds and generous spirits. Now at the University of Southern California, I am challenged and taught by students still in their teens as well as colleagues of every age and in an ever-expanding list of disciplines (today neuroscience seems to produce many of the most intriguing ideas, just as the social sciences once did). Academe is always intellectually charged and stimulating, especially now that technology allows worldwide collaboration at the speed of light. And for decades now I have had the good fortune of being able to interact with great leaders in business, public life, and other fields who have generously shared their insights and discoveries with me.

Looking over a lifetime of work, I see that certain themes have always fascinated me. Early on, I felt that bureaucracy was doomed and that something flatter and more collegial would triumph. The need for candor and transparency has been a frequent cry, because I saw how warped organizations become without them. I've long known that organizational decisions inevitably have a moral dimension. The vital role that great followers play in successful leadership has grown ever more obvious. I am increasingly aware how crucial rhetoric and other performing arts are in making a compelling leader—good or bad. That leaders are inevitably shaped by personal crucibles has been confirmed by hundreds of interviews. And it is clear to me now that the process of becoming a leader and the process of becoming a fully integrated human being are one and the same, both grounded in self-discovery.

One of the great pleasures of putting this collection together has been the wonderful commentary provided by so many friends and collaborators. Each of them did more than gloss the essays; they illuminated them by drawing on their unique experiences and expertise. Who better to comment on "The Seven Ages of the Leader" than Sidney Harman, who has lived them all and who is able to recite great swaths of poetry, including Shakespeare's, from memory. Who better to share her insights on leadership as a performing art than Glenn Close? And who is better equipped to write the foreword than Charles Handy, who, with his wife Elizabeth, nursed me back to health in Windsor Castle forty years ago? Each of the men and women whose names appear on the cover with mine have sharpened my ideas and warmed and enriched my life in countless other ways. I will always be grateful to them.

PART ONE

MY LIFE
AS A LEADER

ALMOST TWENTY YEARS AGO a colleague asked some of us who write about leadership for short autobiographies. My response was "An Invented Life: Shoe Polish, Milli Vanilli, and Sapiential Circles," which became the title essay of a 1993 collection of my pieces. This mini-memoir was an attempt at using events in my life to illuminate aspects of my work. I had earlier looked for leadership lessons, good and bad, in my own experiences in *The Leaning Ivory Tower,* published in 1973. That book deals with my short tenure as an administrator at the State University of New York as part of a team that tried, and ultimately failed, to realize its utopian academic vision. We faltered, in large part, because we forgot that no established organization is a blank slate. Trying to change organizations is fundamentally different from theorizing about organizational change. Theory sheds no blood. When you fail in the real world, the pain is palpable and often widespread. However brief, these forays into autobiography revealed one of the great joys of writing. No matter how painful the events being documented, the writing itself always has a redemptive quality. I laughed out loud when I wrote about the assault by melon ball that was the low point of my interview for the presidency of Northwestern University. As Shakespeare wrote: "All the world's a stage/And all the men and women merely players." But I've learned that what feels like a tragedy in the moment may well be a comedy.

AN INVENTED LIFE: SHOE POLISH, MILLI VANILLI, AND SAPIENTIAL CIRCLES (1993)

I recently sat down and wrote this short autobiography at the request of a colleague who had solicited similar sketches from others in the field. Writing it was one of those heartening experiences, like a successful high school reunion, in which looking back made me not nostalgic for the past but grateful for the present. As I explain in the essay, this is a version of my life—a selection of the facts that tries to illuminate the work I've done that readers are most likely to know. It is more candid than exhaustive (always desirable when people are discussing themselves, I think). And it explains such mysteries as why I hate the accordion.

○

NOT LONG AFTER I SAT DOWN to write this brief intellectual autobiography, I had a small epiphany: I realized that what I was doing was actually *biography*, imagining a narrative about someone named myself. The result is a selection of stories, some called memories, that I—and to some extent others—have created to give coherence and meaning to my life.

What I'm talking about is self-invention. Imagination. That's basically how we get to know ourselves. People who cannot invent and reinvent themselves must be content with borrowed postures, secondhand ideas, fitting in instead of standing out. Inventing oneself is the opposite of accepting the roles we were brought up to play.

This work originally appeared as the title essay in *An Invented Life: Reflections on Leadership and Change* (Basic Books, 1993).

It's much like the distinction I made in my last book, *On Becoming a Leader,* between "once-borns" and "twice-borns."[1] The once-born's transition from home and family to independence is relatively easy. Twice-borns generally suffer as they grow up; they feel different, even isolated. Unsatisfied with life as it is, they write new lives for themselves. I'm one of those twice-born.

I believe in self-invention, have to believe in it, for reasons that will soon enough be clear. To be authentic is literally to be your own author (the words derive from the same Greek root), to discover your native energies and desires, and then to find your own way of acting on them. When you've done that, you are not existing simply to live up to an image posited by the culture, family tradition, or some other authority. When you write your own life, you have played the game that was natural for you to play. You have kept covenant with your own promise.

Shoe Polish

Samuel Beckett is my favorite playwright. Among the major writers of the twentieth century, he perhaps alone understood the relative insignificance of human existence in a vast, indifferent universe. His stage settings were virtually empty, an abyss without a timepiece, a space on the cusp of a precipice. Beckett dismissed the ordinary subject matter of the theater—social relations, struggles for power, and the like—as diversions masking the anguish and despair that are the essential human condition. Instead he asked bleak, existential questions: How do we come to terms with the fact that, without having asked for it, we have been thrown into being? And who are we? What does it mean when we say "I"?

In the 1958 play *Krapp's Last Tape,* Beckett continues his lifelong exploration of the mystery of self. An old man listens to the confessions he recorded in earlier years. To the old Krapp, the voice of the younger Krapp is sometimes that of a total stranger. In what sense, then, can the two Krapps be regarded as the same human being? In this essay I will try to bring the younger Bennis into some uneasy connection with the older one. But don't forget: I'm writing about a person who invented himself.

As I see it now, the landscape of my childhood was very like a Beckett stage set—barren, meager, endless. A little boy waited there for someone who might not, probably would not, show up. There were walk-ons occasionally: twin brothers ten years my senior, a father who worked eighteen hours a day (when he took off his shoes and soiled socks, the ring of dirt around his ankles had to be scrubbed off with a stiff-bristled brush), and a mother who liked vaudeville and played mah-jongg with her friends when she wasn't helping my father eke out an existence.

I was withdrawn, sullen, detached, removed from hope or desire, and probably depressed—"mopey," my father called it. I was also left pretty much alone. I had no close friends. I can't remember how I spent my time, except I know that I made up improved versions of my life that ran like twenty-four-hour newsreels in my mind.

I didn't much like school, and barely remember most of my teachers. Except for Miss Shirer. I liked Miss Shirer enormously. She taught the eighth grade, and she was almost famous because her older brother, William Shirer, was broadcasting from Berlin on CBS. I leaned into the radio whenever Shirer was on. That he was anti-Hitler was thrilling to a kid who, in 1938, often felt like the only Jew in Westwood, New Jersey, a town that richly deserved its reputation as a major stronghold of the German Bund.

On one psychically momentous occasion, Miss Shirer asked us to spend about ten minutes telling the class about our favorite hobby. I panicked. After all, I liked Miss Shirer a lot, but the truth was that I didn't have anything remotely like a favorite hobby. My efforts to develop recreational interests like those of the other guys had failed miserably. I was mediocre at sports. I was bored with stamps. I was too clumsy to tie dry flies, too nervous to hunt, too maladroit to build model airplanes out of balsa wood. What I finally decided to do, in a moment of desperate inspiration, was to bring a shoe box full of shoe polish, different colors and shades in cans and bottles, since the only palpable physical activity I regularly engaged in was shining the family shoes.

And so when it was my turn in the spotlight, I revealed the arcane nature of a new art form. I described in loving detail the nuances of my palette (I was especially good on the subtle differences between oxblood and maroon). I discoursed on the form and function of the various appliances needed to achieve an impressive tone and sheen. I argued both sides of the debate on solid versus liquid wax and wrapped it all up with a spirited disquisition on the multiple virtues of neat's-foot oil. It was a remarkable performance, if only because it was, from start to finish, an act of pure imagination. I could tell from her smile that Miss Shirer thought it was terrific. Even the class seemed impressed in a stupefied way. And there, in a flourish of brushes and shoe polish, a new Warren Bennis was born.

You should know a few other things about me before we draw any conclusions about my intellectual or academic contributions. My favorite essayist, Isaiah Berlin, once remarked that his reputation was based on systematic overestimation of his abilities. ("Long may this continue," he added merrily.) Over three decades I have written a great deal. A small portion of that work has had a life outside the pages of the journals in which it originally appeared. The most enduring examples are the work on planned change, the study of the stages of groups, the essay on the inevitability of democracy that almost miraculously came true twenty-six years after it was written, and the more recent work on leadership, particularly the ongoing analysis of why leaders can't lead. I am proud of that body of work, some written with distinguished colleagues. But there are moments when I look back and have my doubts. Where is the irrefutable masterpiece, the systematic application, the great theoretical treatise? When I think about the achievements of some of my peers, I sense a depth and continuity that is majestically alien to my own.

In an essay on Tolstoy, Berlin notes the distinction Tolstoy makes between foxes and hedgehogs. Foxes know many things of various degrees of importance, while hedgehogs know one big thing. Foxes are conceptualists. While the critics are fussing about the latest vulpine theory, the fox is already working on the next one. Hedgehogs, at their best, produce Darwins; at their worst, pedants. Foxes occasionally can claim an Einstein or an Oppenheimer but more often are simply dilettantes. I'm clearly a fox with a sneaking admiration for the hedgehog.

There's another aspect of my intellectual development that can't be dismissed: that is empathy and the role it has played in both my temperament and my work. I think the ability to read and respond to others has to do with my Jewishness and the sense of marginality that goes with it. Minorities have to be good at picking up subtle cues of rejection. Our moral radar is always switched on, ready to detect what is and what is not acceptable to the majority community. As Lionel Trilling once said, this enables us to understand the mind of the enemy. But Trilling also felt, as did Berlin and as do I, that empathy, or at least that part of it that involves eternal vigilance—the stethoscope always probing for danger—can also undermine one's critical abilities. There is what Berlin called the "fatal desire to please." Over the years I've come to value the ambivalent gift of empathy, but it did lead me, earlier on, to work on projects that a friend once described as "good boy" work—solid books of readings that cited everyone and his or her colleagues and left no idea unturned or fully developed.

Arthur Lovejoy, the historian of ideas, once wrote that every writer possesses, and often tries to hide, his or her distinctive "metaphysical pathos," those subterranean, often unconscious impulses and values that govern our choice of intellectual work. My way of putting it would be less metaphysical and abstract, although it makes the same point. It seems to me that the issues we select to study are almost always the underground churnings of unresolved conflicts—that our ideas stem from an attempt to solve our existential predicaments and that the unlikely force behind all rational problem solving is the need to quiet our demons. (We are all children of our time, and, needless to say, mine includes the golden age of psychoanalysis.)

These, then, are some of the early forces that shaped me:

○ A family structured like a double helix, my brothers, bonded in unimaginable ways, in one strand, and a mother and father who rarely connected, in the other. I felt outside this structure, almost invisible, a non-participant observer. Growing up in a Jewish family in a gentile community, I rejected both. Talk about marginal.

○ A search for power and potency born out of what I perceived as an unsuccessful father, who, prodded by my mother, moved from town to town, opening and soon closing a series of candy stores, malt shops, and soda stands. Like so many of my depression-era generation, I remember the day my father lost his last regular job as one of the most wretched and despondent of my life. Without realizing it then, I vowed never again to feel such utter hopelessness. Understandably, given the disappointments of his own working life, my father kept urging me to learn a trade, by which he meant carpentry or printing or tailoring. My mother, whose unrelenting forcefulness frightened me even more than my father's passivity, thought I should be a child movie star, on the order of Bobby Breen, who sang, on the brink of adolescence, like a castrated cantor. Recognizing that my voice was at best croaky and had a range of about half an octave, she insisted that I take ten accordion lessons from Pietro Agostino of Hackensack, New Jersey, sincerely believing that what my voice lacked, the 120 bass Hohner accordion could easily redeem. I did finally master "The Sharpshooters' March" and "Over the Waves." But even the professionally optimistic Pietro Agostino, who probably needed the $1.50 an hour I paid for my lesson and claimed to admire my "drive" (I schlepped the accordion on the Rockland County bus, ten miles from Westwood and back again, twice a week), felt that I lacked what he charitably described to my mother as "touch." Go figure.

○ A terrible sense of uncertainty, which may be the human condition for non–grown-up humans. My only early certitudes were my ability to observe and an insatiable hunger to learn. The latter arose not out of anything as neutral as curiosity but because I needed the illusion of understanding in order to feel safe. After the shoe polish affair, I developed a growing sense of the power of the imagination, which may be the only real power children have.

I emerged from boyhood sure of only two things: that I never wanted to get on another bus carrying an accordion and that I didn't want to grow up to be like the people I already knew. It was almost time to invent a life of my own.

The U.S. Army: 1943–1947

The Army Specialized Training Program, better known as ASTP, beckoned. To qualify you had to pass a physical and demonstrate an IQ of 125 or so. Camp Hood, Texas (now Fort Hood), was the venue for its seventeen weeks of basic training. Following my stint at Camp Hood, I was shipped to UCLA for the collegiate portion of my army career. The army had no trouble matching my many incompetencies with a career track: I was assigned to major in "sanitary engineering." Fortunately, ASTP was dismantled in order to prepare for the D-day invasion of Normandy. And I was sent to Fort Benning, Georgia, to attend the infantry school there.

The so-called Benning School for Boys was the best-possible education for combat. If education is supposed to prepare you for what you will confront in real life, then the training there was near perfect. German villages and cities were reproduced on the base, and we were drilled in what we were likely to encounter as the Germans desperately resisted the end of the war. While it's fair to say no one is ever truly prepared for combat, Fort Benning came pretty damned close.

In 1944 I was commissioned as a second lieutenant and sent almost immediately to the European theater of operations, first as a platoon commander and later as a company commander. I was nineteen. (Later I learned I had been the youngest infantry officer in the ETO.) The company I joined had been savaged during the Battle of the Bulge. Out of 189 men and six officers, the normal size of an infantry company, only 60 men and two officers remained. One of the two, Claude Williams, had graduated from Benning just two months before I did. The other, the CO, Captain Bessinger, had in civilian life been the caretaker of the Vanderbilt mansion in Asheville, North Carolina. He was old, I thought, almost thirty-five, and half deaf because of the incessant roar of German antitank guns. He was also one of the finest leaders I've ever met.

. . . I had first become interested in leadership watching my twin brothers, one of whom effortlessly initiated activities that attracted other kids (including a rather tame teenage gang), while the other couldn't influence his way into a stickball game. My army experience affirmed my lifelong interest in the topic.

In the army I saw firsthand the consequences of good and bad leadership in the simplest and starkest terms—morale, tank support that would or would not be where it was supposed to be, wounds, body counts. The army was the first organization I was to observe close-up and in-depth. And although I have been in pleasanter classrooms, it was an excellent place to study such organizational realities as the effects of command-and-control leadership and the paralyzing impact of institutional bureaucracy.

Captain Bessinger was a wonder. Despite his poor hearing, he really listened to the men, inspired them, and protected them from the whims of the brass. In every way Bessinger embodied what Doug McGregor, my mentor later in college, immortalized as a "Theory Y" orientation. Bessinger was also my first role model, although I didn't know that phrase then and even now the banality of the term doesn't do justice to the man. A high school dropout, Bessinger literally kept me alive. He taught me how to identify different kinds of German artillery by their sound. He taught me how and when to duck. He also had a quality I deeply respect but have never been able to emulate—the courage to be patient.

After a month or so in combat, I became weakly confident that I wasn't going to bolt or go nuts (I was less sure I wasn't going to die). And in the time-honored army fashion, I began grumbling about the conditions we were fighting in. We had inadequate air cover and tank support, incompetent "forward observers" from the artillery, delays in getting reserves, unspeakable rations, and so on. Each day my voice would grow more strident, and each day Captain Bessinger would chew his tobacco and listen, with less and less of his legendary patience. One day (only a few weeks before the war ended, as it happened) I blurted out, "I, for one, don't know how the hell we're going to win this f—-ing war unless. . . ." Finally, the captain spat out his plug of Red Man, looked at me through sad, beagle eyes, and said, "Shit, kid, they've got an army too."

Bessinger had given me exactly the useful truth I needed. The Germans did have an army, an army composed largely of hungry fourteen- and fifteen-year-old kids, shooting wooden bullets because they had run out of metal casings (the wooden bullets exploded hideously on contact). They were even more frightened than I was and had to contend with a bureaucracy that was at least as bad.

I wonder how much that story conveys to someone who wasn't there. The army in wartime was an organization, unlike most I've studied since, in which miscommunications and errors in judgment could kill you. I was a teenager, desperately trying to make sufficient sense of the general chaos to stay alive, and along came a person who listened, as empathically as possible, and who, despite coming from a totally different culture from my own, was able to transcend age, rank, and ethnic and religious background to help me cope with our mutual dilemma. Bessinger, whom I haven't seen since he was wounded in 1945, wasn't just a leader, he was the kind of leader you read about in the Bible.

I came very close to signing up for a career in the army once the war ended. My division, the Sixty-third, was dismantled, and I was eventually sent to European headquarters in Frankfurt, where I served in the transportation corps. I had a Jeep and a driver, an apartment in the Frankfurt compound, and membership in the officer's club. I was twenty. The army had already served me well, if only by giving me an honorable way to leave my family. It had taught me self-reliance and the extraordinary power that comes of being organized and using your time efficiently. Frankfurt was a kind of finishing school. I learned what fork to use and how dry a martini should be. I took weekend trips to Luxembourg City, Wengen, Switzerland, and Bad Homburg with a sweet "older woman" (she was going on twenty-six), a captain in the WACS. Among the heady things she taught me was how to eat an artichoke.

The main reason I didn't sign up for an army career was that my runner, Gunnar, had beguiled me with stories about the college he had been attending before the war. He loved the school, located in bucolic-sounding Yellow Springs, Ohio, in large measure because it allowed him to work part of the year and attend classes the rest of the time. The college had a strange name: Antioch.

Gunnar told me he wanted to become a clinical psychologist, and he had already worked for the Psychological Corporation, validating tests, and in the personnel department of Macy's, testing job applicants. He said that the courses he had taken had prepared him for the jobs and that the jobs had enhanced his classroom experience. I was fascinated by Gunnar's tales of Antioch. No one in my entire family had gone to college—no one. But Antioch intrigued me, and I figured I could afford it, given both the GI Bill and the co-op job system.

Gunnar was killed by an errant canister of white phosphorus on the last day of fighting in the town of Budesheim, Germany. And I, after serving two more years in Europe, was accepted as a freshman at Antioch.

Antioch College: 1947–1951

I took the train to Antioch. (It actually stopped at Springfield, and I hitchhiked the last ten miles to Yellow Springs.) As we neared my destination, my seatmate couldn't resist asking me why I wanted to go to a "Commie school," with its "nigger-lovers, pinkos, and people who believe in free love." (What, I have wondered ever since, is the opposite of free love—expensive love?)

Antioch was progressive. Even then we called it "politically correct," although without the ironic tone we use today. In many ways it was an ideal community. The campus heroes were intellectuals. There were no Greek societies or social clubs. People of color were celebrated, the Young Communist League and followers of Henry Wallace were taken seriously, and the talk was ferocious, utopian, and unending.

But for all its commitment to diversity and independent thought, Antioch had a definite subculture, an unwritten Antioch way. We ordered our organically grown wheat from Deaf (pronounced Deef) County, Texas; our Telemann from Sam Goody in New York; and Dwight Mac-Donald's *Politics* and *The Nation* from Greenwich Village. The books we read were Erich Fromm's *Escape from Freedom*, Bertrand Wolfe's *Three Who Made a Revolution*, Edmund Wilson's *To the Finland Station* and *Axel's Castle*, Marquis Child's *Sweden: The Third Way*, Djuna Barnes's *Nightwood*, Malcolm Lowrey's *Under the Volcano* (we all knew that it was his one and only novel and that he had died too young from booze), T. S. Eliot's *The Cocktail Party,* and the complete works of Thomas Mann, Hemingway, Fitzgerald, Dos Passos, Ford Madox Ford, and Virginia Woolf. We uniformly vilified the literary upstarts: Norman Mailer, Irwin Shaw, Herman Wouk, and James Jones.

The army taught me the value of being organized. At Antioch I learned to have opinions. That may not sound very important, but it amounted to a personal paradigm shift. Before college, I had been like Olenka in Chekhov's story "The Darling." Olenka, Chekhov writes, "saw the objects about her and understood what was going on, but she could not form an opinion about anything and did not know what to talk about. You see, for instance, a bottle, or the rain, or a peasant driving his cart, but what the bottle is for, or the rain, or the peasant, and what is the meaning of it, you can't say, and could not even for a thousand rubles."

What freedom, what liberation, to have opinions, sometimes based on reason and evidence, sometimes based on nothing more than the liberal campus zeitgeist. There were times at Antioch when a particular politically correct opinion would run through the entire population like a flu epidemic (vegetarianism and the superiority of home weaving were two I recall). But all the same, having opinions was, at least for me, tantamount to developing a personal identity.

Later on, as I became a nimbler, more seasoned Antiochian, I developed a whole set of counteropinions. I began tweaking, sometimes reviling, the campus's more doctrinaire positions in a series of pseudonymous satires in the college literary magazine, writing under the name Dr. Gruppen Aus-gefundener (Dr. Group Finder-Outer). The satires caused George Geiger, our venerable professor of philosophy, to compare me with S. J. Perelman (what a coup!) and made just about everybody look at me differently.

As a result, I was "tapped" (informally, of course) by the campus intellectuals, despite my philistine interest in social psychology and economics. The cognoscenti were easy to spot at Antioch. They wore army fatigues (the women especially); smoked Camels in long black cigarette holders; drank beer at night at Com's, a black bar in town; listened with closed eyes to Johnny Coltrane keening on the jukebox; played esoteric games like Botticelli; regularly threatened to transfer to Columbia or Chicago; and constantly said "fug," emulating James Jones's queer contraction in *From Here to Eternity,* a book everyone claimed to loathe. I trembled with delight when I was invited to join them at Com's.

Henry Broude was one of the Brahmins, then a senior (I was a junior, or, as we, finding all labels of rank offensive, said, "a third-year student"). He was Waldemar Carlson's teaching assistant in Fiscal Policy, which introduced me to Keynes. Henry, now a distinguished economist at Yale, probably doesn't remember this, but after he read my term paper for the course, he said I might want to consider graduate school and mentioned in particular Harvard or MIT. The Nobel laureate James Franck once said that he always knew when he had heard a good idea because of the feeling of terror that seized him. I was seized.

There were at least three other things that influenced me during those Antioch years. First was the famous co-op program, pioneered by one of the college's great presidents, Arthur Morgan, an engineer who was Roosevelt's first head of the Tennessee Valley Authority. Antioch's program was mandatory, complex, and extraordinary. You came to campus for eight weeks; then, with the counsel of an adviser, decided on a job somewhere in the world—usually a fairly large urban center—and worked for twelve weeks; then returned to campus for sixteen weeks. It normally took five years to finish Antioch decades before that became the national norm. I did it in four because, in classic Antioch fashion, I got co-op credit for my four years in the army.

Splicing classroom experience with real-world work was a wonderful way to explore the relationship or lack thereof between theory and practice, word and act, those who make history and those who study it. There was an exquisite tension between the idealistic tilting at windmills that went on on campus and the inevitable compromises of the workplace.

Second, Antioch forced me to confront, for the first of innumerable times, both my desire to achieve personal satisfaction and the often conflicting urge to live up to the motto of Antioch's founding president, Horace Mann: "Be ashamed to die until you have won some victory for humanity." That tension between self-expression and civic responsibility continues to trouble me, perhaps even more now than it did then.

Third, Antioch deserves credit for teaching me to beware of totalized explanations of life and other mysteries. Despite the campus's sometimes unfortunate tendency toward groupthink, there were so many competing ideas poking at you that you couldn't help developing healthy skepticism about commissars of thought. The quest for a Parnassian truth, a rule or rules for everything, was what my heart wanted but my mind rejected. The Spanish film director Luis Buñuel used to say, "I would give my life for a man who is looking for the truth, but I would gladly kill a man who thinks he has found the truth." Although there were a few "true believers" on the faculty, most of the professors were skeptics with little patience for universal systems. Certainly the great lesson of the first half of the twentieth century has been that overarching systems or theories that eliminate the opportunity for independent thought lead to totalitarianism. We had experienced the savagery of Nazism, the horrors of Stalinism, the limits of Marxism and Freudianism. We were sufficiently adolescent to continue to seek the grail of grails. But we also knew, in our disappointed hearts, that the Truth could be fatal to millions.

But my most important influence at Antioch by far was its president, Doug McGregor. He came there in 1948 at the age of forty-two, open, broad-grinned, and tweedy from MIT, where he had started an industrial psychology department. I don't think there was a search committee in those days, or else Arthur Morgan simply ignored it. Morgan visited McGregor at MIT, liked him enormously, and asked him to become college president.

Doug was at Antioch for six years and turned the school on its head. At his very first assembly, he announced, while our collective jaws dropped, that he valued his four years in analysis more than his four years as an undergraduate, that he hadn't the faintest idea what the students or faculty wanted, and that maybe the campus should shut down for a week while we had some "goal discussions" in small groups. Soon after, goal discussions were initiated (much to the consternation of the Brahmins, who thought they amounted to "pooling ignorance"). Those sessions redefined our collective aspirations, focused our vision for our education, and constituted a superb example of how change is facilitated by involving those who will be most affected.

In a foreword to a book of Doug's essays, published after his death at the tragically early age of fifty-nine, I described Doug as "a born innovator, a born experimenter. He refused to accept what was, or the traditional, uncritically, and it may be that his greatest and most permanent achievement was to create an atmosphere in which students, as well as faculty, were stimulated to question and challenge continually in an effort to create an educational program that had a relationship to the whole life of the individual. . . . If there was anything he was trying to overcome or destroy, it was the institutional habit of talking about the virtue of democracy while running affairs autocratically."

By the time Doug returned to MIT in 1954 to start a new program in organizational studies, he had already laid the groundwork for what today is called organizational behavior, human relations, or personnel management. As Mason Haire, one of his colleagues at MIT in the 1940s, pointed out, Doug created much of the professional field in which he operated: "Much of the work that goes on now couldn't have happened if he had never been."

If Captain Bessinger saved my life, Doug McGregor surely shaped it. In my final year at Antioch, I took a tutorial with him on "superior-subordinate relationships and leadership" and several courses on group dynamics, taught by his MIT colleague, the maverick psychologist Irvin Knickerbocker.

I liked everything about Doug and tried to be like him in every conceivable way. I started smoking a pipe, tried to dress the way he did (though I was a 38 short and he was at least a 42 long), and applied to MIT for graduate work, although I had little idea what it would entail or even that it would funnel and focus my later choices. The truth is that I wouldn't have gotten into MIT without his recommendation; nor would I have gotten tenure there without his full-throated endorsement (he threatened to quit if it wasn't granted unanimously); nor would I have sought a university presidency; nor, in short, would my life have taken the direction it has.

In a recent interview a British journalist, David Oates, talks about my dissociation of myself from my family and quotes me as saying, "I was brazen in getting teachers at school to make me the favorite son. I kept being adopted by intellectual father figures and was shameless at sucking up to mentors." Sounds awful, doesn't it? The phrase "sucking up" is appalling, I know. Without repudiating that confession, I'd like to reframe it: I did cultivate major figures in my field—Doug McGregor, Carl Rogers, Abe Maslow, Erik Erikson, Peter Drucker, and others. While I was not unmindful of what their patronage might mean professionally, the truth is that I couldn't resist the power of their ideas and their personalities. I was so drawn to genius, perhaps, because I felt so ordinary myself.

MIT and Milli Vanilli: 1951–1956

MIT was as different from Antioch as Cambridge from Yellow Springs. My straight-A performance at Antioch and Doug's three-page letter of recommendation were the sole reasons I was admitted to the MIT Economics Department. In college I had taken algebra and introductory physics, and that was about it. Most of my new MIT classmates had taken advanced calculus, knew at least the rudiments of set theory, understood Markov chains, and had mastered Boolean algebra. At my first interview, the then-admissions officer, economist Charles P. Kindleberger, outlined the courses I'd have to take to catch up and confessed, "We didn't exactly throw our hats in the air when we saw your application." It was a daunting revelation.

MIT was a confusing cocktail of makeup mathematics; philosophy of science; microeconomics from a great teacher, Bob Bishop; more economics from a great mind, Paul Samuelson; industrial statistics from Bob Solow; consumer economics from Franco Modigliani; and economic history from Walt Rostow (my only honest A). A pop quiz: Three of the above are Nobel laureates. Who are they? (Answer on page 33.)

But there were also George Shultz, who taught labor economics, and Alex Bavelas, who was the most brilliant designer of small-group experiments who ever lived. And then there was another early mentor, the most playful professor during my MIT days, Herb Shepard, who taught me that groups are real, even if they don't have spinal cords, and introduced me to Harry Stack Sullivan, Karen Horney, Erving Goffman, Norbert Wiener, L. J. Henderson, Elton Mayo, Walter Cannon, and a raft of people who were developing networks—not the human networks I was familiar with but electronic ones. In other words, a raft of people who were inventing the present day.

What a dazzling group! I was sometimes befuddled, routinely intimidated, and thoroughly outclassed by these new colleagues of mine, including my fellow graduate students (there were no women in the department then, and the only minority group was Canadians). It is probably true that I was the least prepared, the least mathematically inclined (Samuelson put it charitably when he said I lacked "mathematical flair"), and the only one who really wondered why he was there. The painful truth is that in Samuelson's seminar, whenever he was summing up, saying something like, "Well, that's the theory of duopoly," he would look over at me and ask, "Warren, are you with me?" If I nodded yes, he knew he was free to go on to the next unfathomable point (perhaps the Stackleburg point!), certain that everyone else in the class had got it hours before.

To get through the Ph.D. program, a sometimes uneasy amalgam of economic theory and social science, I began to memorize and mimic. I don't think I really understood what the Walrasian General Theory of Equilibrium was all about, but I was perfectly capable of memorizing the equations. I imitated my professors and the brightest of my fellow graduate students. For roughly two years I lip-synced what I heard, Milli Vanilli style. Eventually the words I formed on my lips came more naturally, but I often wondered whether I was kidding myself and should try my hand at something else (tailoring, Dad?).

Perhaps most of us learn through a form of lip-syncing, but I often found the process terribly confusing. Sometimes I would identify with Herb Shepard, cuddly, empathic, and warm, and at other times with Bob Solow, Brooklyn-tough, caustic, and wonderfully lucid. Sometimes my model was Talcott Parsons, who taught sociology at Harvard (I took up to half my social science courses at Harvard under an agreement between MIT and Harvard that may still be in effect today) and was unfathomable in ways that Samuelson couldn't dream of. Parsons was a Weberian sociologist prone to neologisms whom the graduate students dubbed "Talk-a-Lot" Parsons in our Christmas play. Sometimes my model was Alex Bavelas, with his Gretsky-like touch in setting up small-group experiments, so subtle and brilliant and utterly charming.

I lip-synced all of them. When I began teaching undergraduates, I didn't always know who I'd be that day or what I would sound like. On some days I thought of myself as a total fraud. Especially the day I bought an expensive, nonrequired book on microeconomics at the Harvard Coop after Paul Samuelson had casually mentioned it in class. Written by Stanford professor Tibor Scitovsky, it was called *Competition among the Few*. It cost $5.95 (the rent on my small apartment on Gray Street was only $9.00 a week), and when I handed the clerk my Coop credit card, I became woozy with self-doubt. What was I doing, lip-syncing idols and going broke buying books I could hardly understand?

After completing my thesis in less than a year and a half—something of a miracle, given my state of mind—I taught social psychology for one year (1955–1956) as an assistant professor and then left because the department had a policy against hiring its own until they had taught elsewhere for at least five years.

Actually, I was glad to leave. I still couldn't pass Paul Samuelson in the corridor without stammering over his first name, and I had begun to suspect that the MIT approach to truth, mathematical and quantitative, was not only beyond me but limited as well. Logical positivism had stormed the social sciences in the 1950s with its belief that all certifiable truths about human behavior could be predicted with scientific certainty. I wasn't sure about that then and am even more dubious about it today. However meticulously obtained, facts are rarely unassailable. And I was tired of fighting my natural impulse, revealed as long ago as Miss Shirer's eighth-grade class, to poeticize the materials at hand and give them a distinctive shape.

The thing I feared most, even beyond incompetence (which I thought about constantly), was that I would become an anemic heir to the majestic but alien minds of my teachers. And I was terribly tired of moving my lips to someone else's tune.

Bethel, Boston, and Sapiential Circles: 1955–1967

Life picked up steam that last year at MIT. It's a jumble of memories now, but a nascent career seemed to be taking shape. A career as what was less obvious. While officially my degree was in economics, I knew in my heart I was a generalist. At Cambridge dinner parties, where one's discipline was an identity card, I sometimes blushed when I described myself as an economist. Often I would simply say that I taught at MIT and a respectful hush would fall over the group, as if those letters sufficed for station identification.

The lack of a clear-cut professional identity had its advantages. I was an inkblot on which others could project their needs. Once, for instance, the editor of a mildly radical journal published at Brandeis called and asked if I would join the editorial board. I did so gladly. Later the editor, Lew Coser, told me that the key reason for the invitation was that the journal needed a gentile on its masthead and thought one from MIT would look especially good. Actually, I enjoyed the editing involved, but, more important, our editorial board meetings put me in touch with a group of scholars more interested in ideas than in their measurement—people like Coser and his wife, Rose; Kurt Wolff; and Mary Stein. My Brandeis circle thought of me as an economist, whereas at MIT I was generally regarded as a social psychologist. Not having to be pinned down was fine with me.

In 1955 I was invited to Bethel, Maine, the summer headquarters of the National Training Laboratories. At Bethel, as we all called it, everyone was buzzing about a new social invention called T-groups (the T stood for training). Established in 1947 by the redoubtable refugee psychologist

Kurt Lewin, NTL crackled with intellectual energy and the heady sense that some major discovery about the real nature of groups was taking place.

Bethel was singularly fortunate in having three genuine social revolutionaries on hand to help it weather Lewin's tragically premature death at the age of forty-seven. Ronald Lippitt, Kenneth Benne, and Leland Bradford each brought their own special gifts to bear. A distinguished young social psychologist, Ron Lippitt contributed intellectual rigor and methodological sophistication. No one could articulate the extraordinary spirit of the place better than Ken Benne, Bethel's resident philosopher. He was a dazzling intellectual "fox" who has taught me much. And holding it all together was Lee Bradford, who was both a visionary and a first-rate manager, a man who continued to dream even as he kept an institution full of dreamers running smoothly.

Leading a T-group at Bethel was a wild, exhilarating experience—"a trip," as the nation would begin to say a decade later. For a period of two weeks a group of strangers was brought together and asked to leave behind the roles, constraints, and norms of everyday life. People screamed, people guffawed, people wept, people talked: You never knew what would happen next. In the micro-utopias of Bethel, I discovered what life could be like when the usual mechanisms that govern our quotidian lives are absent. As the group developed and evolved, I saw how we search for structure and support and how we recoil from some individuals and align ourselves with others. I also realized how deeply our attitudes toward authority are buried and how stubborn they are.

In the supercharged atmosphere I was sometimes overwhelmed by what I saw and felt. When a group really came together, when the communication was free and telling and truthful, you could practically feel the bonds between us expanding and deepening like the intertwined roots of enormous trees. Once in a while I felt that our bodies were somehow actually joined, like those of Siamese twins, so that the emotions circulated between the members of the group, creating some superior new social organism. It was heady stuff that made what took place in the typical academic small-group lab look as drab as a black-and-white movie.

Later that year Herb Shepard and I wrote two articles on "natural groups" in which we described the stages of group growth that I had experienced so vividly at Bethel. The articles were published back to back—an unusual move—in *Human Relations,* then the most prestigious journal in social psychology. No mention was made, needless to say, of merging roots or Siamese twins.

Although I was unaware of it at the time, it seems clear to me now that the study of group dynamics that flourished after World War II was as much a response to the recent past as a leap into the future. And in large part, I now believe, it was a reaction to Hitler.

At least two of the giants in the field, Kurt Lewin and Fritz Redl, were Jewish refugees from Hitler's reign of terror. It seems almost inevitable that they would have developed a profound faith in democratic groups, given their firsthand experience of the destructive power of charismatic leaders, including their ability to enslave their followers. Lewin's early experiments, as well as those of his students, seem now almost fore-ordained to demonstrate that democratic groups are not only more ful-filled psychologically but more efficient, especially under complex and changing conditions. The theory that democratic groups are superior struck a sympathetic chord with a whole generation that had heard the ominous roar of a nondemocratic group cheering Hitler at Nuremberg.

Interestingly, those Americans who were drawn to Kurt Lewin's theo-ries were almost all Midwestern populists with a homegrown antiau-thoritarian tradition of their own. I'm referring to Bradford, Benne, and Lippitt, of course, but also to Herb Thelen, Ren Likert, Doug McGregor, and many others. In that postwar period social scientists and related researchers, myself included, tended to view all authority with deep-seated skepticism, if not suspicion. We adopted much the same stance toward leaders that Baudelaire took toward newspapers: that you might learn from them if you read them with the proper contempt.

The three years between the time I left MIT and returned there in 1959 were spent teaching at Boston University. I worked mainly with Ken Benne and Bob Chin, as well as with the head of BU's Psychology Department, Nathan Maccoby. I also taught at Harvard with Freed Bales, Phil Slater, and Ted Mills and did research on groups with Will Schutz and Tim Leary (both at Harvard in the antediluvian age before Esalen and LSD, respec-tively) and with the psychoanalyst Elvin Semrad at what was irreverently called Boston Psycho.

At that time I was also undergoing six years of psychoanalysis with a Boston-trained analyst. That means, for those of you uninitiated in the ther-apeutic and intellectual folklore of the 1950s, a real, orthodox Freudian analysis. My analyst changed the pillow case for each analysand, every fifty-minute hour.

That was a rich, tumultuous, enchanting time in my life. Only my mother seemed unwowed by all I was experiencing. I remember telling her in 1959 that I had been psychoanalyzed. I sensed that she didn't like the thought of me untangling my psyche in the presence of a non-Bennis, but her only response was to ask how much I had paid the doctor. I told her—$3.00 an hour for the first three years, $15.00 an hour after that. "And you went how often?" she asked. I told her—five days a week for the first three years and four days a week for the next three. She was silent for several minutes and then said, "Hmmm . . . that comes to quite a bit of money." Another pause, and she said, "Son, I wish you had taken that money and spent it on yourself."

In 1959 Doug McGregor invited me to return to MIT, where he was heading up a department in the new Sloan School of Management. He had already recruited a formidable team: Don Marquis and Ed Schein, in particular, and later Bill Evan, Per Soelberg, Tom Allen, Mason Haire, Harry Levinson, Bob Kahn, Dave Berlew, and Fritz Steele.

Those years at BU and MIT were my best in academic terms. My output was prodigious—everything from tightly designed experiments in small-group communications to psychoanalytic exegeses of the schism between C. P. Snow's "Two Cultures." With Benne and Chin I produced my first book, a selection of readings titled *The Planning of Change* (1961). I also did another book of readings in interpersonal dynamics, in collaboration with Ed Schein, Dave Berlew, and Fritz Steele.

Both books eventually went into four editions, but even more thrilling than their success was the experience of working as part of an intellectual team. Sometimes when a group of talented people comes together, even if only for a short time, something wonderful happens. Each individual energizes the others, teaches them and learns as well. When everything goes right, this creative collaboration produces something new and important. Twenty-five years ago I mentioned this phenomenon—which has led to such diverse achievements as the Bauhaus School and the atom bomb—to Margaret Mead, who was giving a speech at Harvard. I asked her whether much had been written about it. She said no. "You write about it," she said. "And call the book *Sapiential Circles*." And that, finally, is what I am doing now.

SUNY Buffalo: 1967–1971

I made the pilgrimage to Buffalo, as did many others, largely under the spell of Martin Meyerson's bold dreams and blandishments. I visited the western New York campus, and later, in my Beacon Hill home in Boston, I asked Martin what his own goal for Buffalo was. Always thoughtful, he hesitated a moment and said, "To make it a university where I would like to stay and be a professor after finishing my administrative responsibilities."

Over the next six weeks I spent most of my time trying to decide whether or not I should leave Boston for Meyerson's grand experiment on the shores of Lake Erie. It was an excruciating period, made even more tense by the fact that my wife had had a miscarriage after her first trip to Buffalo and had to spend most of the time in bed. My memory of that late-winter trip to Buffalo is one of exhaustion. And God, was it cold! As I walked down the roll-away stairs into the white swirl of the runway at Buffalo International Airport, all I could think of was someone's bitchy observation that summer in Buffalo was three weeks of bad ice-skating. (Actually, summers there are lovely—as summers are only in places where you fully understand the alternative.)

My colleagues at the Sloan School were unsympathetic when I announced I was considering an offer to be provost at the State University of New York at Buffalo. Their attitude toward administrative jobs at any university bordered on contempt. "God," one asked, "why do you want to spend your time shuffling papers?" And then, of course, there were the snowblower jokes. It was difficult to explain to them what I was going through, but now I realize it was a genuine crisis. I was haunted, almost obsessed, by the need not just to teach and research management and leadership but to experience it firsthand. I wanted, as Shakespeare put it, to know "a hawk from a handsaw."

I turned to everyone I could think of for advice. I remember calling David Riesman at Harvard one day early in March 1967. He had taught at the law school at Buffalo when it was still a private university and was advising Meyerson on social science matters. David gave me a realistic assessment of the academic state of the university (many mediocre departments; some first-rate ones, including the quirky, creative English Department). He also put in a perversely good word for the industrial landscape, with its "chartreuse and black and mauve smoke against the steel-gray sky."

Still perplexed, I approached a friend at the Harvard Business School who studied mathematical models of decision making. He said he had once been in a similar position and had gone to his dean for advice. "Why don't you work it out mathematically?" the dean asked him. My friend howled when he recalled his indignant response: "But this is important!"

Meyerson kept up his dignified campaign of persuasion. His great gift as a recruiter was his ability to transmogrify all the highly visible drawbacks of Buffalo and make them reappear in the guise of exhilarating challenges. What a pleasure it was to be with him! Meyerson has a wonderfully agile, broad-ranging mind; he can think of nine things at once. Moreover, he seemed to know everybody. (It's from him that I learned the importance of the Rolodex.)

In recruiting, Meyerson's ace in the hole was a truly monumental vision for transforming Buffalo from a conventional university to an academic New Jerusalem—"the Berkeley of the East," as he liked to say. The ideas were stunning: decentralization of authority; dozens of new colleges that would function as intimate "intellectual neighborhoods"; universitywide research centers to grapple with urban studies, higher education, and other major issues; a new campus to be built from the ground up—the list went on and on. It was a seductive dream that tended to drive out any trivial-seeming qualms I had about the weather and the number of good bookstores in Buffalo compared with Boston.

While I was pondering the Buffalo offer, I was also considering two others—one from the Salk Institute and the other, ironically, to be vice-president for academic affairs at USC. As I weighed and reweighed alternatives, real life intruded one morning when I discovered that someone had broken into our house and stolen the family's winter coats from the vestibule.

The Boston winter ended that day. Drawn outside by the sweet air of early spring, I took a brisk, pleasant stroll over to Filene's basement, where I bought a new overcoat—the heaviest alpaca snowcoat in the store.

Obviously, without realizing it I had made up my mind.

Two other provost candidates handpicked by Meyerson accepted about the same time. Eric Larrabee, a suave and brilliant New York editor *(Harper's, Horizon)*, became provost of arts and letters, and Karl Willenbrock agreed to leave his post as an associate dean at Harvard to head Buffalo's engineering faculty. Four other provosts were recruited from the existing faculty.

Larrabee, Willenbrock, and I—Meyerson's chief outside recruits—arrived on campus that fall with all the optimism and confidence of young princes joining a crusade. Though only Willenbrock was a seasoned administrator, our relative inexperience didn't deter us in the least. We were sure that in this academic Great Good Place, creativity would count for more than traditional training and ordinary credentials. Meyerson had emphasized this point repeatedly. If in fact his idea of unorthodox training was a degree from Harvard in a field other than the one you were appointed to teach in, then so be it. We had no doubt we could set Buffalo free.

We certainly looked the part. Buffalo is a town where you don't have to make fashion statements. Swathed in down, everybody looks pretty much like the Michelin man for most of the winter. But we three had style, even panache. I remember the entrance we made at the first provosts' meeting. Karl invited me to have breakfast with him before the meeting at the Frank Lloyd Wright–designed house he had picked up for a song on his arrival in Buffalo. Afterward he and I climbed into his white Porsche convertible (a sure sign of an out-of-towner—people in upstate New York tend to favor cars with front-wheel drive in colors that will stand out against the snow, not disappear in it). As we were about to drive away, Karl's wife, Millie, came out to say good-bye and handed us berets to protect us from the wind.

We drove from Willenbrock's Frank Lloyd Wright house to Larrabee's Frank Lloyd Wright house (which was adjacent to Meyerson's Frank Lloyd Wright house). Eric was waiting for us, a homburg perched on his aristocratic head, his umbrella furled. I remember the sense of euphoria I had as we drove toward campus in the warm September sun and my complete confidence that, if nothing else, we epitomized Buffalo's new look. God only knows what the natives thought as we drove onto the tree-lined campus. To some, I'm sure, we must have looked like the vanguard of a particularly spiffy occupying force.

During my first year as provost at Buffalo, I recruited nine new chairs and two new deans, changing about 90 percent of the leadership structure of the social sciences. The faculty gained forty-five new full-time faculty (almost 75 percent of the present Buffalo faculty were appointed under Meyerson). I personally interviewed more than thirty candidates for various jobs. The newcomers were a largely self-selected group who shared the commitment to innovation, risk taking, and excellence that was the credo of the Meyerson presidency.

For that first year Buffalo was a kind of academic Camelot. When we provosts gathered around the president's conference table, we were ready to work miracles. Occasionally, however, signals reached me that not everyone took us quite as seriously as we took ourselves. One morning I found that on my coatrack someone had hung a Batman cape (I eschewed the down parka that was the winter uniform of the campus and wore a Tyrolean cape that I thought was quite dashing). The anonymous critic had a point. Omnipotent fantasy was the delusion of choice that year in the administration building.

The occasional doubt crept in. In my end-of-the-year provost's report, I ticked off the high points of the ambitious reorganization we were undertaking but cautioned that "each of these virtues could be transformed overnight into obstacles and problems." But such reservations were rare.

The commitment to transforming the university shaped my home life as well. Our house was constantly filled with academic superstars and promising newcomers we were desperately trying to recruit and with Buffalonians with whom we were frantically getting acquainted. As one local wag observed, my wife and I were always entertaining "two hundred of

[our] closest friends." That first year we had sixty-five parties—brunches in the garden, afternoon wine-and-cheese parties, but mostly large dinner parties where everyone who mattered was invited to meet whoever was being wooed.

Sometime late in that first spring, my four-year-old daughter, Kate, came into the garden while I was reading the newspapers in a rare moment of stillness. She looked pensive. I asked her what she was thinking. She said she was thinking about what she wanted to do when she grew up.

"What have you decided?" I asked.

She paused for a long time and then said, "When I grow up, I want to be a guest."

I picked her up and laughed. And then later, when I was by myself, I cried. At four Kate was like the psychiatrist's child who wants to grow up to be a patient. Her remark wasn't so much clever as it was true—and terribly sad.

I learned a great deal at Buffalo, but one thing I did not learn was how to integrate intimacy with ambition. I still haven't learned at sixty-eight. Yeats writes that "the intellect of man is forced to choose / Perfection of the life, or of the work, and / if it take the second must refuse / A heavenly mansion, raging in the dark." In real life the dilemma is even more excruciating because it is often the people we love who are left raging in the dark.

Like John Kennedy's Camelot, our academic utopia lasted roughly a thousand days. By 1970 our attempt to transform the university was interrupted by the campus unrest that was sweeping the country. At one point six hundred police officers in full riot gear appeared on campus, ready to use force if protesting students got too uppity. It was not academic life as any of us had known it. A student filmmaker at Buffalo put it nicely when he titled his cinema vérité record of that turbulent semester *Andy Hardly Goes to College*. The halls of ivy were no longer filled with the optimism of a few years earlier but instead were filled with the lingering smell of tear gas.

In the final analysis the Meyersonian spirit at Buffalo was defeated by a changed political and economic reality. Yet there were ways in which we contributed, however unwittingly, to that failure.

Examining what went wrong at Buffalo altered forever the way I think about change. Martin Meyerson had the first thing that every effective leader needs—a powerful vision of the way the organization should be, a vision he was able to communicate to me and many of his other recruits. But unless a vision is sustained by action, it quickly turns to ashes.

The Meyersonian dream never got out of the administration building. In ways that only later became clear, we undermined the very thing we wanted most. Our actions and even our style tended to alienate the people who would be most affected by the changes we proposed. Failing to appreciate the importance to the organization of the people who are already in it is a classic managerial mistake, one that new managers and change-oriented administrators are especially prone to make. We certainly did. In our Porsches and berets, we acted as if the organization hadn't existed until the day we arrived.

There are no clean slates in established organizations. A new administration can't play Noah and build the world anew with two handpicked representatives of each academic discipline. Talk of new beginnings is so much rhetoric—frightening rhetoric to those who suspect that the new signals the end of their own careers. At Buffalo we newcomers disregarded history. But without history, without continuity, there can be no successful change. A. N. Whitehead said it best: "Every leader, to be effective, must simultaneously adhere to the symbols of change and revision and the symbols of tradition and stability."

What most of us in organizations really want (and what status, money, and power serve as currency for) is acceptance, affection, self-esteem. Institutions are more amenable to change when the esteem of all members is preserved and enhanced. Whatever people say, given economic sufficiency they stay in organizations and feel satisfied in them because they feel competent and valued. Change carries the threat of loss. When managers remove that threat, people are much freer to identify with the adaptive process and much better equipped to tolerate the high degree of ambiguity that accompanies change.

When I think of Buffalo, I think of that joke "How many psychiatrists does it take to change a light bulb?" The answer is "One, but the light bulb really has to want to change." Organizations change themselves when the members want to. You can't force them to change, even in a Batman cape.

The University of Cincinnati: 1971–1978

The logical next step after Buffalo was a college presidency. My name began to surface at the meetings of presidential search committees, short-lived organizations I would come to know well over the next two decades. During 1970–1971 my name appeared on several short lists, and in the fall of 1971 I became president of the University of Cincinnati.

Less than a year into my tenure, I had a moment of truth. I was sitting in my office on campus, mired in the incredible stack of paperwork on my desk. It was four o'clock in the morning. Weary of bone and tired of soul, I found myself muttering, "Either I can't manage this place, or it's unmanageable."

As I sat there, I thought of a friend and former colleague who had become president of one of the nation's top universities. He had started out full of fire and vision. But a few years later, he had quit. "I never got around to doing the things I wanted to do," he explained.

Sitting there in the echoing silence, I realized that I had become the victim of a vast, amorphous, unwitting conspiracy to prevent me from doing anything whatsoever to change the status quo. Unfortunately, I was one of the chief conspirators. This discovery caused me to formulate what I thought of as Bennis's First Law of Academic Pseudodynamics, which states that routine work drives out nonroutine work and smothers to death all creative planning, all fundamental change in the university—or any institution, for that matter.

The evidence surrounded me. To start, there were 150 letters in the day's mail that required a response. About a third of them concerned our young dean of education, Hendrik Gideonse. His job was a critical one— to bring about change in the way the university taught teachers and to create a new relationship between the university and the precollege students in the deprived and deteriorating neighborhood around us, the neighborhood from which we drew an increasing number of students.

But the letters were not about education. They were about a baby, Gideonse's ten-week-old son. The young dean was committed to ensuring that his wife had the time and freedom to develop her potential as fully as his own. And so he was carrying the baby to his office twice a week in a portable bassinet that he kept on the desk while he worked. The local paper had run a story on Gideonse and his young office companion, with picture, on page one. National TV had picked up the story. As a result, my in-basket had begun to overflow with letters urging me to dismiss the dean or at least have him arrested for child abuse. My response was to say that if Gideonse could engage in that form of applied humanism and still accomplish the things we both wanted in education, then I, like Lincoln with Grant's whiskey, would gladly send him several additional babies for adoption. But there was no question that Hendrik and his baby took up quite a bit of my time.

Also on my desk was a note from a professor, complaining that his classroom temperature was down to sixty-five degrees. Someone once observed that trying to lead a faculty is like herding cats. What did this man expect me to do—grab a wrench and fix the heating system myself? A parent complained about a four-letter word in a Philip Roth book being used in an English class. The track coach wanted me to come over and see for myself how bad the track was.

And that was the easy stuff. That year perhaps 20 percent of my time had been taken up by a problem at the general hospital, which was owned by the city but administered by the university and which served as the teaching hospital of the UC medical school. A group of terminal-cancer patients had, with their consent, been subjected to whole-body radiation as a possible beneficial therapy. The Pentagon, interested in gauging the human effects of nuclear warfare, had helped subsidize the study.

Like Hendrik's baby, this too became a major story, one in which irresponsible comparisons were made between the cancer study and Nazi experiments on human guinea pigs. The flap eventually subsided after a blue-ribbon task force recommended changes in the experiment's design. But by then I had invested endless time in a matter only vaguely related to the primary purposes of the university—and wound up being accused of interfering with academic freedom in the bargain.

In my cluttered office that morning, I grew up in some fundamental way. I realized that, from now on, my principal role model was going to have to be me. I decided that the kind of university president I wanted to be was one who led, not managed. That's an important difference. Many an institution is well managed yet very poorly led. It excels in the ability to handle all the daily routine inputs yet never asks whether the routine should be done in the first place.

My entrapment in minutiae made me realize another thing: that people were following the old army game. They did not want to take responsibility for the decisions they properly should make. "Let's push up the tough ones" had become the motto. As a result, everybody was dumping his or her "wet babies" (as old hands at the State Department call them) on my desk. I decided then and there that my highest priority was to create an "executive constellation" to run the office of the president. The sole requirements for inclusion in the group were that the individual needed to know more than I did about his or her area of competence and had to be willing to take care of daily matters without referring them back to me. I was going to make the time to lead.

I realized that I had been doing what so many leaders do: I was trying to be everything to the organization—father, fixer, policeman, ombudsman, rabbi, therapist, and banker. As a CEO who was similarly afflicted put it to me later, "If I'm walking on the shop floor and see a leak in the dike, I have to stick my finger in." Trying to be everything to everyone was diverting me from real leadership. It was burning me out. And perhaps worst of all, it was denying all the potential leaders under me the chance to learn and prove themselves.

Things got better after that, although I never came close to the ideal. As I look back at my experience at UC, I compare it with my psychoanalysis: I wouldn't have missed it for the world, and I would never go through it again. In becoming a leader I learned a number of important things about both leadership and myself. As Sophocles observes in *Antigone,* "But hard it is to learn the mind of any mortal, or the heart, 'til he be tried in chief authority. Power shows the man."

Having executive power showed me three personal truths.

First, I was, as the song says, "looking for love in all the wrong places." Intellectually I knew that leaders can't, shouldn't, count on being loved. But I seriously underestimated the emotional impact of angry constituents. I believed the false dream that people would love me if only they really got to know me. I call it the Lennie Bernstein syndrome. Ned Rorem, Bernstein's friend and colleague, recalls how "Lennie" was furious about a negative review in the *New York Times.* "He hates me," Bernstein said of the critic. Rorem suggested gently that Bernstein really couldn't expect everyone to love him. Bernstein was stunned for a moment by his friend's insight. "Oh, yeah," Bernstein finally conceded, "that's because you can't meet everybody."

Even worse than not being loved was not being understood. I found that so dispiriting that I began to develop a whole new theory about the social determinants of depression. It came to me sometime in 1976. I was flying back from a fund-raising trip to Washington, D.C., and idly skimming through the pages of the American Airlines magazine *American Way,* when I came across a fascinating feature about the items various famous Americans would leave in a time capsule to symbolize America on its two hundredth anniversary. The first celebrity was the astronaut Neil Armstrong. I had helped recruit Armstrong to UC and was floored by his response. He chose a credit card (I forget what it was supposed to symbolize).

I was simply amazed that Armstrong thought the credit card was emblematic of the United States in 1976. It seemed so remote from the technological triumph the country had accomplished in space or what Armstrong himself was famous for. By sheer happenstance, when I got back to Cincinnati that night I attended a party to which Armstrong had also been invited. I couldn't resist asking him about the magazine article. I told him I couldn't understand why he hadn't brought up his famous moonwalk or something else about his historic space flight. Why hadn't he chosen the American flag he planted on the moon or his fabled camera instead of a credit card?

He looked at me sadly and answered as if from the Slough of Despond. "You too," he said. "Isn't there any way I can escape the astronaut image? Do you realize that I've been teaching aeronautical engineering at your university for the past five years, getting decent student ratings, working on a few important bioengineering projects at the medical school, and still, all you think of me as is Neil Armstrong, astronaut? No wonder I'm depressed."

Anyone in authority, astronaut or baseball player, university president or national leader, is to some extent the hostage of how others perceive him or her. The perceptions of other people can be a prison. For the first time I began to understand what it must be like to be the victim of prejudice, to be helpless in the steel embrace of how other people see you. People impute motives to their leaders, love or hate them, seek them out or avoid them, and idolize or demonize them independently of what the leaders do or are. Ironically, at the very time I had the most power, I felt the greatest sense of powerlessness.

Finally, at UC I began to work out the relationship every leader must resolve between the self and the organization. One university president I knew took his own life because, according to his best friend, "he cared too much for the institution." I recall giving a lecture at Harvard and going on and on about the difficulties of presiding over a university. Afterward Paul Ylvisaker, then the dean of Harvard's school of education, asked me, "Warren, do you love the university enough?" It was an unsettling question. I said I didn't know for sure and would have to think a lot more about it.

Secretly I had doubts about how much I loved UC. I felt that my predecessor had cared too much for the university, so much so that he thought, in the manner of Louis XIV, "UC, c'est moi." I think it's dangerous to identify so strongly with an institution that your own self-esteem can be affected by the outcome of the campus Big Game.

Ultimately, I think, a leader should love the organization enough to help create a self-activating life for it. He or she has to love it enough to try to turn it into an environment in which others can understand and care for it, even in difficult times. A leader has to care enough about the organization to want it to be autonomous, able to function very nicely without him or her.

And I realized an important personal truth. I was never going to be completely happy with positional power, the only kind of power an organization can bestow. What I really wanted was personal power, influence based on voice.

The Rest So Far

In February 1979 I joined forty other scholars, executives, and futurologists at Windsor Castle for a colloquium on the evolutionary forces at work in society and the ways in which rapid change was likely to affect management.

I learned more about change that week than I had bargained for. At the age of fifty-three I experienced a myocardial infarction, a heart attack that landed me in a fifteen-bed ward at historic Middlesex Hospital, with a glamorous society photographer on my right and an engaging tramp on my left. It was probably the most crucial event of my adult life. I eventually spent three months in England, recuperating. And during that period I had nothing to do but think about what I had learned in the course of five decades and what I wanted to do with the rest of my life.

During the avoidance phase of my recovery, while I was groping for distractions, I learned that Rudyard Kipling had been taken to Middlesex Hospital with a perforated duodenum. When his physician asked Kipling what was the matter, he explained, "Something has come adrift inside" (he died in Middlesex a week later).

I too was acutely aware that something had come adrift inside. Forcibly removed from the overbooked professional life I had created for myself, I began to write poetry for the first time ever. Once again I was discovering what I had learned by putting it into words. My favorite of the poems was one called "Plea Bargaining." In it an authoritative voice asks, "How soon would you like to visit your grave? A. Not for a long, long time."

During my recuperation at Windsor Castle, I received a call from Jim O'Toole, a management professor at USC, wondering if I would be interested in a professorship there. In June 1979 I visited the campus. I was intrigued by then-dean Jack Steele's vision for the School of Business Administration (I'm a sucker for a vision every time) and astonished by the quality of the faculty he had assembled.

I am now in my eleventh year at USC—my longest continuous tenure at any institution. In many ways it has been the happiest period of my life. USC has provided me with exactly the right social architecture to do what seems most important to me now: teaching in the broadest sense.

At USC I have the leisure to consolidate what I've learned—about self-invention, about the importance of organization, about the nature of change, about the nature of leadership—and to find ways to communicate those lessons. Erik Erikson talks about an eight-stage process of human development. I think I have entered Erikson's seventh stage—the generative one—in which self-absorption gives way to an altruistic surrender to the next generation. Although writing is my greatest joy, I also take enormous pleasure in people-growing, in watching others bloom, in mentoring as I was mentored.

USC has provided me with several other structures for transmitting what I know, including a new Leadership Institute that will be an international center for the study of leadership and the development of leaders in every field. Recently I was also able to apply the sometimes painful lessons I learned as a university president, in the course of heading the committee that chose Steven Sample to be the new USC president.

My father died when he was fifty-nine, as did Doug McGregor. Abe Maslow was barely sixty. When I was growing up, that was the norm. But now, at sixty-eight, I find that I need a new role model for the last third of my life, which is shaping up to be the most challenging of all. In a recent television commentary, writer John Leonard praised his mother and his mother-in-law, two remarkable women in their eighties. He said of them that in the course of their lives, they had been pushed out of the windows of a lot of burning buildings. "I need to know," said Leonard, "how they learned to bounce."

I am learning how to bounce from my closest friend, Sam Jaffe, who will be ninety-two this year. (When in his fifties Sam was the Academy Award–winning producer of *Born Free*.) What I have already discovered is that the need to reinvent oneself, to "compose a life," as Mary Catherine Bateson puts it, is ongoing. Three years ago Sam and I took a summer course on Dickens at Trinity Hall, Cambridge. Sam, who recently tried to buy the film rights to a book I had given him, continues to scrimmage in the notoriously competitive subculture of Hollywood. He gives me hope.

I find that I have acquired a new set of priorities. Some of the old agonies have simply disappeared. I have no doubt that my three children are more important than anything else in my life. Having achieved a certain level of worldly success, I need hardly think about it anymore. Gentler virtues seem terribly important now. I strive to be generous and productive. I would hope to be thought of as a decent and creative man.

I think Miss Shirer would be proud.

Answer to the pop quiz: Samuelson, Solow, and Modigliani.

MARTIN KAPLAN ON
"AN INVENTED LIFE:
SHOE POLISH, MILLI VANILLI,
AND SAPIENTIAL CIRCLES"

WARREN BENNIS IS UNDER THE ILLUSION that "An Invented Life: Shoe Polish, Milli Vanilli, and Sapiential Circles" is his own memoir, but what he has in fact written is what Gertrude Stein called *Everybody's Autobiography*. His mother was my mother. His anxieties are my anxieties; his dreams, my dreams. The phrase *mutatis mutandis* turns out to have been coined to explain the relationship between Warren's invented life and mine. And not only mine: I will lay odds on the likelihood that anyone who reads it will discover that Warren's self-portrait actually mirrors their own.

They say that the more particular a piece of writing is, the more universal it becomes. I don't know who "they" are, but they're right.

Is my empathy overblown? After all, I do literally share with him what he calls "my Jewishness and the sense of marginality that goes with it."

I guess it's conceivable that some readers will bring to his memoir such magisterial confidence in their place in the world, such sangfroid about their belongingness, such impeccable ruling-class credentials, that they will encounter it like an ethno-botanist coming upon an exotic flower.

But I don't think it's my Newark childhood in Philip Roth's Weequahic neighborhood or my own career peregrinations that lead me to identify with Warren's story. All it takes to feel like you're his Siamese twin (as he describes a T-group moment during his heady days in Bethel, Maine) is membership in the same species, and being a fellow traveler on the same ineluctable life cycle.

At one point in "An Invented Life," Warren writes of "the ambivalent gift of empathy." Isaiah Berlin, a hero of his, called it the "fatal desire to please." This is not a rare disease. It is what makes this essay so ingratiating, so deliciously painful to read. He is harder on himself than any of his readers will be on him. But in casting a gimlet eye on his own life, he gives his readers permission to do the same for themselves. This is, I think, what he means toward the end of this memoir, when he describes his entering Eric Erikson's seventh stage, "in which self-absorption gives way to an altruistic surrender to the next generation." This is the gift that a master teacher, which is who Warren Bennis turned out to be, gives his students, which is who we readers of *The Essential Bennis* turn out to be.

Martin Kaplan is the Norman Lear Chair in Entertainment, Media and Society at the USC Annenberg School for Communications. He has been a White House speechwriter, journalist, screenwriter, radio host, and a studio executive at Disney.

THE BERKELEY OF THE EAST (1973)
AND
WHAT WENT WRONG (1973)

THE BERKELEY OF THE EAST

My very first telephone call from Buffalo, on December 19, 1966, was from Saul Touster, an assistant to Martin Meyerson, a law professor, a poet, and chairman of the search committee that had lured Meyerson from his acting chancellorship at Berkeley in 1966. Touster began the conversation with almost sinful empathy: "I bet you don't know what's going on here at Buffalo, do you?" I allowed that I didn't, and he continued with exuberant virtuosity, portraying an academic New Jerusalem of "unlimited money, a $650,000,000 new campus, bold and new organizational ideas, President Meyerson, the number of new faculty and administrators to be added, the romance of taking a mediocre up-state university and creating—well—*the Berkeley of the East.*" I was totally captivated by his utopian rhapsody. Even his New Frontier jargon didn't put me off, although Touster blushes now when I revive his memories of the "very first telephone call," when he referred to Meyerson as a "Kennedy type," himself as "McGeorge Bundy," and Meyerson's predecessor, Clifford C. Furnas, as "Eisenhower."

I was smitten by Saul Touster, his verve, his *chutzpah*, his ability to evoke shades of an academic Eden. I was put off only by his "Berkeley of the East" routine. The Avis syndrome, "No. 2 but trying harder," afflicts many universities. Mimicking charismatic institutions in their twilight is no way to build a great university. But the Avis syndrome is deeply embedded. I

The "Berkeley of the East" and "What Went Wrong" originally appeared in *The Leaning Ivory Tower* (Jossey-Bass, 1973).

heard recently that the University of California at Santa Cruz is being touted as the "Buffalo of the West," while the University of Maryland claims to be the "Santa Cruz of the East."

Until Touster approached me, the University of Buffalo was a largely unknown quantity to me. I knew that it was the principal upstate campus of the New York State University system and that earlier it had been a private university whose medical school in particular had earned some distinction. I remember calling David Riesman at Harvard in early March of 1967 to ask him what he thought of Buffalo. He had taught at its Law School in the late 1930s and was now advising President Meyerson on social science matters. Riesman was generally optimistic. He compared Buffalo's academic qualities to marble cake: "Some departments awfully soggy and depressed; others fluffy and rising." Riesman had lived in nearby Canada while teaching at UB. In the days before eco-awareness, he found the view of industrial Buffalo from across Lake Ontario "aesthetically fetching—especially the chartreuse and black and mauve smoke against the steel-gray sky."

Looking into the Buffalo situation closely, I discovered that there was indeed reason for optimism. Buffalo was clearly on the move. Less than five years before, the private University of Buffalo had merged with the public state university system as the campus' one hope for financial solvency. At that time Meyerson's predecessor, Clifford Furnas, had fought courageously to ensure the campus a high degree of autonomy in spite of its affiliation with the state. Furnas was determined that UB would not be, in his own homely term, "a numbered restaurant in a Howard Johnson chain." That remark and others like it (including an outspoken interview with Fred Hechinger in the education section of the *Times*) permanently alienated Furnas from the state university central administration in Albany and ultimately cost him the option of delaying his retirement by several years. His successful negotiation of the merger was the outstanding achievement of the Furnas years at Buffalo. In the four years following the merger Buffalo steadily expanded on many fronts, from hiring a number of outstanding faculty (including novelist John Barth and critic Leslie Fiedler) to preliminary planning for a multimillion dollar new campus. When Furnas retired in 1966, a committee of forward-looking faculty hit on Meyerson as the successor best suited to realize the enormous potential implicit in UB's emergence as a major graduate center in the state university system.

During my first visit to Buffalo, on February 8, 1967, I met with the department chairmen and deans of the social sciences and administration faculty. These fifteen or so men represented some 350 faculty members within the area of the university that I was being asked to lead as provost. Lunch was cordial enough. On my right was Professor Daniel Hamberg, chairman of the department of economics, who bragged playfully about taking a second-rate department and building it into a good one via panzer-like raids on other universities. He was especially proud of "a fabulous package deal" (literally fabulous, it turned out) to recruit eight recent MIT Ph.D.s en bloc. On my left was Professor Albert Somit, chairman of the political science department, who told me that UB had had no political science department until three years before. The department now numbered twenty-seven and in the next five years would be enlarged to forty-five faculty. Other growth promises were formidable. The Buffalo campus was going to be the "jewel in the state university crown," promising to double its student body and professoriat in the next five years' time. This depended, I also learned, on the building of the enormous new campus. When I asked the projected completion date of the new campus, everybody suddenly got very busy with his food—except Saul Touster, better in person even than on the phone. Throughout the meeting, Touster had simultaneously played the parts of MC, interlocutor, moderator, censor, and press agent. Zero Mostel on speed. Touster assured me over the rising clatter of knives and forks that the new campus would go up on schedule. "Figure on five years or so," he said.

Before I could continue this line of questioning, Touster shuttled us to a nearby conference room where, according to my schedule, we were to have a two-hour conference. Touster left for another appointment, to my despair, because it soon became clear that no one knew what the assembled group was supposed to do together for two hours. Absentmindedly I took a place at the head of a long table, then realized it might seem presumptuous, but sat on uncomfortably where I was—very alone and facing rows of empty chairs. Two or three of the group sat away from the table, by the door near the back of the room. A dozen others were clustered at the *very* bottom of the bowling-alley-length table, like tenpins, I thought.

After fifteen minutes or so, I cleared my throat and said, "Maybe we ought to start the meeting." The tenpins nodded, and the group by the door stopped talking and looked my way. But I didn't know where to go from there, and neither did they. There was more silence. Finally, Hamberg, the economics chairman, raised his hand. "Professor Bennis, what do you think the function of provost is?" he asked. I told him I would like that question answered too, since the provost structure had not been explained to me. "I wonder if you could tell me what you *think* the functions of the provost are?" Hamberg would have none of this table-turning; and now, in an

Alphonse-Gaston act that must have lasted ten minutes, we lobbed the question back and forth. "You most certainly did not come to Buffalo without any awareness of the role for which you are now being interviewed?" he said. In fact, I did come to Buffalo with only the fuzziest awareness, since Meyerson and Touster had been long on enthusiasm and very short on such administrative specifics as precise responsibilities. So I said again that I knew little about it and would prefer to hear from them first. Then, I promised rather archly, I would respond. Hamberg and I had reached one of those strange impasses that occur sometimes in interviews. Aside from genuine vagueness about the role, I had a sense that what the group most wanted was a skeet to shoot at, and somehow or other I did not want to give them a target. Hamberg and I continued to wrestle politely, the grunts practically audible in the quiet conference room.

During the encounter, several mentioned Meyerson's interest in "superstars" and "glamor" appointments—glamor being defined, I learned, as a Harvard A.B., an Oxford doctorate, and a BBC accent. There were also chortles about the Frank Lloyd Wright house, purchased by the state for $65,000, which the Meyersons planned to move into.

The interview could not have been much fun for those conducting it. Interviewing potential bosses never is. Besides, in the tussle with Hamberg, I had broken the rule that the candidate gamely answers the question, whatever it is. The interviewers, no doubt, saw me as Meyerson's choice for the job. There was no mistaking an undercurrent of hostility, and I felt that the faculty leaders resented having to participate in what they saw less as an honest, open-ended interview than a formality to be followed by a rubber stamp.

I felt that the deans and chairmen there were generally honest—honest and scared, and probably with good reason. At one of Meyerson's first press conferences as UB president, he was reported to have wondered if the department chairmen would prove big enough men to be capable of hiring people better than they themselves were, a remarkable opener for a new president presumably trying to gain the confidence and support of his faculty. Several questioned me closely about my relationship with Meyerson; somebody even asked whether we were cousins, mentioning a current rumor to that effect. I said I had not yet even *met* Meyerson, was supposed to meet him that morning at the airport on his way to New York, but that my plane had arrived too late.

Driving me back to the airport that evening, Saul Touster went only slightly out of his way to show me still another tantalizing Frank Lloyd Wright house, supposedly for sale not far from Meyerson's. The house, I later learned, had already been sold to another recruit, Karl Willenbrock, the new provost of engineering and applied science. We swung by the Riesman-admired smokestacks along the lake for a romantic finale. As we drove, Touster began a new and puzzling line of questioning on my work at MIT as department chairman, particularly my consulting activities for the Department of State, ALCAN, and other industrial organizations. (Over a year later, in May 1968 at a goodbye party for Touster as he left Buffalo for another assignment, I asked him about those puzzling questions. He told me that a number of faculty members had wondered whether my connection with the "military-industrial complex" and my management-school background were compatible with the liberal educational goals at Buffalo.) The interview that afternoon and the puzzling questions aside, I felt good about the day. One reason was Touster himself. A formidably intelligent, complicated man, Touster had not only charmed me, he had also deeply impressed me with the humaneness of his idea of a university. Whether I go to Buffalo or not, I told Clurie when I arrived home, I've made a friend.

I met Martin Meyerson about a week later, on February 16, 1967, at our house on Beacon Hill. That meeting lasted three hours. I had heard a good deal about Meyerson before, all positive, from Cambridge sources. Meyerson was thought to be unusually well prepared for the kind of turmoil afflicting almost all large universities. From 1959 to 1963 he was the first director of the Harvard-MIT Joint Center for Urban Studies (somewhat overshadowed by his subsequent successor, Daniel Moynihan); he then went to Berkeley as dean of the college of environmental design; as acting chancellor at Berkeley, he administered to the reassembled wreckage after the student upheavals of 1965. Before initiating the joint center, he had been a student in classics at Columbia and had established himself as a leading scholar of urban planning, teaching at Chicago and then at Pennsylvania.

To be with Meyerson was a pleasure. His mind and imagination ranged, both historically and comparatively, over the widest variety of topics. He seemed to know almost everybody. He could think of nine things at once, always with a beautiful anecdote and a conceptual grasp. As a recruiter, Meyerson's ace in the hole was a truly monumental plan for redesigning Buffalo's conventional departments-schools-and-colleges academic structure. His plan had been ratified by the UB faculty senate only two months after his arrival at Buffalo in November 1966. As Meyerson summarized his academic plan for me, the university was undergoing the following changes:

(1) The ninety some existing departments were to be restructured into seven new faculties, each with a provost as the chief academic and admin-

istrative officer. The provosts would be selected for their academic emi-
nence, broad scholarship, and administrative ability. Each faculty would
consist of the basic disciplines within the newly defined area plus relevant
professional schools. The faculty he wanted me to head would be composed of all the basic social science disciplines, from anthropology to psychology, and also (to the chagrin of the arts and letters provost) philosophy
and history as well as the faculty of the schools of management and social
welfare. Interdisciplinary programs would be encouraged, and the provost
would have ample resources and administrative leeway to implement new
education ventures.

(2) Augmenting and complementing the seven-faculty structure, thirty
new colleges, small enough to be intellectual communities, would be built
on the new campus, each housing only four hundred students with up to
six hundred more commuting students as affiliates. These colleges would
serve residential, social, and educational functions. Faculty and students
would live and work together in the meaningful human relationships of
these "intellectual neighborhoods." Meyerson, who had only recently
come from the archetypical multiversity, saw the smaller colleges as a way
to offset the apathy and anomie characteristic of an enormous campus. A
secondary purpose was to counteract the stranglehold that traditional
departments have on the typical university. The colleges would provide a
truly educational experience, not just a narrow academic one, particularly
for undergraduates, who too often receive only a watered-down version
of what professors teach to their graduate students. I thought this idea
stunning. It would develop closer faculty-student relationships while providing the best of two possible worlds: the complex diversity of a large university, the communal advantages of smaller "living and learning" units.

(3) University-wide action-research centers or councils on international
studies, urban studies, and higher educational studies would act as magnets for scholars and students drawn from the entire university (and outside) to work together on such vital central issues.

I was impressed with Meyerson's overall concept. Several aspects of the
plan were especially attractive to me: the decentralization of authority;
the development of a multicircuited university with many different focuses
of collegiality (if you didn't find the right fit in a department, there was
always a college or a center to connect up with); a conviction that administrators should be scholars and that a five-year period was about the optimum number of years one should stay in an administrative capacity
before returning to one's scholarship. I was also impressed with Meyerson's clear intent to raise the self-esteem of the university, the self-esteem
of the faculty and students, and also the self-esteem of the general Buffalo

community—a big working-class population, predominantly Polish in derivation, in a city that is the butt of numberless bad jokes like those that plague less vulnerable Philadelphia.

Meyerson also assured me that with the new campus sufficient resources would be available to build quality on top of the university's inevitable deadwood, the less competent holdovers from previous administrations. By going easy on the University's former power structure, we could avoid a collision course with "old UB." I would also have the resources, and his support, he assured me, for an experimental Ph.D. program that I hoped to develop in the applied social sciences.

When I questioned Meyerson about the political climate of New York State, mindful of Governor Ronald Reagan's campaign against the University of California system, he replied confidently, "Well, Warren, if you compare the former governors of California with those of New York, you can see the difference: Roosevelt, Smith, Lehman, Harriman, Rockefeller . . ."

As we became more at ease with each other, I asked him what his own goal for Buffalo was. He paused for at least thirty seconds and answered: "To make it a university where I would like to stay and be a professor after finishing my administrative responsibilities." When my wife, Clurie, joined us, she asked him what the city of Buffalo offered, say, compared with Boston. The pause that followed grew into a long silence. Finally Meyerson's face brightened. "It's more comprehensible," he said.

I was sold on the man and his conceptual vision. Meyerson's gift as a recruiter was his ability to transmogrify all the highly visible drawbacks of Buffalo and make them reappear in the guise of exhilarating challenges. I knew after those mesmerizing three hours that if he asked me to join this twentieth-century Republic of Virtue, I would accept. The timing seemed perfect; Meyerson's new organizational design would go into effect on the same day as my term of office, September 1, 1967.

Colleagues at the Sloan School of Management, one of the five schools at MIT, were unsympathetic when I announced that I was considering an offer to be provost at Buffalo. Their attitude toward all administrative jobs in the university—any university—bordered on contempt. "God," said one, "why do you want to waste your time shuffling papers?" Then gales of laughter following a crack about snow-blowers being a fantastic growth industry.

I was frankly in conflict about leaving the Boston-Cambridge area. At MIT I enjoyed the comfortable life of a full professor, a life which included lucrative opportunities for consulting, terrifyingly bright students, and excellent colleagues. I had written my clutch of books and had established some repute as an organizational theorist. MIT was paradise for an organizational theorist. It attracted a steady stream of practicing executives who came to the Boston area to acquire advanced degrees in management. For over a decade they were the human crucible in which I was able to test new hypotheses, new approaches. But after ten years the insulated atmosphere of MIT was becoming a little too comfortable, too predictable. I was hungry for practical experience of my own. The provostship at Buffalo might be just the opportunity I wanted to apply social science theory from a position of authority in a complex academic organization.

During the next six weeks, I went through an acutely irresolute, Hamletic phase. My decision-making wasn't helped by the fact that after Clurie and I had flown to Buffalo for her first trip and my second she had a miscarriage. She spent the next month mostly in bed. Even for a recruiting trip, that late winter visit to Buffalo was unusually unpleasant. Being scrutinized every waking minute is exhausting anyway, and the flight took four hours, late each way. And, God, was it cold. As I walked down the roll-away stairs into the white swirl of the Buffalo International runway, I wondered whether it was true, what a disgruntled native son had told me, that summer in Buffalo was three weeks of bad ice-skating.

Before a firm offer came, there were several mildly distressing signals at odds with the utopian view of Buffalo that Meyerson had painted. First, Saul Touster asked me to return to the campus at once. He explained that Meyerson and he were getting flak from certain members of the social sciences faculty in regard to my likely appointment. Apparently, no formal search committee had been set up, and the faculty were now demanding one. Some faculty spokesmen, "with nothing against you personally," Touster assured me, insisted on a formal procedure. I told Saul that I thought I had gone through that already. He answered that generally he was in charge of recruiting provosts and other top administrators. I had assumed that the previous informal procedure with the consultation was adequate, but this time the faculty were pressing for another look. "People are paranoid," he said. I thought I understood.[1]

I also learned that the building plans were not firm but vague and uncertain. Actually, the $650,000,000 figure mentioned during my interview had only once been cited by Governor Rockefeller. The only place it currently appeared in writing was in a *Time* article quoting Meyerson. Furthermore, a major controversy was raging in Buffalo over where the new campus should be located. Three different sites were being advocated: a characterless 1,200-acre suburban tract (where, at this writing, construction of the campus has finally begun), a downtown site, and expansion of the existing 178-acre campus onto an adjacent public golf course.

When news of the campus controversy reached me in Cambridge, I was unpleasantly surprised. Meyerson had never said so, but for some reason I had fantasied an academic Mont-Saint-Michel already substantially existent on the plains of western New York.

Momentary qualms aside, Meyerson and his vision of Buffalo excited me, and I knew that I had wanted to go there almost from the moment Saul Touster first phoned. Notorious weather, paranoia, uncertainty about the building plans, chartreuse industrial smoke, even the thought of life in the provinces—none of these seriously lessened my enthusiasm.

After Touster had assuaged the social sciences faculty, Meyerson made a firm offer. By then I also had offers from two schools in Southern California. Winter was nearly over in Boston. While I weighed alternatives and juggled possible career choices, real life intruded one morning when I discovered that our vestibule had been broken into and all the family's winter coats stolen. The bad weather lifted that day. Drawn outside by the spring air, I took a pleasant stroll over to Filene's basement and mindlessly purchased a new overcoat—the heaviest alpaca snowcoat in the entire store.

In late March I gave Meyerson my answer; "Yes."

Largely under the spell of Meyerson's bold dreams and blandishments, others also made the pilgrimage to Buffalo. Two other provost designees accepted at about the same time I did. Eric Larrabee, a suave and brilliant New York editor (*Harper's, Horizon*), became provost of arts and letters, and Karl Willenbrock, as mentioned earlier, agreed to leave his post as associate dean of applied sciences at Harvard after twenty years to head Buffalo's engineering faculty. The four remaining provosts called for in the reorganization plan were recruited from faculty already at UB.

Larrabee, Willenbrock, and I—Meyerson's three chief outside recruits—arrived on campus that fall with all the confidence and optimism of young princes joining a crusade. Only Willenbrock had had first-hand experience in educational administration above the chairman level, but our inexperience didn't deter us in the least. It only served to make us more confident, more optimistic. In this academic great good place, creativity would count for more than narrowly defined training and credentials.

We were Meyerson's champions in this cause, and we looked the part. I remember the entrance we made at the first provosts' meeting. Karl Willenbrock, who had snatched that other Wright-designed house, invited me to it for breakfast before the meeting. Afterward, as Karl and I climbed into his white Porsche convertible, his wife, Millie, came out to wave good-bye and handed us berets to protect us from the wind. We drove from Willenbrock's Wright house to Larrabee's Wright house (formerly an adjunct to Meyerson's Wright house). Eric was waiting for us with homburg erectly perched and umbrella furled. So caparisoned in homburg and berets, the three of us drove in rising euphoria under the warm September sun onto the small, tree-covered campus. We felt that we epitomized Buffalo's new look. Style was the byword. Whether we succeeded in making Buffalo great, we were confident we would give it style.

"Style" was the magic word that year at Buffalo, one rich with associations with the Kennedy years. Meyerson's urbanity and grace inevitably led to comparisons with John Kennedy's. We outside recruits were Meyerson's New Frontiersmen, and some did feel, clinging to Buffalo's few cultural amenities (notably the Albright-Knox Art Gallery and the Buffalo Philharmonic), as if we were laboring on the extreme edges of the civilized world. Happily, such snobbism was only a minor characteristic of the Meyerson new look. Mostly it consisted of a breathtaking optimism. State University of New York was going to become a new, better California system.

Meyerson brought a subtlety to the institution's hunger for greatness. He eschewed the heavy-handed "Boost Buffalo" approach of his predecessors, but he was no less attuned than folksy Cliff Furnas had been to the necessity of image-building. From the start Meyerson had an enviable national press. His ideas turned up regularly in the education sections of *Time* and *Newsweek*. On campus he began a systematic attack on the aura of provincialism that still clung to UB. Making the Frank Lloyd Wright house the president's new residence was part of it. Designating his new layer of administrators "provosts" was another. Besides a general uncertainty about the proper pronunciation of the word, there was speculation about what a provost could do that a dean or vice president could not. In fact, the distinction was real. Meyerson conceived of the provosts as senior *academic* officers, who would be sensitive to the needs of individual faculty and important educational goals and not simply responsive to organizational requirements. For example, the dean of the college of arts and sciences was replaced by several provosts, each representing a natural family of related disciplines (arts and letters, for example). The idea was simple and admirable, even if the title was a bit pretentious.

Meyerson's taste is extraordinary, and his campaign to change UB's image was remarkably successful. No aspect of university life was unaffected. At one point the university retained the services of graphic designers Chermayeff & Geismar Associates to advise on ways to express UB's new look visually. At a rumored fee of ten thousand dollars, Ivan Chermayeff himself was charged with designing a new logo for the university to replace the clutter and conventional academic symbolism of the old one. The new seal was to appear on everything from catalogs to garbage cans (the latter proved impractical). More than a million pieces of stationery with the new seal were printed up. That changeover took a year of hassling with the state over the grade of paper, a specially mixed ink, and a nonstandard typeface, all specified by the designer in blissful ignorance of state purchasing procedures.

The climax of the image-building effort was the new president's inauguration in late May 1967. Among the forty-two dignitaries on the platform with Meyerson were educational superstars Clark Kerr, a former colleague from the Berkeley of the West, and Yale's charismatic President Kingman Brewster. On an enormous silver screen behind the platform party flashed the larger-than-life image of Governor Nelson Rockefeller, adding his good wishes for the occasion via the medium of sound on film. The theme of Meyerson's inaugural address was the realization of greatness through implementation of the letter and spirit of the academic reorganization. "If we have the courage to be different, we shall not long be different because the model of State University of New York at Buffalo will become a model for many."

Rain forced the inaugural luncheon indoors. When the skies cleared, the guests moved on to the new president's new house for a reception. The Meyersons shook 1,500 hands as guests lined up across the lawn and down the driveway, at one point waiting in the reception line for as long as forty-five minutes. Shuttle busses ran every ten minutes from the parking lot of the nearby Buffalo zoo, where guests had been requested to leave their cars. Once through the line, the guests explored the house itself, a rambling, low-ceilinged gem that Buffalo had ignored for the half century since Wright completed it. The house was almost devoid of furniture. But even bare and unrestored it was a dramatic backdrop for the final moments of a pageant unlike any in the university's first 120 years.

Now that a changed economy has radically altered our perceptions, the Meyerson inauguration seems almost frivolous. But at the time it was simply the least important manifestation of a pervasive commitment to change. Buffalo desperately needed new blood. Meyerson and his men were transfusing her.

My first year as social sciences provost was marked by an impressive list of "transitions," to borrow *Newsweek*'s unemotional term. During 1967–68, I recruited nine new chairmen and two deans for the faculty, changing about 90 per cent of the leadership personnel of the social sciences area. The faculty also gained forty-five new full-time faculty members that year (a net increase of thirty, owing to a number of departures). Almost three fourths of my time that first year was spent recruiting. I interviewed over three hundred candidates.

Buffalo raided from Harvard, Yale, and Princeton. Each new appointment meant an exponential increase in enthusiasm, new ideas, the Meyerson optimism. The tiny crowded campus barely seemed able to contain all the excitement within it. Intellectual neighborhoods sprang up across the campus, each dominated by the personality of a "new look" appointee. Lawrence Chisolm inaugurated a radical American studies program that emphasized the study of non-American cultures as a way of overcoming chauvinistic biases. David Hays inherited a good but narrowly defined linguistics program and made it magnetic by insisting that linguistics was no less than a focus for intellectual integration. John Eberhard, the new dean of architecture and environmental design, attracted a nucleus of nonestablishment designers interested in creating living systems rather than monuments. To head a new library school, a dean with an applied math background was hired. He shocked an assembly of catalogers by asking who exactly Melville (Dewey Decimal System) Dewey *was* and then proceeded to attract to the school a flock of media freaks, sensitivity trainers, and, less unusual for a library school, systems specialists. The new social welfare dean, Franklin Zweig, young enough to be called "boy dean" by his detractors, turned the social work school upside down. Social work at Buffalo was no longer to be the handmaiden of psychiatry. Under Zweig, the emphasis would be on community organization, legal and social policy. Richard Brandenburg, new dean of the school of management, also broadened the scope of the management school to include public institutions. Changes were seen in the least likely places. For example, Leroy Pesch, who came from Stanford to head the medical school, took steps toward streamlining the medical curriculum. Talk at the medical school was somewhat less of the narrow professional concerns of private practice and more of the health-care needs of the public.

The change was pervasive. Almost 75 per cent of the present Buffalo faculty were appointed under Meyerson. The newcomers were largely a self-selected group, committed to innovation and risk-taking. The student body was also changing. By 1968, 80 per cent of the entering freshmen were in the top tenth of their high school graduating classes, compared to only 10 per cent ten years before. This upward trend in the quality of Buffalo's undergraduates had begun when the campus affiliated with the state university. Going state had resulted in an influx of bright applicants from the New York City area. Along with Stony Brook on Long Island, Buffalo was regarded as one of the state university's radical campuses, which left some people wondering whether Meyerson's Berkeley of the East approach may have had an appeal that he had not fully calculated.

For that one year, 1967–68, Buffalo was an academic Camelot. The provosts met around the president's conference table ready to work miracles. Signals occasionally reached me that not everyone on campus took us quite as seriously as we did ourselves. On my coat rack one morning I found that someone had hung a Batman cape. The anonymous critic had a point. The atmosphere in Hayes Hall was a bit heavy with omnipotent fantasy.

Although living quarters on the new campus were still in the future, six "human-sized" colleges got underway at once. Meyerson named a master for each of them. Almost immediately these colleges provoked controversy. Meyerson wanted innovation, yes, but rumors began to circulate that course cards for College A (the six colleges were referred to by initials until formal applications for names were approved) were being sold, snatched up by students who intended to do little or nothing and reward themselves with A's at the end of the semester. "Why do you think they call it College A?" one cynical student asked. There were tales of credit being given for trips to Europe and building bird cages.

The master of College A regarded any impugning of its grading system as an antirevolutionary tactic. No one in the Meyerson administration, including myself, wanted to take a harsh public stand against this nonsense, particularly after College A and its master had become the target of community attack. Foolishly, we let the more change-resistant "old faculty" appropriate to themselves the role of guardians of academic standards.

There were other rumblings in paradise. The centers were not doing well. It was easier to break down barriers than build bridges, we learned. The center for higher education, for example, did not generate new programs or attract faculty and students, as planned. Since Meyerson had never made explicit the goals or functions of the center, its newly appointed head dissipated much of his energy in writing voluminous memos requesting more direction. The center for international studies had existed prior to the reorganization and did function, but not much more effectively than before. More paper, in the form of a newsletter, was the only substantial sign of its new status. The center for urban studies was undertaking a series of much-needed but thoroughly conventional projects in Buffalo's inner city.

In one form or another all the faculties had their problems. Many departments resisted the new faculty structure. I sometimes felt that our many individual accomplishments, a promising new program, the appointment of a particularly good teacher or administrator, somehow did not add up to a significantly changed university; that somehow our gains were not being consolidated and might somehow slip away. These concerns prompted me to write in my provost's report for 1967–68:

Each of [the university's] virtues could be transformed overnight into obstacles and problems. Spectacular growth could lead to a "change for change sake" mentality, culminating in a massive and mediocre institution; the new university organization with its seven faculties, three university-wide deans, seven university vice presidents, three councils, thirty colleges (and what have I forgotten?) could become a wild Night at the Opera with the Marx Brothers; and tax-based universities are vulnerable to the biennial vicissitudes and vagaries of intramural politics.

But such moments of doubt were rare.

In August 1968, Meyerson asked me to step up from social sciences provost to be the university's vice-president for academic affairs. The official press release on my appointment said that my responsibilities included coordination of educational programs, working on the development of educational innovations and policies, and special responsibility for the colleges and the university's communication resources. One surprising consequence was that I was suddenly very much in demand in the Buffalo community. Shortly after the announcement, a group of citizens even asked me to consider running for mayor. "On what ticket?" I asked. "It doesn't matter."

Camelot lasted barely a thousand days.

WHAT WENT WRONG

"You know, I never asked you about this, Warren, but do you ever feel guilty about bringing me to Buffalo?"

Theodore Mills, who had left Yale to head Buffalo's sociology department, had dropped in to say goodbye the weekend before Clurie and I moved to Cincinnati. Mills had had a rough time at Buffalo: responsibility for the campus's most politicized, most polarized department; a scathing public attack in the campus paper; constant run-ins with the new university administration. Since then he has resigned as chairman; but for some time after I had decided to leave, he was still holding on. He laughed as he asked how I felt. *He* clearly was angry.

I thought about the question for a minute. I did feel guilty. "Yes," I said. "Well, you should."

If they were as frank as Mills, many would probably tell Meyerson and me the same thing. They rode into Buffalo on the crest of our enthusiasm. More than four years later, the campus mood is dismal.

I had gone to Buffalo seeking Camelot. Camelot's shining moment was brief indeed.

Three years after my arrival, Buffalo was a different university:

Chancellor Gould and President Meyerson had both departed, as had Peter Regan.

Karl Willenbrock resigned in December 1970, to take a post with the National Bureau of Standards.

Eric Larrabee resigned that same summer to head the New York State Council of the Arts. (A prominent member of the SUNY trustees and fundraiser for the Republican Party tried to sabotage his appointment by Rockefeller simply because Larrabee was associated with the "permissive Meyerson regime.")

The six colleges were struggling for their existence, the initial energies and ideas behind them dissipated.

All directors of the three special centers or councils had resigned, and only one center, that for international studies, was still in operation.

Ground was broken on the new campus in suburban Amherst, New York, by Governor Rockefeller on Halloween Day, 1968. The governor reported to the press that he "struck water with the first shovel." Actual construction got underway in September 1970. The delay, coupled with the extraordinary inflation of the last several years, will result in construction of a much more Spartan campus than originally proposed.

Practically every appointment made by Meyerson and most of the other "Meyerson men" was turned into a resignation or a termination by the new administration headed by Robert Ketter.

One of the original provosts still held his job. One of the last holdouts was my successor as social sciences provost, who was there during the pre-Meyersonian days. The undergraduate dean appointed by Meyerson (a distinguished political scientist then not yet thirty, trained at Harvard and Oxford) was also forced to resign as dean.

The great majority of officials appointed by the new Ketter administration had been at Buffalo for most of their academic lives, predating, in some cases, the Eisenhower years and the tenure of Clifford Furnas. The new provost of the health sciences (now called vice president for health affairs), for example, was sixty-six and had been at the UB school of medicine for thirty-three years.

Several superstars had left. Education critic Edgar Z. Friedenberg had gone to Nova Scotia; C. H. Waddington, the biologist and futurist who held the university's lucrative Einstein chair, had returned prematurely to Britain. Radical historian Gabriel Kolko had gone to York University in Toronto. There was no stampede from the university (Nobel Prize–winning physiologist Sir John Eccles remains), but a steady, outward trickle, unhappily coupled with a state university-wide moratorium on hiring.

Even the Frank Lloyd Wright houses had lost their identification with the university. Karl Willenbrock sold his to an outsider. The Larrabees retained their house, but are no longer affiliated with the university. President Ketter left the Wright house that Meyerson had chosen, claiming publicly that the roof leaked and privately that the ceiling was "too damn low" for his 6-ft-plus. Instead he moved into a residence purchased by the UB Foundation at a cost of $125,000. The Wright house now houses the UB alumni office and the university archives, coupled, for all anyone can determine, only because of their alphabetical proximity.

Much more serious than change in specific personnel was the shifting mood at the university. The atmosphere was one of diminished expectations. To some extent this was a national problem, the function of the recession and great war weariness. But it was more than that. The many faculty who came to Buffalo during Meyerson's brief tenure were understandably unhappy with the conservative administration that replaced him. But the discontent went deeper and was more widespread than that.

Even moderate and conservative faculty were concerned about the malaise that prevailed on campus. As philosophy professor Paul Kurtz wrote in May 1971 in the university paper, the *Reporter:*

> Many faculty within this university now believe . . . that the overriding problem that we now face concerns the apparent *decline in the level of academic aspirations* of the State University of New York at Buffalo. At least there is the widespread impression that the present administration is doing very little to raise our goals. Indeed, it now seems that the vision of a great university that so stirred SUNYAB from the day it went State until 1970 has been seriously narrowed and restricted.
>
> Although many faculty members were critical of President Meyerson's administration, nevertheless his administration demonstrated a concern for stature and it promised greatness. It was motivated by a desire to reach a high level of achievement. One can only regret that this forward-looking leadership has been largely absent in the first year of this new administration. All sectors of the university, the right and the left, the students and faculty now sense the mood of second best that seems to prevail.
>
> From 1962 through 1970 SUNYAB attracted a great number of distinguished scholars, many of them world-renowned. As far as we can tell, there have been few, if any, distinguished appointments made this past year. Indeed, a number of excellent scholars have resigned from

the university, some of them because of the general impression that UB has passed its moment of greatness and is entering a period of decline. Many younger colleagues are exasperated by the recent defense of a quota system for tenure and promotions, which is primarily based upon grounds of economy rather than academic excellence.

The administration should be committed to the building of a *great* university—the leading graduate center in the state university. I am not thinking simply in quantitative fiscal terms but in *qualitative* terms. And I am thinking of the need to develop bold educational programs fused with solid academic criteria. As far as I can tell, very few, if any, educational innovations have been suggested or introduced by this administration.

That analysis was made by one of the more conservative members of the faculty (a man who describes himself as Old Left, lest by conservative I suggest the Goldwater breed). The liberal and radical faculty feel even greater alienation. As the master of one of the colleges wrote to me:

I do not see the colleges as capable of steady growth and persistence. I fear that what we are going to get from the new administration are arguments about scarce resources that are really policy arguments in disguise, and that the tendency of policy will be to squeeze the colleges bit by bit into difficulty—not assault or abolish them. . . . It's hard to see the future as even modestly rosy for the efforts now underway.

So it is a peculiar time. People are working more on matters of direct and personal interest to them, in contrast to the highly political and public year just passed, but this is not the same as a return to academic privatization. Lots of good things are going on, while at the same time the general picture of possibilities—within the university—looks bleaker. An essay in the *Whole Earth Catalogue* recently was entitled, "Think Little." That's where we are.

The diminution of spirit at the university is the result of many factors. The narrower ambition of the current administration is one, a very important one. But another, unfortunately, was the failure of the former administration to deliver a package to match the promise.

Whether anyone could have turned UB into a permanent academic Utopia in three short years is doubtful. But the warning signals of weaknesses that would ultimately prove fatal were there early in the attempt, and we in the Meyerson administration consistently ignored them. In the euphoria of the place we paid little attention to valuable, objective intelligence we occasionally received from the outside. For example, in late

November 1968 the campus was visited by Dr. Dwight Ladd, representing the Carnegie Commission on the Future of Higher Education. Ladd's report, summarized and distributed by the then-director of UB's center of higher education, Edward Joseph Shoben, was uncanny in its perception of the precise areas that subsequently emerged as pitfalls. Had Buffalo changed, Ladd wondered, or had it experienced only the illusion of change? As Shoben summed up:

> Has anything fundamental happened at SUNY-Buffalo, or has only a brilliantly conceived and handsomely engineered superstructure been built over a pretty conventional hull? Except for some of our programs for the disadvantaged, which have evoked both large enthusiasm and critical opposition, he found our reorganization still the big topic for discussion. For Ladd, this fact of local life has an ominous quality. The reorganization is visible, dramatic, massive—and without necessary impact on individual faculty members. In short, it permits people to live in both worlds, that of superficially exciting change and that of actually comfortable academic conventionality. Although the individual professor is free to talk about it with interest and even pride, he is not required by our new organizational patterns to alter his outlook or his professional conduct in any special fashion.

As a corollary, Ladd noticed that many educationally conservative faculty remained in informal positions of influence. He predicted that, if directly challenged, these individuals would exert a considerable force against the pattern of change created by Meyerson. The events following Meyerson's decision to go to Pennsylvania proved Ladd absolutely right. Conservative faculty capitalized on anti-Meyersonian feeling in the Buffalo community, exacerbated by the violence of the student strike, and succeeded in catapulting their own candidate to the university presidency.

The Meyerson administration had been insensitive to the hurtfulness of status deprivation. The old guard were frequently overlooked at such nonacademic but important prestige-building functions as presidential dinner parties for visiting dignitaries. Clifford Furnas may have been short on style, but he knew how to use a committee assignment or a seat in the president's box at a football game to make an ally. Meyerson brought supporters with him. He didn't make many new ones.

Ladd also spotted the extent to which the academic reorganization had complicated the university's already baroque structure. "Repeatedly," Shoben wrote, "people asked whether we were entangling ourselves in a plurality of agencies [faculties, colleges, schools, councils, programs, departments, and workshops, to name only the major units] that define less of an administrative foliage while other and more usual [basic] . . . interests became lost in the unnecessarily created forest."[2] Many individuals, even those in general harmony with Meyerson's goals, felt that the reorganization did little more than add an extra layer to the administration. The addition of provosts with their associates and assistants and staffs to the existing hierarchy of deans and vice presidents did swell the university bureaucracy to a remarkable degree. This administrative redundancy has become an argument for the present administration's plan for yet another academic reorganization. The Ketter proposal would streamline the administration somewhat, but it might also result in stamping out the last vestiges of the Meyerson spirit. No one is sanguine at the prospect of the institution's being completely overhauled every three years as the first order of business of each new administration. The human cost of that would be frightful.

Perhaps if Meyerson had stayed, if there had been no campus strike in 1970, if a less conventional administration had followed, if the money had held out, things would be different. But Buffalo is no longer the academic new frontier. As a major university in the New York State system, it isn't Podunk either. But the pervasive excitement of 1968 and 1969 is gone. Now one finds it only in isolated programs, with individual faculty and students. The law school, for example, provides humane professional education, is innovative and unorthodox, has become a model for law schools throughout the nation. The English department still thrives. There are some others as well that remind one of the former spirit. But for me and many others who left, the Buffalo experience is irretrievably over. I look back on it now with enormous nostalgia. As an educational experiment the Meyerson years at Buffalo were not a major success. No permanent change in the nation's expectations for higher education can be identified with our attempt to radically transform the University. What does remain is a nucleus of people who form an informal Buffalo group, in much the same way one thinks of individuals identified with the University of Chicago or Black Mountain College as a group. All of us were deeply touched by the Buffalo experience. For a time Buffalo was the locus of enormous excitement, as great as any we had experienced in our academic careers. Hopes and ambitions were high. For a time Buffalo transcended the imitative competitiveness that characterizes so many campuses on the make and achieved an excellence that was all its own.

Recently I spent a long weekend with several members of the Buffalo group, many of whom are now in diaspora at other universities. (Interestingly, several are acting university presidents or are currently considering offers of college presidencies.) The talk turned, as it inevitably does, to how thoroughly the Meyersonian spirit has been stamped out at UB. "What went wrong?" someone always asks.

The lion's share of the blame—or the credit, as some people view it—goes to the current university administration. This administration simply denies history. Philosophically the Ketter administration is the successor of the Furnas administration. Meyerson's was the reign of an educational anti-Pope. There is rarely official mention of him or his works. For example, last year the American Council on Education released its current evaluation of the nation's graduate programs. Buffalo improved dramatically in the ACE ratings since the last survey was released, so much so that the jump was cited in the national press. The university proudly held a news conference at which campus officials announced that the upgrading of graduate education at Buffalo was largely accomplished under the late President Furnas. Meyerson had officially disappeared.

What saddens me is a suspicion that this gross assault would not be successful if we had been more effective. The stated goal of the Meyerson academic reorganization was to *transform* the university. How could a new administration turn her back so quickly if progress toward that goal had not been largely illusory or rhetorical? This is not a confession of failure. Nothing is so hard to change as a university, and Meyerson's attempt was courageous. But as one who was involved in many of the crucial decisions, I now see with all the unsettling clarity of hindsight that we undermined many of our own best aspirations for the university. If I were asked today how to bring about change in a university setting, I would offer the following guidelines:

(1) *Recruit with scrupulous honesty.* My personal recruiting at Buffalo depended on a falsely bright picture of the situation. It wasn't that I lied. But, consciously or not, I sweetened the package even when I was trying to be balanced and fair. Recruiting is a courtship ritual. The suitor displays his assets; the recruit, flattered by the attention and the promises, does not examine the assets closely. We were naive. The recruiting pitch at Buffalo depended on the future. We made little of the past and tended to deemphasize the present. Buffalo was the university of the future—of course, it would take time to catch up.

New arrivals had barely enrolled their kids in local schools before reality intruded. A labor-union dispute delayed construction of the promised new facilities. Inflation nibbled away at the buying power of the allocated construction funds at a rate of 1½ per cent a month. It was easy to put up with the inconvenience of overcrowding when one was sure that the condition was temporary. But the dispute dragged on for months, and there was little room on the old campus. The situation might have been challenging if we had not led the new faculty to expect something magical. We had urged them to reveal their most creative, most imaginative educational thinking, then had assured them that their plans would receive generous support. In reality, money to staff new programs was difficult to come by. After one year, the state legislature began to pare the budget. Many new faculty members felt they had been conned. As recruiters we had not pointed out our ultimate inability to control the legislatively determined budget. We had promised a new university when our funds could provide only an architect's model.

Inadvertently, we had cooked up the classic recipe for revolution as suggested by Aaron Wildavsky: "Promise a lot; deliver a little. Teach people to believe that they will be much better off, but let there be no dramatic improvement. Try a variety of small programs but marginal in impact and severely underfinanced. Avoid any attempted solution remotely comparable in size to the dimensions of the problem you are trying to solve."[3]

The intensity of the disaffection felt by some of those I had brought to the university came to me as a shock. We had raised expectations as high as any in modern educational history. When our program met only a part of these expectations, the disillusionment that followed was predictable and widespread. The disparity between vision and reality became intolerable. No one had said a word during the seductive recruiting days about triplicate forms, resentful colleagues, and unheeded requests for help from administrative headquarters.

Those who rose above the mundane annoyances provoked by university bureaucracy felt cheated in other ways. Recruits had joined our academic revolution because they shared our goal and wanted to participate. To keep such a cadre committed, an administration must keep them involved. But the warmth of our man-to-man recruiting interviews was not evident in later meetings with administrators. In fact, such meetings became fairly infrequent. The continuing evidence of personal support that might have overcome the unavoidable lack of concrete support was not forthcoming.

(2) *Guard against the crazies.* Innovation is seductive. It attracts interesting people. It also attracts people who will take your ideas and distort them into something monstrous. You will then be identified with the monster and will have to devote precious energy to combating it. A change-oriented administrator should be damned sure about the persons he recruits, the persons who will be identified as his men and women. A few of the persons who got administrative posts under the new administration, committed though they were to change, were so irresponsible or antagonistic that they alienated more persons than they converted.

It is difficult to distinguish between agents of responsible change and those who rend all they touch. The most successful innovators often are marginal to the institution, almost in a geographical sense. They have contacts in other institutions, other areas. Their credentials are unorthodox. They are often terrible company men with little or no institutional loyalty. Change-oriented administrators must be able to distinguish the innovators, however eccentric they may be, from the crazies. An academic community can tolerate a high degree of eccentricity. But it will brutally reject an individual it suspects of masking mediocrity with a flashy commitment to innovation.

(3) *Build support among like-minded people, whether or not you recruited them.* Change-oriented administrators are particularly prone to act as though the organization came into being the day they arrived. This is an illusion, an omnipotent fantasy. There are no clean slates in established organizations. A new president can't play Noah and build the world anew with two hand-picked delegates from each academic discipline. Rhetoric about new starts is frightening to those who suspect that the new beginning is the end of their own careers. There can be no change without history, without continuity.

What I think most of us in institutions want—and what status, money, and power serve as currency for—is acceptance, affection, and esteem. Institutions are more amenable to change when they preserve the esteem of all members. Given economic sufficiency, persons stay in organizations and feel satisfied in them because they are respected and feel competent. They are much freer to identify with the adaptive process and much better equipped to tolerate the high level of ambiguity that accompanies change when these needs are heeded. Unfortunately, we did not attend to these needs at Buffalo.

The academic code, not the administrative one, determines appropriate behavior in the university. The president is a colleague, and he is expected to acknowledge his intellectual equals whatever their relative position on the administrative chart. Many old-guard professors took the administration's neglect as a personal snub. They were not asked for advice; they were not invited to social affairs. They suspected that we acted coolly toward them because we considered them to be second-rate academics who lacked intellectual chic and who could not cut it in Cambridge or New York.

Ironically, some of the old-guard academic administrators who kept their positions were notoriously second-rate. Meyerson extended the appointments of several such, perhaps hoping to avoid the appearance of a purge. Among the incumbents were a couple whose educational philosophy had rigidified sometime in the early fifties. Instead of appeasing the old guard, these appointments added insult. The old guard suspected that the new administration viewed them as an undifferentiated mass. They wondered why we kept these second-raters and overlooked a pool of potentially fine veteran candidates.

We succeeded in infusing new blood into Buffalo, but we failed to recirculate the old blood. We lost an opportunity to build loyalty among respected members of the veteran faculty. If veteran faculty members had been made to feel that they too had a future in the transformed university, they might have embraced the academic reorganization plan with some enthusiasm. Instead they were hurt, indignant, and—finally—angry.

(4) *Plan for how to change as well as what to change.* Buffalo had a plan for change, but we lacked a clear concept of how change should proceed. A statement of goals is not a program.

The Buffalo reorganization lacked the coherence and forcefulness that would have guaranteed its success. The fault may have been that it was too abstract. Or perhaps it was too much a pastiche. A great many influences were evident: Paul Goodman and the community of colleges; the colleges and sense of academic tradition of Oxbridge; the unorthodoxy and informality of Black Mountain; the blurring of vocational-professional lives practiced at Antioch and Bennington; the collegiality of Santa Cruz; the college-master system of Yale. Each of these elements was both desirable and educationally fashionable, but the mix never jelled. No alchemy transformed the disparate parts into a living organism.

We had no coherent mechanisms for change. Instead we relied on several partially realized administrative models. The burden of change fell upon the Faculty Senate, which emphasized the small-group model. Change depended on three things: participation by the persons involved, trust in the persons who advocated the change, and clarity about the change itself. None of these conditions was fully present at Buffalo, and, as a result, the change was imperfectly realized.

Radical students utilized a revolutionary model. The students saw an opportunity for radical educational change in the Romantic tradition. The administration relied heavily on the model of successive limited comparisons, popularly known as "muddling through." This is the model of most organizational decision-making. It is a noncomprehensive, nontheoretical approach. Most administrators are forced to muddle through because the decisions they are called upon to make are simply too complex to treat comprehensively—even by committees. As a result, we neglected possible outcomes, overlooked alternative solutions, and could not predict the ultimate impact of the resulting policy on values.

Ultimately the reorganization failed to concentrate its energies on the model that would have satisfied the ambitions of all parts of the university: an incremental-reform model. Revolution inevitably produces reaction. All power to the French people one day and to Thermidor the next. If change is to be permanent it must be gradual. The incremental-reform model depends on a rotating nucleus of persons who continuously read the data provided by the organization and the society around it for clues that it is time to adapt. These persons are not faddists but they are hypersensitive to an idea whose hour has come. In a university such persons know when an idea is antithetical to the values of an academic institution and when it extends the definition of a university and makes it viable. One cannot structure these critical nuclei, but an organization cannot guarantee continuous self-renewal without them. At Buffalo a few departments and programs developed these nuclei. Most did not.

(5) *Don't settle for rhetorical change.* We accomplished the change at Buffalo by fiat. The Faculty Senate announced that the president's plan had been ratified.[4] Significant change does not take place that way. An organization has two structures: one on paper and another deep one that is a complex set of intramural relationships. A good administrator creates a good fit between the two. We allowed ourselves to be swept along by our rhetoric and neglected the much more demanding business of building new constituencies and maintaining established ones.

(6) *Don't allow those who are opposed to change to appropriate such basic issues as academic standards.* I became Meyerson's academic vice president in August 1968. Members of the old guard soon began to accuse me of being soft on standards. I had refused to disavow some of the more flagrant abuses of self-evaluation in the new colleges, and I had failed publicly to chastise faculty who subverted traditional academic practices as part of the radical revolution, although I did so unofficially. The problem of academic standards soon became a political issue. Privately we avowed our commitment to standards; publicly we were silent. The approach was notably unsuccessful. We did not want to undermine the fledgling colleges or violate the rights of radical faculty members. After Fascist, McCarthyite is the dirtiest word you can use on a liberal campus, and none of us was eager to hear it. We allowed the least change-oriented faculty members to make the issue of standards their own. They persuaded a great majority of moderate faculty members that the administration was committed to change for change's sake, whatever the price in academic excellence. We made a mistake that no successful reformer should ever make: we did not make sure that respectable people were unafraid of what was about to happen.

(7) *Know the territory.* A peculiar balance exists between the city of Buffalo and its one major university. Buffalo is not a university town like Princeton or Ann Arbor. The university is not powerful enough to impose its style and values on the city. Philadelphia and Los Angeles have several powerful universities that divide attention and diffuse rancor. Buffalo has a single target for its noisy anti-intellectuals. Two years ago some powerful forces in the town tried to close the university down. I don't know of another campus in the country that has had to function with such constant unsympathetic pressure from the surrounding community.[5] Meyerson barely had arrived in Buffalo when a group called Mothers Against Meyerson (MAM) began to petition for his removal. Their argument was that he was a Jew (a charge erroneously made against Meyerson's predecessor by an earlier group, Mothers Against Furnas) and that the campus harbored such dangerous criminal types as critic Leslie Fiedler.

Buffalo blamed the disruptions of 1970 on the "permissiveness" of the new administration. I got mail recommending that Curtis LeMay succeed Meyerson as university president. The local ex-marine who nominated LeMay believed that only the general's exotic blend of authoritarianism and right-wing values could undo the harm that we had perpetrated.

We never mastered the politics of local chauvinism. At the same time that the national press was romancing the university, one of the two local dailies was libeling her unmercifully. We devoted too little energy and imagination to public relations at the local level.

(8) *Appreciate environmental factors.* Like any other human activity, change proceeds more smoothly under optimal environmental conditions. Buffalo's chief environmental problem was not its miserable weather. The problem at Buffalo was (and still is) overcrowding. The faculty we recruited expected to move their books into futuristic offices like those promised by the architect's model of the new campus. Instead, they moved in on top of the faculty already there. The university assembled some prefab annexes for the overflow. Barbara Solomon, writing on the paranoia at Buffalo, noted that we pursued the life of the mind in quarters so ugly as to seem calculated.

The new campus barely had begun to rise by the time we reached the originally proposed completion date of 1972. The university had to lease an interim campus near the new campus site. Eleven academic departments moved out to this temporary facility in the spring 1967. The leased buildings had been designed for commercial and light-industry use. The fifteen-minute bus trip was a drag for students, and the isolation of the interim campus was contrary to the whole spirit of the Meyerson plan.

We neglected to protect new programs from external forces. College A began an experimental program in community action that was housed off-campus because of space priorities. College A is located directly across from a parochial grammar school and a diocesan center for retarded children. Every time a Scarsdale Maoist wrote "F——" on the wall or a bra-less coed played her guitar in front of one of the stores residents of the neighborhood predictably reacted. Students of College A were determined to interact with their neighbors; mothers of the school children were equally determined not to interact. The mothers picketed. The whole business snowballed, increasing the community's usual high level of outrage against the university.

(9) *Avoid future shock.* Buffalo aspired to be The University of the Year 2000. The future limited the campus just as the past limits the neurotic. The future insinuated itself into every attempt to deal with current issues and distorted our perception of the present. The unfinished new campus became an albatross, reminding everyone of the limited progress that was being made toward limitless goals. We put so much stock in the vision of future greatness that our disillusionment was inevitable. The problem with planning for the future is that there are no objective criteria against which to measure alternative solutions. There is not yet a contemporary reality against which to test. As a result the planner generates future schlock along with valid ideas, and there's no sure-fire way to separate the two.

(10) *Allow time to consolidate gains.* The average tenure of a university president is now 4.4 years and decreasing. It is impossible to transform a university in so short a time. Only a year after Meyerson assumed the Buffalo presidency, rumors began to circulate that he was leaving. Supporters of the new administration feared abandonment. Social critic David Bazelon commented to me, "In every other university I've been to, the faculty hated the administration. Here they worry about desertion." The changes proposed by Meyerson depended on continued presidential support for their success. The campus had, in effect, undergone major surgery and did not have sufficient time to heal before a series of altogether different demands, including a semester of unrest, a new president, and a major recession, were made on it. When Meyerson finally did resign in late January 1970, it was as though someone had prematurely pulled out the stitches.

The last guideline I offer to the would-be university reformer is so basic that it might well come first:

(11) *Remember that change is most successful when those who are affected are involved in the planning.* This is a platitude of planning theory, and it is as true as it is trite. Nothing makes persons as resistant to

new ideas or approaches as the feeling that change is being imposed upon them. The members of a university are unusually sensitive to individual prerogatives and to the administration's utter dependence on their support. Buffalo's academic plan was not popularly generated. Students and faculty did not contribute to its formulation. People resist change, even of a kind they basically agree with, if they are not significantly involved in the planning. A clumsier, slower, but more egalitarian approach to changing the university would have resulted in more permanent reform.

The problems surrounding innovation and change in an entrenched bureaucracy are not peculiar to universities. Every modern bureaucracy—university, government, or corporation—is essentially alike and responds similarly to challenge and to crisis.

Bureaucracy is the inevitable—and therefore necessary—form for governing large and complex organizations. Essentially, we must find bureaucratic means to stimulate the pursuit of truth—the true nature of the organization's problems—in a spirit of free inquiry and with democratic methods. This search calls for those virtues our universities and colleges have proved so capable of inspiring in others: an examined life, a spirit of inquiry and genuine experimentation, a life based on discovering new realities, of taking risks, of suffering occasional defeats, and of not fearing the surprise of the future.

The model for truly innovative and creative organizations in an era of enormous change becomes nothing less than the scientific spirit. The model for science becomes the model for all.

PATRICIA WARD BIEDERMAN ON "THE BERKELEY OF THE EAST" AND "WHAT WENT WRONG"

WARREN SWEPT INTO HIS NEW LIFE as an academic administrator with panache, aided by a Tyrolean cape. As he writes in *The Leaning Ivory Tower,* his 1973 account of his experiences at State University at Buffalo, the locals did not favor fancy-schmancy capes as winter garments. Puffy down parkas were the best defense against lake-effect blizzards, and so Buffalonians—male and female—tended to favor Inuit-style outerwear from November through March. Although *The Leaning Ivory Tower* is one of Warren's few titles to go out of print, it remains one of my favorites, if only because it was our first collaboration. It was also the first of his autobiographical books, and one of the most courageous in its candor, especially in the clear, cold eye he casts upon himself. Recounting how a prankster left a Batman cape on his office coat rack, Warren gently mocks himself for making so theatrical a fashion statement and lets the cape represent the myriad things—large and small—that can go wrong in a new leader's critical first days.

Buffalo was a leap of faith for Warren—an opportunity to test his growing, largely theoretical understanding of leadership in the real world. He gave up an enviable full professorship at MIT to become provost of social sciences and later vice president for academic affairs and acting executive vice president at the western New York campus. He chose accountability as a practitioner over the arm's-length responsibility of the theoretician. The siren that wooed Warren away from the cachet and certainty of Cambridge/ Boston was Martin Meyerson's audacious plan to transform the upstate campus into a grand educational experiment, an "academic New Jerusalem," the "Berkeley of the East."

The university was ambitious before the arrival of Meyerson's recruits and had pockets of greatness in the music and English departments, among others. But Buffalo was a once glorious American city that had been in decline for decades when its would-be saviors arrived in 1967, and its university inevitably reflected that diminution. A smart and edgy local graphics firm produced a best-selling T-shirt that proclaimed: "Buffalo, City of No Illusions." In fact, the city and its namesake university wore its reputation for being not quite first rate like a hair shirt. Not long ago I came across a choice example of the genteel abuse the university long had to contend with in David S. Brown's 2006 "intellectual biography" of historian Richard Hofstadter. A Buffalo native and UB graduate, Hofstadter once told his son: "Everybody wants to go to a great university, but I went to the University of Buffalo and got a very good education." Ouch.

Those of us who had preceded the newcomers to the Buffalo campus watched, often amused, sometimes horrified, as Meyerson and his new hires collected Frank Lloyd Wright houses and paid a high-profile graphic designer $10,000 to create a chic new image-changing seal for the university. No one in the president's office seemed to notice that the redesigned seal, which featured a stylized book whose open pages were meant to represent the university's seven new divisions, showed only six pages, not seven. Despite its soaring ambition, Martin Meyerson's tenure was as short as JFK's. Meyerson left his barely launched experiment in Buffalo to become president of an Ivy League school, the University of Pennsylvania.

But the late 1960s and early 1970s would have been tumultuous on campus with or without avowed change agents in charge. The entire country was in turmoil, as the New Left flourished and students fought for free speech and an end to the war in Vietnam. At Buffalo forty-five faculty were arrested while supporting the student protestors, and at one point hundreds of police in riot gear swarmed the campus. Between manifestoes, people turned on and tuned out; at a Janis Joplin concert on campus, Allen Ginsberg and Peter Orlovsky contentedly shared a joint wrapped in bright turquoise paper. By the time Warren decided to resign as acting executive vice president, unrest at the university had segued into virtual paralysis. As Warren notes, a student's documentary film about the troubled campus was titled "Andy Hardly Goes to College."

Characteristically, Warren extracted valuable lessons from both his successes and failures at Buffalo. As a result, these excerpts amount to a mini-blueprint for spinning the messy straw of experience into the gold of practical wisdom. One of the realities those hoping to change the university initially failed to appreciate was how often people already there felt dismissed or diminished by the new administration, however unwittingly. Re-reading Warren's analysis from more than thirty-five years ago, I thought how much Carly Fiorina might have benefited from a copy of *The Leaning Ivory Tower* when she was trying to transform the culture of Hewlett-Packard as its new CEO. Right there in black and white, Warren warns that a new leader cannot change an organization without honoring its past and, in effect, recruiting those already in place: "There are no clean slates in established organizations," he writes. "A new president cannot play Noah and build the world anew with two hand-picked delegates from each academic discipline. . . . There can be no change without history, without continuity."

Whether the organization is a college or a corporation, new leaders ignore that enduring truth at their peril.

A longtime collaborator with Warren Bennis, Patricia Ward Biederman is a prize-winning reporter and columnist, and former staff writer for the *Los Angeles Times*. She is co-author of the best-selling *Organizing Genius* (Perseus, 1997).

SEARCHING FOR THE "PERFECT" UNIVERSITY PRESIDENT (1971)

During the past twelve months more than 170 colleges and universities have chosen new presidents, including two men who failed to survive even their first year in office. As of February this year, at least 112 schools were still looking for a chief executive; Harvard had finally concluded its infinitely publicized search for Nathan Pusey's replacement; and tiny Franconia College, in New Hampshire, had observed its first six months under the leadership of twenty-four-year-old Leonard Botstein, certainly the youngest, if not the best known, presidential appointee of the year.

The job pays well—from $15,000 to $50,000 in most schools—and often includes housing, a generous expense account, and a comforting, if occasionally deceiving, illusion of power. But more and more college presidents have found themselves caught squarely between the zealously defended claims of a self-protective, professionalist faculty, a restive and extravagantly idealistic student body, antiquarian state legislators, and a fusty old-guard group of trustees, alumni, and businessmen, whose generosity, nevertheless, is largely responsible for keeping open the university's doors. To deal fairly with these frequently competing interests, and see to the business of providing an education for the students, has often been more than one ordinarily civilized man could manage—though the fact has not, apparently, reduced the allure of the job for a good many ambitious educators and administrators.

What follows is the story of a college presidency dangled before Warren Bennis, a forty-five-year-old sociologist, author, and veteran administrator; of a selection process that befuddled at least one candidate and pleased practically no one; and of a decision that never came.

This article originally appeared in the *Atlantic Monthly*, April 1971.

"DID YOU SEE THE MEYERSON ANNOUNCEMENT? It's awful, just awful."
Seymour Knox was lamenting Martin Meyerson's decision, announced in
January, 1970, to step down from the presidency of State University of New
York at Buffalo in order to succeed Gaylord Harnwell as president of the
University of Pennsylvania. As chairman of the Buffalo Council, Knox had
been crucial in bringing Meyerson to Buffalo over the cries of a local fac-
tion determined to block the appointment of "that Jew from Berkeley."
Therefore, Knox was not happy about Meyerson's decision to move on.

"I feel like a crumb-bum," he complained. "Yesterday, in Philadelphia, I
ran into an old friend, Bill Day, who is now chairman of the Penn Board of
Trustees. Was he gloating! God, it was awful. I felt like he'd stolen my cook."

The stolen cook was not the first analogy to come to my mind, but I
knew what Knox meant. University presidents are currently somewhat
harder to find and keep than competent domestic help. The numbers fluc-
tuate, but a sizable list of colleges and universities are currently conducting presidential searches. Why are there so many openings at the top?
There are many reasons, but a root cause is the altered nature of the job
itself. There was a time when a university president did little more than
officiate at commencements and raise funds; when his tenure was roughly
equal to that of a Supreme Court Justice. Not today; in the aftermath of
Berkeley, Columbia, Harvard, and Kent State, a university president is a
full-time crisis manager. He remains in office less than five years on the
average, and is usually glad to retire. Annual turnover of university and
college presidents has jumped nearly 30 percent in the last three years. In
the first two months of 1970, new presidents were named at forty-two
colleges, while one hundred resigned during the first six months of 1970.
One analyst has compared the job unfavorably with that of a pro hockey
referee. I don't think he's far off the mark. The work is rough, physically
exhausting, even dangerous. University presidents may lose fewer teeth than
hockey officials, but they have a startling number of heart attacks. A modern university president is expected to have practical vision, a good track
record in administration, and national prominence as a scholar. He must
be a good public speaker, fundraiser, writer, analyst, friend and colleague,
manipulator of power, planner, co-worker, persuader, and disciplinarian.
He must have an attractive family and an indefatigable and effortlessly
sociable wife. He must be a Money Man, Academic Manager, Father Figure, Public Relations Man, Political Man, and Educator. In short, as one
Harvard man put it, looking toward Nathan Pusey's successor, "He must
be a messiah with a good speaking voice." Or as Herman B. Wells, former
president of Indiana University, said in a rather more earthy way: "He
should be born with the physical strength of a Greek athlete, the cunning

of a Machiavelli, the wisdom of a Solomon, the courage of a lion, if possible. But in any case he must be born with the stomach of a goat."

During the last several years, while serving in various administrative posts at State University of New York at Buffalo, I was considered for the presidencies of at least a dozen colleges and universities. Since scrutiny works both ways, the time I spent with search committees (being examined rather like a bolt of felt, as I sometimes thought) gave me an excellent opportunity to study the process by which our universities choose presidents. Each of the twelve or so searches in which I was a participant-observer was unique. However, one search in particular—Northwestern University's—illustrates better than fiction the clash of formal machinery and partisan pressures in which American university presidents are made.

In simpler, less turbulent times, the presidential search process was handled pretty much the way an exclusive men's club chooses a new member. John G. Bowman, chancellor of the University of Pittsburgh in the twenties, recalls his own selection by this method in a chapter of his autobiography, entitled *You Must Go*. As Bowman writes:

> On an afternoon in October, 1920, in my work as the Director of the American College of Surgeons, I made a talk in Pittsburgh. The room was full of people, most of them interested in hospitals and the practice of medicine. After the talk, two or three men asked me to have dinner with them and some others that evening at the Duquesne Club. I said yes.
>
> In the evening I met about a score of men, most of them strangers to me, gathered around a table in a private dining room. During the dinner and after the dinner they asked questions: Do university presidents have business sense? What in your opinion is the top value of a college education? Is a college education a good thing for everybody? On and on the questions went. We had a lively talk and a good time. At about ten o'clock, one of the men at the table asked me to step into the hall with him. We went out of the room and walked down the hall toward a window hung with heavy draperies.
>
> We had covered only half the distance to the window, however, when another man of the group opened the door and asked us to come back. Then, all at the table again, George H. Clapp, head of Pittsburgh Testing Laboratories, said to me, "These men are trustees of the University of Pittsburgh. For some weeks we have been gathering information about you. We are glad now to invite you to become Chancellor of the University."

Bowman's story has a nostalgic quaintness to it, like a Dreiser novel, but the process he describes wasn't at all unusual. Douglas McGregor, president of Antioch College (1948–1954), once told me about his selection. He was in his office, at MIT, when his secretary told him that a Mr. Arthur Morgan was waiting to see him. McGregor knew little of Antioch and nothing of Morgan, who had been president of the college. Morgan offered him the presidency of Antioch after a few minutes of polite conversation which ran the gamut from the weather to the Charles River, snaking below the window of McGregor's office. They talked a while longer, and the next afternoon, the two of them took the train from the Back Bay Station for Yellow Springs, Ohio.

Even in the old days, naming one's successor was rather unusual (although after David Jordan left Indiana University to become president of Stanford, the Indiana board asked him to name not only his immediate successor but the next three presidents as well). The selection of a new president was most often the once-in-a-lifetime task of the board of trustees or the university corporation. Board members usually knew a few well-placed individuals to call on to suggest nominees, and people like Andrew S. White, the first president of Cornell University, Nicholas Murray Butler, or Chancellor William Tolley of Syracuse were frequently consulted. White, for example, personally picked two presidents for Michigan, one for Indiana, one for California, and one for Brown, and he also suggested the men who became the first presidents of Stanford and Johns Hopkins. In the 1920s, few boards reached their final decision without having consulted the Rockefeller Foundation. More recently, the Ford and Carnegie Foundations have played crucial roles in identifying potential presidents.

But times have changed. Today, universities are expected to choose presidents in the open by a process which involves students and faculty in some meaningful way. The process is expected to be a democratic one. In my experience, what actually happens when universities choose presidents falls considerably short of that ideal.

Take Northwestern. Sometime in mid-November, 1969, my office received a call from the Chicago office of the management consulting firm of Booz, Allen & Hamilton. I didn't return the call until Thanksgiving week because of university pressures and more or less mindless lethargy. Also, a sense of low priority. I had mistakenly assumed that Booz, Allen was going to ask me to give a speech on management. I had stopped giving speeches on management sometime before, again because of university chores, and because I felt increasingly squeamish lecturing on problems I had written books about now that my own institution was suffering with symptoms very like those I was reputedly an expert in curing. Midspeech I tended to recall Auden's character "who lectured on navigation while the ship was going down."

When I finally returned the call, two days before Thanksgiving, I learned that the firm was contacting me as a consultant for Northwestern University. Their man wanted to know if I might be available for, "or at least interested enough to explore," the Northwestern presidency. "I'm not really sure," I answered. "I don't know a great deal about Northwestern and what it wants. But I would certainly be interested in discussing it with you." He asked me when I could come out to Chicago or make time available for him at Buffalo. I told him that it would be extremely tough to find any free time before mid-January, but that I would be in Cleveland over the Thanksgiving weekend, and if he could manage to come there, I could certainly see him on Friday or Saturday. He jumped at this and said that a man in their Cleveland office "who has been working on the Northwestern case" would be able to see me at my in-laws' home in Cleveland.

I cannot recall Booz, Allen's Cleveland man by name. He reminded me of many youngish management consultants I have known who worked for any of the Big Three: Booz, Allen & Hamilton; McKinsey & Co.; Cresap, McCormick and Paget. He was a Harvard Business School graduate, WASPish, attractive, crisp, alert, and formidably informed. We spent about three hours together and hit it off immediately. I felt he was as straightforward and honest as he could be about the Northwestern situation. He gave me an exhaustive survey of the present status and future of Northwestern, told me a little about the search activities to date, generally what kind of man they were looking for, how Booz, Allen came to be involved in "coordinating the search process," and an informal rundown of some of the people on the board of trustees. At the end of the discussion, I presented my "C.V." (my *curriculum vitae*, without which any academic man is *sans* identity). He told me that I would be hearing from them in the future.

What I learned at that time was this. Northwestern sounded first-rate. It had a healthy endowment, distinguished faculty, top-caliber students, and rich and prominent trustees. Moreover, it was untainted, so far, by "the troubles" its more distinguished neighbor, the University of Chicago, had experienced during the past three years or so. Undertaking the presidential search was an omnibus committee which consisted of nine trustees, four faculty members (elected by the faculty), and three students. Booz, Allen had collected the names of more than three hundred possible candidates from the faculty, the board of trustees, and students. The incumbent president, a former dean of the Northwestern Medical School, Rocky Miller, was close to sixty-eight years old, mandatory retirement age, and had been in office for about twenty years. He had been, according to my informant, a good, somewhat conservative president who was instrumental in bringing about a substantial building program at Northwestern. With Booz, Allen's help, the search committee had drawn up a three-page document describing the kind of man they were looking for to replace Miller. Dr. Right was married, between thirty-five and forty years of age, with a strong, broad academic background, administrative experience, vision, energy, good health, and an ability to talk with diverse constituencies, and someone who could keep the campus relatively free from disruption. Booz, Allen was in the act because the board felt that a good consulting firm, with a strong track record for executive "headhunting," could assist in the normally chaotic selection process. I also learned that Jim Allen, a Northwestern trustee, was the "Allen" in Booz, Allen & Hamilton.[1]

I was very taken with Northwestern after that talk and felt highly complimented by their interest in me. Of the colleges and universities that had contacted me in the past year, I had taken two of them seriously enough to visit, but they weren't in the same league as Northwestern as far as resources, talent, and future potential were concerned. Several factors contributed to my initial enthusiasm: Northwestern was in an important urban area which the university had virtually ignored in the past and with which it now wanted to get involved. The university had yet to achieve "greatness" in the same sense that Harvard or Yale or even Stanford had (Stanford most of all, since twenty years ago Stanford was in about the same league as Northwestern) despite their valid claim to top-rank faculty and students; there was not yet a truly unique character associated with Northwestern, no Northwestern*ness*, but the search committee obviously wanted such a character to emerge under new leadership. All of these suggested to me that Northwestern was on the verge of major growth, and that its new president would play a key role in directing its emergence as a major university.

Whatever doubts I had centered on whether Northwestern and I fit. From all I knew of Northwestern, it was conservative, rich, suburban, and Midwestern—what in the 1950s would have been called a "white shoe" campus. The trustees were the biggest question in my mind. For the most part they came from the large banks, law firms, and businesses in Chicago. They not only read the *Chicago Tribune* editorials daily, but according to my Booz, Allen & Hamilton man, they actually *believed* them. Boards have an understandable tendency to pick presidents who incline to agree with their values, if not their politics. (One study of 110 state college and university presidents showed that 88 percent stated their political affiliations as identical with the governors of their respective states.) Whether or not they would find me acceptable remained to be seen. That a consulting firm had been called in—no matter one of the best—also registered a blip of concern. Previous experience with presidential searches led me to believe that this was extremely atypical. So I had a few qualms, and I knew there would be surprises ahead. But even when one is prepared for surprises, they do surprise all the same.

A week or so later, Booz, Allen called again. Without really using these words, their man told me that I had passed the first hurdle and in a month or so I would hear from him again. Apparently, there were other people to screen, and if I stood up well, a contingent from Northwestern would visit me in Buffalo. He was extremely friendly, even solicitous. "Do you want any more information about Northwestern?" he asked before ringing off.

Sometime in the first half of January, 1970, I was called again. The search was going along nicely, my Booz, Allen contact reported. The list was now pared down to fifteen or twenty names. He said that I was still very much in the running, and, indeed, he wondered if I could meet with the chairman of the search committee, who was also a Northwestern trustee and chairman of the board of Harris Trust Company in Chicago; the associate dean of Northwestern's School of Speech and Drama, representing the faculty; and the president of the Northwestern Student Association. We set the time for February 4 in my office at Buffalo.

The group arrived in my office around 10 o'clock in the morning and left for the airport at 4 in the afternoon. Lunch was brought in. It was a six-hour talk show. After the initial awkwardness was smoothed over with orders for coffee or tea and talk of their flight, we settled down for some serious conversation. We covered a range of topics: from my attitudes about student participation, campus unrest, and my role at Buffalo, all the way to social activities and family. (They did not ask whether I had a "Hebrew strain," as one trustee of Penn State University had the year before when he visited me at Buffalo. At that time I had replied that not only did I have a strain, I was, indeed, a "Hebrew." "I knew it! I knew it!" the trustee had exclaimed enthusiastically.)

The time with the three search committee members was well spent. We covered a lot of ground, and it was clear that they not only permitted but encouraged me to indicate how I stand and who I am. They had read some of my books and articles, and referred several times to a revealing interview with me which had appeared in the February, 1969, *Psychology Today*. (Actually, candidates are rarely as satisfied with their interviews as I was. According to a recent study conducted by the Committee on Educational Leadership in New York State, only a small number of college presidents felt that the selection process had permitted them to show their strengths for the position in a significant manner. I figured that even if Northwestern were to favor someone else, at least they would do so with a knowledge of my strengths as well as my weaknesses.) My strategy in dealing with search committees, if it can be called a strategy, is to be myself as much as is humanly possible to be oneself with a group of caliper-eyed strangers. If they *really* want someone like me, then there is none better.

In any case, all of us seemed to enjoy the day. The faculty member was interested to learn if I cared more about academic pursuits than administrative affairs and whether or not I would work with, rather than against, the faculty. Faculty tend to view or want to view the president as their servant, not their seer, he said. The student clearly wanted a president who would take the students into account, not just in a token way, and he dwelt on problems of student involvement in the political processes of the university. We got into a little argument concerning the tenure of presidents. I said rather firmly that I believed in a term appointment of about seven years, as Kingman Brewster had recently advocated at Yale, rather than a lifelong appointment. This caused the chairman to ask if I really was interested in Northwestern and "might it not be a mistake to set a definite period of office?" The discussion was easy, flowing, informal, and without a great deal of anxiety.

The sticky points were all predictable. I asked them a battery of questions about Northwestern's culture and style, its financial status and outlook, what kind of guy "Rocky" Miller was, why they were interested in me (Why was I interested in them? they asked back, quite reasonably), what was Northwestern's relationship with other universities in the area and with the cities and state, how many "disadvantaged" students are admitted, about black studies programs in general, some notion of presidential discretion and power, the structure of the search committee, the weaknesses in the present organization of the university, an evaluation of the present administration, relations with alumni, and so on.

I *liked* them, particularly the student, who asked the most penetrating and direct questions. The faculty representative appeared to be gentle and perceptive and a remarkable listener. The chairman was the least relaxed and sometimes irrelevant, going off on a tack of his own which I couldn't always understand. He was clearly concerned about campus disorders, but he appeared to be a broad-minded and open man.

When the three returned to Northwestern, they met with Booz, Allen for a two- or three-hour "debriefing." On the basis of their reports, Booz, Allen prepared the following summary of their impressions:

SUMMARY COMMENTS FROM SUBCOMMITTEE MEETING WITH PROSPECTIVE CANDIDATE	WARREN G. BENNIS Acting Executive Vice President and Vice President-Academic Development State University of New York at Buffalo, Buffalo, New York
ACADEMIC QUALIFICATIONS AND EXPERIENCE	Strong qualifications and credentials. Full professor—two institutions. Innovative and progressive. Some national eminence through extensive writing and lecturing. Favorably inclined to professional fields as well as academic—"cultural pluralism." Both a teacher and writer. Evidently strong faculty/student relations and sensitivity. Former President Meyerson's selection of him is tribute to his academic as well as administrative credentials. Buffalo and state university affiliation should not be held against him. The university has made many significant changes and improvements. A dissenting opinion by one subcommittee member—"compulsive speaker and writer—perhaps has overdone it."
EXECUTIVE EXPERIENCE	Has handled key issues of the "number-two" job at Buffalo very well under heavy pressure. Clear understanding of how the administrative structure can complement, even aid, the development of new progressive currents in the field of higher education. Has played key role in the improvements made at Buffalo. Is an innovative administrator—many new programs evidently well planned and executed. Delegates well. Personally well organized; firm-minded; appears to be decisive and no impressions of limitations in leadership. Consensus opinion that he can contribute, but we must check his track record—Is he a senior executive or merely an able, persuasive administrator?
MAGNITUDE OF PRESENT MANAGEMENT RESPONSIBILITY	Experience is applicable but effectiveness has not been proven over extended period. Chief operating officer for past several months of sizable, complex, urban, public university. Larger in enrollment than Northwestern but not as broad in scope. Helped effect necessary and important changes from private

	to public institution management. Important to recall that he had significant experience as a professor and department chairman at a large, private university (MIT). Is not tied to any system of organization and expressed reservations on Buffalo multi-area provost system. Also raised questions on NU organization, but appears to be objective and open-minded. Works hard at managing and evidently is very demanding.
PERSONAL QUALIFICATIONS	Medium height, "tweedy," "modernish" but neat. Personal bearing "taller than his physical stature." Poised, articulate, charming, genuine, and business-like warmth. A quality man. Smart, analytical— once he makes decisions will be demanding and perhaps unbending. Could work well at all levels. Will want authority but suspect he would be sensitive to others. Community-minded and gives impression that his wife is equally extroverted (although subcommittee did not meet her). While affable and thoughtful, there is clear indication of firm-mindedness and high opinion of self. [A possible, but not serious, reservation that his manner might not "sit well" with some faculty, trustees, and alumni.]
APPARENT INTEREST IN THE POSITION	Very high. Really "did his homework" on NU. Asked extremely good questions. Sees Northwestern as logical and attractive next step for him. Sees the university as an academic institution of great accomplishment and potential. [Would want to come only if he were convinced he could ultimately become the chief executive.] Was sensitive to the importance of the relationship with the Chancellor— raised subject himself.
SUMMARY COMMENTS	A good meeting. Personally and professionally attractive. Handled himself well. Has a style that might be just right for the coming era at Northwestern. An impressive, innovative, competent, and accomplished administrator. May be limited in experience and a bit too aggressive and demanding, but is a strong candidate who should be considered further.

Similar profiles were drawn up on each of the stronger candidates and distributed among the entire search committee. (The members of the search committee had specially made black notebooks, with their names embossed in gold on the covers, in which to keep the profiles and all their other search materials together.) Of course, as a candidate I knew none of this at the time. What was happening at the Northwestern end of their yearlong search was told to me only recently by one of the on-campus participants.

Two weeks passed after my interview, and the Booz, Allen representative phoned again, this time with positive joy in his voice. The search committee wanted me to come to Northwestern *as soon as possible* to spend at least a day or two talking with people. He was annoyed by the fact that two key Northwestern faculty committees had "demanded" the right to interview all "serious" candidates, and he hoped I wouldn't mind if they were included in my visit. "There is now a short list of candidates," he told me, "and you are on the short list. Only the top four on the short list are being invited to the campus." I was leaving for Mexico City in a few days and told him that I would call him as soon as I got back. I called on February 23, and we settled on March 7 for my visit to Northwestern, the day of the eclipse.

Between my phone call to Booz, Allen on February 23 and March 7, the Buffalo campus exploded into one of the worst crises that have hit major campuses in America. Strangely enough, except for faculty member Edgar Z. Friedenberg's articles in the *New York Review of Books,* a squib in *Newsweek,* and an occasional story in the *New York Times,* the *Post,* and the *National Observer,* there was surprisingly little national coverage of the Buffalo crisis. Perhaps people were getting bored or inured to the guerrilla activities of students and the police (this was *before* Kent State and Jackson State), or maybe the Santa Barbara bank-burning about the same time eclipsed everything else. I don't know. In any case, the Buffalo campus experienced an unparalleled convulsion, with the local press reporting news of "fresh disasters" daily. More than 125 students, police, and others required medical attention. Forty-five faculty members were arrested and booked on three separate charges (the largest number of faculty ever arrested for a campus activity; the previous record was sixteen Harvard faculty arrested for protesting the Spanish-American War). Another six faculty members were arrested on other counts. More than fifty students were charged on criminal counts. Over $300,000 in property damage was reported.

At seven that morning, March 7, on the plane for Chicago, I wasn't at all certain that I should be going. I had averaged only two hours sleep per night over the last three weeks. (If there is any advice I would give campus administrators during a crisis, it is this: GET SLEEP. The kids are younger and there are more of them. They can run in relays.) I felt like limp pasta as I flopped into my seat. I was no more up to what I knew would be a grueling day of scrutiny than I was to another day of manning the barricades on my own campus.

Worse by far than the fatigue was the recognition that I *should* remain in Buffalo that day in order to stave off a decision made by certain members of the university's administration the night before. The acting president, Peter Regan, and some of his advisers were convinced that the only way to stop the student disruption was through a massive police intervention, virtually an occupation of the campus, by four hundred Buffalo city police. I was convinced this would be a catastrophic mistake, that it would destroy whatever legitimacy and trust the present administration tenuously held; that it would depress morale below the tolerable limits; and, finally, that it would be playing into the hands of the most militant students, who badly needed another clumsy overreaction by the administration to survive. Calling in four hundred police was the single way to "radicalize" the majority of moderate students, forcing them to join and augment the usually thin ranks of committed revolutionaries; at Buffalo, a corps of perhaps 100 students out of a total student body of almost 24,000.

I had argued vehemently against the police intervention, for these and other reasons, for the preceding eighteen hours without success. When I left Buffalo the police were expected to move onto the campus twenty-four hours later, Sunday morning, March 8. My only hope—or rationalization—in leaving town was that the acting president would recover from this lapse of judgment when he could get some sleep, and when he was no longer involved in a "win-lose" argument with me, his number-two man.

All these things were on my mind when I finally met my Booz, Allen contact at O'Hare Airport, at 7:30 AM, Chicago time. He escorted me directly into the chauffeured Cadillac owned by the search committee chairman and drove to the chairman's house for coffee. On the way, I was shown the schedule for the day. It was more clogged than usual because I had insisted (and everyone fully understood) that conditions at Buffalo were such that I could spend only one day for this visit. After coffee, I was to be driven over to the president's house for a two-hour talk with Rocky Miller. Then the chairman would pick me up just before noon and drive me out to the Glenview Country Club, where I would have lunch with a group of about ten trustees. (Booz, Allen proposed a later meeting with several absent trustees in Palm Beach.) Following lunch, I would meet with the two insistent faculty committees who "demanded" the opportunity to interview and register their responses to all "serious" candidates.

Following that, I would have dinner with all those faculty members and students on the search committee who had not been able to come to Buffalo in February. This series of meetings would last through 9:00 PM, allowing just time enough to return to O'Hare for the 10:05 PM flight back to Buffalo.

The man from Booz, Allen was visibly glad to see me. I remember him rubbing his hands together in delight when he told me that the search was down to four candidates, "two insiders and two outsiders." This was more information than I had expected, though I had heard that Northwestern's dean of the arts and sciences, Dr. Robert Strotz, was a very strong contender. He also surprised me when he mentioned the name of the other inside candidate, a man whom *I* was trying to recruit for a top administrative post at Buffalo. When I said that we, too, were interested in him, my Booz, Allen contact seemed both surprised and annoyed. "Haven't you guys looked seriously into his record here? Haven't you called *anybody* from Northwestern about him?" I replied that I wasn't on the search committee but I had every reason to believe that they had taken all the necessary steps, including informal "prowling," in order to arrive at their assessment. Our mutual candidate, it turned out, was the man responsible for the Northwestern "faculty intrusion" into the university's search for a new president. He was generally making life miserable for the search committee, which did not, of course, endear him to Booz, Allen. My internal radar, dormant throughout the lulling airplane trip, was suddenly reactivated by the inappropriateness of the Booz, Allen man's remarks. As he grumbled on about faculty troublemakers, the candidate began to sound better and better to me. (He eventually accepted the position at Buffalo, by the way.)

The day was predictably grueling. The two hours with Rocky Miller were extremely cordial but basically a "nonevent." We covered nothing of consequence, although I tried on several occasions to bring him out. We spent most of our time in his car, driving around the campus. He pointed out buildings, told me what year they went up and which of the trustees had paid for them. I hadn't realized how bland it all was until Eva Jefferson, one of the students at dinner (soon to be president of Northwestern's student body), asked me what I thought of him. I really didn't have any response at all, except that he had certainly helped raise a lot of money for buildings.

The two faculty meetings were condensed into one session because lunch took longer than was expected and because the search committee chairman had trouble finding the room in which I was scheduled to meet with the two "ad hoc" faculty committees. So instead of meeting with them back to back, I saw all twenty-five of the faculty at the same time. That was a good session, as I remember. The questions were sharp and incisive, and I was heartened by an intuitive feeling that they were looking for someone like me. The dinner with the four faculty and three students was also active, penetrating, and pleasant. In addition to the drama and speech dean, who left early, the other faculty members included Raymond Mack, a first-rate sociologist and head of the Northwestern Urban Center, and, as I remember, faculty members from the Technology Institute and the health science areas. I felt very keen support from the students, moderate to strong support from the faculty.

Lunch at the country club provided the one remarkable moment of the day. It was a beautiful early spring day, with the eclipse throwing the bare-limbed trees into relief in the strong but muted sun, as if the sun were filtered through the edge of a fingernail. At times, I could barely look through the windows because of the strange brightness of the light. About ten people were present, including the omnipresent Booz, Allen man, the search committee chairman, and a representative of the Northwestern alumni organization. He was memorable because he was clearly the youngest in the group. The rest, with one exception, were in their fifties and over. But they were a handsome bunch of people, extremely cordial for the most part.

After Bloody Marys and sherry, we sat down at the table. Just as I began attacking the fresh fruit cup, the person seated two seats to my left, whom I remember as the alumni representative, cleared his throat and floated a question down to me. I was tempted to let it pass, but it was evident that he had been working on that question a long time, and, I thought—mistakenly, in retrospect—that taking a cut at it would get him over the embarrassment the question seemed to cause him.

"Who," he asked, "do you think are the three greatest university presidents and why?"

I returned my spoon with a melon ball resting on it to the plate and said, looking up into the oak beams, "Well, Howard Johnson of MIT, for one. In my view he is the administrator-manager *par excellence*. And imagine overcoming a name like that."

That seemed to relax everybody, and I continued. "My second choice would have to be Kingman Brew . . . " At that very point, somewhere between the "Brew" and the unuttered "ster," the man opposite me began to choke as if something were caught in his throat. Two red-jacketed waiters ran over to him and started pounding him on the back. This lasted a good thirty seconds, until he seemed to recover his breath. His breath but not his composure. As he came up into a vertical position for air, the man shouted something to me. I couldn't hear him, although he wasn't more than three and a half feet across the table from me, and as I leaned forward, the ball of honeydew that had lodged in his throat at the mention of Brewster left it at a muzzle velocity of at least 1000 feet per second and smashed against my forehead.

At the moment of impact, the Booz, Allen representative, seated directly to my right, kicked my leg, and I began to wonder if this was some kind of perverse stress test they gave to all candidates. As the waiter dried my face nervously, my red-faced assailant increased the volume. He screamed, choking again. "DID YOU SAY BREWSTER? WOULD *YOU* KEEP THAT IDIOT COFFIN ON YOUR PAYROLL?"

I ducked involuntarily and then replied, more dogmatically than I actually felt about the whole business, that, yes, the Reverend Coffin apparently serves an important purpose at Yale, despite his radical views, or at least, Brewster thinks so, and furthermore, I'm not sure that Brewster has the power or right to contravene what are basically faculty prerogatives, and . . . " My questioner's coughing had subsided to heavy breathing, but his face was still alarmingly red. A trustee seated at the head of the table asked in a commanding voice if I wouldn't turn to my third choice, and we continued, almost pleasantly, as if what had happened were a trifling *faux pas* that we had collectively agreed to ignore.

The "honeydew statement" aside, the Northwestern search to this point is more or less typical of how most universities go about selecting a new president. The only unusual feature, as I said earlier, was the use of an outside consulting firm to coordinate the search process. (Later on this backfired.) Of the 2500 or so accredited colleges in the United States, only the most parochial (say, Bob Jones University in South Carolina) would proceed on a presidential search without a faculty, student, and possibly an alumni committee, working with a small group of trustees.[2] Northwestern also had alumni representation on the board. When a community college is searching for a president, the committee almost always includes prominent members of the community.

The search that Harvard undertook before selecting Derek Bok to succeed Nathan Pusey may well emerge as the new model for selection processes, at least at major institutions. Harvard's Committee on Governance (appointed by President Pusey in September, 1969, a product of the spring crisis) circulated a fifteen-page booklet, *Discussion Memorandum Concerning the Choice of a New President*. Published in April, 1970, it called for the most thorough participation in the presidential search known to Harvard, certainly, and perhaps known to any campus. Aside from an incredible number of consultations with "key groups," both inside and outside the University, the Harvard Corporation started its search with the distribution of some 200,000 letters inviting suggestions for candidates from (among others) faculty members, students, key alumni, and employees. This correspondence alone took almost the full time of a professional staff member with a large staff of assistants and clerks. That first step was only a small part of the total effort, which cost an estimated half million dollars. (By way of comparison, James Conant was selected after only one appearance before the total search committee, during which he gave a clear analysis of the man needed and urged the candidacy of one of his closest friends.)

In one magnificently prescient paragraph entitled, "How might the foreseeable negative consequences be minimized?" the Harvard *Discussion Memorandum* lists these five stumbling blocks which may cripple a search committee:

1. Sheer volume of work.

2. The selection process may divide and polarize rather than unify the university.

3. Candidates surviving the scrutiny of many diverse groups may be the same hackneyed names who always turn out to be unavailable— what I refer to as the "John Gardner" syndrome—or, among those who are available, they may be essentially "low risk," mediocre candidates.

4. A "credibility gap" may occur between the search committee and various groups within and without the university over the extent to which their advice is being sincerely sought, objectively evaluated, and imaginatively interpreted.

5. Potential candidates may be alienated by premature publicity, gossip about their candidacy, and vigorous opposition, even if ill-informed and limited.

Northwestern's search process left none of these "negative consequences" unturned. In fact, it uncovered several "negative consequences" undreamt of in Harvard's list.

Quite often, especially if the university is prestigious, there is a good deal of publicity that attends and sometimes complicates the search. In the Northwestern case, for example, the student newspaper, the *Daily Northwestern*, managed, somehow, to obtain dossiers on each of the three finalists as well as their ranking. How they succeeded is one of the miracles of the age, since all search committee members are sworn to secrecy and the candidates themselves are usually in no mood to discuss the race.

For obvious reasons. Nobody wants to have "honorable mention," even on the "short list." Active candidates try to appear majestically aloof from the politics of candidacy. Overt campaigning is as alien to the academic man, and as endemic, as it is to the College of Cardinals during papal election. All that is missing when a university picks a president is the puff of smoke.[3]

The *Daily Northwestern* scoop of April 15 revealing the names of the three finalists—New York University's Chancellor Allan Cartter, Northwestern's Dean Robert Strotz, and myself—was immediately picked up by all the Chicago dailies and in the hometown newspapers of the two outside candidates. The next day the student paper ran an editorial scourging the search committee for ignoring student opinion in the selection process so far. Everyone concerned refused to comment, although the leaked story was completely accurate, so accurate, as a matter of fact, that one candidate decided to withdraw from the race shortly after the story appeared.

Owing to poor weather conditions, the 10:05 plane from Chicago to Buffalo on March 7 was unable to land, and I arrived in Buffalo around 11 AM, Sunday morning, March 8. The acting president had called a noon meeting of all faculty, administrative officers, and student officers, and I rushed over to the campus to learn what was going on. The entire perimeter of the campus was surrounded, bumper to bumper, with Buffalo City Police vehicles. As I walked into the building where the meeting was to be held, policemen were already marching across the campus, Army-style, twelve to sixteen per group in columns of two. When I arrived, Acting President Regan was explaining his reasons for calling the police onto the campus, a speech greeted for the most part with a lobotomized silence. Only three people spoke up. The vice president for student affairs said that "it was about time," and a member of the faculty senate who supported Dr. Regan's action reported that "my department would certainly support the police action." Mark Huddleston, president of the Student Association, said that he and the other students were totally against the police occupation, and that he was even more thoroughly disgusted with the acting president for going back on his word that students would be consulted on all decisions related to police intervention. The meeting dissolved after Huddleston's statement.

Afterwards, I walked with Dr. Regan to a nearby office and told him that I intended to resign, not only to disassociate myself from the police intervention, but for other reasons that made my future cooperation with his administration impossible.

In writing my letter of resignation that evening (which was personally delivered to Regan the next morning, March 9), I was not totally unaware of the consequences of the act and how it would be perceived, both inside and outside the university. If there were still any doubts about the Northwestern presidency, I felt this act could be interpreted, particularly by the Northwestern trustees, in any number of unfavorable ways, from being "too permissive" or "soft on law and order" to "desertion." My fears were confirmed during the next few months in a series of unusual exchanges with Northwestern.

POINTS TO REMEMBER ON
CHOOSING A COLLEGE PRESIDENT

1. *Remember that there is no single quality, trait, characteristic, style, or person that guarantees presidential capability.* A century and a half of psychological research confirms this point. An Ivy League degree or a "low profile" is not in itself going to ensure the bearer of success in dealing with an adamant board or angry students. Being from the "outside" is no talisman either. The outsider may fail if he is unable to master quickly the special terrain of his institution—fail just as dismally as the insider whose judgment is skewed by partisan loyalties held over from his pre-presidential days. There is no one presidential "type," no presidential personality. The time is past when a Stanford or a Columbia can be described as the lengthened shadow of any one man.

Many different approaches to university management have been successful in the recent past. Among possible presidential styles are:

The problem-solver/manager. Howard Johnson, the retiring president of MIT, has used this approach most successfully. Johnson's concern has been, How can I identify problems (real problems, not temporal issues) and engage the best minds and most important constituencies to work on them?

The managerial style is often confused with that of *low-profile/technocrat*. Similarities are superficial. Instead of putting the right people to work on the right problems, the technocrat tries to find *systems* that will somehow transcend human error. The concerns of the technocrat are all pragmatic. He cuts through moral and ideological dilemmas with a callousness that soon has students and faculty aligned against him.

The leader/mediator. Based on the labor relations model, this style is just coming into its own. If one conceives of the university in terms of constituencies seeking to maximize self-interest, a place where there is no way to make decisions without pleasing some and making some angry, then this style is very effective. In fact, there may be no decent alternative. A number of men from industrial relations backgrounds have become very successful presidents recently, most notably, Robben Fleming at the University of Michigan. (Howard Johnson also has a labor relations background; he first came to MIT as dean of the School of Industrial Management.) A problem that such men have is that since they cannot help making one side on any issue angry, at a certain point in time the accumulated anger overtakes the goodwill. So the tenure of such a president will be problematical unless he possesses, in addition to mediating skills, a degree of charisma that keeps him personally above conflict.

The value of labor relations experience does not seem to have escaped the Harvard Corporation, which recently named Derek C. Bok as Harvard's twenty-fifth president. Bok, who has been dean of Harvard Law School, is an authority on labor law and has been an arbitrator in several major disputes.

The collegiate manager. This is the style of the academic administrator in the strict sense of the term—the man whose primary commitment is to a scholarly discipline, who assumes the presidency as a faculty colleague rather than as a professional administrator. This man is very like a *representative* leader. The model is Parliament, with the faculty as the House of Commons and the trustees rather like the House of Lords.

Faculties have already acquired substantial influence at the great American universities. Non-academic leaders can forget just how powerful the faculty is within these institutions. General Eisenhower, during his Columbia presidency, had to be reminded by the vice-chairman of the faculty senate that "the faculty *is* the university, sir!"

The communal-tribal or postmodern leader. Leaders of this style are emerging in many of our institutions, not just universities. The academic leader of this style usually heads a college, not a university. The tribal leader typically identifies strongly with students; he not only backs them, he often joins with them, whether on marches to Washington or on strike. He is himself an activist, and likely to be young. John R. Coleman of Haverford or Harris Wofford at Old Westbury College (he is now at Bryn Mawr, where his style may be somewhat different) are examples of this style.

The charismatic leader. John Summerskill, who preceded Robert Smith (who preceded S. I. Hayakawa) at San Francisco State, was a charismatic president, but the exemplar of this style is Kingman Brewster of Yale. Brewster's personal attractiveness makes it possible to transcend obstacles.

In addition to these more or less acceptable presidential styles, there are several other possible approaches to university governance that should be mentioned. The following styles are currently out of favor or actually undesirable, but all of us have known men who practiced them:

The law-and-order president. Hayakawa, with his tam o'shanter and megaphone, is the epitome of this style. Ronald Reagan's behavior as the self-selected head of the University of California is also fairly typical.

The absentee-pluralist. This style, rapidly losing favor, has been highly regarded in the past. The president who adopts this approach sees his primary function as raising money for buildings and other needs and appointing competent subordinates. He hires those he considers to be good deans, spends his time on ceremonial functions, and "lets things happen." This is a spectacularly effective model when the university is rich, the subalterns capable, and the students and faculty relatively homogeneous and docile. In other words, if the university is like an elite men's club or the year is 1915.

The bureaucrat/entrepreneur. This style drives faculty to despair. The academic entrepreneur *par excellence* was Millard George Roberts, who with phenomenal *chutzpah* transformed a marginal sectarian college in the Midwest into a booming financial success and a national scandal. Before the bubble burst, Roberts succeeded in running Parsons College in Fairfield, Iowa, less like an academic institution than like a railroad. A *Swiss* railroad.

When all else fails, and the search committee and board cannot reach agreement on any of the above presidential styles, there is always the *interregnum* (or Pope John) solution. Interregnum leaders often do much better than might be expected. A good secular example is Dr. Andrew Cordier, who surprised almost everybody with his able management at Columbia.

There is at least one other presidential style, that of the *Renaissance or protean man.* This is the elusive superman that so many search committees pursue, the man who is all things to all constituencies. The protean president can role-play, presenting himself as a *communal-tribal leader* on some matters, a *bureaucratic-entrepreneur* on other matters, and on still others a *problem-solver/manager.* One of these protean men can also make life excruciatingly difficult for his constituents, who never know from one day to the next exactly what to expect.

2. *Determine the university's particular metaphor, the collectively held image of what the university is or could become.* Just as there are a number of successful presidential types, there are many university metaphors. The State University of New York at Buffalo comes close, in my view, to a "labor relations" metaphor. There are many other usable metaphors: Clark Kerr's "City," Mark Hopkins' "student and

teacher on opposite ends of a log," "General Systems Analysis," "Therapeutic Community," "Scientific Management," my own "temporary systems," and so on, competing with the pure form of bureaucracy.

3. *Forgo the costly hit-or-miss search and tailor the search process to the special requirements of the individual university.* Once the university's metaphor—its collective self-image or ideal self—is determined, the type of president sought is automatically less problematical.

The university's metaphor should determine not only the style of the president sought but also the composition and relative weighting of the search committee. For example, if the university requires a *collegiate manager,* an individual with strong academic qualifications and faculty identification, then faculty should have the decisive voice on the search committee.

As corollary to Number 3, it is increasingly clear that *a presidential search committee should undertake only an intelligently limited canvass, not a national quest.* When a university picked a new president every twenty years or so, it was reasonable to underwrite a far-flung search, sparing no effort or expense to screen conceivable candidates. But the national search is beginning to appear as extravagant as the elaborate inauguration.

4. *Assuming that the search committee is representative, the committee should select the president as well as screen candidates.* Demoralizing conflicts can be avoided by making sure that trustees serving on the search committee are powerful enough and numerous enough to represent the total board throughout the search. This seems to be the only sure way to avoid the enormous frustration that results when a board of trustees overrules the decision of a responsible and representative search committee.

On Wednesday, March 11 (the day after the story of my resignation appeared in the *New York Times*), Booz, Allen called to say that the tentative meeting called in Palm Beach, Florida, during which I was supposed to meet a contingent of Northwestern trustees who spend the winter there, had been canceled. Their man, no longer a disembodied voice, also pumped me about the resignation, clearly trying to establish the background for my decision. Before the conversation ended, he assured me that he would "keep in touch." Around the end of the month, having heard nothing in the meantime, I phoned him to find out how things were progressing with the search. He seemed very flustered and said that things were in a mess and that he didn't have any news for me as yet. He said that he wished he'd never gotten involved in this mess and that he hoped to have a chat with me, "man to man, after this whole thing blows over." "Then," he said, "I can really level with you." I thanked him and hung up, wondering what was really going on.

So, apparently, did the *Daily Northwestern*. An editorial in late April criticized the board for retaining, presumably at substantial cost, a management-consulting firm whose senior partner, James Allen, also happened to sit on both the Northwestern board and the search committee.

Between late March and the first week in May, the only news I received about the Northwestern candidacy came through informal sources. A student journalist at Northwestern called to extract a story from me and in the process related a good deal of inside information. On the basis of a purloined copy of the complete search-committee proceedings and other leaks, she indicated that the students and most of the faculty favored me, but that the board of trustees, ultimately responsible for naming the president, was, as expected, polarized; that Robert Strotz, who has been at Northwestern for practically his entire academic life, was seen by the board as the "safest" candidate; that Chancellor Cartter of NYU was moderately acceptable to the board and some students, but that the faculty was opposed to him. (I heard in early May, from Booz, Allen, that Cartter withdrew after the publicity upon the advice of his wife.) The students were so upset about the prospect of Strotz (for reasons which were unclear to me) that they intended to do everything possible to block his appointment and to insist that only Cartter or I was acceptable. They intended to use all means necessary to delay, obstruct, and ultimately subvert the Strotz appointment. According to the girl, the students were not ecstatic about Cartter, but were sure that the faculty would blackball him. I was, she thought, the candidate most likely.

Leaks often ended up as headlines in the Buffalo press and on local TV. Both of the Buffalo dailies used their Chicago contacts to ferret out any news from there, and the *Chicago Tribune* sent a reporter to Buffalo to do a piece on me for background. On May 3, the *Trib* ran side-by-side stories on both Cartter and me under the headline "TWO EDUCATORS SEE OTHER MAJOR ROLES FOR U.S. INSTITUTIONS." Excerpts appeared in the Buffalo papers.

I also heard, about this time, that the Northwestern trustees were in touch with some of the Buffalo Council members, establishment types for the most part, and that the chairman of the Buffalo Council was saying publicly that he had inside information and "knew that Bennis was not going to be appointed president of Northwestern." The precise nature and frequency of communication between the two groups were not known to me. I did hear that there was a good deal, none of it particularly helpful to my Northwestern chances. Meanwhile, a strong contingent on the Buffalo campus began urging me to run at home against odds far greater than Northwestern held for me.

Sometime around mid-May, I decided to call the chairman of the search committee directly, rather than going the Booz, Allen route. It was not particularly pleasant to initiate these calls. I always felt that it made me appear more eager than I really felt. On this occasion I called because two other universities were interested in "exploring" presidencies with me, and I wanted to be certain that Northwestern was really out of the question before investing time and energy on other prospects.

The committee chairman was reported by his secretary to be "tied up," and did not return my call. Booz, Allen's man did instead. If his mood in late March was disconsolate, he was practically teary on this occasion. He startled me by suggesting that I call the committee chairman. "Tell him that you want to withdraw," he advised after I remarked that I was getting concerned about the search's lack of progress, information, and the other spooky vicissitudes of the search process. I asked him what I would learn or gain by withdrawing my name at this point. "Well," he said, "this way they'll know you're really serious." "Is there any doubt about my *seriousness* at this point?" I asked. "Well, you never can tell. And it will serve them right."

My level of paranoia, usually abnormally low, was rising, along with increasing doubts about Northwestern. I did call the committee chairman back a few days later. He began by apologizing for not returning my call. Trying to get clear and direct information from him in person was difficult enough, but on the phone it was like trying to nail a chiffon pie to a wall. I did not mention my most recent conversation with Booz, Allen, nor did he. He finally said that the search was taking longer than they had expected, but that I was still in the running. "Hang in there," he encouraged me.

In early July, I called Booz, Allen for the last time. Their man indicated that he really didn't know what was going on at this point, but that I should consider myself "out of the running." The following day I received a call from the chairman of the search committee, who, to my amazement, informed me that I was still "a very active candidate" and that he hoped to have word for me no later than July 21 or 22. He also reported that he had just been elected president of the Northwestern Board of Trustees. In order to facilitate the whole search process and to select a president no later than the third week in July, when the full board (about forty members) had its regular meeting, he was going to meet individually with each trustee. I told him that I was leaving for Europe on the sixth of August for a month, but he assured me that I would hear from him no later than July 21.

I should have listened to Booz, Allen.

In the week preceding July 21, Buffalo radio and TV stations reported that Northwestern would appoint a new president at its regular meeting of the board on July 20 and that the race was between Dean Strotz and myself. On Saturday morning, July 18, Eppie Lederer (better known to millions of her readers as Ann Landers), an old friend, called to tell me of several articles which had appeared in the Chicago press on July 17.

Eppie was convinced that student leader Eva Jefferson's strongly worded statement against Strotz as the "old guard" choice would discourage the Northwestern board from appointing Strotz. In her view, I still had a pretty good chance for the post, and she advised me not to "give up hope." I told her I thought that for once she was dead-wrong, that my chances for the Northwestern presidency were nil, particularly since the Kent State–Cambodia crisis. Besides, my own university had, within the past three weeks, appointed a president over even stronger student *and* faculty objections. As it turned out, Ann Landers *was* wrong, a first perhaps, although I didn't know this until the first week in September.

When my family and I sailed for Europe on August 6, I was still in the dark about the Northwestern selection. The committee chairman's promise of "getting in touch no later than July 22" never materialized. After the front-page hullabaloo over student opposition to Strotz, I wagered that the whole search process to date would be scrapped and revived only with the appointment of a new search committee.

In early September, I returned from Europe via Miami to give a talk to the American Psychological Association. At a convention cocktail party, a vaguely familiar-looking man came over to me and reminded me that he was a member of one of the faculty groups at Northwestern who had interviewed me. "I'm just so sorry that you turned us down," he said. I wasn't sure how to respond to that gracious and tactful opener. So I said, "I appreciate your tact and graciousness, but I was never asked. Was it Strotz?" He said that it was.

To this day, I have not received official word from Northwestern concerning my candidacy or Strotz's appointment. Not from the search committee or from Booz, Allen. Finally, out of sheer perverseness, I suspect, I sent the following letter to the committee chairman:

When I returned from Europe on the 7th of September I quite by accident heard that Dr. Strotz was appointed President of Northwestern University. For any number of reasons, I am certain that you are delighted that the search is over and that you have found a first-rate person to lead Northwestern at this point. I congratulate you and the Board on its choice and wish you the very best of luck—which all of us will be needing—in the years ahead.

In light of my own candidacy for the post, I wonder if you could write me a note, totally off the record, that would help me understand the reasons for the Board's final selection. Obviously, I am aware that privileged communication and tact, and the usual practices, do not allow the frankest or most open discussion of this issue or the reasons why any candidate is chosen over any other, but I would like and would deeply appreciate "feedback" from you especially.

I might also say that I was surprised to hear the news in the manner I did. You had originally told me that you would be back in touch with me before leaving the country and when I did not hear from you through August 6 when I left with my family for Europe I had just assumed that no decision would be made until I had been told, before learning about it in the inadvertent way I did.

Anyway, I would appreciate hearing from you whenever time permits.

Sincerely yours,
Warren G. Bennis

He has never answered my letter.

STEVEN B. SAMPLE ON "SEARCHING FOR THE 'PERFECT' UNIVERSITY PRESIDENT"

WARREN BENNIS WAS CHAIRMAN of the search committee that in 1991 recruited me to be president of the University of Southern California. For me USC's recruitment process was thoroughly professional and humane, from which I draw the clear inference that Warren took his scathing experience at Northwestern and did with it what a truly wise person does after enduring an ordeal: He emerged with deeper insight and sensitivity. I am not alone in having benefited from Warren's wisdom and experience.

Over the years in which I've observed presidential search committees and candidates, I've concluded that most are curious creatures. On the surface, they seem to be united in a common goal—namely, to determine whether the fit is right, as the cliché goes, from each party's perspective. But they are also likely to be united in another way, and this one is often beneath the surface. The best way I can describe this submerged common trait is to call it *delusion*. The search committee, on one side, desires, as Warren's title indicates, a "perfect" president. They want God on a good day. The university wants someone who can set goals that are both aspirational and achievable, a president who can lead the university in measurable progress, who is at once tenacious *and* willing to change *and* opportunistic. They want a chief executive who can inspire, choose good lieutenants, and build disparate people and personalities into a great, cohesive team. They want a rare hybrid—chief, scholar, and (supremely and most Herculean) fundraiser.

On the other side, candidates often believe that they really want to *be* president, but the sad reality is that very few want to *do* president. I'm afraid that many of them see the office through rose-colored glasses, believing that their constituents will be deferential, conciliatory, intellectually stimulating, and broadening, while they themselves will be like a beneficent Pope, dispensing goodwill and purpose with a benign, wise countenance.

Search committees often believe they will be able to recruit a superhuman, and candidates often believe they can work wonders.

But look at the demands placed on today's university presidents. We are operating in a climate in which higher education is more competitive than ever. There is stiff competition for the best students, for the best faculty, for government grants and contracts, and in climbing in the rankings of the nation's best colleges and universities. And there is *very* stiff competition for gifts and donations.

Moreover, there is greater and greater pressure on colleges and universities to operate in the black, while holding down the price that students must pay for a college education. Each year we are expected to improve the quality of our educational programs with few if any additional resources.

My experience over the last thirty years has confirmed to me that, given this complex portfolio of duties and array of constituencies—let alone others' high expectations—the pool of candidates who can succeed as university presidents is very small indeed. Consequently search committees must often make difficult compromises. My experience has also shown me that likewise many candidates are often dazzled by the prospect of leadership and its perquisites, only to find out that they don't really want to do what it is that the position of university or college leadership requires.

My profession is overflowing with unhappy people who worked assiduously and made enormous sacrifices to become presidents of prestigious universities, simply because they believed that was what they were *supposed* to do, and in the process gave up their chance to do what it was they really wanted to do and were really good at. Many people aren't aware of the fact that leaders must frequently subordinate the things they're most interested in, or feel are most important, to the urgent (but often ephemeral) and sometimes trivial demands of others. I always tell those who aspire to academic leadership, "Along with helping to guide and shape one of the most noble and important institutions in society, a university president must also kiss a lot of frogs!"

When a search committee convenes, what it must try to discern is: Does this candidate want simply to *be* president, or does he or she really want to *do* president? If the latter, the candidate might contribute something great and lasting for followers and the organization they constitute. But if the candidate only wants to *be* president, everyone is in for a sour time of it, and it would have been better for everyone concerned, including the would-be president, if delusions had been mercilessly dispelled at the start. This kind of discernment takes keen skill, observation, instinct, and wisdom. But if a search committee and candidates can muster these qualities—and along the way treat one another with sensitivity and respect—the result will benefit everyone.

Steven B. Sample, Ph.D., has been a university president for twenty-seven years, first at SUNY Buffalo and currently at the University of Southern California, where he co-teaches an annual course with Warren Bennis, "The Art and Adventure of Leadership." He is an electrical engineer who has created several widely used inventions, and is the author of *The Contrarian's Guide to Leadership* (Jossey-Bass, 2002).

FOREWORD TO
THE AGE OF HERETICS (2008)

ART KLEINER'S *THE AGE OF HERETICS* is that rarest of books, one that is both important and a pleasure to read. Its subtitle—*A History of the Radical Thinkers Who Reinvented Corporate Management*—lets readers know at the outset that they are about to encounter something other than the standard cast of characters who write or star in most business books today, the exemplary leaders whose names we know almost as well as our own. This highly original history is devoted to the mostly forgotten pioneers, including the eccentrics and rogues, who have shaped American and increasingly world business and organizational life since World War II.

That is a huge swath of history to take on, and it is evidence of Kleiner's ambition. A comprehensive account of those sixty years would be invaluable, but it would also be too heavy to lift and all but unreadable. And so the author has made the wise decision to illustrate key events by telling emblematic stories featuring colorful, often unconventional individuals.

As Kleiner reveals, when postwar American business was a vast sea of gray flannel suits and tasteful ties, a few unorthodox individuals were not so quietly shifting the paradigm toward the breezier, Googlier workplace of today. These change agents include a raft of idealistic social scientists as well as nonacademics, like labor organizer Saul Alinsky, who pioneered the use of shareholder activism to open Kodak's doors to more African Americans. Alinsky, who was literally willing to smash dishes to get attention, was the embodiment of the activist principle that behaving badly is sometimes necessary because, in the words of the civil-rights anthem, "The nice ways always fail."

This work originally appeared in *The Age of Heretics* by Art Kleiner (Wiley, 2008).

Kleiner uses religious terms to title each of the chapters of his book—
"Monastics," "Pelagians," "Mystics," and so forth. At first that seems an
odd choice for a study of modern corporations and other secular institutions. But Kleiner is insightful to do so. Like the heretic whose rejection of
religious orthodoxy might send him to the pyre, Kleiner's organizational
heretic "is someone who sees a truth that contradicts the conventional wisdom of the institution to which he or she belongs—and who remains loyal
to both entities, to the institution and the new truth." The person who is
willing to make a great sacrifice to change an institution he or she loves is a
hero as well as a heretic because, Kleiner writes, "the future of industrial
society depends on our ability to transcend the destructive management of
the past, and build a better kind of business."

One of the transformations that Kleiner's heretics brought about is a
modern workplace that increasingly recognizes the centrality of work to
a person's deepest needs and aspirations. The author uses the word "vernacular" to describe the sense of community and personal integration that
so many of today's workers long for, a desire that is reflected in everything
from corporate matching of employees' charitable contributions to the
recognition by enlightened employers that workers want to do the right
thing as well as put food on their tables. In this sense, Google's motto
"Don't be evil" is an even more seductive lure to many gifted potential
hires than its free gourmet meals.

At its heart, Kleiner's book is a history of ideas, some good, some less
so. One of the trends he documents is the absorption into the Western
mainstream of aspects of Eastern spirituality advocated by such once
influential gurus as G. I. Gurdjieff. It is fascinating to read how Pierre
Wack helped prepare Royal Dutch/Shell decades ago for present-day oil
politics in part because of his exposure to Gurdjieff and the wisdom of a
Japanese master gardener, who taught Wack to see truly what was in front
of him. Wack's consciousness seems to have genuinely expanded because
of these teachers. But one wonders how many others have simply used the
language of Eastern enlightenment to justify substituting gut instinct for
a sounder, if more strenuous blend of intuition and old-fashioned Western style analysis.

Kleiner writes with verve and a novelist's or filmmaker's appreciation for
the value of a scene. The reader is unlikely to forget the image of a group
of United States rear admirals on their knees trying to identify "their"
lemon among a pile of lemons on the floor during a National Training Labs
session. Equally memorable is the moment when my sometime coauthor
and longtime friend Chris Argyris used a shocking demonstration to shat-
ter the antibusiness bias of his Harvard education students.

One of the pleasures of this book is its expansive frame of reference. I cannot think of another volume that refers to Heloise and Abelard, Norwegian resistance fighters of World War II, my mentor Doug McGregor, consumer crusader Ralph Nader, *and* counterculture cartoonist R. Crumb (he of "Keep on Truckin'"). Moreover, the book is studded with delicious, unexpected factoids. Did you know that the term "scenario," now ubiquitous in corporate planning, was first suggested by a sometime writer for the Rand Corporation—Leo Rosten, later author of *The Joys of Yiddish?*

Although it is unsettling to discover how others see and write about you, I am happy to be one of the many heretical change agents who appear in this book. As Kleiner points out, all of us—heroes and outlaws alike—are the spiritual and intellectual children of the great social psychologist Kurt Lewin and, almost two millennia before him, of the heretical British monk Pelagius. Both believed in the perfectibility of humankind and helped us to believe in it as well. To a greater or lesser degree, each of us helped destroy, if not the Man in the Gray Flannel Suit, the soulless organization that stole his labor and his days. And in doing so, each of us contributed to a new organizational reality in which the personal and business are inextricably linked and success is measured in human terms as well as dollars and euros. That is a worthy history to have been part of, and this is a worthy account of that history.

PART TWO

HOW ORGANIZATIONS CREATE OR THWART LEADERS

DURING THE LATE 1950S AND 1960S the future became the next new thing and many of us made forays into the prognostication business, for better or for worse. I recall writing a piece titled "A Funny Thing Happened on the Way to the Future." In 1964 I teamed with Phil Slater, then teaching at Harvard, on a piece for the *Harvard Business Review* predicting the eventual triumph of democracy. In retrospect, it may seem obvious that the Soviet Union would eventually fail if only because of its grim rigidity, but in 1964 many people thought the West would be contending indefinitely with its Cold War rival. Phil and I titled the piece "Democracy Is Inevitable." Our editors, however, weren't so sure and recast the title statement as a question. The fall of the Berlin Wall confirmed our prediction and gave us a moment of triumph. But, reconsidering the essay for this book, I think the most interesting thing about it is the way it lays out many of the factors that would transform organizations, including corporations, in the decades to come. Updated for republication in *HBR* in 1990, the piece is really about the death of hierarchy and the increasing importance to organizations of people with ideas and expertise, whatever their rank. The ability to adapt to accelerating change, especially technological change, and the growing importance of communication and consensus are among the attributes of today's most successful organizations, including Google. In the essay we also predict the end of the Great Man, a theme that Pat Ward Biederman and I would take up again in our study of Great Groups, *Organizing Genius: The Secrets of Creative Collaboration.* In 1966 I again made the case for flatter, more egalitarian organizations in "The Coming Death of Bureaucracy." Both articles argue that an organization's structure helps determine its success or failure. Organizations (and their leaders) also thrive or fail because of their values. "When to Resign" is a very personal account of my own struggle with the perennial question of what to do when you find yourself in an organization whose policies you can no longer support. That is the dilemma of every whistleblower and, indeed, all those whose personal beliefs conflict with those of their employer, church, or government. How an individual resolves that conflict is always of great weight and can be a matter of life or death. Often, the decision to resign follows a failed attempt to speak truth to power, in the form of an organization or a superior who won't listen or can't hear an uncomfortable truth.

DEMOCRACY IS INEVITABLE
(1964, 1990, 1998)

(coauthored by Philip Slater)

Today the inevitability of democracy might seem obvious, but in the mid-sixties, when we first argued that democracy would eventually dominate in both the world and the workplace, a nuclear war between the United States and the Soviet Union seemed more likely than a McDonald's in Moscow.[1]

It all started because Bennis had seen a common thread running through the most exciting organizations of that time: as the once absolute power of top management atrophied, a more collegial organization was emerging where good ideas were valued—even if they weren't the boss's ideas. We became convinced that democracy would triumph for a simple but utterly compelling reason: it was working. It was, and is, more effective than autocracy, bureaucracy, or any other nondemocratic form of organization. We went on later to develop these ideas more fully: Bennis through his extensive work on leadership and organization,[2] and Slater in an exploration of democracy's cultural and psychological underpinnings.[3]

In international politics democratization is a very recent phenomenon, albeit a profound one. A decade ago Nicolae Ceausescu had the

This work originally appeared in *Harvard Business Review,* March/April 1964, and was reprinted with a new preface in September/October 1990. This version appeared in the revised edition of *The Temporary Society* (Jossey-Bass, 1998).

power to ban birth control in Romania and require that every typewriter be registered. The state even regulated the temperature of Romanian households. The collapse of his regime was even more remarkable for being so long in coming.

The democratization of the workplace has made fewer headlines but has been no less dramatic. In the sixties participative management was considered so radical that some of the Sloan Fellows at the Massachusetts Institute of Technology accused Bennis of being a communist for espousing it. Today most major corporations practice some form of egalitarian management. The pyramid-shaped organization chart is going the way of the Edsel.

The change is pervasive. Self-managed work groups are replacing assembly lines in auto plants. Organizations as disparate as Herman Miller (the manufacturer of office furniture) and Beth Israel Hospital in Boston have adopted the democratic management techniques of the late Joseph Scanlon—one of the first to appreciate that employee involvement is crucial for quality control. At Hewlett-Packard's facility in Greeley, Colorado, most decisions are made not by traditional managers but by frontline employees who work in teams on parts of projects. Even project coordination is done by team representatives, working on committees known as "boards of directors."

No longer a monolith, the successful modern corporation is like a Lego set whose parts can be regularly reconfigured as circumstances change. The old paradigm that exalted control, order, and predictability is giving way to a nonhierarchical order in which all employees' contributions are solicited and acknowledged and in which creativity is valued over blind loyalty. Sheer self-interest motivates the change. Organizations that encourage broad participation, even dissent, make better decisions. Rebecca A. Henry, a psychology professor at Purdue University, found that groups are better forecasters than individuals are.[4] And the more the group disagrees initially, the more accurate the forecast is likely to be.

We said that adaptability would become the most important determinant of an organization's survival and that information would drive the organization of the future. This seems even more true today. The person who has information wields more power than ever before. But although we sensed how important processing technology would be, we didn't fully appreciate the extent to which the new technology would accelerate the pace of change and help create a global corporation if not a global village. New York Life Insurance, for example, processes its claims not in New York or even the United States but in Ireland. And a decade ago, when Bennis invited the Dalai Lama to participate in a seminar for CEOs at the University of Southern California, the embodiment of thousands of years of Tibetan spiritualism graciously declined by fax.

Our crystal ball let us down in a few other areas. We failed, for example, to foresee the extraordinary role Japan would play in shaping U.S. corporate behavior in the 1980s. The discovery that another nation could challenge U.S. dominance in the marketplace inspired massive self-evaluation and forever disrupted the status quo. Nothing contributed more to the democratization of business than the belief—true or false—that Japanese management was more consensual than U.S. management. To meet Japanese competition, U.S. leaders were willing to try anything—even share their traditional prerogatives with subordinates.

More surprising is our failure to anticipate the women's movement—a failure reflected in the gender-biased language scattered throughout the 1968 first edition of *The Temporary Society*. For while the women's movement was only embryonic in the sixties, we of all people might have been expected to comment on it since nothing could have been a stronger validation of the points we were making. We said that those who are not overcommitted to the status quo are in the best position to take advantage of change and innovation, and this certainly applies to women, who have pretty much been excluded from the authoritarian hierarchical structures that have dominated human existence for the past 6,000 years. As men were squeezed by authoritarian culture into the emotional corset of macho competitiveness, it fell to women to take care of all other human needs—emotional expression, relationships, cooperation, nurturance, and so on. They were forced to become skilled at diplomacy, mediation, negotiation, compromise, recognition of the needs and rights of others, and so on. But these are precisely the skills that are needed in a democracy. Men who practice democracy tend still to be caught up in the belligerent assumptions of the authoritarian past: they talk constantly of "standing up to" and "not being swayed by" and "not giving in to" and being "firm" or "tough," as if rigidity were a virtue and problem solving a form of hand-to-hand combat.

Men have committed themselves to an individualistic, linear, competitive, atomistic, and mechanistic conceptual world—one which they now dominate. But ironically, science—once the most extreme expression of this world—has now rendered it obsolete. Recent advances in physics and biology have opened up an entirely new conceptual universe.[5] The cosmos, scientists have begun to realize, is not a mechanism constructed of little particles that can be taken apart and put together—it is a gigantic unity of which the significant elements are relationships.

In the past men disparaged this way of looking at the world as "magical thinking," typical of women, children, and the inhabitants of nonliterate societies. But now it has become the accepted conceptual framework as we enter the next century. Nature, it seems, is relentlessly nonlinear, and those who fail to recognize this simple truth are destined to be left behind, mired in an antiquated mind-set.

Women are better adapted to the confusion and chaos that chronic change, democracy, and the new sciences together produce. Their control needs, on average, tend to be less exaggerated than those of men, who like to dominate their environment and make it simple and predictable. Women are more comfortable with the chaos that small children generate and are better able to cope with several different processes at the same time. The traditional housewife trying to cook, clean, and shop while noisy children were racing everywhere received optimum training for democratic living.

Some will object, of course, that women who become corporate managers do not necessarily exhibit these traits but are often more controlling, rigid, competitive, and authoritarian than men. This will be true as long as women are a small minority in a "man's world," having to prove they have traits they are not expected to have—having to show they are "tough" enough to do the job. In the same way, blacks who have succeeded in the same situation have often had to be "whiter" than whites—more conservative, uptight, restrained, and so forth. Once a group ceases to be a rarity, this need to over-conform to tradition eases.

In the first edition we predicted that industrial nations would eventually be forced to democratize, and this prediction has been borne out. Democracy movements in satellite states such as Poland and Czechoslovakia, as well as in capitalist countries like South Korea and South Africa, continue to demonstrate the long-range incompatibility of modern technological innovation and authoritarianism.

We also predicted that dictatorships would characterize developing nations in their early stages, and this, too, has been borne out. While the more viable states of Latin America and Asia are being pushed toward democracy, most third-world countries still find themselves mired in autocratic regimes. Yet even in Africa—plagued in recent decades by war, famine, and poverty—signs of change have been observed: "After decades of trying to impose centralized systems, governments [are beginning to] allow businessmen and villagers to take the lead . . . Democracy has softened dictatorial rule in a score of countries. Although flawed and often fixed, elections allow harsh criticism of leaders who once stifled any hint of dissent." And in a rare reversal of the macho ethic that has helped keep so much of Africa enslaved and impoverished for so long,

Senegalese President Abdou Diouf observed that "women are the key" to this development.[6]

In recent years our understanding of democracy has been enhanced by new data on early civilizations, particularly the work of Riane Eisler.[7] Drawing on a wealth of archeological data,[8] Eisler effectively demolishes the popular assumption that authoritarianism and war are somehow "natural" to human beings. She demonstrates that the "Golden Age" so often mentioned by the Greeks refers to an actual period of peace and equality in Europe and the Mediterranean, with a much higher level of culture than previously believed. In Minoan Crete, for example, there were no kings or nobles, and war was almost unknown until Crete's last days. Yet a level of civilization had been achieved that was not equaled for more than a millennium.

Eisler also lays to rest the notion that authoritarianism and belligerence are somehow part of our primate heritage, pointing to the Bonobos—a species closely related to the chimpanzee, but one in which dominating behavior is absent, conflicts are resolved through sexual seduction, and the least aggressive males are those chosen by the females as partners.[9] Slater elaborates the relationship between democracy and the women's movement in A Dream Deferred.[10]

The growth of democratic systems in industry has accelerated since the first edition. In a survey of 1,000 corporations Lawler[11] found that 80 percent used some form of participatory management. And as we noted then, it is particularly common in companies engaged in invention, such as electronics. Companies on the cutting edge of technological change tend to be forced by their very nature to operate by democratic principles, and those that become bureaucratized and hierarchical usually find themselves quickly upstaged by egalitarian newcomers. Adams and Brock[12] point out that "very small firms produce twenty-four times as many innovations per research and development dollar as large corporations," and although size is not inherently related to authoritarianism, the correlation is historically a large one.

One of the concerns of 1968 that we refer to seems rather quaint today. This was the fear that the trend toward more democratic structures in the corporate world would lead to a nation of homogeneous "Organization Men"—colorless and interchangeable ciphers, willingly serving an impersonal corporate machine. The key word here is willingly. Although a great many workers and managers today may feel themselves caught in such a predicament—as they have for the last century or more—the notion that they will somehow have been brainwashed into accepting it seems dated. And homogeneity, which once held a proud position in the top ten of our national fears, right after the

Red Menace, has become, in the age of multiculturalism and our obsession with "lifestyles," merely the fond dream of a few bigoted white males.

Transitions are difficult. The gradual global shift from authoritarianism to democracy—from war to peace, from machismo to cooperation, from domination to attunement, from linear science to nonlinear science—is a paradigm shift of unprecedented magnitude. Such a change inevitably causes great strain and confusion for us poor human beings hungry for stability and familiarity. We reach excitedly toward the future with one hand and cling desperately to our old concepts with the other. Is it any wonder we feel pulled apart at times? We can see this strain in the so-called lack of civility in our daily lives today, in the frustration that produces so much ranting on the airwaves and so often leads to violence. We see our ambivalence in our high-tech sci-fi fantasies that begin with so much sophistication but usually end in some form of hand-to-hand combat. We see it again in our many movies about brutal post-apocalyptic worlds—worlds created by the disastrous macho values we now embrace, yet at the same time rendering those same values once again meaningful and desirable.

Reality is less dramatic. Change is a gradual, two-steps-forward-one-back process, but we may reasonably be expected to muddle through. There will be plenty of disasters and atrocities along the way for change never comes cheaply. Nobody likes becoming obsolete, and those who hold advantages seldom give them up without a struggle. But the process cannot be stopped without a global catastrophe; it gathers momentum every day. It will never be easy for us, but it may help a little to recognize what's happening and to admit that it all makes us a little uncomfortable, whether we think we welcome change or fight it tooth and nail.

We argued in the first edition that the military-bureaucratic model was becoming increasingly obsolete and being replaced by a scientific one. This is still true. Science not only tolerates change, it creates change. And as we wrote, science flourishes only in a democracy—the one form of organization recognizing that creativity is invaluable, unpredictable, and can come from any quarter.

------------ o ------------

CYNICAL OBSERVERS HAVE ALWAYS been fond of pointing out that business leaders who extol the virtues of democracy on ceremonial occasions would be the last to think of applying them to their own organizations. To the extent that this is true, however, it reflects a state of mind that by no means is peculiar to businessmen but that characterizes all Americans—perhaps all citizens of democracies.

This attitude, briefly, is that democracy is a nice way of life for nice people, despite its manifold inconveniences—a kind of expensive and inefficient luxury, like owning a large medieval castle. Feelings about it are for the most part affectionate, even respectful, but a little impatient. There are probably few men of affairs in America who have not at some time nourished in their hearts the blasphemous thought that life would go much more smoothly if democracy could be relegated to some kind of Sunday morning devotion.

The bluff practicality of the "nice-but-inefficient" stereotype masks a hidden idealism, however, for it implies that institutions can survive in a competitive environment through the sheer goodheartedness of those who maintain them. We would like to challenge this notion and suggest that even if all of those benign sentiments were eradicated today, we would awaken tomorrow to find democracy still firmly entrenched, buttressed by a set of economic, social, and political forces as practical as they are uncontrollable.

We will argue that democracy has been so widely embraced, not because of some vague yearning for human rights but because *under certain conditions* it is a more "efficient" form of social organization. We do not regard it as accidental that those nations of the world that have endured longest under conditions of relative wealth and stability are democratic, whereas authoritarian regimes have, with few exceptions, either crumbled or maintained a precarious and backward existence.

Despite this evidence, even so acute a statesman as Adlai Stevenson argued in a *New York Times* article on November 4, 1962, that the goals of the Communists are different from ours. "They are interested in power," he said, "we in community. With such fundamentally different aims, how is it possible to compare communism and democracy in terms of efficiency? You might as well ask whether a locomotive is more efficient than a symphony orchestra."

Isn't this simply the speech of an articulate man who believes that democracy is inefficient and doesn't like to say so? Actually we are concerned with locomotives *and* symphony orchestras, with power *and* community. The challenges for communism and democracy are, in fact, identical: to compete successfully for the world's resources and imagination.

Our position is, in brief, that democracy (whether capitalistic or socialistic is not at issue here) is the only system that can successfully cope with the changing demands of contemporary civilization. We are not necessarily endorsing democracy as such; one might reasonably argue that industrial civilization is pernicious and should be abolished. We suggest merely that given a desire to survive in this civilization, democracy is the most effective means to achieve this end.

There are signs, in fact, that our business community is becoming aware of this law. Several of the newest and most rapidly blooming companies in the United States boast unusually democratic organizations. Even more surprising is the fact that some of the largest of the established corporations have been moving steadily, if accidentally, toward democratization. Frequently they began by feeling that administrative vitality and creativity were lacking in the older systems of organization. In increasing numbers, therefore, they enlisted the support of social scientists and of outside programs, the net effect of which has been to democratize their organization. Executives and even entire management staffs have been sent to participate in human relations and organizational laboratories to learn skills and attitudes that ten years ago would have been denounced as anarchic and revolutionary. At these meetings, status prerogatives and traditional concepts of authority are severely challenged.

Many social scientists have played an important role in this development toward humanizing and democratizing large-scale bureaucracies. The theories of McGregor, Likert, Argyris, and Blake paved the way to a new social architecture. Research and training centers at the National Training Laboratories, Tavistock Institute, Massachusetts Institute of Technology, Harvard Business School, Boston University, University of California at Los Angeles, Case Institute of Technology, and others have pioneered in the application of social-scientific knowledge to the improvement of organizational effectiveness. So far, the data are not all in; conclusive evidence is missing, but the forecast seems to hold genuine promise: it is possible to bring about greater organizational effectiveness through the utilization of valid social knowledge.[13]

What we have in mind when we use the term *democracy* is not *permissiveness* or *laissez-faire* but a system of values—a climate of beliefs governing behavior—that people are internally compelled to affirm by deeds as well as words. These values include

1. Full and free *communication,* regardless of rank and power

2. A reliance on *consensus,* rather than the more customary forms of coercion or compromise to manage conflict

3. The idea that *influence* is based on technical competence and knowledge rather than on the vagaries of personal whims or prerogatives of power

4. An atmosphere that permits and even encourages emotional expression as well as task-oriented acts

5. A basically human bias, one that accepts the inevitability of conflict between the organization and the individual but that is willing to cope with and mediate this conflict on rational grounds

Changes along these dimensions are being promoted widely in American industry. Most important, for our analysis, is what we believe to be the reason for these changes: *democracy becomes a functional necessity whenever a social system is competing for survival under conditions of chronic change.*

The most familiar variety of such change to the inhabitants of the modern world is technological innovation. Because change has now become a permanent and accelerating factor in American life, adaptability to change becomes increasingly the most important single determinant of survival. The profit, the saving, the efficiency, the morale of the moment becomes secondary to keeping the door open for rapid readjustment to changing conditions.

Organization and communication research at the Massachusetts Institute of Technology reveals quite dramatically what type of organization is best suited for which kind of environment. Specifically: for simple tasks under static conditions, an autocratic, centralized structure, such as has characterized most industrial organizations in the past, is quicker, neater, and more efficient. But for adaptability to changing conditions, for rapid acceptance of a new idea, for "flexibility in dealing with novel problems, generally high morale and loyalty the more egalitarian or decentralized type seems to work better." One of the reasons for this is that the centralized decision maker is "apt to discard an idea on the grounds that he is too busy or the idea too impractical."[14] The failure of Nazi Germany to develop the atom bomb is a telling example of this phenomenon.

Our argument for democracy rests on an additional factor, one that is fairly complicated but profoundly important in shaping our ideas. First of all, it is interesting to note that modern industrial organization has been based roughly on the antiquated system of the military. Relics of the military system of thought can still be found in terminology such as "line and staff," "standard operating procedure," "table of organization," and so on. Other remnants can be seen in the emotional and mental assumptions regarding work and motivation held today by some managers and industrial consultants.

By and large these conceptions are changing, and even the military is moving away from the oversimplified and questionable assumptions on which its organization was originally based. The Israeli army, for example, is unsurpassed throughout the world for sheer military effectiveness. It is also one of the most slovenly, equalitarian, and democratic. Spit and polish is ignored; social barriers between officers and men are almost nonexistent; and communication of ideas proceeds up as well as down the rank hierarchy. Even more striking, as we have mentioned, are developments taking place in industry. These are no less profound than a fundamental change away from the autocratic and arbitrary vagaries of the past toward democratic decision making.

This change has been coming about because of the palpable inadequacy of the military-bureaucratic model, particularly its response to rapid change, and also because the institution of science is now emerging as a more suitable model.[15]

But why is science gaining acceptance as a model? Most certainly, it is *not* because we teach and conduct research within research-oriented universities. Curiously enough, universities have been stubbornly resistant to democratization, far more so than most other institutions.

We believe that science is winning out because the challenges facing modern enterprises are, at base, knowledge-gathering, truth-requiring dilemmas. Managers are not scientists, nor do we expect them to be. But the processes of solving problems, resolving conflicts, and recognizing dilemmas have great kinship with the academic pursuit of truth. The institution of science is the only institution based on and geared for change. It is built not only to adapt to change but to overthrow and create change. So it is—and will be—with modern industrial enterprises.

And here we come to the point. In order for the spirit of inquiry—the foundation of science—to grow and flourish, a democratic environment is a necessity. Science encourages a political view that is egalitarian, pluralistic, liberal. It accentuates freedom of opinion and dissent. It is against all forms of totalitarianism, dogma, mechanization, and blind obedience. As a prominent social psychologist has pointed out, "Men have asked for freedom, justice and respect precisely as science has spread among them."[16] In short, we believe that the only way in which organizations can ensure a scientific *attitude* is by providing conditions where it can flourish. Very simply, this means democratic social conditions.

In other words, democracy in industry is not an idealistic conception but a hard necessity in those areas in which change is ever-present and in which creative scientific enterprise must be nourished. For democracy is the only system of organization that is compatible with perpetual change.

It might be objected here that we have been living in an era of rapid technological change for a hundred years without any noticeable change in the nature of the average industrial firm. True, there are now many restrictions on the power of the executive over his subordinates compared with those prevailing at the end of the nineteenth century. But this hardly constitutes industrial democracy; the decision-making function is still an exclusive and jealously guarded prerogative of the top echelons. If democracy is an inevitable consequence of perpetual change, why then have we not seen more dramatic changes in the structure of industrial organizations? The answer is twofold.

First, the rate of technological change is rapidly accelerating. Take advance in scientific knowledge as one criterion: it doubles every ten years. Casimir calculated that if the *Physical Review* continued to grow as rapidly as it had between 1945 and 1960, it would weigh more than the earth during the next century.[17] Prior to World War I a businessman might live a productive and successful life and find himself outmoded at the end of it. By the end of World War II a similar man could find that his training, skills, outlook, and ways of thinking were obsolescent in the middle of his career. James R. Killian, Jr., chairman of the Corporation of Massachusetts Institute of Technology, estimated that already [in 1963] several hundred thousand engineers are obsolete.[18] This is undoubtedly matched by an equal number of managers.

We are now beginning an era when a man's knowledge and approach can become obsolete before he has even begun the career for which he was trained. The value of what one learns is always slipping away, like the value of money in runaway inflation. We are living in an era that could be characterized as a runaway inflation of knowledge and skill, and it is this that is, perhaps, responsible for the feelings of futility, alienation, and lack of individual worth that are said to characterize our time.

Under such conditions, the individual is of relatively little significance. No matter how imaginative, energetic, and brilliant he may be, time will soon catch up with him to the point where he can profitably be replaced by someone equally imaginative, energetic, and brilliant but with a more up-to-date viewpoint and fewer obsolete preconceptions. As Martin Gardner says, with regard to the difficulty some physicists have in grasping Einstein's theory of relativity, "If you are young, you have a great advantage over these scientists. Your mind has not yet developed those deep furrows along which thoughts so often are forced to travel."[19] This situation is just beginning to be felt as an immediate reality in American industry, and it is this kind of uncontrollably rapid change that generates democratization.

The second reason is that the mere existence of a dysfunctional tendency, such as the relatively slow adaptability of authoritarian structures, does not automatically bring about its disappearance. This drawback must either first be recognized for what it is or become so severe as to destroy the structures in which it is embedded. Both of these conditions are only now beginning to make themselves felt, primarily through the peculiar nature of modern technological competition.

The crucial change has been that the threat of technological defeat no longer comes necessarily from rivals within the industry, who usually can be imitated quickly without too great a loss, but often from outside—from new industries using new materials in new ways. One can therefore make no intelligent prediction about "what the next likely development in our industry will be." The blow may come from anywhere. Correspondingly, a viable corporation cannot merely develop and advance in the usual ways. In order to survive and grow it must be prepared to go anywhere—to develop new products or techniques even if they are irrelevant to the present activities of the organization.[20] It is perhaps for this reason that the beginnings of democratization have appeared most often in industries (such as electronics) that depend heavily on invention. Marshall McLuhan [influential social scientist of the 1960s and 1970s] no doubt exaggerated when he said that "no new idea ever starts from within a big operation. It must assail the organization from outside, through some small but competing organization."[21] But it helps explain why more and more sprawling behemoths are planning consequential changes in their organizational structures and climates toward releasing democratic potentiality.

This issue is frequently misunderstood. People argue that Nazi Germany was an exception to our rule, because it was at once highly authoritarian and highly efficient. But the fact that the organization destroyed itself in foolish military adventures is excluded from the criterion of efficiency in this example, as if survival were a detail of no importance. This is a common fallacy in industry: a management that saves a hundred thousand dollars through cost-cutting measures and provokes, in the process, a million-dollar wildcat strike, is more likely to be called efficient than one that saves $900,000 by doing neither! Men strive for efficiency within a narrowly defined range of familiar acts and relegate all other events to the category of "acts of God," as if no one could expect to exert any control over them. The martinet general whose beautifully disciplined fighting machine is wiped out by guerrillas will probably still lay claim to efficiency, but we need not agree with his assumption that efficiency consists in doing an irrelevant thing well. By such a definition the March Hare was efficient when he used the "best butter" to repair the Mad Hatter's watch. The Greeks cautioned against calling a man happy before he had achieved a peaceful death; we would caution against calling any organization efficient until it has met at least one new and unexpected threat to its existence.

The passing of years has also given the *coup de grâce* to another force that retarded democratization—the Great Man who with brilliance and farsightedness could preside with dictatorial powers at the head of a growing organization and keep it at the vanguard of American business. In the past he was usually a man with a single idea, or a constellation of related ideas, which he developed brilliantly. This is no longer enough (and the Great Man may, in fact, be a Great Woman).

Today, just as the head of an organization begins to reap the harvest of his imagination, he finds that someone else (even, perhaps, one of his stodgier competitors, aroused by desperation) has suddenly carried the innovation a step further, or has found an entirely new and superior approach to it, and he is suddenly outmoded. How easily can he abandon his idea, which contains all his hopes, his ambitions, his very heart? His aggressiveness now begins to turn in on his own organization, and the absolutism of his position begins to be a liability, a dead hand, an iron shackle upon the flexibility and growth of the company. But he cannot be removed. In the short run the firm would even be hurt by his loss, since its prestige derives to such an extent from his reputation. And by the time he has left, the organization will have receded into a secondary position within the industry. It may even decay further when his personal touch is lost.

The cult of personality still exists, of course, but it is rapidly fading. More and more large corporations predicate their growth not on heroes but on solid management teams.

Taking the place of the Great Man, we are often told, is the organization man. A good many tears have been shed over this transition by liberals and conservatives alike. The liberals, of course, have in mind, as the individual, some sort of creative deviant—an intellectual, artist, or radical politician. The conservatives are thinking of the old captains of industry and perhaps some great generals.

Neither is at all unhappy to lose the individuals mourned by the other, dismissing them contemptuously as Communists and rabble-rousers, on the one hand, and criminals and Fascists, on the other. What is particularly confusing in terms of the present issue is a tendency to equate conformity with autocracy, to see the new industrial organization as one in which all individualism is lost except for a few villainous individualistic manipulators at the top.

But this, of course, is absurd in the long run. The trend toward the organization man is also a trend toward a looser and more flexible organization in which roles are to some extent interchangeable and no one is indispensable. To many people this trend is a monstrous nightmare, but one should at least not confuse it with the nightmares of the past. It may mean anonymity and homogeneity, but it does not and cannot mean authoritarianism, in the long run, despite the bizarre anomalies and hybrids that may arise in a period of transition.

The reason it cannot is that it arises out of a need for flexibility and adaptability. Democracy and the dubious trend toward the organization man (for this trend *is* a part of democratization, whether we like this aspect of democracy or not) both arise from the need to maximize the availability of appropriate knowledge, skill, and insight under conditions of great variability.

While the organization man idea has titillated the imagination of the American public, it has masked a far more fundamental change now taking place: the rise of the "professional man." Professional specialists, holding advanced degrees in such abstruse sciences as cryogenics or computer logic, as well as the more mundane business disciplines, are entering all types of organizations at a higher rate than any other sector of the labor market.

And these men can hardly be called organization men. They seemingly derive their rewards from inward standards of excellence, from their professional societies, from the intrinsic satisfaction of their standards, and not from their bosses. Because they have degrees, they travel. They are not good company men; they are uncommitted except to the challenging environments where they can "play with problems."

These new professional men are remarkably compatible with our conception of a democratic system. For, like these new men, democracy seeks no new stability, no end point; it is purposeless, save that it purports to ensure perpetual transition, constant alteration, ceaseless instability. It attempts to upset nothing but only to facilitate the potential upset of anything. Democracy and our new professional men identify primarily with the adaptive process, not the establishment.

Yet it must also be remembered that all democratic systems are not entirely so—there are always limits to the degree of fluidity that can be borne. Thus, it is not a contradiction to the theory of democracy to find that a particular democratic society or organization may be more conservative than some autocratic one. Indeed, the most dramatic violent and drastic changes have always taken place under autocratic regimes, for such changes usually require prolonged self-denial, while democracy rarely lends itself to such voluntary asceticism. But these changes have been viewed as finite and temporary, aimed at a specific set of reforms, and moving toward a new state of nonchange. It is only when the society reaches a level of technological development in which survival is dependent on the institutionalization of perpetual change that democracy becomes necessary.

The [former] Soviet Union experienced this change; the United States has also. Yet democratic institutions existed in the United States when it was still an agrarian nation. Indeed, democracy has existed in many places and at many times, long before the advent of modern technology. How can we account for these facts?

In the first place, it must be remembered that modern technology is not the only factor that could give rise to conditions of necessary perpetual change. Any situation involving rapid and unplanned expansion, sustained over a sufficient period of time, will tend to produce great pressure for democratization. Second, when we speak of democracy we are referring not only, or even primarily, to a particular political format. Indeed, American egalitarianism has perhaps its most important manifestation, not in the Constitution, but in the family.

Historians are fond of pointing out that Americans have always lived under expanding conditions—first the frontier, then the successive waves of immigration, now a runaway technology. The social effects of these kinds of expansions are, of course, profoundly different in many ways, but they share one impact in common: all have made it impossible for an authoritarian family system to develop on a large scale. Every foreign observer of American mores since the seventeenth century has commented that American children have no respect for their parents, and every generation of Americans since 1650 has produced forgetful native moralists complaining about the decline in filial obedience and deference.

It was not so much American ways that shook up the old family patterns but the demands and requirements of a new situation. How could the young look to the old as the ultimate fount of wisdom and knowledge when, in fact, the old knowledge was irrelevant—when, indeed, the children had a better practical grasp of the realities of American life than did their elders? How many of the latter can keep up with their children in knowledge of the sciences, for example? Santayana put it beautifully when he said: "No specific hope about distant issues is ever likely to be realized. The ground shifts, the will of mankind deviates, and what the father dreamt of the children neither fulfill nor desire."[22]

It is this fact that reveals the basis for the association between democracy and change. The old, the learned, the powerful, the wealthy, those in authority—these are the ones who are committed. They have learned a pattern and have succeeded in it. But when change comes, it is often the *uncommitted* who can best realize it, take advantage of it.

Democracy is a superior technique for making the uncommitted more available. The price it exacts is the pain of uninvolvement, alienation, and skepticism. The benefits it gives are flexibility and the joy of confronting new dilemmas.

Indeed, we may even in this way account for the poor opinion democracy has of itself. We underrate the strength of democracy because democracy creates a general attitude of doubt, of skepticism, of modesty. It is only among the authoritarian that we find the dogmatic confidence, the self-righteousness, the intolerance and cruelty that permit one never to doubt oneself and one's beliefs. The looseness, the sloppiness, and the untidiness of democratic structures express the feeling that what has been arrived at today is probably only a partial solution and may well have to be changed tomorrow.

In other words, one cannot believe that change is in itself a good thing and still believe implicitly in the rightness of the present. Judging from the report of history, democracy has always underrated itself—one cannot find a democracy anywhere without also discovering (side-by-side with expressions of outrageous chauvinism) an endless pile of contemptuous and exasperated denunciations of it. And perhaps this is only appropriate. For when a democracy ceases finding fault with itself, it has probably ceased to be a democracy.

But feeling doubt about our own social system need not lead us to overestimate the virtues and efficiency of others. We can find this kind of overestimation in the exaggerated fear of the Red Menace, mere exposure to which is seen as leading to automatic conversion. Few authoritarians can conceive of the possibility that an individual could encounter an authoritarian ideology and not be swept away by it.

Of a similar nature, but more widespread, is the "better dead than Red" mode of thinking. Here again we find an underlying assumption that communism is socially, economically, and ideologically inevitable—that once the military struggle is lost, all is lost. It is interesting that in all our gloomy war speculations, there is never any mention of an American underground movement. It is everywhere assumed that if a war had been fought in which anyone survived and the Soviet Union had won, then:

> All Americans would immediately become Communists.
>
> The Soviet Union would set up an exact replica of herself in this country.
>
> It would work.
>
> The Soviet system would remain unchanged.
>
> The Soviets in America would be uninfluenced by what they found here.

Not only are these assumptions patently ridiculous; they also reveal a profound misconception about the nature of social systems. The structure of a society is not determined merely by a belief. It cannot be maintained if it does not work, that is, if no one, not even those in power, is benefiting from it. How many times in history have less-civilized nations conquered more-civilized ones only to be entirely transformed by the cultural influence of their victims? Do we then feel ourselves to be less civilized than the Soviet Union? Is our system so brittle and theirs so enduring?

Actually, quite the contrary seems to be the case. For while democracy seems to be on a fairly sturdy basis in the United States (despite the efforts of self-appointed vigilantes to subvert it), there is considerable evidence that autocracy is beginning to decay in the Soviet Union and in Eastern Europe.

Most Americans have great difficulty in evaluating the facts when confronted with evidence in the Soviet Union of decentralization, of relaxation of repressive controls, or of greater tolerance for criticism. We seem bewildered. And we do not seem to sense the contradiction when we say that these changes were made in response to public discontent. For have we not also believed deeply that an authoritarian regime, if efficiently run, can get away with ignoring the public's clamor? Yet it is now evident that "de-Stalinization" took place because the rigid, repressive authoritarianism of the Stalin era was inefficient, and that many additional relaxations have been forced on the Soviet Union by the necessity of remaining amenable to technological innovation.

But the inevitable Soviet drift toward a more democratic structure is not dependent on the realism of leaders. Leaders come from communities and families, and their patterns of thought are shaped by their experiences with authority in early life, as well as by their sense of what the traffic will bear. We saw that the roots of American democracy were to be found in the nature of the American family. What does the Russian family tell us in this respect?

Pessimism regarding the ultimate destiny of Soviet political life has always been based on the seemingly endless capacity of the Russian people for submission to authoritarian rule. Their tolerance for autocratic rulers was only matched by their autocratic family system, which was equal to the German, the Chinese, or that of many Latin countries in its demand for filial obedience. On this early experience in the family the acceptance of authoritarian rule was based.

But modern revolutionary movements, both fascist and communist, have tended to regard the family with some suspicion as the preserver of old ways and as a possible refuge from the state. Fascist dictators have extolled its conservatism but have tended at times to set up competitive loyalties for the young. Communist revolutionaries, on the other hand, have more unambivalently attacked family loyalty as reactionary, and have deliberately undermined familial allegiances, partly to increase loyalty to the state and partly to facilitate industrialization and modernization by discrediting traditional mores.

Such destruction of authoritarian family patterns is a two-edged sword, which eventually cuts away political autocracy as well as the familial variety. The state may attempt to train submission in its own youth organizations, but so long as the family remains as an institution, this earlier and more enduring experience will outweigh all others. And if the family has been forced by the state to be less authoritarian, the result is obvious.

In creating a youth that has a knowledge, a familiarity, and a set of attitudes more appropriate for successful living in the changing culture than those of its parents, the autocratic state has created a Frankenstein monster that will eventually sweep away the authoritarianism in which it is founded. Russian attempts during the late 1930s to reverse their stand on the family perhaps reflect some realization of this fact. More recent denunciations of Soviet artists and intellectuals also reflect fear of a process going beyond what was originally intended.

Further, what the derogation of parental wisdom and authority has begun, the fierce drive for technological modernization will finish. Each generation of youth will be better adapted to the changing society than its parents. And each generation of parents will feel increasingly modest and doubtful about overvaluing its wisdom and superiority as it recognizes the brevity of its usefulness.[23]

We cannot, of course, predict what forms democratization might take in any nation of the world, nor should we become unduly optimistic about its impact on international relations. Although our thesis predicts the ultimate democratization of the entire globe, this is a view so long-range as to be academic. There are infinite opportunities for global extermination before any such stage of development can be achieved.

We should expect that in the earlier stages of industrialization dictatorial regimes will prevail in all of the less-developed nations. We may expect many political grotesques, some of them dangerous in the extreme, to emerge during this long period of transition, as one society after another attempts to crowd the most momentous social changes into a generation or two, working from the most varied structural baselines.

But barring some sudden decline in the rate of technological change, and on the (outrageous) assumption that war will somehow be eliminated during the next half-century, it is possible to predict that after this time democracy will be universal. Each revolutionary autocracy, as it reshuffles the family structure and pushes toward industrialization, will sow the seeds of its own destruction, and democratization will gradually engulf it. Lord Acton once remarked about Christianity that it isn't that people have tried it and found it wanting. It is that they have been afraid to try it and found it impossible. The same comment may have once applied to democracy, but the outlook has changed to the point where people may have to try it.

We may, of course, rue the day. A world of mass democracies may well prove homogenized and ugly. It is perhaps beyond human social capacity to maximize both equality and understanding, on the one hand, and diversity, on the other. Faced with this dilemma, however, many people are willing to sacrifice quaintness to social justice, and just as Marx, in proclaiming the inevitability of communism, did not hesitate to give some assistance to the wheels of fate, so our thesis that democracy represents the social system of the electronic era should not bar these persons from giving a little push here and there to the inevitable.

ROSABETH MOSS KANTER ON
"DEMOCRACY IS INEVITABLE"

"DEMOCRACY IS INEVITABLE" is a timeless classic. It was a prescient statement that anticipated some organizational and political trends of the next decades. Bennis and Slater predicted that democracy would burgeon everywhere because of rapid technological change, and that it represented the ultimate stage of development. While emerging countries at earlier points of the development continuum might remain autocratic (just as, one presumes, founder-led companies in early stages of growth might remain paternalistic), further development would inevitably lead them to democratize or perish, they argued. Adapting to change requires a democratic form, the essay argues, because that is the only way to get the best ideas, arising from new sources, and build support for progress.

When the article first appeared in the 1960s, its central notion was an appealing one for the times and particularly for America and Western Europe. The essay foreshadowed the fall of Communism in Eastern Europe and the triumph of liberal democracies. It heralded the end of rigid bureaucracies and the widespread diffusion of employee participation. It provided momentum for the infant field of organization development, which in practice meant training people for more participatory work environments. It was compatible with youth-led social movements that challenged hierarchies and orthodoxies. It promised fresh new leadership, or at least to add a focus on leadership to the task of managing organizations.

While this is a powerful humanistic manifesto with people at the core, the ultimate argument of the essay is a pragmatic one. Democracy is inevitable because it is an ideal that is also practical, one that will result in higher performance. Much of that argument has stood the test of time. Rapid technological change continues at an accelerating pace, with information and communications technology (ICT) penetrating every part of the world, through cell phones if not computers.

In my recent study of leading multinational companies in the twenty-first century for my book *Supercorp*, I found that the complexity of globalization tends to induce and favor distributed rather than concentrated leadership. That is, fewer people act as power-holders, monopolizing information or decision making, and more people serve as integrators, using relationships and persuasion to get things done. Circles of influence supplement or replace chains of command—as is appropriate in a networked world. Organization structures involve multi-directional responsibilities, with an increasing emphasis on horizontal relationships rather than vertical reporting as the center of action that shapes daily tasks and one's portfolio of projects, in order to focus on serving customers and society. This is a hallmark of a flatter and more innovative organization, which I suppose Bennis and Slater would label more "democratic." Knowledge workers cannot be controlled by coercive means anyway; the very nature of their work requires more autonomy and voluntary decisions. In keeping with the expectations of highly skilled employees, who seek meaningful work that includes a positive impact on society, organizations and their leaders must empower people with opportunities for input and entrust people with choices, including, in some cases, where, when, and with whom they work. Indeed, the rise of self-organizing social networks, once called the "informal organization," which is itself facilitated by the newest ICT tools, has become essential to the success of many of the companies I studied. Even in countries known for revering authority, in which managers would tell me that "their people" do not need participation because they prefer following orders, high-performance companies such as Banco Real in Brazil or Shinhan Financial Group in Korea embrace high degrees of employee involvement and are preferred employers as a result.

Overall, this model is consistent with the humanistic values and open communication urged in this essay. Still, I would not call this organizational paradigm "democracy." It offers participation, voice and choice, open communication and wider distribution of power—all good motivational processes, but they do not exactly constitute democracy in the political sense. Labor leaders, for example, would argue that the only democracy in employment organizations comes from labor unions, in which people vote for leaders to represent them. Professional associations are democracies in that sense; business corporations are not. And, sadly, too many scandals have revealed that many organizations are not even well governed under legal mandates. The best companies keep employees happy, but employees do not vote for CEO or for representatives at the governing table, and the idea that boards are chosen by shareholder democracies is equally laughable. The closest analogy in the private sector to political democracy is not ESOPs (employee stock ownership programs) in which employee representatives serve on the board of directors, but 360-degree performance appraisals with information going up the line, so that employees have a modest say in executive job tenure. Executives serve not at the will of the people nor to represent their priorities; they serve at the will of the board that is supposed to represent shareholder interest in financial performance.

We should not confuse mechanisms for voice and participation within organizations with political democracy, nor force private sector organizations into the same box with the public sector. Political democracy is sometimes shaky, but it does involve elections and representation, theoretical accountability to the people, and a certain transparency of decision making not true even in high-participation organizations. C-Span lets us see Congress in action; the best one can see in a company is a webcast of a well-orchestrated training event. Political democracy involves both the formal apparatus of voting, legislation, and judicial process, and also a variety of institutions, sometimes called civil society, that organize and mobilize citizens for action, including debate and opposition.

Political democracy is threatened from within and without. Within the United States, subversion of the public agenda and electoral process by lobbyists and moneyed interests has been a continuing and perhaps growing problem, especially in the twenty-first-century Bush administration. Concentration of power in the White House has led to some rather undemocratic, or publicly unpopular, actions that have subverted legal protections and undermined respect for democratic ideals in other parts of the world. And whether the rest of the world is heading toward democracy in the Western sense, despite ballot boxes for local elections, is less clear than it was twenty years ago, when the Berlin Wall fell. Asian leaders such as former Malaysian Prime Minister Mahatir Mohammed have juxtaposed Western and Asian values, arguing that capitalism and advanced development can occur without every trapping of Western democracy, including encouragement of a free press, opposition parties, and dissent. Singapore, a prosperous developed country, is a democracy only in some respects, and power is inherited. Furthermore, another challenge to the inevitability of democracy is coming from Asia and the Middle East. "Democracy is a superior technique for making the uncommitted feel committed," Bennis wrote in the essay—but religion has proven remarkably adept at such conversions, without democracy. Although political democracy in the

West tends to strictly separate politics from religious orthodoxies and exclude orthodoxies from workplaces, that is not true everywhere. India is a democracy; China is not (and open-communication-oriented Google agreed to constraints on information in China). Turkey is secular (so far); Malaysia is not. Maybe democracy is inevitable in Iran if we wait long enough, but right now imams hold a great deal of power.

Thus globalization has brought a range of democracy-impeding forces, as well as ethnic and religious groups desiring sovereignty, but not necessarily democracy in the Western liberal tradition. That leads me to a puzzle in the essay: the statement that democracy leads to homogenization. Democracy might lead to opportunity for social mobility, but the biggest democracies now have to grapple with and acknowledge diversity in a significant way, sometimes indigenous diversity and sometimes because of immigration, whether North Africans in France, Pakistanis in England, Turks in Germany, or Mexicans and other Hispanics in the United States. Furthermore, political science theory connecting democratic institutions and harmony to pluralism put a certain kind of diversity at the heart of democracy. Diversity thrives in political democracy, giving voice to minorities and enabling identity groups to come forth to demand inclusion. This happens also inside companies that open communication to give voice to people in new ways, as I found in my research for *Supercorp;* IBM, Procter & Gamble, Cisco, and Banco Real are among those with global cultures that also acknowledge and give expression to a range of identity groups.

When the essay was written, there was exuberance for linear progress, theories of the inevitability of development stages, arguments about the end of history and the decline of totalitarian ideologies. In 2009, after terrorism, corporate corruption, and the rise of powerful economies that are not democracies, we would approach generalizations about trends in a more sober and more cautious mood. Some analysts have dared to pose the question not of the inevitability of democracy but whether it was a temporary phenomenon, a two-to-three-hundred-year exception in human history. When might democracy lead to empire? When might it close rather than open opportunity? Inequality in income and education have been growing in the United States, and unregulated excesses led to financial collapse that spread around the world. And the rise of fundamentalism has occurred in Western democracies, too; it is hard to maintain fact-based meritocracies when religious fundamentalists control—and then close the minds of—school boards. Those who value democracy as an ideal have applauded the election of President Barack Obama as a sign that the democratic process of electing a new president will counter anti-democratic tendencies.

Is the power of technology and globalization enough to empower the masses with information so that democrats will prevail over demagogues? I certainly hope so. But I must wonder.

I write this in the midst of the world's worst financial crisis since the Great Depression, apparently caused by very undemocratic and occasionally corrupt business decisions, and in which a new U.S. president, Barack Obama, must restore faith that American democracy is up to the challenges of helping reduce conflicts and deal with the dark side of globalization. It is tempting to change Bennis's title from a statement to a question: "Is Democracy Inevitable?" and then ask a subset of questions about when, where, and how variants and degrees of democracy take root.

Democracy is a human system that requires continual investment in the best leaders and the strongest humanistic values. Democracy can be a goal, a standard, and an ideal. But it is no longer a foregone conclusion.

Rosabeth Moss Kanter holds the Ernest L. Arbuckle Professorship at Harvard Business School, where she specializes in strategy, innovation, and leadership for change. Her strategic and practical insights have guided leaders of large and small organizations worldwide for over twenty-five years, through teaching, writing, and direct consultation to major corporations and governments. She has authored seventeen books, such as *Confidence: How Winning Streaks & Losing Streaks Begin & End* (a *New York Times* business and #1 *Business Week* best seller) and *Men & Women of the Corporation*.

THE COMING DEATH OF
BUREAUCRACY (1966, 2000)

Originally published in 1966, this piece argues that bureaucracy is an institution whose time has past. The essay falters in some of its particulars—certainly General Motors is not the formidable empire it was thirty-five years ago. But the basic premise is truer today than it ever was. The wisdom of "destroying the pyramids," as Jan Carlzon called it, has become a First Principle of successful leaders ranging from Jack Welch to Percy Barnevik.

○

NOT FAR FROM THE NEW GOVERNMENT CENTER in downtown Boston, a foreign visitor walked up to a sailor and asked why American ships were built to last only a short time. According to the tourist, "The sailor answered without hesitation that the art of navigation is making such rapid progress that the finest ship would become obsolete if it lasted beyond a few years. In these words which fell accidentally from an uneducated man, I began to recognize the general and systematic idea upon which your great people direct all their concerns."

The foreign visitor was that shrewd observer of American morals and manners, Alexis de Tocqueville, and the year was 1835. He would not recognize Scollay Square today. But he had caught the central theme of our country: its preoccupation, its *obsession* with change. One thing is, however, new since de Tocqueville's time: the *acceleration* of newness, the changing scale and scope of change itself. As Dr. Robert Oppenheimer said, " . . . the world alters as we walk in it, so that the years of man's life

---

This work originally appeared in *Think Magazine*, Nov./Dec. 1966. This version appeared in the collection *Managing the Dream* (Perseus, 2000).

measure not some small growth or rearrangement or moderation of what was learned in childhood, but a great upheaval."

How will these accelerating changes in our society influence human organizations?

A short while ago, I predicted that we would, in the next 25 to 50 years, participate in the end of bureaucracy as we know it and in the rise of new social systems better suited to the twentieth-century demands of industrialization. This forecast was based on the evolutionary principle that every age develops an organizational form appropriate to its genius, and that the prevailing form, known by sociologists as bureaucracy and by most businessmen as "damn bureaucracy," was out of joint with contemporary realities. I realize now that my distant prophecy is already a distinct reality so that prediction is already foreshadowed by practice.

I should like to make clear that by bureaucracy I mean a chain of command structured on the lines of a pyramid—the typical structure which coordinates the business of almost every human organization we know of: industry, government, universities and research and development laboratories, military, religious, voluntary. I do not have in mind those fantasies so often dreamed up to describe complex organizations. These fantasies can be summarized in two grotesque stereotypes. The first I call "Organization as Inkblot"—an actor steals around an uncharted wasteland, growing more restive and paranoid by the hour, while he awaits orders that never come. The other specter is "Organization as Big Daddy"—the actors are square people plugged into square holes by some omniscient and omnipotent genius who can cradle in his arms the entire destiny of man by way of computer and TV. Whatever the first image owes to Kafka, the second owes to George Orwell's *1984*.

Bureaucracy, as I refer to it here, is a useful social invention that was perfected during the industrial revolution to organize and direct the activities of a business firm. Most students of organizations would say that its anatomy consists of the following components:

1. A well-defined chain of command.
2. A system of procedures and rules for dealing with all contingencies relating to work activities.
3. A division of labor based on specialization.
4. Promotion and selection based on technical competence.
5. Impersonality in human relations.

It is the pyramid arrangement we see on most organizational charts.

The bureaucratic "machine model" was developed as a reaction against the personal subjugation, nepotism and cruelty, and the capricious and subjective judgments which passed for managerial practices during the early days of the industrial revolution. Bureaucracy emerged out of the organizations' need for order and precision and the workers' demands for impartial treatment. It was an organization ideally suited to the values and demands of the Victorian era. And just as bureaucracy emerged as a creative response to a radically new age, so today new organizational shapes are surfacing before our eyes.

First I shall try to show why the conditions of our modern industrial world will bring about the death of bureaucracy. In the second part of this article, I will suggest a rough model of the organization of the future.

Four Threats

There are at least four relevant threats to bureaucracy:

1. Rapid and unexpected change.
2. Growth in size where the volume of an organization's traditional activities is not enough to sustain growth. (A number of factors are included here, among them: bureaucratic overhead; tighter controls and impersonality due to bureaucratic sprawls; outmoded rules and organizational structures.)
3. Complexity of modern technology where integration between activities and persons of very diverse, highly specialized competence is required.
4. A basically psychological threat springing from a change in managerial behavior.

It might be useful to examine the extent to which these conditions exist *right now:*

Rapid and Unexpected Change

Bureaucracy's strength is its capacity to efficiently manage the routine and predictable in human affairs. It is almost enough to cite the knowledge and population explosion to raise doubts about its contemporary viability. More revealing, however, are the statistics which demonstrate these overworked phrases:

a. Our productivity output per man hour may now be doubling almost every 20 years rather than every 40 years, as it did before World War II.

b. The Federal Government alone spent $16 billion in research and development activities in 1965; it will spend $35 billion by 1980.

c. The time lag between a technical discovery and recognition of its commercial uses was: 30 years before World War I, 16 years between the Wars, and only 9 years since World War II.

d. In 1946, only 42 cities in the world had populations of more than one million. Today there are 90. In 1930, there were 40 people for each square mile of the earth's land surface. Today there are 63. By 2000, it is expected, the figure will have soared to 142.

Bureaucracy, with its nicely defined chain of command, its rules and its rigidities, is ill-adapted to the rapid change the environment now demands.

Growth in Size

While, in theory, there may be no natural limit to the height of a bureaucratic pyramid, in practice the element of complexity is almost invariably introduced with great size. International operation, to cite one significant new element, is the rule rather than exception for most of our biggest corporations. Firms like Standard Oil Company (New Jersey) with over 100 foreign affiliates, Mobil Oil Corporation, The National Cash Register Company, Singer Company, Burroughs Corporation and Colgate-Palmolive Company derive more than half their income or earnings from foreign sales. Many others—such as Eastman Kodak Company, Chas. Pfizer & Company, Inc., Caterpillar Tractor Company, International Harvester Company, Corn Products Company and Minnesota Mining & Manufacturing Company—make from 30 to 50 percent of their sales abroad. General Motors Corporation sales are not only nine times those of Volkswagen, they are also bigger than the Gross National Product of the Netherlands and well over the GNP of a hundred other countries. If we have seen the sun set on the British Empire, we may never see it set on the empires of General Motors, ITT, Shell and Unilever.

Labor Boom

Increasing Diversity

Today's activities require persons of very diverse, highly specialized competence.

Numerous dramatic examples can be drawn from studies of labor markets and job mobility. At some point during the past decade, the U.S. became the first nation in the world ever to employ more people in service occupations than in the production of tangible goods. Examples of this trend:

a. In the field of education, the *increase* in employment between 1950 and 1960 was greater than the total number employed in the steel, copper and aluminum industries.

b. In the field of health, the *increase* in employment between 1950 and 1960 was greater than the total number employed in automobile manufacturing in either year.

c. In financial firms, the *increase* in employment between 1950 and 1960 was greater than total employment in mining in 1960.

These changes, plus many more that are harder to demonstrate statistically, break down the old, industrial trend toward more and more people doing either simple or undifferentiated chores.

Hurried growth, rapid change and increase in specialization—pit these three factors against the five components of the pyramid structure described earlier, and we should expect the pyramid of bureaucracy to begin crumbling.

Change in Managerial Behavior

There is, I believe, a subtle but perceptible change in the philosophy underlying management behavior. Its magnitude, nature and antecedents, however, are shadowy because of the difficulty of assigning numbers. (Whatever else statistics do for us, they most certainly provide a welcome illusion of certainty.) Nevertheless, real change seems underway because of:

a. A new concept of *man*, based on increased knowledge of his complex and shifting needs, which replaces an oversimplified, innocent, push-button idea of man.

b. A new concept of *power*, based on collaboration and reason, which replaces a model of power based on coercion and threat.

c. A new concept of *organizational values*, based on humanistic-democratic ideals, which replaces the depersonalized mechanistic value system of bureaucracy.

The primary cause of this shift in management philosophy stems not from the bookshelf but from the manager himself. Many of the behavioral scientists, like Douglas McGregor or Rensis Likert, have clarified and articulated—even legitimized—what managers have only half registered to themselves. I am convinced, for example, that the popularity of McGregor's book, *The Human Side of Enterprise,* was based on his rare empathy for a vast audience of managers who are wistful for an alternative to the mechanistic concept of authority, i.e., that he outlined a vivid utopia of more authentic human relationships than most organizational practices today allow. Furthermore, I suspect that the desire for relationships in business has little to do with a profit motive per se, though it is often ratio-nalized as doing so. The real push for these changes stems from the need, not only to humanize the organization, but to use it as a crucible of per-sonal growth and the development of self-realization.[1]

The core problems confronting any organization fall, I believe, into five major categories. First, let us consider the problems, then let us see how our twentieth-century conditions of constant change have made the bureaucratic approach to these problems obsolete.

Integration

The problem is how to integrate individual needs and management goals. In other words, it is the inescapable conflict between individual needs (like "spending time with the family") and organizational demands (like meet-ing deadlines).

Under twentieth-century conditions of constant change there has been an emergence of human sciences and a deeper understanding of man's complexity. Today, integration encompasses the entire range of issues con-cerned with incentives, rewards and motivations of the individual, and how the organization succeeds or fails in adjusting to these issues. In our society, where personal attachments play an important role, the individ-ual is appreciated, and there is genuine concern for his well-being, not just in a veterinary-hygiene sense, but as a moral, integrated personality.

Paradoxical Twins

The problem of integration, like most human problems, has a venerable past. The modern version goes back at least 160 years and was precipitated by an historical paradox: the twin births of modern individualism and mod-ern industrialism. The former brought about a deep concern for and a pas-sionate interest in the individual and his personal rights. The latter brought about increased mechanization of organized activity. Competition between the two has intensified as each decade promises more freedom and hope for man and more stunning achievements for technology. I believe that our society *has* opted for more humanistic and democratic values, however unfulfilled they may be in practice. It will "buy" these values even at loss in efficiency because it feels it can now afford the loss.

Social Influence

This problem is essentially one of power and how power is distributed. It is a complex issue and alive with controversy, partly because studies of leadership and power distribution can be interpreted in many ways, and almost always in ways which coincide with one's biases (including a cultural leaning toward democracy).

The problem of power has to be seriously reconsidered because of dramatic situational changes which make the possibility of one-man rule not necessarily "bad" but impractical. I refer to changes in top management's role.

Peter Drucker, over 12 years ago, listed 41 major responsibilities of the chief executive and declared that "90 percent of the trouble we are having with the chief executive's job is rooted in our superstition of the one-man chief." Many factors make one-man control obsolete, among them: the broadening product base of industry; impact of new technology; the scope of international operation; the separation of management from ownership; the rise of trade unions and general education. The real power of the "chief" has been eroding in most organizations even though both he and the organization cling to the older concept.

Collaboration

This is the problem of managing and resolving conflicts. Bureaucratically, it grows out of the very same process of conflict and stereotyping that has divided nations and communities. As organizations become more complex, they fragment and divide, building tribal patterns and symbolic codes which often work to exclude others (secrets and jargon, for example) and on occasion to exploit differences for inward (and always fragile) harmony.

Recent research is shedding new light on the problem of conflict. Psychologist Robert R. Blake in his stunning experiments has shown how simple it is to induce conflict, how difficult to arrest it. Take two groups of people who have never before been together, and give them a task which will be judged by an impartial jury. In less than an hour, each group devolves into a tightly-knit band with all the symptoms of an "in group." They regard their product as a "master-work" and the other group's as "commonplace" at best; "Other" becomes "enemy." "We are good, they are bad; we are right, they are wrong."

Rabbie's Reds and Greens

Jaap Rabbie, conducting experiments on intergroup conflict at the University of Utrecht, has been amazed by the ease with which conflict and stereotype develop. He brings into an experimental room two groups and distributes green name tags and pens to one group, red pens and tags to the other. The two groups do not compete; they do not even interact. They are only in sight of each other while they silently complete a questionnaire. Only ten minutes are needed to activate defensiveness and fear, reflected in the hostile and irrational perceptions of both "reds" and "greens."

Adaptation

This problem is caused by our turbulent environment. The pyramid structure of bureaucracy, where power is concentrated at the top, seems the perfect way to "run a railroad." And for the routine tasks of the nineteenth and early twentieth centuries, bureaucracy was (in some respects it still is) a suitable social arrangement. However, rather than a placid and predictable environment, what predominates today is a dynamic and uncertain one where there is deepening interdependence among economic, scientific, educational, social and political factors in the society.

Revitalization

This is the problem of growth and decay. As Alfred North Whitehead has said: "The art of free society consists first in the maintenance of the symbolic code, and secondly, in the fearlessness of revision. . . . Those societies which cannot combine reverence to their symbols with freedom of revision must ultimately decay. . . ."

Growth and decay emerge as the penultimate conditions of contemporary society. Organizations, as well as societies, must be concerned with those social structures that engender buoyancy, resilience and a "fearlessness of revision."

I introduce the term "revitalization" to embrace all the social mechanisms that stagnate and regenerate, as well as the process of this cycle. The elements of revitalization are:

1. An ability to learn from experience and to codify, store and retrieve the relevant knowledge.
2. An ability to "learn how to learn," that is, to develop methods for improving the learning process.
3. An ability to acquire and use feed-back mechanisms on performance, in short, to be self-analytical.
4. An ability to direct one's own destiny.

These qualities have a good deal in common with what John Gardner calls "self-renewal." For the organization, it means conscious attention to its own evolution. Without a planned methodology and explicit direction, the enterprise will not realize its potential.

Integration, distribution of power, collaboration, adaptation and *revitalization*—these are the major human problems of the next 25 years. How organizations cope with and manage these tasks will undoubtedly determine the viability of the enterprise.

Against this background I should like to set forth some of the conditions that will dictate organizational life in the next two or three decades.

The Environment

Rapid technological change and diversification will lead to more and more partnerships between government and business. It will be a truly mixed economy. Because of the immensity and expense of the projects, there will be fewer identical units competing in the same markets and organizations will become more interdependent.

The four main features of this environment are:

1. Interdependence rather than competition.
2. Turbulence and uncertainty rather than readiness and certainty.
3. Large-scale rather than small-scale enterprises.
4. Complex and multinational rather than simple national enterprises.

"Nice"—and Necessary

Population Characteristics

The most distinctive characteristic of our society is education. It will become even more so. Within 15 years, two-thirds of our population living in metropolitan areas will have attended college. Adult education is growing even faster, probably because of the rate of professional obsolescence. The Killian report showed that the average engineer required further education only ten years after getting his degree. It will be almost routine for the experienced physician, engineer and executive to go back to school for advanced training every two or three years. All of this education is not just "nice." It is necessary.

One other characteristic of the population which will aid our understanding of organizations of the future is increasing job mobility. The ease of transportation, coupled with the needs of a dynamic environment, change drastically the idea of "owning" a job—or "having roots." Already 20 percent of our population change their mailing address at least once a year.

Work Values

The increased level of education and mobility will change the values we place on work. People will be more intellectually committed to their jobs and will probably require more involvement, participation and autonomy.

Also, people will be more "other-oriented," taking cues for their norms and values from their immediate environment rather than tradition.

Tasks and Goals

The tasks of the organization will be more technical, complicated and unprogrammed. They will rely on intellect instead of muscle. And they will be too complicated for one person to comprehend, to say nothing of control. Essentially, they will call for the collaboration of specialists in a project or a team form of organization.

There will be a complication of goals. Business will increasingly concern itself with its adaptive or innovative creative capacity. In addition, supragoals will have to be articulated, goals which shape and provide the foundation for the goal structure. For example, one might be a system for detecting new and changing goals; another could be a system for deciding priorities among goals.

Finally, there will be more conflict and contradiction among diverse standards for organizational effectiveness. This is because professionals tend to identify more with the goals of their profession than with those of their immediate employer. University professors can be used as a case in point. Their inside work may be a conflict between teaching and research, while more of their income is derived from outside sources, such as foundations and consultant work. They tend not to be good "company men" because they divide their loyalty between their professional values and organizational goals.

Key Word: "Temporary"

Organization

The social structure of organizations of the future will have some unique characteristics. The key word will be "temporary." There will be adaptive, rapidly changing *temporary* systems. These will be task forces organized around problems to be solved by groups of relative strangers with diverse professional skills. The groups will be arranged on an organic rather than mechanical model; they will evolve in response to a problem rather than to programmed role expectations. The executive thus becomes a coordinator or "linking pin" between various task forces. He must be a man who can speak the polyglot jargon of research, with skills to relay information and to mediate between groups. People will be evaluated not vertically according to rank and status, but flexibly and functionally according to skill and professional training. Organizational charts will consist of project groups rather than stratified functional groups. (This trend is already visible in the aerospace and construction industries, as well as many professional and consulting firms.)

Adaptive, problem-solving, temporary systems of diverse specialists, linked together by coordinating and task evaluating executive specialists in an organic flux—this is the organization form that will gradually replace bureaucracy as we know it. As no catchy phrase comes to mind, I call this an organic-adaptive structure. Organizational arrangements of this sort may not only reduce the intergroup conflicts mentioned earlier; they may also induce honest-to-goodness creative collaboration.

Motivation

The organic-adaptive structure should increase motivation and thereby effectiveness, because it enhances satisfactions intrinsic to the task. There is a harmony between the educated individual's need for tasks that are meaningful, satisfactory and creative and a flexible organizational structure.

I think that the future I describe is not necessarily a "happy" one. Coping with rapid change, living in temporary work systems, developing meaningful relations and then breaking them—all augur social strains and psychological tensions. Teaching how to live with ambiguity, to identify with the adaptive process, to make a virtue out of contingency, and to be self-directing—these will be the tasks of education, the goals of maturity, and the achievement of the successful individual.

No Delightful Marriages

In these new organizations of the future, participants will be called upon to use their minds more than at any other time in history. Fantasy, imagination and creativity will be legitimate in ways that today seem strange. Social structures will no longer be instruments of psychic repression but will increasingly promote play and freedom on behalf of curiosity and thought.

One final word: While I forecast the structure and value coordinates for organizations of the future and contend that they are inevitable, this should not bar any of us from giving the inevitable a little push. The

French moralist may be right in saying that there are no delightful marriages, just good ones. It is possible that if managers and scientists continue to get their heads together in organizational revitalization, they *might* develop delightful organizations—just possibly.

I started with a quote from de Tocqueville and I think it would be fitting to end with one: "I am tempted to believe that what we call necessary institutions are often no more than institutions to which we have grown accustomed. In matters of social constitution, the field of possibilities is much more extensive than men living in their various societies are ready to imagine."

TOM PETERS ON "THE COMING DEATH OF BUREAUCRACY"

In 1966, when "The Coming Death of Bureaucracy" was published, I was an ensign in the U.S. Navy, serving in a combat engineering battalion ("Seabees") in Da Nang, Vietnam. Ensigns are the most junior of officers, and I was clearly part of the "military model" of organization—though I'd never heard that moniker. I'd trained as a civil engineer, and even stuck around Cornell to get a master's in construction engineering—though the management of people had not earned even a single lecture!

Per the Navy Seabee routine, I was deployed to Vietnam for nine months, came home for three, and went back over for another nine. With the Tooth Fairy looking over my shoulder, I lucked out and had two wildly different COs (Commanding Officers); taken as a pair, their impact on my world view remains enormous forty-three years later.

To this day, I call them "day" and "night." My first CO, Dick Anderson (*Captain* Anderson) was "day." Our job was to build stuff—roads, bridges, camps, gun emplacements, and so on—mostly for the U.S. Marine Corps. Captain Andy's approach could be summarized in three words, subsequently made immortal by Nike; namely, "Just do it." Or, more accurately in our case, "Just get the damn thing built—as fast as you can." He made it clear to the very junior officers, like me, that we were to do whatever the hell our Chief Petty Officers told us to do. (These were the senior enlisted men whom, in theory, *we* had life and death authority over—as far as our CO was concerned, it was pretty much the other way around.) Above all, Captain Andy wanted no damned excuses—monsoon rains that made everything impassible were our problem, not God's. "What, do you only build when it's sunny, Mr. Peters?" (Typical Andersonism—by the way, junior naval officers are addressed as "Mr.") Captain Andy, in retrospect, gave us a ridiculous amount of autonomy—and expected us to rise to the occasion. Oh, and when he gave us hell, which was frequently, it always ended with a smile from his weather-beaten face: "You'll sort it out, Tom, I have no doubt." The upshot was that we got a lot of work done, and done well, in short order. (Incidentally, one of the by-products of Captain Andy's approach to chief petty officers was that I got along well with my chiefs, took them very seriously as he'd suggested, and became a regular at the Chiefs Club—by invitation only to officers—and benefited enormously from this informal web of relationships with the real movers and doers in our 850-person outfit.)

Deployment #2 brought Captain "Night," whose name shall not be mentioned (sort of like Voldemort). He had a different style of "leadership" entirely. It's often called "by the book." He was a stickler for the formalities. My de facto membership at the Chiefs Club was frowned upon—and I sometimes thought and think that he was more interested in typo-free reports than completed construction. I had a crappy time, as did pretty much the whole set of junior officers. For me the quintessential event came when I was summoned to the CO's office and lectured on the difference between "tangible" and "palpable" in a report I'd prepared that was going up the chain of command—to this day, at age sixty-six, I have no idea what the difference is between the two words.

Salvation came when Captain Anderson summoned me back to Washington to work for him in the Pentagon. There he continued my education in how to get things done way beyond one's rank by mastering what I subsequently learned was called the "informal organization."

The Navy done, and with nothing better to do (that's not an exaggeration), I aimlessly, like a lot of my friends, moseyed off to business school; in my case Stanford. (Palo Alto weather was better than Harvard's—that was the key factor.) One of our core courses in the first semester was something called "organization behavior." There was no text, and my professor (and subsequently mentor), Gene Webb, constructed a book of eclectic readings. You guessed it, one was brother Bennis's "The Coming Death of Bureaucracy." I despise such language, but the fact is that there really was a "flash of recognition." Warren imagined a world that was pretty darned close to the wonderful world of Captain Day (Anderson). And the world slipping away (hopefully!) was the world of Captain Night (Voldemort).

And the rest, as they say, is history. Warren's work, introduced to me with a big bang courtesy of this article, and that of Stanford's "OB" foursome (Webb, Hal Leavitt, Mason Haire, and Jim March), provided a peculiar view of organizations that has been at the center of my approach to my work since that autumn of 1970 when I matriculated at Stanford.

In short, I became obsessed with the oddball way things *really* work in effective organizations—Bob Waterman and I later saw it at the likes of a smaller Hewlett-Packard, and at 3M, when we did the research that led to *In Search of Excellence*. Power was pretty much associated with the "temporary" work of project teams. Worker engagement was sky high—abetted by high levels of trust and autonomy. Whoever had the best idea of what needed to be done pretty much took charge for a while until the next stage emerged. And so on. After my first book, I settled down in Silicon Valley for a wonderfully turbulent quarter century—and courtesy of the Apples and Electronic Arts, and then of the Googles, watched the new organization forms that Warren had foreseen in 1966 come of age.

I'd be stretching things to say that "The Coming Death of Bureaucracy" was the butterfly without which the rest would not have happened. But I surely can say it was one of a scant handful of items that made my world what it is today.

I am eternally grateful.

Tom Peters is one of the world's most influential business thinkers. He coauthored the milestone book *In Search of Excellence* (HarperCollins, 1982) and has written many others including *Re-imagine: Business Excellence in a Disruptive Age* (DK, 2003). He founded tompeterscompany!, a global training and consulting organization, and has previously been a partner at McKinsey & Co. and a White House senior adviser.

THE END OF THE
GREAT MAN (1997)

(coauthored by Patricia Ward Biederman)

None of us is as smart as all of us.

---○---

THE MYTH OF THE TRIUMPHANT INDIVIDUAL is deeply ingrained in the American psyche. Whether it is midnight rider Paul Revere or basketball's Michael Jordan in the 1990s, we are a nation enamored of heroes—rugged self-starters who meet challenges and overcome adversity. Our contemporary views of leadership are entwined with our notions of heroism, so much so that the distinction between "leader" and "hero" (or "celebrity," for that matter) often becomes blurred. In our society leadership is too often seen as an inherently individual phenomenon.

And yet we all know that cooperation and collaboration grow more important every day. A shrinking world in which technological and political complexity increase at an accelerating rate offers fewer and fewer arenas in which individual action suffices. Recognizing this, we talk more and more about the need for teamwork, citing the Japanese approach to management, for example, as a call for a new model of effective action. Yet despite the rhetoric of collaboration, we continue to advocate it in a culture in which people strive to distinguish themselves as individuals. We continue to live in a by-line culture where recognition and status are accorded to individuals, not groups.

This work originally appeared in *Organizing Genius* (Perseus, 1997).

But even as the lone hero continues to gallop through our imaginations, shattering obstacles with silver bullets, leaping tall buildings in a single bound, we know there is an alternate reality. Throughout history, groups of people, often without conscious design, have successfully blended individual and collective effort to create something new and wonderful. The Bauhaus school, the Manhattan Project, the Guarneri Quartet, the young filmmakers who coalesced around Francis Ford Coppola and George Lucas, the youthful scientists and hackers who invented a computer that was personal as well as powerful, the creators of the Internet—these are a few of the Great Groups that have reshaped the world in very different but enduring ways.

That should hardly surprise us. In a society as complex and technologically sophisticated as ours, the most urgent projects require the coordinated contributions of many talented people. Whether the task is building a global business or discovering the mysteries of the human brain, one person can't hope to accomplish it, however gifted or energetic he or she may be. There are simply too many problems to be identified and solved, too many connections to be made. And yet, even as we make the case for collaboration, we resist the idea of collective creativity. Our mythology refuses to catch up with our reality. We cling to the myth of the Lone Ranger, the romantic idea that great things are usually accomplished by a larger-than-life individual working alone. Despite the evidence to the contrary, we still tend to think of achievement in terms of the Great Man or Great Woman, instead of the Great Group.

But in a global society, in which timely information is the most important commodity, collaboration is not simply desirable, it is inevitable. In all but the rarest cases, one is too small a number to produce greatness. A recent study of senior executives of international firms published by Korn-Ferry, the world's largest executive search firm, and *The Economist* resoundingly confirms our thesis that tomorrow's organizations will be managed by teams of leaders. Asked who will have the most influence on their global organizations in the next ten years, 61 percent responded "teams of leaders"; 14 percent said "one leader." That does not mean, however, that we no longer need leaders. Instead, we have to recognize a new paradigm: not great leaders alone, but great leaders who exist in a fertile relationship with a Great Group. In these creative alliances, the leader and the team are able to achieve something together that neither could achieve alone. The leader finds greatness in the group. And he or she helps the members find it in themselves.

Organizing Genius examines Great Groups systematically in the hope of finding out how their collective magic is made. We could have chosen any number of creative collaborations, from the artists who made up the Harlem Renaissance to the scientists of the Human Genome Project, but we decided to focus on seven that have had enduring impact. They are the Walt Disney studio, which invented the animated feature film in 1937 with *Snow White and the Seven Dwarfs;* the Great Groups at Xerox's Palo Alto Research Center (PARC) and Apple, which first made computers easy to use and accessible to nonexperts; the 1992 Clinton campaign, which put the first Democrat in the White House since Jimmy Carter; the elite corps of aeronautical engineers and fabricators who built radically new planes at Lockheed's top-secret Skunk Works; the influential arts school and experimental community known as Black Mountain College; and, finally, what may be the paradigmatic Great Group, the Manhattan Project.

Why these seven? We chose to emphasize twentieth-century groups based in the United States because this has been a golden age of collaborative achievement in America. (As French observer Alexis de Tocqueville noted more than 150 years ago, Americans seem to have a genius for collective action.) And we decided to focus only on groups that have altered our shared reality in some significant way. The Manhattan Project, which ushered in the nuclear age with all its benefits and horrors, obviously fits this criterion. But so does, less obviously, Disney Feature Animation. Guided by an unlikely visionary named Walt, the artists at Disney did more than create an enduring new art form. The studio that Walt and brother Roy built continues to set the standard, both creatively and economically, for the entertainment and leisure industries worldwide.

All seven groups are great in several senses. Each was or is made up of greatly gifted people. Each achieved or produced something spectacularly new, and each was widely influential, often sparking creative collaboration elsewhere. To echo Steve Jobs, whose Great Group at Apple created the Macintosh, each of these groups "put a dent in the universe." It is worth noting that all but one—Black Mountain College—were engaged in creating something substantive and external to the group: a film, a computer, the first stealth plane. Groups seem to be most successful when undertaking tangible projects, as Black Mountain was when building its second campus. The project brings them together and brings out their collective best. When the thing is finished, the group often spins apart.

Given our continuing obsession with solitary genius, reflected in everything from the worship of film directors to our fascination with Bill Gates and other high-profile entrepreneurs, it is no surprise that we tend to underestimate just how much creative work is accomplished by groups. Today, an important scientific paper may represent the best thinking and patient lab work of hundreds of people. Collaboration continually takes place in the arts as well, despite our conviction, as the great French physiologist Claude Bernard observed, that "art is I; science is we." A classic example is Michelangelo's masterpiece the ceiling of the Sistine Chapel. In our mind's eye, we see Michelangelo, looking remarkably like Charlton Heston, laboring alone on the scaffolding high above the chapel floor. In fact, thirteen people helped Michelangelo paint the work. Michelangelo was not only an artist, he was, as biographer William E. Wallace points out, the head of a good-sized entrepreneurial enterprise that collaboratively made art that bore his name (an opinion piece by Wallace in the *New York Times* was aptly headlined "Michelangelo, CEO").

Other painters have worked collaboratively as well. In a landmark article titled "Artists' Circles and the Development of Artists," published in 1982, sociologist Michael P. Farrell describes the synergistic circle of French artists, including Monet, Manet, Degas, and Renoir, who pioneered Impressionism. Monet and Renoir often painted next to each other in the Barbizon woods. For a time, their work was so similar that Monet had to look at the signature to tell whether a particular canvas for sale in a Parisian gallery was his or Renoir's. Braque and Picasso also had an intense creative collaboration, which gave birth to Cubism. For several years, they saw each other almost every day, talked constantly about their revolutionary new style, and painted as similarly as possible. They even dressed alike, in mechanics' clothes, and playfully compared themselves to the equally pioneering Wright brothers (Picasso called Braque, "Wilbourg"). Braque later described their creative interdependence as that of "two mountaineers roped together."

Creative collaboration occurs in other arts as well. Filmmaking is collaborative almost by definition. And Pilobolus, the marvelous dance troupe named after an unusually mobile fungus, began when a couple of Dartmouth jocks took a class from Alison Chase, a rare dance teacher who valued collective discovery over years of training. As one member of the pioneering group later recalled, most of them had zero dance technique to fall back on so they had to invent their own. "We definitely couldn't have done this alone," cofounder Jonathan Wolken told writer John Briggs. Writers, too, often reap the benefits of creative collaboration. The Bloomsbury Group is only one of dozens of such groups, albeit one whose antics have been chronicled at numbing length. Dorothy Parker and her vicious circle—the writers who exchanged barbs at Manhattan's Algonquin Hotel during the 1920s—is a home-grown example of a group whose whole seems to have been significantly greater than the sum of its acerbic parts.

Farrell's article on artists' circles begins with a quote from Henry James in praise of group creativity: "Every man works better when he has companions working in the same line, and yielding to the stimulus of suggestion, comparison, emulation. Great things have of course been done by solitary workers; but they have usually been done with double the pains they would have cost if they had been produced in more genial circumstances."

James's point is well taken. Gifted individuals working alone may waste years pursuing a sterile line of inquiry or become so enamored of the creative *process* that they produce little or nothing. A Great Group can be a goad, a check, a sounding board, and a source of inspiration, support, and even love. Songwriter Jules Styne said he had to have a collaborator: "In the theater you need someone to talk to. You can't sit by yourself in a room and write."

We chose our seven Great Groups to underscore the range of fields, including education, in which creative collaboration can take place. We also picked these seven because each makes a fascinating story. Vibrant with energy and ideas, full of colorful, talented people playing for high stakes and often racing against a deadline, Great Groups are organizations fully engaged in the thrilling process of discovery. It is our hope that everyone will be interested in some of these groups. (We have a nagging suspicion that we may have lost a few prospective readers by not chronicling a great sports team, such as the Boston Celtics of the 1980s, but we felt that was the one variety of Great Group that had been analyzed to death.) All such groups are engaged in creative problem solving, but the specific problems each of these seven faced and the solutions it found makes each distinctive. In the story of each Great Group, you will find the themes and ideas introduced in this chapter illustrated, illuminated, and expanded. But you will also find the brilliant answers to specific puzzles, such as how the Macintosh computer came to have icons that make us smile.

You might ask why we chose to focus exclusively on Great Groups when the majority of the institutions in which we work, teach, and otherwise participate are anything but. The reason is our conviction that excellence is a better teacher than is mediocrity. The lessons of the ordinary are everywhere. Truly profound and original insights are to be found only in studying the exemplary. We must turn to Great Groups if we hope to begin to understand how that rarest of precious resources—genius—can be successfully combined with great effort to achieve results that enhance all our lives.

The need to do so is urgent. The organizations of the future will increasingly depend on the creativity of their members to survive. And the leaders of those organizations will be those who find ways both to retain their talented and independent-minded staffs and to set them free to do their best, most imaginative work. Conventional wisdom about leadership and teams continues to glorify the leader at the expense of the group. Great Groups offer a new model in which the leader is an equal among Titans. In a truly creative collaboration, work is pleasure, and the only rules and procedures are those that advance the common cause.

Psychologically and socially, Great Groups are very different from mundane ones. Great Groups rarely have morale problems. Intrinsically motivated, for the most part, the people in them are buoyed by the joy of problem solving. Focused on a fascinating project, they are oblivious to the nettles of working together in ordinary circumstances.

Obviously, there are lessons here for transforming our classrooms, our offices, even our communities. Traditionally, collaboration in the classroom, for instance, has been taboo, condemned as a form of cheating. Yet what we discover in Great Groups is that collaboration can only make our classrooms happier and more productive. What lessons do Great Groups have for our workplaces, where so many people feel stifled, not stimulated? Look how hard people in Great Groups work, without anyone hovering over them. Look how morale soars when intelligent people are asked to do a demanding but worthy task and given the freedom and tools to do it. Imagine how much richer and happier our organizations would be if, like Great Groups, they were filled with people working as hard and as intelligently as they can, too caught up for pettiness, their sense of self grounded in the bedrock of talent and achievement.

Every Great Group is extraordinary in its own way. Yet all of them have much in common. Imagine that it is twenty-five years ago and you are a fly on the wall at Xerox PARC where the first user-friendly computer is being invented. The offices themselves are nondescript. But the atmosphere is charged, electric with the sense that great things are being accomplished here. Most of the members of the group are young—in their twenties or thirties—and each knows that having been recruited for this project is a badge of honor. Although Xerox is a corporate behemoth, there is no sense at PARC of being part of a major corporation. No "suits" from headquarters are in evidence. Instead, the atmosphere is much like that of a graduate department at a first-rate university. People wear Birkenstocks and T-shirts. For the weekly meeting, everybody grabs a beanbag chair. Although the group is too busy working to philosophize much, any participant would tell you that he or she would rather be here than anywhere else. The money doesn't matter, career doesn't matter, the project is all. In some cases, personal relationships have been interrupted or deferred. It's hard to have a life when you're up half the night in the lab working on your part of a compelling problem, often with one of your equally obsessed colleagues at your side. This is not a job. This is a mission, carried out by people with fire in their eyes.

Great Groups have some odd things in common. For example, they tend to do their brilliant work in spartan, even shabby, surroundings. Someday someone will write a book explaining why so many pioneering enterprises, including the Walt Disney Company, Hewlett-Packard, and Apple, were born in garages. Disney's animators have often worked in cluttered temporary quarters. Black Mountain College managed with a leased campus during its exciting early years, despite the inconvenience of having to store all college property in the attic over the summer while the church organization that owned the buildings moved back in and conducted its programs. The Skunk Works did its clandestine work in a windowless building next to the airport in notoriously bland Burbank, California (the home of Disney Animation as well). According to late Skunk Works head Ben Rich, the place was "about as cheery as a bomb shelter."

We can speculate on why great things are often accomplished in dull or tacky surroundings. Perhaps a bland or unattractive environment spurs creativity, functioning as an aesthetic blank slate that frees the mind to dream about what might be. Maybe a great view and chic decor are distractions and thus counterproductive when important work is being done. But the truth is that most people in Great Groups spend very little time thinking about their surroundings. They have wonderful tunnel vision. The project, whether it's building the bomb before the Germans do or creating a computer easy enough for a child to use, is what's important. The right tools are essential, but fancy digs aren't. As a result, the offices of Great Groups often look, as Tracy Kidder writes of the Eagle computer offices in *The Soul of a New Machine*, "like something psychologists build for testing the fortitude of small animals."

All Great Groups have other commonalities. They all have extraordinary leaders, and, as a corollary, they tend to lose their way when they lose their leadership, just as Disney did after Walt's death in 1966. It's a paradox, really. Great Groups tend to be collegial and nonhierarchical, peopled by singularly competent individuals who often have an antiauthoritarian streak. Nonetheless, virtually every Great Group has a strong and visionary head. These leaders may be as patrician as J. Robert Oppenheimer of the Manhattan Project and the Kennedyesque Bob Taylor at PARC. They may be as seemingly simple, even cornball, as Walt Disney. They are sometimes outrageous in a juvenile kind of way, as Steve Jobs was at Apple and James Carville, the Ragin' Cajun, was during Clinton's 1992 campaign. But all these leaders share certain essential characteristics.

First, each has a keen eye for talent. Sometimes Great Groups just seem to grow. Some places and individuals become so identified with excellence and excitement that they become magnets for the talented—think of the physics program at Göttingen that drew Oppenheimer and so many other great minds or the San Francisco scene that lured the writers of the Beat Generation. But Great Groups are made as well. Recruiting the right genius for the job is the first step in building many great collaborations. Great Groups are inevitably forged by people unafraid of hiring people better than themselves. Such recruiters look for two things: excellence and the ability to work with others. Computer pioneer Alan Kay recalls that Bob Taylor at PARC was a "connoisseur of talent" who recruited people both for their intellectual gifts and for their ability to work collaboratively. At Disney Feature Animation, head Peter Schneider also looks for both talent and the ability to work side by side, pursuing a common dream instead of a purely personal vision. Schneider doesn't want animators, however able, "who don't play well in the sandbox with others."

Being able to work with others does not necessarily mean fitting in in a conventional sense. Phil Jackson, coach of basketball's Chicago Bulls, treasures what Dennis Rodman brings to the championship team, despite—indeed, because of—his flamboyance. Says Jackson, who often uses Sioux and other Native American traditions to motivate the team, "Dennis has been a real blessing for us, because he's like a heyoka, the clown of the tribe. The heyoka was a cross-dresser, a unique person who walked backwards. He was respected because he brought a reality change when you saw him."

How do you find people who are capable of extraordinary work? Some leaders talk about looking for people "with fire in their eyes." Others rely on tests. Inventor Thomas Alva Edison was both an intuitive recruiter and a systematic one. He liked to give job applicants timed tests containing 150 questions dealing with science, history, engineering, and other subjects. Believing that a good memory was the basis for good decision making, he asked everything from "How is leather tanned?" to "What is the price of twelve grains of gold?" J.C.R. Licklider, the psychologist who helped launch the Internet, trusted the Miller Analogies Test (the one that asks, "North is to South as blue is to . . . ?" The correct answer is gray.). Licklider believed that someone who did well on the test had a promising combination of broad general knowledge and the ability to see relationships. "I had a kind of rule," Licklider said. "Anybody who could do 85 or better on the Miller Analogies Test, hire him, because he's going to be very good at something."

The process of recruitment is often one of commitment building as well. At Data General, Tom West and his subordinates told prospective recruits to their secret computer project how good a person had to be to be chosen and how few were actually tapped. As a result, those who were brought on board saw themselves as an enviable elite, however overworked and underpaid. Kelly Johnson, the legendary founder of the Skunk Works, sought to recruit only the best person in each specialty the project required (Disney tried to do the same). As one of Johnson's lieutenants wrote to Tom Peters, "Each person was told why he had been chosen: He was the best one to be had. Whether it was absolutely true or not, each one believed it and did his darndest to live up to it."

Who becomes part of a Great Group? Participants are almost always young. In most of these groups, thirty-five was regarded as elderly. Historically, women have created some extraordinary groups. Consider the largely female coalition that mounted the New York City shirtwaist strikes of 1909–10. An alliance of women labor organizers, teenage factory workers (most of them Italian and Jewish immigrants), college students, and a "mink brigade" of wealthy society women organized walkouts by nearly 30,000 workers from the sweat shops of the Lower East Side. Committed to collective action and social justice and dressed alike in white shirtwaists and long skirts, the women showed solidarity in the face of beatings, arrests, and, for some, economic ruin. Although their protest led to few long-term reforms and was overshadowed by the tragic fire in the Triangle Shirtwaist factory a year later, the action was a model of women working together to effect change. A number of participants were involved in other Great Groups. Strike leader Leonora O'Reilly, for example, was both a suffragist and a founding member of the NAACP.

Although women played roles in all seven of our groups, most of the participants were male, in large part, we can assume, because of lack of professional opportunities for women. Even when most members have been men, however, Great Groups are rarely stodgy Old Boys' Clubs. Typically, theirs is a playful, decidedly adolescent subculture.

We are deep in Peter Pan territory in many Great Groups, whether they include women or not (think of Black Mountain College under Charles Olson, who believed women made better mommies than poets, or the gifted but sophomoric engineers of the Skunk Works, who once had a contest to see who had the biggest rump). Although sexism surely kept women out of some Great Groups, there may be something in the group dynamic itself that has discouraged participation by women. (This is clearly an area for serious research, if only to find ways to tap the entire talent pool, not just the male portion.) Minorities have been under-represented as well, even at Black Mountain, the first non–African American college in the South to enroll black students and hire black faculty. Great

Groups often tend to attract mavericks, such as Black Mountain founder John Andrew Rice, who was fired from Florida's Rollins College for bucking its president, and the irrepressible physicist, prankster, and future Nobel laureate, Richard Feynman, at Los Alamos. If not out-and-out rebels, participants may lack traditional credentials or exist on the margins of their professions.

Certainly youth can bring enormous energy to these enterprises, and not being a mainstream success can liberate an individual from too much respect for orthodoxy. But probably the most important thing that young members bring to a Great Group is their often delusional confidence. Kidder cites the recruiting strategy Tom West picked up from Seymour Cray, the legendary designer of high-speed computers. Cray liked to hire talented but newly minted engineers. He believed lack of experience was an asset, not a liability, because, as Kidder writes, these unseasoned recruits "do not usually know what's supposed to be impossible." The French composer Berlioz made a similar observation about fellow composer Saint-Saëns. "Saint-Saëns knows everything," Berlioz said. "All he lacks is inexperience."

Thus many Great Groups are fueled by an invigorating, completely unrealistic view of what they can accomplish. Not knowing what they can't do puts everything in the realm of the possible. In a radio interview, director John Frankenheimer, whose work includes the unforgettable film *The Manchurian Candidate,* said that the Golden Age of television resulted, at least in part, from his naïveté and that of his fellow video pioneers. "We didn't know we couldn't do it, so we did it," said Frankenheimer of making such classic dramas as "Marty" in a demanding new medium, live TV. Time teaches many things, including limitations. Time forces people, however brilliant, to taste their own mortality. In short, experience tends to make people more realistic, and that's not necessarily a good thing. As psychologist Martin Seligman has shown, realism is a risk factor for depression and its attendant ills, including an inability to act and the loss of self-trust. Great Groups often show evidence of collective denial. And "Denial ain't just a river in Egypt," as twelve-steppers like to say. Denial can obscure obstacles and stiffen resolve. It can liberate. Great Groups are not realistic places. They are exuberant, irrationally optimistic ones.

Many of the people in our Great Groups are tinkerers—the kind of people who, as children, took the family television apart and tried to put it together again. They are people willing to spend thousands of hours finding out how things work, including things that don't yet exist. There's a joke about engineers that captures the spirit of many participants in creative collaborations. An engineer meets a frog who offers the engineer anything he wants if he will kiss the frog. "No," says the engineer. "Come on," says the frog. "Kiss me, and I'll turn into a beautiful woman." "Nah," says the engineer. "I don't have time for a girlfriend . . . but a talking frog, that's really *neat*." Members of Great Groups don't fear technology, they embrace it. And they all think that creating the future is really neat.

Curiosity fuels every Great Group. The members don't simply solve problems. They are engaged in a process of discovery that is its own reward. Many of the individuals in these groups have dazzling individual skills—mathematical genius is often one. But they also have another quality that allows them both to identify significant problems and to find creative, boundary-busting solutions rather than simplistic ones. They have hungry, urgent minds. They want to get to the bottom of everything they see. Many have expansive interests and encyclopedic knowledge. Alan Kay, for instance, one of the wizards of PARC and now an Apple fellow, is a polymath accomplished in math, biology, music, developmental psychology, philosophy, and several other disciplines. During an interview with us, he talked insightfully about political discourse, economic theory, and the optimal size of a town before turning to his memories of PARC. Kay is the kind of person who says, with authority, "Computer science is a bit like a Gregorian chant—a one-line melody changing state within larger scale sections. Parallel programming is more like polyphony." Kay takes his insights wherever he finds them. What he knew about how children learn helped him imagine a computer that would teach them how to use it. A technique that Stewart Brand used in *The Whole Earth Catalog* to force readers to make a serendipitous journey through the book instead of a preplanned one influenced Kay and his colleagues in designing PARC's revolutionary network browser. People like Kay are able to make connections that others don't see, in part because they have command of more data in the first place. It is one of the unique qualities of Great Groups that they are able to attract people of Kay's stature, then provide an atmosphere in which both individual and collective achievements result from the interplay of distinguished minds.

The truism that people don't want to be managed, that they want to be led, is never more true than when orchestrating a group of Alan Kays. ("Knowledge workers" can't be managed, according to Peter Drucker, who coined the term. For that reason alone, Great Groups warrant close study by anyone interested in running an information-based enterprise.) The leaders who can do so must first of all command unusual respect. Such a leader has to be someone a greatly gifted person thinks is worth listening to, since genius almost always has other options. Such a leader must be someone who inspires trust, and deserves it. And though civility is not always the emblematic characteristic of Great Groups, it should be a trait of anyone who hopes to lead one. It was the quality that Maestro Carlo Maria Guilini thought most important in allowing the gifted individuals of the Los Angeles Philharmonic to achieve their collective goal of making truly beautiful music. "Even in delicate situations," he recalls, "I explained my views to the orchestra. I did not impose them. The right response, if forced, is not the same as the right response when it comes out of conviction." Those leaders of Great Groups who don't behave civilly (as Jobs sometimes failed to do, and Disney) put their very dreams at risk.

Members of Great Groups don't have to be told what to do, although they may need to be nudged back on task, as educators like to say. Indeed, they typically can't be told what to do: Being able to determine what needs to be done and how to do it is why they are in the group in the first place. In the collaborative meritocracy, people who are talented enough and committed enough are rightly seen as indispensable. The late Jerry Garcia, the great, gray presence of the Grateful Dead, once observed, "You do not merely want to be considered just the best of the best. You want to be considered the only ones who do what you do." Such people need to be freed to do what only they can do. Great Groups are coordinated teams of original thinkers. Kidder has a wonderful term to describe the structures that result in creative collaboration. They are, he writes, "webs of voluntary, mutual responsibility." Such groups are obsessionally focused on their goal. They could not care less about the organizational chart (which often becomes a dartboard in such a group), unless there is something on there that might get in the way of the project.

Our suspicion is that one of the reasons so many members of Great Groups are young is that, given a choice, more mature and confident talent opts for more autonomy, choosing to work collectively only when the project is irresistible. Disney Animation, for instance, is currently losing some of its best and most seasoned animators in part, Peter Schneider believes, because midlife priorities make creative collaboration less attractive.

Who succeeds in forming and leading a Great Group? He or she is almost always a pragmatic dreamer. They are people who get things done, but they are people with immortal longings. Often, they are scientifically minded people with poetry in their souls, people like Oppenheimer, who turned to the Bhagavad Gita to express his ambivalence about the atom and its uses. They are always people with an original vision. A dream is at the heart of every Great Group. It is always a dream of greatness, not simply an ambition to succeed. The dream is the engine that drives the group, the vision that inspires the team to work as if the fate of civilization rested on getting its revolutionary new computer out the door. The dream—a new kind of entertainment, a new political era, a radical new take on what learning is all about—is a kind of contract, a mutual understanding that the product, and even the process itself, will be worth the effort to create it. The dream is also a promise on the visionary's part that the goal is attainable. Each time Disney asked his artists to push the envelope of animation, he told them, "If you can dream it, you can do it." He believed that, and, as a result, they did too.

Truly great leaders such as Oppenheimer seem to incarnate the dream and become one with it. They do other crucial things as well. Psychologist Teresa M. Amabile and others have established that the way an environment is structured can have an enormous impact on creativity, for good or for ill. The atmosphere most conducive to creativity is one in which individuals have a sense of autonomy and yet are focused on the collective goal. Constraint (perceived as well as real) is a major killer of creativity, Amabile has found. Freedom or autonomy is its major enhancer.

Effective leaders are willing to make decisions, but they typically allow members of the group to work as they see fit. It was the director's skill at moving the project forward while letting each participant do his or her best work that art director Robert Boyle so valued in Alfred Hitchcock. Boyle recalls working with Hitchcock on *North by Northwest* (1959). From an art director's point of view, it was an especially challenging film because Boyle was forced to find ways around such obstacles as the Department of the Interior's refusal to allow Cary Grant and the other actors to be filmed in front of the presidential faces on the real Mount Rushmore. Having tough problems to solve was one of the pleasures of making the movie, Boyle recalls. (He was lowered down the face of the mountain and took photos of the sculptures that were then rear-projected when the climactic scene was shot back in the studio.) "Hitchcock was very demanding, but he was also the most collaborative of any director I ever worked with," Boyle said. "Since you were professional, he expected you to do your job. *He* made the unity possible."

Leaders also encourage creativity when they take the sting out of failure. In creative groups, failure is regarded as a learning experience, not a pretext for punishment. Creativity inevitably involves taking risks, and, in Great Groups, it is understood that the risk taker will sometimes stumble. CEO Michael Eisner says that Disney aspires to be a place "in which people feel safe to fail." An atmosphere in which people dread failure or fear that they will be ridiculed for offbeat ideas stifles creativity, Eisner believes. He often quotes hockey great Wayne Gretzky's observation that "You miss 100 percent of the shots you don't take." At Disney, Eisner says, adding an important caveat, "Failing is good, as long as it doesn't become a habit."

Although strong leadership is typical of Great Groups, its form may vary. The innovative and highly collaborative Orpheus Chamber Orchestra has no maestro as such. Instead it has different member-leaders for different concerts.

Many Great Groups have a dual administration. They have a visionary leader, and they have someone who protects them from the outside world, the "suits." Great Groups tend to be island societies. They are often physically isolated, as were the Manhattan Project in the New Mexico desert and Black Mountain College in the foothills of western North Carolina. While Oppenheimer was the creative head of Los Alamos, General Leslie R. Groves was its protector. Unloved by the scientists he served so well, Groves patrolled the border between the creative group and the exterior forces, notably the military bureaucracy that controlled the group's resources and could interfere at any time. Great Groups tend to be nonconformist. Their members sometimes dress haphazardly (Black Mountaineers dismayed the local townsfolk by wearing sandals or going barefoot). But whatever their appearance, they are always rule busters. People in Great Groups are never insiders or corporate types on the fast track: They are always on their *own* track.

As a result, they often need someone to deflect not just the criticism, but even the attention of the bureaucrats and conventional thinkers elsewhere in the organization. According to Kay, Bob Taylor did that superbly well at PARC. "Taylor put his body between Xerox and us," Kay recalled two decades later. The protectors typically lack the glamour of the visionary leaders, but they are no less essential, particularly in enterprises that require official sanction or that cannot realize their dream without institutional consent. This was the fate of the group at PARC. Taylor was able to protect his group from interference at Xerox, but he wasn't able to convince Xerox to actually put the revolutionary PARC computer into commercial production. In the Manhattan Project, Groves freed Oppenheimer to deal with the science and his independent-minded staff. Oppenheimer was able to get what he needed from the scientists, and Groves could get the scientists what they needed from the brass. Both men made the project a success.

The zeal with which people in Great Groups work is directly related to how effectively the leader articulates the vision that unites them. When heading up the team that made the Macintosh, Steve Jobs inspired his staff with the promise that they were creating something not just great, but "insanely great." He was able to urge them on not with a detailed plan for the Mac (which they were creating as they went along), but with slogans that reflected and reinforced the spirit of the project. "It's better to be a pirate than join the navy!" Jobs exhorted, and they raised a skull and crossbones over their offices. Leaders find ways to say or do whatever it takes to galvanize the group. When Frank Dale was managing editor of the now defunct *Herald-Examiner* in Los Angeles, he rallied his underdog journalists to struggle against the dominant *Los Angeles Times* by equipping his office chair with an airplane seatbelt. The message: The *Herald-Examiner* was taking off in its battle against the establishment paper.

Such leaders understand very basic truths about human beings. They know that we long for meaning. Without meaning, labor is time stolen from us. We become, like Milton's fallen Samson, "a slave at the wheel." Jobs and the others also understand that thought is play. Problem solving is the task we evolved for. It gives us as much pleasure as does sex. Leaders of Great Groups grasp this intuitively. They know that work done for its own sake becomes a wonderful game. No matter what our kindergarten teachers tell us, we are all Darwin's children. We love to compete. And so virtually every Great Group defines itself in terms of an enemy. Sometimes the enemy is real, as the Axis powers were for the Manhattan Project. But, more often, the chief function of the enemy is to solidify and define the group itself, showing it what it is by mocking what it is not. At Apple, IBM functioned as the Great Satan, IBM's best-selling computers as big, inelegant symbols of a reactionary corporate culture Apple despised. Jobs and his pirates took IBM on as single-mindedly and gleefully as a cell of teenage Resistance fighters going up against the Nazis. In Great Groups the engagement of the enemy is both dead serious and a lark. Thus in the landmark ad that announced the Mac during the 1984 Super Bowl, Apple tweaked IBM by suggesting that people who used its computers were Orwellian zombies, slaves to number-crunching conventionality. In a video reel shown to Apple shareholders the same day, a playful talking computer, obviously not an IBM behemoth, teased, "Never trust a computer you can't lift."

In the scramble to discover the structure of DNA, James Watson and Francis Crick cast scientific rival Linus Pauling as the villain. But nobody demonized the opposition to greater effect than did Clinton strategist James Carville during the 1992 presidential campaign. A master of memorable vilification, Carville heaped the kind of scorn on Bush and other Republicans usually reserved for people who do unnatural things to farm animals. Carville insists that every campaign needs an enemy in order to keep its energy high and focused. Leaders in other fields agree. In a dialogue with General Electric CEO Jack Welch published in *Fortune* magazine, Coca-Cola chairman Roberto Goizueta said that organizations that don't have an enemy need to create one. When asked why, he explained, "That's the only way you can have a war." In public, Coca-Cola may want to teach the world to sing, but in its corridors the motto is "Destroy

Pepsi!" For the group, the bigger the enemy, the better. Great Groups always see themselves as winning underdogs, wily Davids toppling the bloated Goliaths of tradition and convention.

All leaders of Great Groups find ways to imbue the effort with meaning. Sometimes the goal is such a lofty one that the meaning is self-evident. Oppenheimer's group knew that its mission was the preservation of democracy. The scientists of PARC knew they were creating a radically new technology. But inspirational leaders can transform even mundane projects, turning them, too, into missions from God. It can be argued that the sale of Craftsman tools is not an intrinsically noble cause. But when Arthur Martinez took over Sears's retail unit in 1992, he recruited executives by promising them a challenge worthy of a Crusader. "I felt I had to be an evangelist," he told a reporter from *Fortune*. "I really was enrolling people in a mission." Turning Sears around, Martinez told prospective staffers, "would be one of the greatest adventures in business history. . . . There's no model for what we're gonna do. It's very risky. You have to be courageous, filled with self-confidence. If we do it, we'll be wealthier, yes. But more than that, we'll have incredible psychic gratification. How can you *not* do it?" Leaders are people who believe so passionately that they can seduce other people into sharing their dream.

People in Great Groups often seem to have struck a Faustian bargain, giving up their normal lives, if not their souls, in exchange for greatness. Because they are mission maniacs, obsessed with the project at hand, relationships outside the group often suffer. The wife of one of the engineers involved in Data General's Eagle project had no trouble believing her husband when he teasingly told her that the company offered alimony benefits as well as health-care ones. Inside the group, the intensity often has a sexual edge. Prosecutors Marcia Clark and Chris Darden had a romance, if not an affair, during the seemingly endless course of the first O. J. Simpson trial. As Darden subsequently explained, "We were working together fifteen or sixteen hours a day, watching each other's backs in court and commiserating over the media and other things no one else understood." At Black Mountain College, the passionate exchange of views sometimes became simple passion. Two of the school's three charismatic leaders, John Andrew Rice and Charles Olson, had affairs with students (Olson left his common-law wife and moved in with his lover, with whom he had a child). As Robert Cringely notes of Apple in its heyday, Great Groups are sexy places.

In almost all creative collaborations roles and relationships change according to the dictates of the project. In less distinguished groups, the leader would have a fair amount of managing to do. But Great Groups require a more flexible kind of leadership that has more to do with facilitating than with asserting control. Like cats, the talented can't be herded. The military model of leadership, with its emphasis on command and control, squelches creativity. Great Groups need leaders who encourage and enable. Jack Welch once said of his role at General Electric, "Look, I only have three things to do. I have to choose the right people, allocate the right number of dollars, and transmit ideas from one division to another with the speed of light." Those three tasks are familiar to almost everyone involved in creative collaboration. Many leaders of Great Groups spend a lot of time making sure that the right information gets to the right people—this was a primary purpose of the mandatory weekly meetings at PARC. Members of Great Groups may be so attuned to each other and to the nature of the task that they hardly have to speak at all, but they do have to have access to relevant data.

Leaders of Great Groups perform less obvious functions as well. Actor George Clooney, one of the stars of NBC's fast-paced medical drama, *ER*, says that one of the most important contributions its creator, Michael Crichton, makes to the show is his clout. As the author of one of the most lucrative entertainments of all time, *Jurassic Park,* Crichton is one of the entertainment industry's 800-pound gorillas. He gets whatever he wants. Clooney says he can name other projects that looked almost as promising and innovative as the highly acclaimed hospital show, but their creators had less juice than Crichton and their projects were eventually second-guessed and fatally compromised.

The best thing a leader can do for a Great Group is allow its members to discover their own greatness. But creative collaboration is a two-way street. Either because they lack the requisite skills or because the dream itself is so complex, leaders often find themselves driven by an aching powerlessness to realize their vision in any other way but collaboratively. Disney could dream it, but, in truth, he couldn't do it unless he got hundreds of other talented people to go along. The leader may be the person who needs the group the most. Luciano De Crescenzo's observation that "we are all angels with only one wing, we can only fly while embracing each other" is just as true for the leader as for any of the others.

Although Great Groups experience their moments of near despair, they are more often raucous with laughter. In the midst of the Clinton campaign, Carville took time out to crack eggs over the head of one of his colleagues, letting accumulated tensions drain away in an absurd but effective way. Epic company-wide water fights have become a fixture of life in Silicon Valley. Creative collaborators become members of their own tribe, with their own language, in-jokes, dress, and traditions. Apple became famous for its team T-shirts. Question: "How many Apple staffers does it take to screw in a lightbulb?" Answer: "Six. One to turn the lightbulb and five to design the T-shirt." Generations of Disney animators have seen how many pushpins they can throw at one time, the sort of mildly dangerous competitive play that the young have engaged in for millennia.

In a true creative collaboration, almost everyone emerges with a sense of ownership. In the early 1940s, students and faculty at Black Mountain built their main college building with their own hands (each student got to finish his or her room, with the predictable variations in workmanship). The Mac team expressed that sense of ownership by having all their signatures displayed inside each machine. It was a way of leaving their mark, of laying claim to a tiny piece of the new world they had created.

What keeps extraordinary groups from becoming cults? The fact that many are engaged in scientific enterprises may be one reason, since science, with its constant testing and habitual skepticism, is less likely than some other disciplines to breed fanaticism. Great Groups also tend to be places where dissent is encouraged, if only because it serves the spirit of discovery that is at the heart of these enterprises. These collaborations also tend to be collegial, with the leader perceived as one among equals, rather than as one in possession of unique skills or knowledge. Egos in Great Groups are often fully developed. Such individuals are unlikely to regard the person they report to as the Messiah.

Great Groups often fall apart when the project is finished. They are like animals that die soon after they breed. Why do these often short-lived associations burn so brightly in the memories of former members? Why does George Stephanopoulos look back on months of campaign drudgery and tell the president elect, "It was the best thing I ever did"? There are a host of reasons. Life in the group is often the most fun members ever have. They revel in the pleasure that comes from exercising all their wits in the company of people, as Kay said of his colleagues at PARC, "used to dealing lightning with both hands." Communities based on merit and passion are rare, and people who have been in them never forget them. And then there is the sheer exhilaration of performing greatly. Talent wants to exercise itself, *needs* to.

People pay a price for their membership in Great Groups. Postpartum depression is often fierce, and the intensity of collaboration is a potent drug that may make everything else, including everything after, seem drab and ordinary. But no one who has participated in one of these adventures in creativity and community seems to have any real regrets. How much better to be with other worthy people, doing worthy things, than to labor alone ("When I am alone," writer Carlos Fuentes says, "I am poverty-stricken").

In a Great Group you are liberated for a time from the prison of self. As part of the team, you are on leave from the mundane—no questions asked—with its meager rewards and sometimes onerous obligations. Nobody who was at PARC or involved in the making of *Snow White and the Seven Dwarfs* ever talks about the long days or who got credit for what. All they remember is the excitement of pushing back the boundaries, of doing something superbly well that no one had ever done before. Genius is rare, and the chance to exercise it in a dance with others is rarer still. Karl Wallenda, the legendary tightrope walker, once said, "Being on the tightrope is living; everything else is waiting." Most of us wait. In Great Groups, talent comes alive.

In writing this book, we depended heavily on existing histories and other secondary sources, augmented by interviews with participants in many Great Groups. This book could not exist without such superlative histories as Martin Duberman's *Black Mountain: An Exploration in Community;* Richard Rhodes's *The Making of the Atomic Bomb;* Douglas K. Smith and Robert C. Alexander's book on Xerox and the personal computer, *Fumbling the Future;* Steven Levy's story of the Macintosh, *Insanely Great;* Robert X. Cringely's Silicon Valley saga, *Accidental Empires;* Ben Rich and Leo Janos's *Skunk Works;* and the encyclopedic account of Clinton's first campaign, *Quest for the Presidency 1992,* written by a team from *Newsweek.* Tracy Kidder's classic study of a nearly Great Group, *The Soul of a New Machine,* was also invaluable.

SCOTT SNOOK AND RAKESH KHURANA ON "THE END OF THE GREAT MAN"

FROM WALL STREET TO MAIN STREET, we hear the all-too-familiar cry, "Where are the leaders?" Perhaps the question itself reveals both the problem as well as a potential solution. Clinging desperately to an antiquated model of heroic leadership, we have unwittingly become trapped in an infinite loop that is driven by our overly simplistic tendency to see our leaders as either heroes or bums! When things go well, we treat them as celebrities, often elevating them to near divine status. Similarly, when things go badly, we are equally quick to vilify and toss them under the nearest bus. Once-worshipped gods are quickly transformed into scapegoats, imperfect mortals who are summarily dismissed for failing to deliver on "the promise." Not to worry, however—new saviors are quickly found and crowned. Hope is once again restored and we sleep well at night, at least for a while. Eventually, however, when they too fail to meet our heroic expectations (and given enough time, they always do!), the entire cycle begins anew. All the while, important problems go unresolved. And society suffers.

But not equally. When leaders fail, it's followers who suffer the most. When politicians fail, countries go to war. When generals fail, soldiers die. When business executives fail, workers lose their jobs. When bankers fail, families lose their homes. When religious leaders fail, the faithful lose hope. Perversely, this very same heroic model of leadership dictates that when leaders succeed, they also benefit the most. No wonder everyone wants to be a leader. "WANTED: Leaders—minimal risk, maximal gain!"

It was 1997 when Warren called for "The End of the Great Man." And yet, we still cling to it today. But why? Our addiction to heroic leaders is supported by a triangle of familiar forces. At the apex sits our heroic leader, symbolic font of official inspiration, the literal embodiment of personal authority. Along one side of the triangle rises the bureaucratic organization. Hierarchical in structure, bureaucracies both sustain and concentrate authority at the top. Lending support on the other side stands the ideology of individualism, a powerful narrative that sustains our heroes by supplying a powerful source of legitimacy with a deeply ingrained mythology that both breeds and celebrates great men. The base of our heroic triangle consists of followers, the great masses who willingly submit to the authority of a single individual, thereby effectively avoiding personal responsibility. At the very heart of the Great Man model spins a highly seductive cycle of co-dependency between leader and led. Followers enjoy laying their problems at the feet of their heroes almost as much as leaders enjoy solving them. Followers depend on leaders for wisdom and courage, and in turn, leaders depend on followers for status and legitimacy. It is this mass abdication of ownership and responsibility, reinforced by a mutually beneficial co-dependency, that ultimately produces and reproduces our heroic model of leadership.

Warren's chapter, "The End of the Great Man" suggests a way out. Instead of asking the question, "Where are the leaders?" he asks, "How can groups exercise effective leadership? Framed in this way, leadership is a set of activities, not necessarily tied to a specific person or position. Moreover, the functions of leadership can be divided into roughly two categories, one more substantive and concrete, and the other more symbolic and value-laden.

By arguing for a functional approach to leadership in teams, Hackman and Walton offer an alternative to "The Great Man." According to this perspective, a leader's "'main job is to do, or get done, whatever is not being adequately handled for groups' needs.' . . . If a leader manages, by whatever means, to ensure that all functions critical to both task accomplishment and group maintenance are adequately taken care of, then the leader has done his or her job well."[1] In essence, effective leaders do whatever needs to be done to maximize collective performance. Conceptualizing leadership in this way effectively releases us from the vicious cycle created by our traditional model of heroic leadership. In theory, anyone is free to step up and fill critical tasks within a team; no formally appointed leader is required. By shifting the emphasis from "what leaders should do," to "what needs to be done for effective performance," in one fell swoop, Hackman and Walton take down both sides of our heroic triangle. On the one side, bureaucratic hierarchies are no longer seen as the only way to organize, and on the other, the ideology of individualism can flourish in a new form. In theory, a diverse group of talented individuals can share the responsibilities of leading—each contributing uniquely when required, thereby tapping individuals' natural desire to contribute, while at the same time shifting the locus of legitimacy from the heroic leader to the collective genius.[2]

A key element of the groups Warren describes is that they do not simply see their work in utilitarian terms. Rather, they see themselves—as a group—"putting a dent in the universe." Effective leadership therefore cannot simply be measured by whether a task is accomplished. That can be done through effective planning and management. Effective leadership creates meaning. A number of scholars have offered various frameworks and principles to inform our thinking about the constituent elements of creating meaning. Some of the key factors include formulating a vision that is a realization of each follower's core beliefs and values, maintaining a community committed to that vision, and establishing the connection between individual action and the vision. What is at the core of these ideas is a recognition that meaning is rooted in the group and the collective. It is what we are doing in concert with others and for others. Practically none of us can single-handedly have a transformative impact on the world. We can only have this type of impact when we feel ourselves as critical linchpins in a collective effort. We need to feel part of something greater than ourselves and simultaneously know that our "self" is essential to that greater effort's success. This is the symbolic day-to-day work of a leadership. The activity that is most time-consuming, that is most constant, that is most essential is connecting—connecting that well-formulated vision to the actions of each individual, connecting individuals to each other, and in the process transforming a collection of individuals into a real community.

In one of the most enduringly popular expressions of the traditional American ideals of self-reliance and self-determination, *The Wizard of Oz,* we are taught an important lesson: By pulling back the veil with which power masks its inner workings, we learn not only how the illusions that dominate us are manufactured but also how their maintenance depends on our ignorance of our own powers and abdication of responsibility for ourselves. Along with much else that can be said about them, the cult of the great man and the cultural beliefs that sustain it depend on mystifications fully equal in their power of enchantment to any of the wonders of Oz. Just as Dorothy did, we need to summon the courage to look behind the curtain if we are to become a more mature, self-aware, and responsible society. As Warren has so often reminded us, the all-powerful Oz is us after all.

Scott Snook is associate professor of business administration at Harvard Business School. He was a highly decorated colonel in the U.S. Army Corps of Engineers and also taught at the U.S. Military Academy. He is the author of *Practical Intelligence in Everyday Life* (Cambridge University Press, 2000).

Rakesh Khurana is Marvin Bower Professor of Leadership Development at Harvard Business School and former founding member of Cambridge Technology Partners. He is author of *Searching for a Corporate Savior* (Princeton University Press, 2002) and *From Higher Aims to Hired Hands* (Princeton University Press, 2007).

THE PORNOGRAPHY
OF EVERYDAY LIFE (1976)

CINCINNATI—WHEN THE PENTAGON PAPERS were published, what disturbed me more than the deceits, the counter-deceits, the moral numbness and ethical shortcircuiting of our leaders, was the pornography of it all. The hubris of those men, thousands of miles away, making life-and-death decisions for others, manipulating the most modern tools of technology, using game theory with models so abstract they could reproduce one another in one joyless, screamless parthenogenetic act. But not once, these men, not once could they experience the epiphany of childbirth—or the smell of burning flesh.

I thought of pornography because that, also, is distanced from reality, from direct experience. Actors in porn films are not real people making love, but appendages of sexual organs engaged in mechanical acts. These appendages are so without personalities or identifiable social characteristics that, as one movie critic pointed out, they are more about physical engineering than love—so many pistons and valves. Loveless sex. Distant, remote, calculated, vicarious.

The "war room" at the Pentagon is as distant from the reality of war as downtown Boston's so-called "combat zone," the festooned, free area for porno sales, is from the reality of sex.

In these now yellowing Papers, we see Secretary of Defense Robert S. McNamara busying himself with the minutiae of war planning because lists of numbers and cost estimates have a distracting if illusory moral neutrality.

Toward the end of his tenure, he stops questioning the military or political significance of sending 206,000 more troops into Indochina, into a war he now knew could not be won, and concentrates, instead, on the logistical

---

This work originally appeared in the *New York Times*, November 28, 1976.

problems of getting them there. That's administration. And as he fulfilled the requirements of efficiency and effectiveness, during his own final days his wife reports that he began to grind his teeth—every night—while tossing fitfully.

Albert Speer elevated the promises of Hitler's "technocracy" to a point where these promises quickly became shields against any inclination to think of the human and social consequences of his actions. The challenges, the deadlines, the deadly routines of the Third Reich—as of the Defense Department, or any large bureaucracy become tasks to be performed, power to be exercised, problems to be solved, monuments to be designed (or demolished).

Is it the nature of large-scale organizations to make it possible for an ethical person such as a McNamara—or unethical Watergaters—to work toward an ultimately immoral end—without an immediate sense of personal responsibility or guilt? Bureaucracies are, by definition, systems of increased differentiation and specialization, and thus the ultimate morality of bureaucracy is the amorality of segmented acts.

Coming home:

On the first real day of spring, two beautiful trees in the infancy of bloom are chopped down to make more room for cars to turn down a campus driveway. Everybody is outraged. Students pack into my office to tell me about it. A few are hysterical and crying. I leave my office and walk over to the little grass plot—there is so little green on our campus—to see a man with a small hand power saw, cleaning and stacking up the milk-white wood into neat piles.

A crowd of some 200 students and faculty stand around and hiss me as I break through the circle to speak to him. "Man, am I glad you're here. They're ready to crucify me." It turns out he's not employed by the university. He works for a local contractor. I could never find out who was responsible: the landscape artist who designed the new plot with poodle hedges, or his boss, the landscape architect; the director of planning, or his boss, the head of the physical plant; the vice president for management and finance, the university building committee, the executive vice president the committee reports to . . .

When I called them all together they numbered twenty, and they were innocents all. All of us. Bureaucracies are beautiful mechanisms for the evasion of responsibility and guilt.

Too far from the classroom, from the munitions plant, from the battlefield, from the people, from love. That's pornography.

There are no easy answers or options. The problem is immense and invades all of our lives. Recently the Bureau of Census reported that only

1.5 percent of our employment rolls are made up of the "self-employed"; the rest work, as you and I do (if we work) in large organizations. Less than 75 years ago, that ratio was the opposite.

And it's far too simple (and unrealistic) to talk about "small is beautiful." Smallness helps only if it prevents the episodic, disconnected experience that characterizes so many of our leaders and administrators. And it does no good to pretend closeness and a direct relationship with "the people," displaying the candidate or governor wearing saffron robes, walking to work, eating vegetarian dinners to a recording of Fritz Perls reading Zen Haiku. The "simple" life—through a technotronic, quadraphonic TV tube. That's "soft porn" for the intellectual, falsely lulling, and just as corrupt as the hard kind.

What's important, it seems to me, is the capacity to see things in wide perspective, to receive impressions and gain experiences directly—not vicariously—that point beyond the experiences and data themselves. Continuity and purpose.

To the pornographic leader, things and events of the world appear as portable fragments. The long view is replaced by shortsightedness. Detail, but no pattern. The fresh outlook yields to a stereotyped and biased one. Experiences and impressions, what there are of them seen through the Lucite gray of a limousine window, cannot be fully valued and enjoyed because their character is lost.

Our leaders must learn to embrace error and take risks, to explore in the presence of others. Almost like learning how to play the violin in public.

Unless they do (and we permit them to), they will continue to sound as if they are talking through a plate-glass window, distant, isolated, removed from the complex lives of living people on the other side.

WINNING AND LOSING (1988)

Thinking of business in sports terms is risky; a company competes more with itself than with its competition.

○

WE TALK OFTEN OF WINNING AND LOSING, scoring touchdowns, close calls, going down to the wire, extra innings, and while we may like movie, television and music stars, we admire sports stars. Every father wants his sons to shine on the playing fields, which is why Little League games frequently have all the carefree air of the London blitz.

Preachers and politicians, among others, see this national obsession as healthy, portraying us as good, clean people interested in good, clean fun. Universities, including the University of Southern California where I teach, celebrate and reward their hero-athletes. On the day of the Super Bowl, the entire country's collective consciousness is focused on The Game.

Time for a New Paradigm

I am admittedly as obsessed as anyone. I can remember great plays, great players, even scores of great games forever, though I sometimes can't remember whom I sat next to at dinner three nights ago. But I am also convinced that it's time to find a new paradigm.

Life is not a baseball game. It's never called on account of darkness, much less cancelled due to inclement weather. And while major sports are big business now, business is not a sport, and never was. Indeed, thinking

This work first appeared in the journal *Executive Excellence,* July 1988. It appeared in the collection *Managing People Is Like Herding Cats* (Executive Excellence Books, 2000).

of business as a kind of game or sport was always simplistic. Now it's downright dangerous.

A game is of limited duration, takes place on or in a fixed and finite site, is governed by predetermined rules which are enforced on the spot by neutral professionals, and is performed by evenly matched teams of one or more who are counselled and led through every move by seasoned hands. Absolute scores are kept, and at the end of the game, an absolute winner is declared.

If there is anyone out there who can say that his or her business is of limited duration, takes place on a fixed site, is governed by rules which are enforced on the spot by neutral professionals, competes only with evenly matched businesses, and can describe its wins and losses in absolute terms, then he or she is either extraordinarily lucky or seriously deluded.

The Risks

The risks in thinking of business in sports terms are numerous.

First, to measure a business on the basis of wins and losses is to misunderstand both the purposes of a specific business and the nature of business itself. No business—whether it sells insurance or manufactures cars—can or should be designed to win. It must rather be designed to grow, on both quantitative and qualitative levels. In this sense, it vies more with itself than with its competition. This is not to say that, in head-to-head contests, as when two ad agencies are competing for the same account, there are not ever winners and losers. It is to say, in paraphrase of Vince Lombardi's legendary dictum, winning isn't everything, it's one of many things a business must accomplish. Thus, a company that is designed only to deliver the knock-out punch will probably lose in the long run.

Second, it is perilous to think of limits, rules, and absolutes in business. Athletes compete for a given number of hours in a given number of games over a given period of weeks or months. Businesses are in the arena for decades, sometimes centuries. Though the action may rise and subside, it never stops. It does not offer any time-outs, much less neatly defined beginnings and endings. As they say, it ain't over till it's over.

American business has traditionally been schizophrenic about rules. When it's flourishing, it wants no rules or regulations. When it's failing, it wants a plethora of rules. Some of the airlines which lobbied vigorously for deregulation have now, ironically, gone down in flames, victims of the very instrument they agitated for. In the same way, Detroit saw Washington as its nemesis, until foreign cars began to take over the market. Suddenly, Chrysler went to the feds for a loan, and now Detroit begs Washington to

regulate the imports, but continues to lobby against federal safety and quality controls.

Athletes perform in a static environment—the size of the field, the length
of the contest, even the wardrobes of the players remain the same day after
month after year. Businesses function in a volatile universe, which changes
from moment to moment, and is hardly ever repeated. It is affected by
droughts half a world away, a new gizmo down the street, consumer attitudes and needs, a million things. Given this mercurial context, any business which relies on absolutes will soon be out of step or out of business.

Clearly, then, there are far more differences between sports and business than similarities. But the real danger in the paradigm is not its bad
match, but its bad example.

The best-run and most successful companies in America do not think
in terms of victories and defeats, shining moments or last-minute saves.
They do not count on regulations or referees. Instead, they think in terms
of staying power, dedication to quality, and an endless effort to do better
than they have done. They see change as their only constant and count on
their own ability to adapt to the world, rather than expecting the world
to adapt to them. Indeed, it is a business's ability to adapt to an ever-
changing world that is the basis for both its success and progress.

The truth is that there is no workable or appropriate paradigm for business, except business itself, and that should be sufficient. Like a well-played
game, a well-run business is something to see, but, unlike a well-played game,
it is not a diversion; it is life itself—complex, difficult, susceptible to both
success and failure, sometimes unruly, always challenging, and often joyful.

So let's leave the home runs to Mike Schmidt and the touchdowns to
Walter Payton, and get down to business.

LESSONS FROM LARRY (2006)

IT WOULD BE A HUGE MISTAKE to believe that the main reason for Harvard University President Larry Summers' downfall was Larry Summers. Nobody would question that he had his faults—big ones, especially for a university president. His inability to subordinate his ego to the talents of others didn't help, nor did he seem to have the patience to develop and build coalitions that would support his noble and important educational goals, like improving undergraduate education, placing greater emphasis on math and the life sciences, and increasing direct faculty-student contacts. Summers had a great vision for Harvard that would likely have allowed it to thrive in a changing world. But what he never quite got is that leaders—especially those who are change agents—can only succeed when they have a reservoir of goodwill that allows them to convince followers that their fates are correlated.

Yet it wasn't Larry Summers' shortcomings that were at the center of his downfall. Some far more fundamental issues (pretty much obscured by the public's obsessive fascination with Summers' personality) were at work. And although these factors were just surfacing 35 years ago when I presided over the University of Cincinnati, I fear they will undermine future relationships between college presidents and all their stakeholders, especially faculty and students.

First, running a major research university today is far more complex and demanding than running any large, global corporation. And make no mistake, that's what Harvard or USC or NYU are: huge, global operations with bad parking. But there is no institution more vulnerable to, and hence more dependent on, external forces than the American university. One major reason is that such schools are not self-supporting. Tuition

---

This work originally appeared in *Business Week*, March 6, 2006.

pays only a small percentage of the costs of running a university; most of the rest comes from alumni, foundations, sponsored research, or, in some cases, the state. The lulling image of the university as a bucolic outpost of learning both removed from and somewhat "above" the outside society that nourishes it is not only outdated but, if believed and acted on, will actually bring about the university's decline or destruction.

Even worse, university leaders possess far less power than any CEO I know. While campuses aren't exactly parliamentary democracies, they do have often-strident faculties—with tenure—who have a redoubtable habit of speaking out and up. They are also often extraordinarily talented, self-absorbed "abdicrats" who don't want to lead—and don't want to be led. The Harvard faculty prayer, it is said, goes like this: "Dear Lord, deliver us from the heinous sin of intellectual arrogance . . . which for your information, means. . . . "

One analyst even likened the job of university president to that of a pro hockey referee, and he's not far off the mark. The work is rough, physically exhausting, even dangerous. Presidents may lose fewer teeth than hockey officials, but they still have a startling number of stress-related problems. In the old days, skeptics like Thorstein Veblen referred to university administrators as "Captains of Erudition." Today a more fitting title would be "Captives of Constituencies."

So, unlike autocratic CEOs of yore, the would-be Larry Summerses of today's academic world face the near-impossible task of forming and managing coalitions. That's no easy feat when you consider the often warring factions within individual constituencies. Indeed, the primary supporters of Summers were the students (only 19% were in favor of his resignation) and most of the faculty associated with the life and natural sciences. Meanwhile, with some important exceptions, the faculty most opposed to Summers and who initiated the votes of "no confidence" that eroded his leadership, are associated with the softer sciences (like sociology and gender studies) and the humanities. That's understandable since both undergraduate and graduate students, especially PhDs, can't find jobs in those disciplines. (As they say in Washington, "Follow the money.") And if dollars aren't flowing in to support jobs, fellowships or post-docs in your discipline, you're less likely to support the administrators that are holding the purse strings. And that's a conflict that's present at all major research universities.

That's why I hope Larry Summers' resignation will create an unintended legacy: an understanding of the systemic forces that could undermine all of our institutions of higher learning.

WHEN TO RESIGN (1972)

NO MATTER HOW OFTEN DANIEL ELLSBERG reminds the public that not he but a seemingly endless war in Indochina is at issue, I find that it is Ellsberg the man who touches the imagination. One can't help speculating on his personal odyssey from loyal insider to defiant outsider, from organization man to prison-risking dissident. It is the process of that change of heart that fascinates me. What interaction of man and organization produces a commitment like the younger Ellsberg's and then leads only a few years later to equally passionate rejection? How much, I wonder, of the Ellsberg affair is idiosyncratic and how much reflects general principles of organizational life? After all, Ellsberg is not the first government adviser to become suspicious of the work in which he has engaged. What is singular about Ellsberg is that he has found a dramatic way to make his dissent articulate. The organizational ethic is typically so strong that even the individual who dissents and opts for the outside by resigning or otherwise dissociating himself does so with organization-serving discretion. Ellsberg may not have broken the law, but he surely did something more daring. He broke the code. He has not only spoken out, he has produced documentation of his disillusionment.

The stakes are rarely as great, but many people who work in large, bureaucratic organizations find themselves in a position similar to Ellsberg's. They oppose some policy, and they quickly learn that bureaucracies do not tolerate dissent. What then? They have several options. They can capitulate. Or they can remain within the group and try to win the majority over to their own position, enduring the frustration and ambiguity that goes with this option. Or they can resign. Remaining can be an excruciating experience of public loyalty and private doubt. But what of

This article was written in collaboration with Patricia Ward Biederman. It originally appeared in *Esquire* magazine, June 1972.

resigning? Superficially resignation seems an easy out, but it also has its dark and conflictful side. As the Stevenson character in *MacBird!* says:[1]

> In speaking out one loses influence.
> The chance for change by pleas and prayer is gone.
> The chance to modify the devil's deeds
> As critic from within is still my hope.
> To quit the club! Be outside looking in!
> This outsideness, this unfamiliar land,
> From which few travelers ever get back in . . .
> I fear to break; I'll work within for change.

If resignation is the choice, the problem of how to leave, silently or openly voicing one's position, still remains.

These options are a universal feature of organizational life and yet virtually nothing has been written on the dynamics of dissent in organizations, although a recent book by Harvard political economist Albert O. Hirschman almost single-handedly makes up for past deficiencies. Oddly enough, the book still remains "underground," largely unread by the wide audience touched by the processes Hirschman describes. I first began seriously considering the question of resignation and other expressions of dissent as organizational phenomena in the Spring of 1970. At that time I had just resigned as Acting Executive Vice-President of State University of New York at Buffalo. As so often happens, my interest in the phenomenon grew out of unpleasant personal experience. I had resigned in protest against what I considered undue use of force on the part of the University's Acting President in dealing with a series of student strikes on our campus that spring. In my case, resigning turned out to be a remarkably ineffective form of protest.[2] When I tried to analyze why, I found that my experience was hardly unique, that most large organizations, including government agencies and universities, have well-oiled adaptive mechanisms for neutralizing dissent. The individual who can force the organization into a public confrontation, as Ellsberg did, is rare indeed.

The garden-variety resignation is an innocuous act, no matter how righteously indignant the individual who tenders it. The act is made innocuous by a set of organization-serving conventions that few resignees are able (or even willing, for a variety of personal reasons) to break. When the properly socialized dissenter resigns, he tiptoes out. A news release is sent to the media on the letterhead of the departing one's superior. "I today accepted with regret the resignation of Mister/Doctor Y," it reads. The *pro forma* statement rings pure tin in the discerning ear, but this is the accepted ritual nonetheless. One retreats under a canopy of smiles, with verbal bouquets and exchanges, however insincere, of mutual respect. The last official duty of the departing one is to keep his mouth shut. The rules of play require that the last word goes to those who remain inside. The purpose served by this convention is a purely institutional one. Announcement of a resignation is usually a sign of disharmony and possibly real trouble within an organization. But without candid follow-up by the individual making the sign, it is an empty gesture. The organization reasons, usually correctly, that the muffled troublemaker will soon be forgotten. With the irritant gone, the organization pursues its chosen course, subject only to the casual and untrained scrutiny of the general public.

The striving of organizations for harmony is less a conscious program than a consequence of the structure of large organizations. Cohesiveness in such organizations results from a commonly held set of values, beliefs, norms, and attitudes. In other words, an organization is also an appreciative system in which those who do not share the common set, the common point of view, are by definition deviant, marginal, outsiders.

Ironically, this pervasive emphasis on harmony does not serve organizations particularly well. Unanimity leads rather quickly to stagnation which, in turn, invites change by nonevolutionary means. The fact that the organizational deviant, the individual who "sees" things differently, may be the institution's vital and only link with, for lack of a better term, some new, more apt paradigm does not make the organization value him any more. Most organizations would rather risk obsolescence than make room for the nonconformists in their midst. This is most true when such intolerance is most suicidal, that is, when the issues involved are of major importance (or when important people have taken a very strong or a personal position). On matters such as whether to name a new product "Corvair" or "Edsel," or whether to establish a franchise in Peoria or Oshkosh, dissent is reasonably well tolerated, even welcomed, as a way of insuring that the best of all possible alternatives is finally implemented. But when it comes to war or peace, life or death, growth or organizational stagnation, fighting or withdrawing, reform or status quo—desperately important matters—dissent is typically seen as fearful. Exactly at that point in time when it is most necessary to consider the possible consequences of a wide range of alternatives, public show of consensus becomes an absolute value to be defended no matter what the human cost.

Unanimity, or at least its public show, is so valued within the organizational context that it often carries more weight with an individual than his own conscience. Thus, we see in the March 31, 1971, issue of the *New York Times* that "Muskie regrets silence on war" and wishes that he had made public as far back as 1965 his "real doubts about involvement in the Vietnam war." Instead, he said, "he voiced his concerns privately to President Johnson." "There are two ways," he said, "and they're both legitimate ways of trying to influence public policy. And I can guess the tendency is, when the President is a member of your own party and you're a Senator, to try to express your doubts directly to him, in order to give him a chance to get the benefit of your views." Senator Muskie said he often had done that, "but wished that I'd expressed my doubts publicly at that time." The article goes on to say that Muskie "was far less hesitant to criticize President Nixon's conduct of the war." In an adjoining article about Humphrey, the *Times* reports him as describing to a student audience "publicly for the first time the pressure he had been under from President Johnson not to speak out on the Vietnam issue. Many times during the first month of the 1968 campaign, he recalled, he had wanted to speak out more forcefully on the Vietnam issue only to be dissuaded by the President. This, he said, posed a personal dilemma. On the one side, he said, he saw his chances for winning the Presidency slipping away. But if he sought headlines on the Vietnam issue by taking a more critical stance, he said, he was being warned by the President that he would jeopardize the delicate negotiations then under way to bring South Vietnam and the Vietcong to the Paris negotiating table."

"That's the God's truth. . . . How would you like to be in that jam?" Humphrey asked a student.

Actually, Humphrey's "jam" is a classic one. A member in good standing of an organization, in this case the Johnson Administration, suddenly finds himself opposed to his superior and his colleagues in regard to some policy. If the policy is relatively unimportant or not yet firm, the objection may be absorbed by bargaining or compromise. If the issue at stake is actually trivial, it may simply be avoided. But if the issue is important and the dissenter adamant, the gulf begins to widen. At first, the dissenter tries to exert all possible influence over the others, tries to bring the others around. In Albert Hirschman's compact terminology, this is the option of *voice*. Short of calling a press conference, this option can be exercised in several ways from simply grumbling to threatening to resign. But usually the individual gives voice to his dissatisfaction in a series of private confrontations like those of Muskie and Humphrey with Johnson. When these fail, as they usually do, he must face the possibility of resigning (or, as Hirschman calls it, exercising the option to *exit*). Resigning becomes a reasonable alternative as soon as voice begins to fail. The individual realizes that hours of sincere, patient argument have come to nothing. He realizes that his influence within the organization is waning, and so probably is his loyalty. If he stays on, he risks becoming an organizational eunuch, an individual of no influence publicly supporting a policy against his will, judgment, personal value system, at times even his professional code.

As bleak as this prospect is, exit on matters of principle is still a distinctly uncommon response to basic institutional conflict. This is particularly true of American politics. In many nations with parliamentary systems, principled resignation from high office is common. But in the United States the concept of exit as a political act has never taken hold. The Walter Hickels are the exception. The last time a cabinet official left in protest and said why was when Labor Secretary Martin Durkin resigned because President Eisenhower refused to support his proposed amendments to the Taft-Hartley Act. As James Reston wrote recently in a postmortem on the Johnson Administration:

"One thing that is fairly clear from the record is that the art of resigning on principle from positions close to the top of American government has almost disappeared. Nobody quits now, as Anthony Eden and Duff Cooper left Neville Chamberlain's cabinet, with a clear and detailed explanation of why they couldn't be identified with the policy any longer. . . . Most [of those who stayed on] at the critical period of escalation gave to the President the loyalty they owed to the country. Some . . . are now wondering in private life whether this was in the national interest."

What accounts for our national reluctance to resign and our willingness, when forced to take the step, to settle for a "soft exit," without clamor, without a public statement of principle, and ideally without publicity? Tremendous institutional pressures and personal rationalizations work together to dissuade the dissident from exit in favor of voice. Most of us would much rather convince the boss or top group to see "reason" rather than quit. Resignation is defiant, an uncomfortable posture for most organization men (including politicians and academics). Worse, it smacks of failure, the worst of social diseases among the achievement-oriented. So instead of resigning, we reason to ourselves that the organization could go from bad to worse if we resigned. This may be the most seductive rationalization of all. Meanwhile, we have become more deeply implicated in the policy that we silently oppose, making extrication progressively more difficult. If resignation cannot be avoided, there are selfish reasons for doing it quietly. Most resignees would like to work again. Only Nader's Raiders love a blabbermouth. Speaking out is not likely to enhance one's marketability. A negative aura haunts the visibly angry resignee, while the individual who leaves a position ostensibly to return to business, family, teaching or research reenters the job market without any such cloud. Many resignees prefer a low profile simply because they are aware that issues change. Why undermine one's future effectiveness by making a noisy but ineffectual stand? However selfish the reasons, the organization reaps the major benefits when an individual chooses to resign quietly. A decorous exit conceals the underlying dissension that prompted the resignation in the first place. And the issue at contest is almost sure to be obscured by the speechmaking.

Like the Zen tea ceremony, resigning is a ritual, and woe to the man who fails to do it according to the rules. For example, when Fred Friendly resigned as President of CBS News in 1966 over the airing of Vietnam hearings, he sinned by releasing a news story *before* the Chairman of the Board, William S. Paley, could distribute his own release. Friendly writes in his memoir of this episode:

"Around two o'clock a colleague suggested that I should have called Paley, who was in Nassau, and personally read my letter [of resignation] to him over the phone. When I called Stanton to ask him if he had read my letter to the chairman, he said that he had just done so, and that Paley wanted me to call him. When I did, Paley wanted to know only if I had released my letter; when I told him that I had, all useful communication ceased. 'You volunteered to me last week that you would not make a public announcement,' he said. . . . The last thing the chairman said to me was: 'Well, if you hadn't put out that letter, maybe we could still have done something.' I answered that my letter was 'after the fact, long after.'"

Paley's response is explicable only if we remember that the *fact* of resignation and the *reasons* behind it are subordinated in the organizational scheme to the issue of institutional face-saving. A frank resignation is regarded by the organization as an act of betrayal. (To some degree, this is, of course, an issue of personal face-saving. Those in power may wish for institutional harmony in part as a protection against personal criticism.)

Because a discreet resignation amounts to no protest at all, a soft exit lifts the opprobrium of organizational deviation from the resignee. When Dean Acheson bowed out as Under Secretary of the Treasury in 1933 after a dispute with F.D.R. over fiscal policy, his discretion was boundless and F.D.R. was duly appreciative. Some years later, when another official left with less politesse, sending the White House a sharp criticism of the President's policies, Roosevelt returned the letter with the tart suggestion that the man ought to "ask Dean Acheson how a gentleman resigns."

But "hard" or "soft," exit remains the option of last resort in organizational life. Remarkably, the individual who is deeply opposed to some policy often opts for public acquiescence and private frustration. He may continue to voice his opposition to his colleagues but they are able to neutralize his protest in various ways. Thus we see George Ball becoming the official devil's advocate of the Johnson Administration. As George E. Reedy writes:

"During President Johnson's Administration I watched George Ball play the role of devil's advocate with respect to foreign policy. The cabinet would meet and there would be an overwhelming report from Robert McNamara, another overwhelming report from Dean Rusk, another over-whelming report from McGeorge Bundy. Then five minutes would be set aside for George Ball to deliver his dissent, and because they expected him to dissent, they automatically discounted whatever he said. This strength-ened them in their own convictions because the cabinet members could quite honestly say: 'We heard both sides of this issue discussed.' Well, they heard it with wax in their ears. I think that the moment you appoint an official devil's advocate you solidify the position he is arguing against."

One can hardly imagine a predicament more excruciating than Ball's. Often an individual in such conflict with the rest of his organization sim-ply removes himself, if not physically then by shifting his concern from the issues to practical problems of management and implementation. He distracts himself. Townsend Hoopes suggests that this was the case with Robert McNamara. According to Hoopes, who was Under Secretary of the Air Force, there was growing evidence in the Autumn of 1967 that the President and McNamara were growing further and further apart in their attitudes toward escalating the Vietnam war. Hoopes saw in McNamara the fatigue and loneliness of a man "in deep doubt" as to the course the war was taking. But, writes Hoopes:

"*Owing to his own strict conception of loyalty to the President, McNamara found it officially necessary to deny all doubt and, by his silence, to discour-age doubt in his professional associates and subordinates.* . . . The result of McNamara's ambivalence; however, was to create a situation of dreamlike unreality for those around him. *His staff meetings during this period were entirely barren affairs: a technical briefing, for example, on the growing strength of air defenses around Hanoi, but no debate on what this implied for the U.S. bombing effort, and never the slightest disclosure of what the Presi-dent or the Secretary of State might consider the broad domestic and inter-national implications to be.* It was an atmosphere that worked to neutralize those who were the natural supporters of his concerns about the war." (Ital-ics are for emphasis.)

What Hoopes describes is ethical short-circuiting. Conflict-torn Mc-Namara busies himself with the minutiae of war planning because lists of numbers and cost estimates have a distracting if illusory moral neutrality. According to Hoopes, toward the end of McNamara's tenure, the despair-ing Secretary stopped questioning the military and political significance of sending 206,000 more troops into Indochina and concentrated in the short time he had on the logistical problems of getting them to the port of debarkation safely and efficiently.

One sees a remarkably similar displacement of energy from moral or political concerns to managerial or technological ones in the career of Albert Speer. I do not mean to label McNamara a Fascist by literary association. But the pages of *Inside the Third Reich* reveal that Speer dealt with ambivalence brought on by intense organizational stress in a remarkably similar way. Speer did not allow his growing personal reservations about Hitler to interfere with his meticulous carrying out of administrative duties. Speer kept the Nazi war machine running in high gear and increasingly productive until 1945. As Eugene Davidson writes: "A man like Speer, working with blueprints, ordering vast projects, is likely to exhaust himself in manipulation, in transforming the outer world, in carrying out production goals with all the means at hand."

Whether such activity exhausts an individual to the point of moral numbness is questionable, but certainly the nature of the large organization makes it possible for a McNamara or an Albert Speer or an Ellsberg (while at Rand), for that matter, to work toward an ultimately immoral end without an immediate sense of personal responsibility or guilt. Organizations are by definition systems of increased differentiation and specialization, and, thus, the morality of the organization is the morality of segmented acts. As Charles Reich wrote in the *New Yorker*, "A scientist who is doing his specialized duty to further research and knowledge develops a substance called napalm. Another specialist makes policy in the field of our nation's foreign affairs. A third is concerned with the most modern weaponry. A fourth manufactures what the defense authorities require. A fifth drops napalm from an airplane where he is told to do so." In this segmented environment, any one individual can easily develop tunnel vision, concentrating on the task at hand, completing his task with a sense of accomplishment, however sinister the collective result of all these individual jobs well done. This segmented structure characteristic of all large organizations encourages indifference and evasion of responsibility. A benefit of membership in such an organization is insurance against the smell of burning flesh. Speer, for example, still does not seem particularly troubled by the horrors of slave labor in his wartime munitions plants even when making his unique public confession.

Speer reports that it never occurred to him to resign even though he was aware of what his loss would do to hasten the end of Hitler's regime. Faced with a much more subtle and complex situation, McNamara seriously considered resigning, according to Hoopes. But that he did not do so in 1967 when his doubts were so oppressive is remarkable. Hoopes provides a fascinating clue to McNamara's reluctance to resign or even to voice his uneasiness in any except the most private audiences with the President. In the following short portrait by Hoopes in his book *The Limits of Intervention,* we see McNamara wrestling with an ingrained organizational ethic stronger than his own intelligence and instinct:

"Accurately regarded by the press as the one moderate member of the inner circle, he continued to give full public support to the Administration's policy, including specific endorsement of successive manpower infusions and progressively wider and heavier bombing efforts. Inside the Pentagon he seemed to discourage dissent among his staff associates by the simple tactic of being unreceptive to it; he observed, moreover, so strict a sense of privacy in his relationship with the President that he found it virtually impossible to report even to key subordinates what he was telling the President or what the President was saying and thinking. . . . All of this seemed to reflect a well-developed philosophy of executive management relationships, derived from his years in industry; its essence was the belief that a busy, overworked chairman of the board should be spared the burden of public differences among his senior vice-presidents. Within such a framework, he could argue the case for moderation with the President—privately, selectively, and intermittently. But the unspoken corollary seemed to be that, whether or not his counsel of moderation were followed, there could arise no issue or difference with President Johnson sufficient to require his resignation—whether to enlighten public opinion or avoid personal stultification. It was this corollary that seemed of doubtful applicability to the problems and obligations of public office. *McNamara gave evidence that he had ruled out resignation because he believed that the situation would grow worse if he left the field to Rusk, Rostow, and the Joint Chiefs. But also because the idea ran so strongly against the grain of his temperament and his considered philosophy of organizational effectiveness.*"

Does this mean that McNamara would not resign because quitting violated some personal notion of honor? Or does it mean that he believed that dissent and "organizational effectiveness" are negatively correlated? I suspect that the latter is closer to the truth. Like any other corporation president, McNamara was raised on organizational folklore. One of the central myths is that the show of unanimity is always desirable. That this belief is false and even dangerous does not limit its currency. Yes, there are times when discretion is required. Clearly organizations should not fight constantly in public. But what is the gain of forbidding at all costs and at all times any emotional give-and-take between colleagues? A man has an honest difference of opinion with the organizational powers. Why must he be silenced or domesticated or driven out so that the public can continue to believe—falsely—that organizational life is without strife? And yet organizations continue to assume the most contrived postures in order to maintain the illusion of harmony. Postures like lying to the public.

Our inability to transcend the dangerous notion that we don't wash our dirty linen in public verges on the schizophrenic. It implies that dissent is not only bad but that our public institutions such as government are made up not of men but saints who never engage in such vulgar and offensive activities. Thus, government strives to be regarded as a hallowed shrine where, as George Reedy reports from his experience as White House press secretary under President Johnson, "the meanest lust for power can be sanctified and the dullest wit greeted with reverential awe." In fact, organizations, including governments, are vulgar, sweaty, plebeian; if they are to be viable, they must create an institutional environment where a fool can be called a fool and all actions and motivations are duly and closely scrutinized for the inevitable human flaws and failures. In a democracy, meanness, dullness, and corruption are always amply represented. They are not entitled to protection from the same rude challenges that such qualities must face in the "real" world. When banal politeness is assigned a higher value than accountability or truthfulness, the result is an Orwellian world where the symbols of speech are manipulated to create false realities.

"Loyalty" is often given as a reason or pretext for muffling dissent. A variation on this is the claim that candor "gives comfort to the enemy." Ellsberg's national loyalty was repeatedly questioned in connection with his release of the so-called Pentagon Papers. In the first three installments of the document as run in the *Times*, practically nothing that wasn't well known was revealed. A few details, an interesting admission or two, but basically nothing that had not come to light earlier in other less controversial articles and books on the Indochina war. But government officials trying to suppress the publication of the classified material chose to make much of the "foreign consequences" of its release. "You may rest assured," a government official was quoted as saying by the Buffalo *Evening News*, "that no one is reading this series any more closely than the Soviet Embassy."

All of the foregoing pressures against registering dissent can be subsumed under the clumsy label of "loyalty." In fact, they represent much more subtle personal and organizational factors including: deep-rooted psychological dependence, authority problems, simple ambition, co-optive mechanisms (the "devil's advocacy" technique), pressure to be a member of the club and fear of being outside looking in, adherence to the myth that gentlemen settle their differences amicably and privately, fear of disloyalty in the form of giving comfort to "the enemy," and, very often, that powerful Prospero-aspiration: the conviction that one's own "reasonable" efforts will keep things from going from bad to worse.

There is a further broad cultural factor that must be considered before the other defenses against exit can be understood. It simply doesn't make sense for a man as intelligent and analytically sophisticated as our nation's Number One Problem Solver, Robert McNamara, to delude himself that he couldn't quit because "duty called." Duty to whom? Not to his own principles? Nor, as he saw it, to the nation's welfare. McNamara's real loyalty was to the code of the "organizational society" in which most of us live out our entire active careers. Ninety percent of the employed population of this country works in formal organizations. Status, position, a sense of competence and accomplishment are all achieved in our culture through belonging to these institutions. What you *do* determines, to a large extent, what you *are*. "My son, the doctor" is not only the punch line of a thousand Jewish jokes. It is a neat formulation of a significant fact about our culture. Identification with a profession or other organization is a real-life passport to identity, to self-hood, to self-esteem. You are what you do, and work in our society (as in all other industrialized societies) is done in large, complex, bureaucratic structures. If one leaves the organization, particularly with protest, one is nowhere, like a character in a Beckett play, without role, without the props of office, without ambience or setting.

In fact, a few more resignations would be good for individual consciences and good for the country. Looking back, veteran diplomat Robert Murphy could recall only one occasion when he thought he should have resigned. The single instance was the Berlin Blockade of 1948–49, which he thought the U.S. should have challenged more vigorously. "My resignation almost certainly would not have affected events," he wrote in regret, "but if I had resigned, I would feel better today about my own part in that episode." *Time* magazine, from which Murphy's quotation was taken, goes on to say in its essay:

"In the long run, the country would probably feel better, too, if a few more people were ready to quit for their convictions. It might be a little unsettling. But it could have a tonic effect on American politics, for it would give people the assurance that men who stay truly believe in what they are doing."

My own resignation was a turning point. The decision represented the first time in many years of organizational life that I had been able to say, No, I cannot allow myself to be identified with that particular policy, the first time I had risked being an outsider rather than trying to work patiently within the system for change. Many factors entered into the decision but in the last analysis my reason for resigning was an intensely personal one. I did not want to say, a month or two months after the police came onto campus, "Well, I was against that move at the time." I think it is important for everyone in decision-making positions in our institutions to speak out. And if we find it impossible to continue on as administrators because we are at total and continuous odds with institutional policy, then I think we must quit and go out shouting. The alternative is petit-Eichmannism, and that is too high a price.

A CORPORATE FEAR OF
TOO MUCH TRUTH (2002)

But I'd shut my eyes in the sentry-box,
So I didn't see nothin' wrong.

—Rudyard Kipling

THE SENTRY BOXES OF CORPORATE AMERICA are its boards of directors, and there is ample evidence that Enron's directors kept their eyes
shut when they should have been perusing the company's books. But all
the sound and fury about Enron, whose collapse has led to Congressional
hearings and media outrage, obscures a more basic problem that is ubiquitous in corporate life today: organizational structures that discourage
honesty and suppress truth.

Let us deal with the board issue first. Yes, it is still the case that most
board members are, in fact, willing dupes of management. Too many are
overpaid, rubber-stamping corporate celebrities. Dogged by the constant
threat of litigation, boards are selected by their subordinates—the company officers. (Shareholders nominally choose them, but typically they
vote for the directors the company recommends.) They seldom understand
their function and are prone to meddle too much—or, worse, not enough.

Three of the six directors who served on Enron's auditing committee—
the people responsible for double-checking Enron's bookkeeping—were
executives at firms in the faraway locales of Hong Kong, London and Rio
de Janeiro. You can guess how much time they had for the vigilant oversight
required of an effective audit committee. And like directors on many other
boards, some had served too long. How Enron's directors could have stood

---

This work originally appeared in the *New York Times,* February 17, 2002.

by while top Enron executives cashed out more than $1 billion in company stock in the last two years is unfathomable.

But it's not only about the boards. The Enron collapse is emblematic of a problem that is far more imbedded, more intractable and, alas, far more universal than the board failures and malfeasance of a single company. In any one case, you can always fire the chief and other executives, reconstitute the board and file for bankruptcy; that's the easy part. The hard part inheres in the very nature and design of large-scale organizations, whose ethos and leadership too often create mindless and complacent cultures with vacant sentry boxes.

Unless the leadership and the social architecture of these behemoths change, I can promise you Congressional regulations will get tighter, the Securities and Exchange Commission more vigilant—and the problems worse. The basic problem in most organizations today, both public and private, is that they work to block transparency. Most are conveniently designed so that everyone seems to know what's wrong—but nobody admits it or tells anyone else.

A case in point: When I consulted for the State Department, I quickly learned that junior Foreign Service officers often decided not to tell their bosses what they had learned in the field because they believed the bosses wouldn't like it. In fact, their bosses often felt exactly the same way about telling their own bosses what they knew. One State Department panjandrum told me that they gave their fledgling diplomats two rules: Never tell a lie. But never the tell the whole truth, either.

It is never easy for subordinates to be honest with their superiors. After a string of box-office flops, Samuel Goldwyn is said to have told a meeting of his top staff, "I want you to tell me exactly what's wrong with me and M.G.M.—even if it means losing your job." Unfortunately, Enron's chief financial officer, Andrew Fastow, didn't have Mr. Goldwyn's sense of humor. When Sherron Watkins sent Kenneth Lay, Enron's chief executive, a letter warning him about Enron's accounting practices, she said, Mr. Fastow tried to fire her.

Unlike top management at Enron, exemplary leaders reward dissent. They encourage it. They understand that, whatever momentary discomfort they experience as a result of being told they might be wrong, it is more than offset by the fact that the information will help them make better decisions. And the trend toward outlandish executive compensation should surely be enough to salve the pricked ego of any leader whose followers speak their minds.

Organizations tend to fail when decision making is based on feedback from yes men. Mr. Lay's failing is not simply his myopia or cupidity or incompetence. It is his inability to create a company culture open to reality, one that does not discourage managers from delivering bad news. No organization can be honest with the public if it is not honest with itself.

So how does an organization institutionalize honesty, the way so many corporations have institutionalized the suppression of it? There is no easy answer. Honesty and candor at the top helps; executives should speak their minds and encourage their peers and subordinates to do so. Many organizations have found ways to generate honest communication—even urging employees to make anonymous suggestions if necessary.

But a culture of honesty, like a healthy balance sheet, is an ongoing effort. It requires sustained attention and constant vigilance.

JAMES O'TOOLE ON "WHEN TO RESIGN" AND "A CORPORATE FEAR OF TOO MUCH TRUTH"

YOU DON'T HAVE TO CHANGE A WORD in Warren's 1972 *Esquire* article, just update the cast of characters. Some forty years ago, the players in the White House tragedy included Messrs. Johnson, Humphrey, McNamara, Rusk, Rostow, and Ball. Recently, the setting was the same, only this time the names of the main characters were Bush, Cheney, Rumsfeld, Tenet, Rice, and Powell. In the '60s, one courageous insider, Daniel Ellsberg, had dared to take a principled stand against the prevailing, and delusional, Washington groupthink with regard to Vietnam. Four decades later, the list of brave—and quasi-brave—civil servants was a bit longer: Treasury Secretary Paul O'Neil, economic adviser Lawrence Lindsey, pollster Matthew Down, national security expert Richard Clarke, and ex-Army chief General Eric Shinseki. But the script for the two sad tales—Vietnam and Iraq—played out in much the same way. Most of those with access to their president dared not speak truth to power; those who did were accused of disloyalty. As in a Sophoclean tragedy, the nation's blind and deaf leaders twice brought death to countless innocents, shame to their nation, and ruin to their careers. History actually repeated itself. Apparently, in the many years since Warren's article was published, few had heeded his timeless lesson that leaders must create cultures of candor, organizations marked by transparency and the ability for those down the line to get unpalatable but vital information into the hands of those at the top. And, above all, that leaders must learn to listen, listen, and listen more.

I now vaguely remember Warren giving me a copy of this article when we first met in Aspen in 1973. I obviously didn't get the message. Too young and inexperienced to appreciate its importance, I promptly forgot that it even existed. It appears that even Warren may have forgotten about it—not about his own principled resignation at SUNY Buffalo, or the general lessons for leaders that he drew from that painful personal experience—but about the fact that he has been writing all his life about the same timeless and seminal themes that occupy his mind today. One theme that runs through his writing is the necessity for truth in organizations (he returns to the theme in his 2002 *New York Times* op-ed "A Corporate Fear of Too Much Truth"). He warns leaders that it is as unhealthy for organizations to fool themselves as it is for individuals to do so. Warren recently enlisted Daniel Goleman and me to join him in writing about that theme in *Transparency: How Leaders Create a Culture of Candor*. Somehow, in the process, he forgot to tell us about his 1972 paper. We neglected to quote from, or even to cite, it. That is doubly ironic because, in the 2008 book, we used the example of the Bush administration's mishandling of the Iraq war in exactly the way Warren had used the Johnson administration's fears of transparency with regard to Vietnam to exemplify his broader organizational point about truth telling.

Honestly, it was painful for me in late 2008 to re-discover Warren's 1972 essay. And the pain wasn't simply the embarrassment that I had reinvented the wheel while writing the chapter in *Transparency* on "speaking truth to power"; more to the point, it was the bitter pain of envy. Warren's thirty-five-year-old piece not only makes all the points I make years later, it makes them better (in describing McNamara's misplaced sense of loyalty, note Warren's apt and elegant phrase "ethical short-circuiting").

I think what distinguishes Warren from other business writers is his understanding of human relationships. When you read Warren's resignation piece you can't help but think that the hardest part about any relationship is ending it. The ethics—and emotions—of the why, when, and how to end a relationship are complex and heart wrenching: aren't divorces emotionally devastating for most people? While not quite to the same degree, resigning from a job raises the same set of issues and feelings. Why—that is, with what moral justification—should you say "enough" and walk away from an organization you have served loyally? When—under what circumstances and timing—should you say "adieu"? And how should it be done—privately and stealthily, or publicly and noisily? Or, as Warren puts the question, does a resignation on a matter of principle demand a public explanation in order to be both virtuous and effective?

If anyone thinks these questions are dated, they were re-raised in 2008 when former-Bush administration press secretary Scott McClellan wrote a revealing memoir about the Bush administration's fabricated rationale for invading Iraq. What bothered many people about the book was that

McClellan had waited until he was out of harm's way—safe from fury and reprisals from Cheney and Rumsfeld—before mustering the moxie to speak up. But before dismissing McClellan's recent revelations as simply a spineless kiss-and-tell exercise by a disgruntled former employee, it is worth weighing the moral value of McClellan's act in light of Warren's 1972 essay.

In all social organizations—families, sports teams, businesses, and government agencies—those lower down the pecking order experience the terror involved in having to tell unpalatable truths to those ranked above them. While few of us have had direct experience calling attention to Iraq-scale fraud and deception, almost all of us have stories to tell of retaliatory fury from the enraged "alpha dogs" we mustered the courage to confront. Daring to speak truth to power often entails considerable risk—whether at the hands of an irate parent, a neighborhood bully, or an incensed boss. Imagine the courage it would have taken for an Enron employee to confront Jeff Skilling with the facts of the company's (and his) financial deception? Or even the courage required by a GE employee simply to question the company's former CEO, Jack Welch? According to *Fortune,* former GE employees reported that dissenters were berated, insulted, and abused: "Welch conducts meetings so aggressively that people tremble. He attacks almost physically with his intellect—criticizing, demeaning, ridiculing, humiliating."

Warren's article reminds us that, in the early '70s, Albert O. Hirschman posited that employees who disagree with company policy have only three options: "exit, voice, and loyalty." That is, they can offer a principled resignation, or try to change the policy (speak truth to power), or remain loyal team players despite their opposition. Experience shows that most people choose option three, the path of least resistance. They swallow whatever moral objections they have to questionable dictates from above, concluding they lack power to change things or, worse, will be punished if they attempt to do so. Recent data make the case: In a survey of a cross-section of American workers, over two-thirds report having personally witnessed unethical behavior on the job, but only about a third of those say they reported what they observed to their supervisors. The reasons given for their reticence range from fear of retaliation to the belief that management would not act on the information appropriately.

Such docile employee behavior is assumed: most executives expect their people to be "good soldiers" and not question company policy (or, if they do, that they will go away quietly). Indeed, as Warren writes, "disloyalty" is the organization's trump card in dealing with those who dare to voice truth internally in the hope of changing policy, and against those who exit and tell tales out of school. Experience shows that employees who muster the courage to question the prevailing groupthink in an organization open themselves to charges of being traitors, and that's why most workers have to be totally teed off before they will speak up publicly. To get angry enough to face an onslaught on one's character requires not only fundamental disagreement over policy—typically involving the conviction that a moral principle has been violated—but also deep personal hurt. Such were the mixed motivations in high-profile corporate cases of whistleblowing at cigarette-maker Brown and Williamson and at Unum Provident Insurance. In both instances, corporate leaders responded with the standard organizational defense that the whistleblowers' testimony should be discounted because they were "disgruntled" (the ex-employees were portrayed as angry nutcases with enough skeletons in their closets to outfit a Halloween ball). McClellan got much the same treatment.

The charge of disloyalty is as easy for leaders to bring against followers as it is difficult for the accused to counter and disprove. As such former members of the Bush administration as O'Neil, Lindsey, Down, Clarke, and Shinseki found, they were attacked for being "disloyal" and said to be "too angry" for their criticisms to be trusted. Of course they were angry. If they weren't, they might have stayed inside the administration, loyally carrying out orders, or trying to voice disagreement through established processes. But they had tried that, failed in their attempts to be heard, and opted for "hard exits" (in Warren's words).

Doubtless, it would be prettier if whistleblowers weren't so angry, but anger is often a necessary spur to doing the right thing. Reading Warren's speculations about the passivity of Rusk and McNamara in light of their doubts about the Vietnam war, we might ask what might have happened had Secretary of State Powell allowed his reported anger over the decision to invade Iraq to overcome his military-disciplined instinct to loyally fall into line with administration policies? Had he, instead, resigned and publicly voiced his concerns, would Americans then have been so accepting of the questionable evidence on weapons of mass destruction? Who knows? But it does seem clear that if we too quickly ignore the angry words of disgruntled former officials, fewer of them will be willing to step forward, and there will be fewer safeguards of the public interest. Warren was right: principled resignations are generally good things.

Scott McClellan was no hero with regard to protesting the Bush administration's rationale for the Iraq war. Still, for the reasons Warren identified years ago, we should cut him some slack for not speaking up while still in office. We need to keep in mind that speaking truth to power requires not only a courageous speaker but also a willing listener—and, realistically, the truth that makes us free is often the truth leaders prefer not to hear. I can't help but wonder what might have been had George W. Bush read, discussed, and understood Warren's article while studying for his Harvard MBA.

James O'Toole is Daniels Distinguished Professor of Business Ethics at the Daniels College of Business, University of Denver. He has also been a research professor at USC's Center for Effective Organizations and a senior fellow at the Aspen Institute. His books include *Transparency* (Jossey-Bass, 2008), *The Executive's Compass* (Oxford University Press, 1995), and *Creating the Good Life* (Rodale, 2005).

MARCH OF FOLLY REDUX:
IRAQ (2003)

---

*The men who create power make an indispensable
contribution to the nation's greatness, but the men who
question power make a contribution just as indispensable . . .
for they determine whether we use power or power uses us.*

—John F. Kennedy

IN *MARCH OF FOLLY,* AUTHOR BARBARA TUCHMAN identifies several types of "misgovernment," the most tragic of which is folly. Folly occurs when a government pursues policies contrary to the nation's self-interest. To be classified as folly, misgovernment must satisfy three conditions. First, the misguided policy must be perceived as counter-productive, *in its own time;* that is, the decision not only looks stupid now, through the shining ether of time, but it looked hugely problematical in its day. Second, other feasible options must be known but rejected. Finally, the questionable policy must be more than the will of an individual leader. It must be shared and propped up by those around the leader, the product of a sort of group-think. Through that prism, Tuchman analyzes four egregious leadership failures: King Priam opening the gates of Troy to the Greeks; the actions of the Renaissance Popes that hastened the Reformation they so feared; King George III's loss of the American colonies; and, finally and perhaps most relevant today, the Vietnam war.

In writing about Vietnam, George Kennan observed that Lyndon Johnson and his inner circle—Dean Rusk, Walt Rostow, and the Joint Chiefs—were like "men in a dream, incapable of any realistic assessment of the

---

This previously unpublished work was written in 2003.

effects of their own acts." Today, we see the cortege of folly moving us inevitably toward a war with Iraq. And eerily like LBJ's "men in a dream," President Bush and his advisors are leading the march, acting out of sheer wish and will, not allowing nettlesome facts and uncertainties to deter them.

To those who don't share the President's conviction, the facts are obvious:

A war will result in a tragic loss of lives—not just our own, but those of our allies, Iraqis and their neighbors.

The financial burden will be enormous. According to economist William Nordhaus, a prolonged war will cost at least $1.2 trillion, a short war, at least $120 billion. Meanwhile, every corporation I know is holding its breath, deferring capital expenditures until something—anything—happens, delaying indefinitely the economic recovery the United States so desperately needs.

Our credibility will suffer enormously. The alarm in NATO and the European Union caused by our attempt to use Turkey as a base for hostilities is only the most recent example. If we go to war without widespread European support, we can count on permanent damage to our influence in the United Nations, NATO and the European Union. Meanwhile, the number of Americans who see Iraq as an "immediate threat" has fallen dramatically over the past few weeks, down to less than 35% from 64%. According to the most recent *New York Times*/CBS poll, fewer than half of those surveyed are in favor of invading Iraq without UN support. In a sense, we are already fighting a three-front war—with Iraq, with "old Europe," and, as evidenced by the recent anti-war marches, with our own people.

No one has to be convinced of the murderous intentions of Saddam, especially a Saddam with nuclear weapons. But as Tuchman reminds us, it is folly to ignore feasible options other than invasion for disabling Saddam. And there are far better options available to us.

Beyond weaning ourselves of dependence on foreign oil, the most promising long-term option is one that has been strangely overlooked, given the appalling prospect of a protracted war that could metastasize overnight into World War III. Columnist Thomas L. Friedman hinted at this recently when he observed that China is behaving about Iraq "as if the whole issue were for America to resolve." This "deeply mistaken view" appears to be shared by France, Germany, and Russia, the nations Friedman calls the "four pillars of the World of Order." In his open letter to them, he asks, "I understand why you don't want us to be so impulsive, but why are you so passive?"

In grappling with that question, I found myself recalling a principle I learned more than 50 years ago while attending the London School of

Economics. I was invited to participate in a training group at the famed Tavistock Clinic for those interested in the emerging practice of group psychotherapy. Its leader was renowned psychiatrist Wilfred Bion, who understood the dynamics of group behavior as well as anyone I've ever known. Bion's insights were simple and profound. And, first among them, was that the leader must avoid, at all costs, getting overly-involved with the sickest member of the group.

Focus on the sickest, he warned prospective leaders, and you will undermine yourself in numerous ways. You will polarize the group. The healthier members will begin to resent you and even question the legitimacy of your leadership. They will tend to sit sulkily by while you try single-handedly to detoxify the troublemaker. The *only* way to deal with the sickest member, Bion counseled, is to leave space for the healthier ones to take the problem on collectively. Over-reacting to extreme pathology is the most predictable and serious mistake a leader can make, Bion argued, because it steals responsibility from those who should assume it—the healthier members of the group.

It seems to me that Bion's insight applies to the leaders of nations as well as groups. Why are China, France, Germany and Russia so passive in the face of the real threat presented by Saddam? Is it not because the United States is behaving as if he were our problem alone? Like a good group leader, shouldn't the United States give the other nations of the world room to act in their own self-interest? Instead of trying to be a unilateral problem-solver, shouldn't we be working collaboratively with the health that exists in the European Union, the UN, and NATO, and among the moderates in those Middle-Eastern states whose fates are even more closely intertwined with Iraq than ours? Until we abandon our attempt to take on Iraq single-handedly, we can only expect more passivity from our natural allies and an even more dangerous resistance.

Working as part of the group does not imply passivity on our part. Just the opposite. It will entail a variety of creative and pro-active responses. It will mean intervening more forcefully than ever in settling the protracted conflict between Israel and the PLO. It will mean persuading the leaders of the Four Pillars that Iraq is an even more immediate threat to them than to us. It will mean strengthening our ties with our partners in more meaningful ways than by sending Secretary Powell, now our only credible representative abroad, to chat them up. It will mean helping Afghanistan become a genuinely democratic republic. And, most of all, it will entail our nation's proving its capacity to grow up and become a genuine citizen of the world.

That last, essential response is one that our current administration seems dangerously out of touch with. "Wooden-headedness, the source of self-deception, is a factor that plays a remarkable role in individuals," Tuchman writes. "It consists in assessing a situation in terms of pre-conceived fixed notions while ignoring or rejecting any contrary signs." She writes that it was epitomized by Phillip II of Spain, "the surpassing wooden-head of all sovereigns: 'No experience of the failure of the policy could shake his belief in its essential excellence.'"

We can only hope Tuchman's cautionary tale is on the White House reading list.

PART THREE

ON BECOMING
A LEADER

ALMOST AS OLD AS THE NATURE-NURTURE DEBATE is that over whether leaders are born or made. Everything I learn about leadership makes me more certain that people can be taught the competencies of leadership. At the same time, it is obvious that some individuals have attributes, such as empathy or a superior ability to communicate, that make it more likely they will become leaders. In order to learn all I could about leadership in all its forms, I long ago began interviewing leaders in many different fields. These intense conversations inevitably revealed something surprising about the process, evidence that everyone becomes a leader in his or her own way, despite the many commonalities. In the 1980s I attempted to synthesize what I knew about the subject in a format that would help would-be leaders succeed in whatever field they chose. The result was 1985's *Leaders: Strategies for Taking Charge,* with Burt Nanus. A few years later came *On Becoming a Leader.* Based on many more in-depth interviews of leaders, that book has since been revised twice, each time to update descriptions of the all-important context every leader must master. For the twentieth-anniversary edition, I added an epilogue that analyzes the extraordinary and illuminating campaign that led to Barack Obama's historic election as the forty-fourth president of the United States. Over the years I have become increasingly aware that leaders are inevitably marked by the eras in which they grew up. To explore that and other generational aspects of leadership, Robert Thomas and I questioned two very different cohorts of leaders—those, like Mike Wallace, in their seventies and eighties who were shaped by the Great Depression, World War II, and the postwar boom, and those mostly under thirty, like Teach for America founder Wendy Kopp, who grew up wired. In 2002 we published the result, *Leading for a Lifetime* (originally titled, more descriptively and controversially, *Geeks & Geezers*). In writing that book we discovered that leadership always emerges in a personal crucible, some transformative experience such as business leader Sidney Rittenberg's sixteen years of imprisonment, often in solitary confinement, in Chairman Mao's China. We also developed a model of how the remarkable alchemy of leadership takes place.

LEARNING SOME
BASIC TRUISMS ABOUT
LEADERSHIP (1976, 1996)

A MOMENT OF TRUTH CAME TO ME toward the end of my first ten months as president of the University of Cincinnati. The clock was moving toward four in the morning, and I was still in my office, still mired in the incredible mass of paper stacked on my desk. I was bone weary and soul-weary, and I found myself muttering, "Either I can't manage this place, or it's unmanageable." I reached for my calendar and ran my eyes down each hour, half hour, quarter hour, to see where my time had gone that day, the day before, the month before.

Nobel laureate James Franck has said he always recognizes a moment of discovery by "the feeling of terror that seizes me." I felt a trace of it that morning. My discovery was this: *I had become the victim of a vast, amorphous, unwitting, unconscious conspiracy to prevent me from doing anything whatever to change the university's status quo.* Even those of my associates who fully shared my hopes to set new goals, new directions, and to work toward creative change were unconsciously often doing the most to make sure that I would never find the time to begin. I found myself thinking of a friend and former colleague who had taken over one of our top universities with goals and plans that fired up all those around him and who said when he left a few years later, "I never could get around to doing the things I wanted to do."

This discovery, or rediscovery, led me to formulate what might be called Bennis's First Law of Academic Pseudodynamics: Routine work drives out

---

This work originally appeared in *The Unconscious Conspiracy: Why Leaders Can't Lead* by Warren Bennis (AMACON, 1976). This updated version appeared in the *Harvard Business Review*, January/February 1996.

195

nonroutine work and smothers to death all creative planning, all fundamental change in the university—or any institution.

These were the illustrations facing me: To start, there were 150 letters
in the day's mail that required a response. About 50 of them concerned
our young dean of the School of Education, Hendrik Gideonse. His job
was to bring about change in the teaching of teachers, in our university's
relationship to the public schools and to students in the deprived and deteriorating neighborhood around us. Out of these urban schools would
come the bulk of our students of the future—as good or as bad as the
schools had shaped them.

But the letters were not about education. They were about a baby, the
dean's ten-week-old son. Gideonse felt very strongly about certain basic
values. He felt especially so about sex roles, about equality for his wife,
about making sure she had the time and freedom to develop her own
potentials fully. So he was carrying the baby into his office two days a
week in a little bassinet, which he kept on his desk while he did his work.
The daily *Cincinnati Enquirer* heard about it, took a picture of Hendrik,
baby, and bassinet, and played it on page one. TV splashed it across the
nation. And my "in" basket began to overflow with letters that urged his
arrest for child abuse or at least his immediate dismissal. My only public
comment was that we were a tax-supported institution, and if Hendrik
could engage in that form of applied humanism and still accomplish the
things we both wanted done in education, then, like Lincoln with Grant's
whiskey, I'd gladly send him several new babies for adoption.

Hendrik was, of course, simply a man a bit ahead of his time. Today,
his actions would be applauded—maybe even with a Father of the Year
award. Then, however, Hendrik and his baby ate up quite a bit of my time.

Also on my desk was a note from a professor, complaining that his classroom temperature was down to sixty-five degrees. Perhaps he expected me
to grab a wrench and fix it. A student complained that we wouldn't give
him course credit for acting as assistant to a city council member. Another
was unable to get into the student health center. The teacher at my child's
day school, who attended the university, was dissatisfied with her grades.
A parent complained about four-letter words in a Philip Roth book being
used in an English class. The track coach wanted me to come over to see
for myself how bad the track was. An alumnus couldn't get the football
seats he wanted. Another wanted a coach fired. A teacher had called to tell
me the squash court was closed at 7 PM when he wanted to use it.

Perhaps 20 percent of my time that year had been taken up by a problem at the general hospital, which was city-owned but administered by
the university and served as the teaching hospital of the university med-

ical school. Some terminal-cancer patients, with their consent, had been subjected to whole-body radiation as possibly beneficial therapy. Since the Pentagon saw this as a convenient way to gather data that might help protect civilian populations in nuclear warfare, it provided a series of subsidies for the work.

When this story broke and was pursued in such a way as to call up comparisons with the Nazis' experiments on human guinea pigs, it became almost impossible for me or anybody else to separate the essential facts from the fantasized distortions. The problem eventually subsided, after a blue-ribbon task force recommended significant changes in the experiment's design. But I invested endless time in a matter only vaguely related to the prime purposes of the university—and wound up being accused by some of interfering with academic freedom.

The radiation experiment and Hendrik's baby illustrate how the media, particularly TV, make the academic cloister a goldfish bowl. By focusing on the lurid or the superficial, they can disrupt a president's proper activities while contributing nothing to the advancement of knowledge. This leads me to Bennis's Second Law of Academic Pseudodynamics: Make whatever grand plans you will, you may be sure the unexpected or the trivial will disturb and disrupt them.

In my moment of truth, that weary 4 AM in my trivia-cluttered office, I began trying to straighten out in my own mind what university presidents should be doing and not doing, what their true priorities should be, how they must lead.

Lead, not *manage:* there is an important difference. Many an institution is very well managed and very poorly led. It may excel in the ability to handle each day all the routine inputs yet may never ask whether the routine should be done at all.

All of us find ourselves acting on routine problems because they are the easiest things to handle. We hesitate to get involved too early in the bigger ones—we collude, as it were, in the unconscious conspiracy to immerse us in routine.

My entrapment in routine made me realize another thing: People were following the old army game. They did not want to take the responsibility for or bear the consequences of decisions they properly should make. The motto was, "Let's push up the tough ones." The consequence was that everybody and anybody was dumping his "wet babies" (as the old State Department hands call them) on my desk, when I had neither the diapers nor the information to take care of them. So I decided that the president's first priority—the sine qua non of effective leadership—was to create an "executive constellation" to run the office of the president. It could be a mixed bag, some vice-presidents, some presidential assistants. The group would have to be compatible in the sense that its members could work together but neither uniform nor conformist—a group of people who knew more than the president about everything within their areas of competency and could attend to daily matters without dropping their wet babies on the president's desk.

What should the president him- or herself do? The president should be a *conceptualist*. That's something more than being just an "idea man." It means being a leader with entrepreneurial vision and the time to spend thinking about the forces that will affect the destiny of the institution. The president must educate board members so that they not only understand the necessity of distinguishing between leadership and management but also can protect the chief executive from getting enmeshed in routine machinery.

Leaders must create for their institutions clear-cut and measurable goals based on advice from all elements of the community. They must be allowed to proceed toward those goals without being crippled by bureaucratic machinery that saps their strength, energy, and initiative. They must be allowed to take risks, to embrace error, to use their creativity to the hilt and encourage those who work with them to use theirs.

These insights gave me the strength to survive my acid test: whether I, as a "leading theorist" of the principles of creative leadership, actually could prove myself a leader. However, the sum total of my experiences as president of the University of Cincinnati convinced me that most of the academic theory on leadership was useless.

After leaving the university, I spent nearly five years researching a book on leadership. I traveled around the country spending time with ninety of the most effective, successful leaders in the nation, sixty from corporations and thirty from the public sector. My goal was to find these leaders' common traits, a task that required more probing than I had expected. For a while, I sensed much more diversity than commonality among them. The group included both left-brain and right-brain thinkers; some who dressed for success and some who didn't; well-spoken, articulate leaders and laconic, inarticulate ones; some John Wayne types and some who were definitely the opposite.

I was finally able to come to some conclusions, of which perhaps the most important is the distinction between leaders and managers: Leaders are people who do the right thing; managers are people who do things right. Both roles are crucial, but they differ profoundly. I often observe people in top positions doing the wrong thing well.

This study also reinforced my earlier insight—that American organizations (and probably those in much of the rest of the industrialized world) are underled and overmanaged. They do not pay enough attention to doing the right thing, while they pay too much attention to doing things right. Part of the fault lies with our schools of management; we teach people how to be good technicians and good staff people, but we don't train people for leadership.

The group of sixty corporate leaders was not especially different from any profile of top leadership in America. The median age was fifty-six. Most were white males, with six black men and six women in the group. The only surprising finding was that all the CEOs not only were still married to their first spouses but also seemed enthusiastic about the institution of marriage. Among the CEOs were Bill Kieschnick, then chair and CEO of Arco, and the late Ray Kroc, of McDonald's.

Public-sector leaders included Harold Williams, who then chaired the Securities and Exchange Commission (SEC); Neil Armstrong, a genuine all-American hero who happened to be at the University of Cincinnati; three elected officials; two orchestra conductors; and two winning athletics coaches. I wanted conductors and coaches because I mistakenly believed that they were the last leaders with complete control over their constituents.

After several years of observation and conversation, I defined four competencies evident to some extent in every member of the group: management of attention; management of meaning; management of trust; and management of self. The first trait apparent in these leaders is their ability to draw others to them, not just because they have a vision but because they communicate an extraordinary focus of commitment. Leaders manage attention through a compelling vision that brings others to a place they have not been before.

One of the people I most wanted to interview was one of the few I could not seem to reach—Leon Fleischer, a well-known child prodigy who grew up to become a prominent pianist, conductor, and musicologist. I happened to be in Aspen, Colorado, one summer while Fleischer was conducting the Aspen Music Festival, and I tried again to reach him, even leaving a note on his dressing-room door. Driving back through downtown Aspen, I saw two perspiring young cellists carrying their instruments, and I offered them a ride to the music tent. They hopped in the back of my jeep, and as we rode I questioned them about Fleischer. "I'll tell you why he's so great," said one. "He doesn't waste our time."

Fleischer finally agreed not only to be interviewed but to let me watch him rehearse and conduct music classes. I linked the way I saw him work with that simple sentence, "He doesn't waste our time." Every moment Fleischer was before the orchestra, he knew exactly what sound he wanted. He didn't waste time because his intentions were always evident. What united him with the other musicians was their concern with intention and outcome.

When I reflected on my own experience, it struck me that when I was most effective, it was because I knew what I wanted. When I was ineffective, it was because I was unclear about it.

So the first leadership competency is the management of attention through a set of intentions or a vision, not in a mystical or religious sense but in the sense of outcome, goal, or direction.

The second leadership competency is management of meaning. To make dreams apparent to others and to align people with them, leaders must communicate their vision. Communication and alignment work together. Consider, for example, the contrasting styles of Presidents Reagan and Carter. Ronald Reagan is called "the Great Communicator"; one of his speech writers said that Reagan can read the phone book and make it interesting. The reason is that Reagan uses metaphors with which people can identify. In his first budget message, for example, Reagan described a trillion dollars by comparing it to piling up dollar bills beside the Empire State Building. Reagan, to use one of Alexander Haig's coinages, "tangibilitated" the idea. Leaders make ideas tangible and real to others, so they can support them. For no matter how marvelous the vision, the effective leader must use a metaphor, a word or a model to make that vision clear to others.

In contrast, President Carter was boring. Carter was one of our best-informed presidents; he had more facts at his fingertips than almost any other president. But he never made the meaning come through the facts. I interviewed an assistant secretary of commerce appointed by Carter, who told me that after four years in his administration, she still did not know what Jimmy Carter stood for. She said that working for him was like looking through the wrong side of a tapestry; the scene was blurry and indistinct.

The leader's goal is not mere explanation or clarification but the creation of meaning. My favorite baseball joke is exemplary: In the ninth inning of a key playoff game, with a three-and-two count on the batter, the umpire hesitates a split second in calling the pitch. The batter whirls around angrily and says, "Well, what was it?" The umpire snarls back, "It ain't *nothing* until *I* call it!"

The third competency is management of trust. Trust is essential to all organizations. The main determinant of trust is reliability, what I call *constancy.* When I talked to the board members or staffs of these leaders, I heard certain phrases again and again: "She is all of a piece." "Whether you like it or not, you always know where he is coming from, what he stands for."

When John Paul II visited this country, he gave a press conference. One reporter asked how the pope could account for allocating funds to build a swimming pool at the papal summer palace. He responded quickly, "I like to swim. Next question." He did not rationalize about medical reasons or claim that he got the money from a special source. A recent study showed that people would much rather follow individuals they can count on, even when they disagree with their viewpoint, than people they agree with but who shift positions frequently. I cannot emphasize enough the significance of constancy and focus. Margaret Thatcher's reelection in Great Britain is another excellent example. When she won office in 1979, observers predicted that she quickly would revert to defunct Labor Party policies. She did not. She has not turned; she has been constant, focused, and all of a piece.

The fourth leadership competency is management of self, knowing one's skills and deploying them effectively. Management of self is critical; without it, leaders and managers can do more harm than good. Like incompetent doctors, incompetent managers can make life worse, make people sicker and less vital. There is a term—*iatrogenic*—for illnesses caused by doctors and hospitals. There should be one for illnesses caused by leaders, too. Some give themselves heart attacks and nervous breakdowns; still worse, many are "carriers," causing their employees to be ill.

Leaders know themselves; they know their strengths and nurture them. They also have a faculty I think of as the Wallenda Factor. The Flying Wallendas are perhaps the world's greatest family of aerialists and tightrope walkers. I was fascinated when, in the early 1970s, seventy-one-year-old Karl Wallenda said that for him living was walking the tightrope, and everything else was waiting. I was struck with his capacity for concentration on the intention, the task, the decision. I was even more intrigued when, several months later, Wallenda fell to his death while walking a tightrope without a safety net between two high-rise buildings in San Juan, Puerto Rico. Wallenda fell still clutching the balancing pole he had warned his family never to drop lest it hurt somebody below. Later, Wallenda's wife said that before her husband had fallen, for the first time since she had known him he had been concentrating on falling, instead of on walking the tightrope. He had personally supervised the attachment of the guy wires, which he had never done before.

Like Wallenda before his fall, the leaders in my group seemed unacquainted with the concept of failure. What you or I might call a failure, they referred to as a mistake. I began collecting synonyms for the word *failure* mentioned in the interviews, and I found more than twenty: *mistake, error, false start, bloop, flop, loss, miss, foul-up, stumble, botch, bungle* . . . but not *failure*. One CEO told me that if she had a knack for leadership, it was the capacity to make as many mistakes as she could as soon as possible, and thus get them out of the way. Another said that a mistake is simply "another way of doing things." These leaders learn from and use something that doesn't go well; it is not a failure but simply the next step.

Leadership can be felt throughout an organization. It gives pace and energy to the work and empowers the work force. Empowerment is the collective effect of leadership. In organizations with effective leaders, empowerment is most evident in four themes:

○ *People feel significant.* Everyone feels that he or she makes a difference to the success of the organization. The difference may be small—prompt delivery of potato chips to a mom-and-pop grocery store or developing a tiny but essential part for an airplane. But where they are empowered, people feel that what they do has meaning and significance.

○ *Learning and competence matter.* Leaders value learning and mastery, and so do people who work for leaders. Leaders make it clear that there is no failure, only mistakes that give us feedback and tell us what to do next.

○ *People are part of a community.* Where there is leadership, there is a team, a family, a unity. Even people who do not especially like each other feel the sense of community. When Neil Armstrong talks about the Apollo explorations, he describes how a team carried out an almost unimaginably complex set of interdependent tasks. Until there were women astronauts, the men referred to this feeling as "brotherhood." I suggest they rename it "family."

○ *Work is exciting.* When there are leaders, work is stimulating, challenging, fascinating, and fun. An essential ingredient in organizational leadership is pulling rather than pushing people toward a goal. A "pull" style of influence attracts and energizes people to enroll in an exciting vision of the future. It motivates through identification, rather than through rewards and punishments. Leaders articulate and embody the ideals toward which the organization strives.

People cannot be expected to enroll in just any exciting vision. Some visions and concepts have more staying power and are rooted more deeply in our human needs than others. I believe the lack of two such concepts in modern organizational life is largely responsible for the alienation and lack of meaning so many experience in their work. One of these is the concept of quality. Modern industrial society has been oriented to quantity, providing more goods and services for everyone. Quantity is measured in money; we are a money-oriented society. Quality often is not measured at all but is appreciated intuitively. Our response to quality is a feeling. Feelings of quality are connected intimately with our experience of meaning, beauty, and value in our lives.

Closely linked to the concept of quality is that of dedication to, even love of, our work. This dedication is evoked by quality and is the force that energizes high-performing systems. When we love our work, we need not be managed by hopes of reward or fears of punishment. We can create systems that facilitate our work, rather than being preoccupied with checks and controls of people who want to beat or exploit the system.

Ultimately, in great leaders and the organizations surrounding them, there is a fusion of work and play to the point where, as Robert Frost says, "Love and need are one." How do we get from here to there? I think we must start by studying change.

UNDERSTANDING THE BASICS
(1989, 2003)

As we survey the path leadership theory has taken, we spot the wreckage of "trait theory," the "great man" theory, and the "situationist" critique, leadership styles, functional leadership, and, finally, leaderless leadership, to say nothing of bureaucratic leadership, charismatic leadership, group-centered leadership, reality-centered leadership, leadership by objective, and so on. The dialectic and reversals of emphases in this area very nearly rival the tortuous twists and turns of child-rearing practices, and one can paraphrase Gertrude Stein by saying, "a leader is a follower is a leader."

—*Administrative Science Quarterly*

LEADERS COME IN EVERY SIZE, shape, and disposition—short, tall, neat, sloppy, young, old, male, and female. Nevertheless, they all seem to share some, if not all, of the following ingredients:

○ The first basic ingredient of leadership is a *guiding vision*. The leader has a clear idea of what he or she wants to do—professionally and personally—and the strength to persist in the face of setbacks, even failures. Unless you know where you're going, and why, you cannot possibly get there. That guiding purpose, that vision, was well illustrated by Norman Lear.

This work originally appeared in *On Becoming a Leader* (Addison-Wesley, 1989). This version is from the revised edition (Basic Books, 2003).

○ The second basic ingredient of leadership is *passion*—the underlying passion for the promises of life, combined with a very particular passion for a vocation, a profession, a course of action. The leader loves what he or she does and loves doing it. Tolstoy said that hopes are the dreams of the waking man. Without hope, we cannot survive, much less progress. The leader who communicates passion gives hope and inspiration to other people. This ingredient tends to come up with different spins on it—sometimes it appears as enthusiasm. . . .

○ The next basic ingredient of leadership is *integrity*. I think there are three essential parts of integrity: self-knowledge, candor, and maturity.

"Know thyself," was the inscription over the Oracle at Delphi. And it is still the most difficult task any of us faces. But until you truly know yourself, strengths and weaknesses, know what you want to do and why you want to do it, you cannot succeed in any but the most superficial sense of the word. Leaders never lie to themselves, especially about themselves, know their faults as well as their assets, and deal with them directly. You are your own raw material. When you know what you consist of and what you want to make of it, then you can invent yourself.

Candor is the key to self-knowledge. Candor is based in honesty of thought and action, a steadfast devotion to principle, and a fundamental soundness and wholeness. An architect who designs a Bauhaus glass box with a Victorian cupola lacks professional integrity, as does any person who trims his or her principles—or even ideas—to please. Like Lillian Hellman, the leader cannot cut his or her conscience to fit this year's fashions.

Maturity is important to a leader because leading is not simply showing the way or issuing orders. Every leader needs to have experienced and grown through following—learning to be dedicated, observant, capable of working with and learning from others, never servile, always truthful. Having located these qualities in themselves, leaders can encourage them in others.

○ Integrity is the basis of *trust*, which is not as much an ingredient of leadership as it is a product. It is the one quality that cannot be acquired, but must be earned. It is given by co-workers and followers, and without it, the leader can't function. . . .

○ Two more basic ingredients of leadership are *curiosity* and *daring*. Leaders wonder about everything, want to learn as much as they can, are willing to take risks, experiment, try new things. They do not worry about failure, but embrace errors, knowing they will learn from them. Learning from adversity is another theme that comes up again and again in this book, often with different spins. In fact, that could be said of each of the basic ingredients.

Even though I talk about basic ingredients, I'm not talking about traits that you're born with and can't change. As countless deposed kings and hapless heirs to great fortunes can attest, true leaders are not born, but made, and usually self-made. Leaders invent themselves. They are not, by the way, made in a single weekend seminar, as many of the leadership-theory spokesmen claim. I've come to think of that one as the microwave theory: pop in Mr. or Ms. Average and out pops McLeader in sixty seconds.

Billions of dollars are spent annually by and on would-be leaders. Many major corporations offer leadership development courses. And corporate America has nevertheless lost its lead in the world market. I would argue that more leaders have been made by accident, circumstance, sheer grit, or will than have been made by all the leadership courses put together. Leadership courses can only teach skills. They can't teach character or vision—and indeed they don't even try. Developing character and vision is the way leaders invent themselves.

The Great Depression was the crucible in which Franklin D. Roosevelt was transformed from politician to leader. Harry Truman became president when FDR died, but it was sheer grit that made him a leader. Dwight Eisenhower, the nation's only five-star general, was underestimated by Republican party bosses who saw only his winning smile. He turned out to be his own man, and a leader. Pols like Chicago's mayor Richard Daley gave John Kennedy a boost into the White House, but he shone there on his own. Like them or not, FDR, Truman, Ike, and JFK were all true leaders.

Truman never saw himself as a leader and was probably as surprised as anyone else when he became president. Eisenhower was a good soldier blessed with a constellation of better soldiers who made both his military and political victories possible. Those charming rich boys Roosevelt and Kennedy were, in the vernacular of the time, traitors to their class, but heroes to the people. Each of these men was his own invention: Truman and Eisenhower, the quintessential small-town boys rising to the top; Roosevelt and Kennedy, driven by ambitious and powerful parents, worldly but conventional, remaking themselves and their worlds.

Being self-made is, of course, not all of it. Lyndon Johnson, Richard Nixon, and Jimmy Carter could be described as self-made men, but they failed to win our hearts or engage our minds, and finally failed as national leaders.

All three were highly competent, but their ambitions overrode their talent. Johnson set out to make a Great Society, but made a bad war instead. Nixon wanted less to lead us than to rule us. It was never clear what Carter wanted, besides the White House. In each case, their minds seemed to be closed—to us, at least, and perhaps to themselves as well. Whatever vision each may have had went unexpressed (or in Johnson's case unfulfilled). Each was given to saying one thing and doing another, and each seemed to look on the American people as adversaries. When we questioned the Vietnam War, Johnson questioned our loyalty. Nixon had an enemies list. And Carter accused us of malingering.

As presidents, Johnson, Nixon, and Carter were all more driven than driving, and each seemed trapped in his own shadows. They were haunted men, shaped more by their early deprivations than by their later successes. They did not, then, invent themselves. They were made—and unmade— by their own histories.

When Henry Kissinger was asked what he had learned from the presidents he had worked with—a list that started with Kennedy, through whom he met Truman—Kissinger replied, "Presidents don't do great things by dwelling on their limitations, but by focusing on their possibilities." They leave the past behind them and turn toward the future.

Just as Roosevelt and Kennedy made themselves new, and therefore independent and free, Johnson and Nixon were used goods, no matter how far they got from their pinched beginnings, no matter how high they rose. Roosevelt, Truman, Eisenhower, and Kennedy invented themselves and then invented the future. Johnson and Nixon were made by their pasts. They imposed those mean lessons of their pasts on the present, enshrouding the future. Good leaders engage the world. Bad leaders entrap it, or try.

Jimmy Carter, who never managed to put a distinctive stamp on his one-term presidency, was able to reinvent himself as an international peace-maker. His 1980 re-election doomed as long as American hostages remained in Iran, he continued to be shaped out of office by his passionate Christianity. But his unshakeable convictions were a far better fit with a career as an almost saintly ambassador of peace than with the office of president of the United States. Carter became an inspiring symbol of what a former president, or any person who has attained and lost great power, can achieve. With wife Rosalynn ever at his side, Carter builds homes for the poor with Habitat for Humanity. And whenever Carter feels he is needed, he jets off to far-flung trouble spots to monitor elections and insure human rights. Some see his efforts as naive. Many more see them as evidence of authentic moral leadership, for which he received the Nobel Peace Prize in 2002.

In the years since Carter left office in 1981, we have had self-made men in the White House (Ronald Reagan and Bill Clinton) and American aristocrats (George Herbert Walker Bush and his son George W. Bush). The first Hollywood president, former actor Reagan proved that leadership is, to an extraordinary degree, a performance art. He earned his reputation as "the Teflon president" largely because of his winning manner even when faced with the Iran-contra scandal and a stock market plunge, on October 19, 1987, inevitably attributed to Reaganomics. Whether Reagan's affable sincerity was genuine, we will never know. But he was a model of successful self-invention who projected authenticity and a lack of pretense that made him one of the most popular presidents in recent history.

The senior George Bush was an American Brahmin on a more modest scale than FDR or JFK. With Reagan, he was the last of our presidents to have been forged in the crucible of World War II, in which he served as a very young and much decorated pilot. Bush received some of the highest acceptance ratings in polling history during his campaign against Iraq's Saddam Hussein, Desert Storm. And it was on Bush's watch that the Soviet Union—the "Evil Empire," as Reagan called it—dissolved in 1991. But Bush was ultimately undone by his inability to distance himself from his aristocratic roots. Constantly reminded by the brilliant, relentless coalition that put Clinton in the White House in 1992, the American public never forgot the image of Bush staring in wonder at an electronic supermarket scanner. The voting public may forgive you for going to Choate, but it will never forgive you for not knowing how the other half shops.

An orphan raised by an alcoholic step-father, President Clinton was brilliantly self-made, a man who was swept into office in 1992 by making voters believe in a place called Hope, the stranger-than-fiction name of his Arkansas birthplace. Clinton had the intelligence, the charm, the ability to find common ground—everything he needed to be one of the greatest presidents in history. Everything, that is, except the strong moral compass that all great leaders have. Clinton's case is tragic in the classical sense, that of a hero brought down by his own fatal flaw. Hounded throughout his two terms by conservative opponents with Javert-like tenacity, Clinton still managed to preside over a period of prosperity, fueled by the soaring New Economy, unmatched in modern American history. He was ultimately impeached on, and acquitted of, charges that included perjuring himself about a dalliance with White House intern Monica Lewinsky.

Clinton's ability to recover from setbacks during his years in Arkansas politics won him the nickname "The Come-Back Kid." Time will tell if Clinton is able to re-invent himself out of office, as Carter did. Certainly

Clinton has the talent and the drive to do so. Whether he has the requisite integrity—a quality that transcends traditional notions of propriety—remains to be seen.

President George W. Bush is another work in progress. He took office without a clear public mandate and was soon faced with the unprecedented events of 9/11. He proved to be a better crisis manager than his critics dreamed possible. But a year later, he was championing a war with Iraq that a significant minority opposed and the United States had slipped into the worst recession since the Carter administration. Put in Shakespearean terms, it was not yet clear, in 2002, whether America's fun-loving, Texas-style Prince Hal would evolve into an American Henry V.

Like Clinton, "W." represents a new generation of leaders, whose crucible was not World War II, but the more ambiguous proving ground of the 1960s and early '70s, with their sex, drugs, rock 'n' roll, and mistrust of traditional authority. No one yet knows who the great leaders of that generation will be, or the distinctive leadership styles they will create, given their era and its distinctive values.

The Greeks believed that excellence was based on a perfect balance of eros and logos, or feeling and thought, which together allow us to understand the world on all levels, from "the concrete contemplation of the complete facts." True understanding derives from engagement and from the full deployment of ourselves. As John Gardner once said, talent is one thing, while its triumphant expression is another. Only when we are fully deployed are we capable of that triumphant expression. Full deployment, engagement, hone and sharpen all of one's gifts, and ensure that one will be an original, not a copy.

Leaders, Not Managers

I tend to think of the differences between leaders and managers as the differences between those who master the context and those who surrender to it. There are other differences, as well, and they are enormous and crucial:

- The manager administers; the leader innovates.
- The manager is a copy; the leader is an original.
- The manager maintains; the leader develops.
- The manager focuses on systems and structure; the leader focuses on people.
- The manager relies on control; the leader inspires trust.
- The manager has a short-range view; the leader has a long-range perspective.

- o The manager asks how and when; the leader asks what and why.
- o The manager has his or her eye always on the bottom line; the leader's eye is on the horizon.
- o The manager imitates; the leader originates.
- o The manager accepts the status quo; the leader challenges it.
- o The manager is the classic good soldier; the leader is his or her own person.
- o The manager does things right; the leader does the right thing.

To reprise Wallace Stevens, managers wear square hats and learn through training. Leaders wear sombreros and opt for education. Consider the differences between training and education:

EDUCATION	TRAINING
inductive	deductive
tentative	firm
dynamic	static
understanding	memorizing
ideas	facts
broad	narrow
deep	surface
experiential	rote
active	passive
questions	answers
process	content
strategy	tactics
alternatives	goal
exploration	prediction
discovery	dogma
active	reactive
initiative	direction
whole brain	left brain

life	job
long-term	short-term
change	stability
content	form
flexible	rigid
risk	rules
synthesis	thesis
open	closed
imagination	common sense
THE SUM: LEADER	MANAGER

If the list on the left seems strange to you, it's because that isn't the way we are usually taught. Our educational system is really better at training than educating. And that's unfortunate. Training is good for dogs, because we require obedience from them. In people, all it does is orient them toward the bottom line.

The list on the left is of all the qualities that business schools don't encourage enough, as they too often opt for the short-run, profit-maximizing, microeconomic bottom line. Bottom lines have nothing to do with problem-finding. And we need people who know how to find problems, because the ones we face today aren't always clearly defined, and they aren't linear. Modern architects are moving away from the divinity of the right angle to rhomboids, to rounded spaces and parabolas. For leaders to develop the necessary competencies, they must start to think about rhomboids.

Leaders have nothing but themselves to work with. It is one of the paradoxes of life that good leaders rise to the top in spite of their weakness, while bad leaders rise because of their weakness. Abraham Lincoln was subject to fits of serious depression, yet he was perhaps this country's best president, guiding this country through its most severe crisis. On the other hand, Hitler imposed his psychosis on the German people, leading them through delusions of grandeur into the vilest madness and most horrific slaughter the world has ever known.

What is true for leaders is, for better or for worse, true for each of us: we are our own raw material. Only when we know what we're made of and what we want to make of it can we begin our lives—and we must do it despite an unwitting conspiracy of people and events against us. It's that tension in the national character again. As Norman Lear put it, "On the one hand, we're a society that seems to be proud of individuality. On the other hand, we don't really tolerate real individuality. We want to homogenize it."

For Oscar-winning movie director Sydney Pollack, the search for self-knowledge is a continuing process. "There's a sort of monologue or dialogue going on in my head all the time," he said. "Some of it's part of a fantasy life, some is exploratory. Sometimes I can trick myself into problem-solving by imagining myself talking about problem-solving. If I don't know the answer to something, I imagine being asked the question in my head. Faulkner said, 'I don't know what I think until I read what I said.' That's not just a joke. You learn what you think by codifying your thinking in some way."

That's absolutely true. Codifying one's thinking is an important step in inventing oneself. The most difficult way to do it is by thinking about thinking—it helps to speak or write your thoughts. Writing is the most profound way of codifying your thoughts, the best way of learning from yourself who you are and what you believe.

Newspaper executive Gloria Anderson added, "It's vital for people to develop their own sense of themselves and their role in the world, and it's equally vital for them to try new things, to test themselves and their beliefs and principles. I think we long for people who will stand up for what they believe, even if we don't agree with them, because we have confidence in such people."

Scientist Mathilde Krim agreed. "One must be a good explorer and a good listener, too, to take in as much as possible but not swallow anything uncritically. One must finally trust his own gut reactions," she said. "A value system, beliefs, are important so you know where you stand, but they must be your own values, not someone else's."

If knowing yourself and being yourself were as easy to do as to talk about, there wouldn't be nearly so many people walking around in borrowed postures, spouting secondhand ideas, trying desperately to fit in rather than to stand out. Former Lucky Stores CEO Don Ritchey said, on the need for being oneself, "I believe people spot phonies in very short order, whether that be on an individual basis or a company basis. As Emerson says, 'What you are speaks so loudly I cannot hear what you say.'"

Once Born, Twice Born

Harvard professor emeritus Abraham Zaleznik posits that there are two kinds of leaders: once-borns and twice-borns. The once-born's transition from home and family to independence is relatively easy. Twice-borns generally suffer as they grow up, feel different, even isolated, and so develop an elaborate inner life. As they grow older, they become truly independent, relying wholly on their own beliefs and ideas. Leaders who are twice born are inner-directed, self-assured, and, as a result, truly charismatic, according to Zaleznik.

Once-borns, then, have been invented by their circumstances, as in the case of Johnson and Nixon, while twice-borns have invented themselves, as in the case of Roosevelt and Truman.

A couple of studies underscore the benefits, even the necessity, of self-invention. First, middle-aged men tend to change careers after having heart attacks. Faced with their own mortality, these men realize that what they've been doing, what they've invested their lives in, is not an accurate reflection of their real needs and desires.

Another study indicates that what determines the level of satisfaction in post-middle-aged men is the degree to which they acted upon their youthful dreams. It's not so much whether they were successful in achieving their dreams as the honest pursuit of them that counts. The spiritual dimension in creative effort comes from that honest pursuit.

There is, of course, evidence that women, too, are happier when they've invented themselves instead of accepting without question the roles they were brought up to play. Psychologist and author Sonya Friedman said, "The truth of the matter is that the most emotionally disturbed women are those who are married and into traditional full-time, lifetime homemaker roles. Single women have always been happier than married women. Always. And there isn't a study that has disproved that."

Staying single has historically been the only way most women were free to invent themselves. Nineteenth-century poet Emily Dickinson, a reclusive woman who never married and who surely invented herself, is supposed to have said to one of the rare visitors to her room, "Here is freedom!"

Fortunately, the changing times have meant changes in relationships, too. Many of the women leaders I talked with have managed to invent themselves even though married—as has Friedman herself.

I cannot stress too much the need for self-invention. To be authentic is literally to be your own author (the words derive from the same Greek root), to discover your own native energies and desires, and then to find your own way of acting on them. When you've done that, you are not existing simply in order to live up to an image posited by the culture or by some other authority or by a family tradition. When you write your own life, then no matter what happens, you have played the game that was natural for you to play. If, as someone said, "it is the supervisor's role in a modern industrial society to limit the potential of the people who work for him," then it is your task to do whatever you must to break out of such limits and live up to your potential, to keep the covenant with your youthful dreams.

Norman Lear would add to this that the goal isn't worth arriving at unless you enjoy the journey. "You have to look at success incrementally," he said. "It takes too long to get to any major success. . . . If one can look at life as being successful on a moment-by-moment basis, one might find that most of it is successful. And take the bow inside for it. When we wait for the big bow, it's a lousy bargain. They don't come but once in too long a time."

Applauding yourself for the small successes, and taking the small bow, are good ways of learning to experience life each moment that you live it. And that's part of inventing yourself, of creating your own destiny.

To become a leader, then, you must become yourself, become the maker of your own life. While there are no rules for doing this, there are some lessons I can offer from my decades of observation and study. And we'll turn to those lessons now.

FRANCES HESSELBEIN ON
"UNDERSTANDING THE BASICS"

WHEN THE FIRST EDITION of *On Becoming a Leader* was published, it was so wildly successful that the decision was made to make a video of the book, to be called *The Leader Within*. Three of the leaders featured in the book were chosen to be in the video. I had the honor of being one of the three, along with General Dave R. Palmer, superintendent of West Point, and Max De Pree, chairman of Herman Miller Company.

I was deeply honored to be chosen, yet I wondered what cadets at West Point, office furniture, and a Girl Scout troop in a park in South Central Los Angeles would have in common. We were all filmed separately, not knowing what the others were doing, then the great day came when we could see the tape in its final form.

Warren had taken our childhoods, our families, our growing up years, our values, and all the commonalities that moved through our work, our lives to deliver a basic. And at one point, Warren looks into the camera and says, "These three people never started out to be leaders. They began by expressing themselves in their work, and along the way they became leaders." Warren wrote the book with ten chapters, then distilled the lives and work of three leaders from the book into a basic, and a message no one can ever forget.

So we learned from Warren Bennis, our greatest teacher, a basic, we express ourselves in our work, and along the way, we become leaders.

The more we study Warren, the more we understand that we—the leader, the person—cannot be separate. Ourselves and our work are one, and if we are faithful to our calling, "along the way" we become the leader we strive to be, are determined to be. The message is that the leader within has to be the leader the people see, know, experience. Our values, our principles, our morals, our ethics, everything we strive to live by has to be expressed in every encounter.

In the workplace, our people watch us, observe us, sometimes test us. When we preach one thing and practice another, the result can be a disillusioned workforce, low in morale, low in productivity. But when the leader lives the values proclaimed, the result is high morale, high productivity, a bright future for the team.

Max De Pree dazzles us in *The Leader Within* with his wisdom, his authenticity. I carry around in my bag a Max De Pree reminder: *"The first responsibility of a leader is to define reality. The last is to say thank you. In between, the leader is a servant and a debtor."*

General Palmer, his life and the cadets at West Point, were equally inspiring, unforgettable. The videotape—no theory, just on-the-ground experience, lives lived, and Warren Bennis documenting a basic for the world of leaders. Basic is basic.

On November 12 in Los Angeles, the International Leadership Association honored six leaders including Warren Bennis for "being instrumental in the founding of the discipline of leadership"—with the Lifetime Achievement Award. Instead of making an acceptance speech upon receiving this distinguished award, he said "thank you" and gave each participant the Epilogue to the twentieth-anniversary edition of *On Becoming a Leader,* published in 2009. A perfect example of a basic we don't often observe: "It is not about me; it's all about them."

I received the same award the next morning, and in my acceptance I talked about the four great leaders who have had the deepest impact upon my life and my work. Peter Drucker, John W. Gardner, Warren Bennis, and my grandmother Sadie Pringle Wicks have provided me with my "guiding vision."

Warren in this book inspires leaders to recognize the qualities and to express the indispensable ingredients of leadership: guiding vision, passion, integrity, trust, curiosity, and daring.

Every leader—no matter where we are in our lives, our careers, will cherish *The Essential Bennis,* our companion for the journey to leadership.

Frances Hesselbein is former CEO of The Girl Scouts of the USA and founding president of the Leader to Leader Institute (formerly the Peter F. Drucker Foundation for Nonprofit Organizations). She is author of *Hesselbein on Leadership* (Jossey-Bass, 2002) and *Be Know Do: Leadership the Army Way* (Jossey-Bass, 2004), as well as editor-in-chief of the journal *Leader to Leader.*

DEPLOYING YOURSELF: STRIKE HARD, TRY EVERYTHING (1989)

There is a self, and what I have sometimes referred to as
"listening to the impulse voices" means letting the self emerge.
Most of us, most of the time (and especially does this apply to
children, young people), listen not to ourselves but to Mommy's
introjected voice or Daddy's voice or to the voice of the
Establishment, of the Elders, of authority, or of tradition.

—*Abraham Maslow*, Farther Reaches of Human Nature

"LETTING THE SELF EMERGE" is the essential task for leaders. It is how
one takes the step from being to doing in the spirit of expressing, rather
than proving. The means of expression discussed in this chapter unfold
from one another as the opening petals of a flower.

Suppose you were required, as a child, to recite a poem in front of your
class. You forgot the second verse, were scolded by your teacher, and
laughed at by your classmates, and ever since you've broken into a cold
sweat at the thought of speaking in public.

Now you've been offered a job that requires making regular speeches
to large groups. You want the job very much, but your fear of public
speaking prevents you from accepting it immediately. In other words, your
feeling of fear overpowers your confidence in your ability to do the job
and prevents you from acting. You have three choices:

This work originally appeared in *On Becoming a Leader* (Addison-Wesley, 1989).

- You can surrender to your fears and pass on the job.

- You can attempt to analyze your fear objectively (but as analyst Roger Gould points out, that will probably not result in any significant change).

- You can reflect on your original experience in a concrete way. You were, after all, a child. And you probably didn't like the poem very much, so it was hard to memorize. But most important, although you got scolded and laughed at, your life was not changed in any significant way by the lapse. Neither your grades nor your standing with your classmates suffered. Indeed, everyone forgot your lapse immediately—except you. You have clung to that feeling all these years, without ever thinking about it. Now is the time to think about it.

Reflection and Resolution

Reflection is a major way in which leaders learn from the past. Jim Burke told me, "At Holy Cross, studying with the Jesuits, I had to take twenty-eight hours of scholastic philosophy, which forces you through a logical, disciplined way of thinking. I've often felt this was very important to my business success, because I was naturally intuitive and instinctive, so this overlay of logic was useful. It helped me get through Harvard Business School, which reinforced it. Most of what I've done in business is to look at something and say, 'That's the way to go.' Then I pull myself back and subject it to a very rigorous logic. I'm much more inclined to emotionally arrive at a decision than I am to use logical resources, and the blend has caused me to be reflective. Also, I've always felt that society lacks philosophers. We ought to have people who dedicate their lives just to thinking. We have plenty of economists, and we have all the sciences covered, but only a handful of thinkers. So maybe that makes me reflective. But I think of myself as an activist."

In fact, what we do is a direct result of not only what and how we think, but what and how we feel as well. Roger Gould agreed: "It's how you feel about things that dictates how you behave. Most people don't process their feelings, because thinking is hard work. And abstract thinking doesn't usually lead to a change in behavior. It leads to conflict about change. I use two analytic skills in everything. One is perspective—I always like multiple frames of reference. And I always look for the heart of the issue, the core."

Reflection may be the pivotal way we learn. Consider some of the ways of reflecting: looking back, thinking back, dreaming, journaling, talking

it out, watching last week's game, asking for critiques, going on retreats—
even telling jokes. Jokes are a way of making whatever-it-was understandable and acceptable.

Freud said that the goal of analysis is to make the unconscious conscious. He talks about the importance of anniversaries, for example—the
number of men who die on the same day their fathers died. The anniversary had remained trapped in the unconscious, never reflected on. The
wound experienced on the day had never been given air and allowed to
heal. Reflection is a way of making learning conscious. Reflection gets to
the heart of the matter, the truth of things. After appropriate reflection,
the meaning of the past is known, and the resolution of the experience—
the course of action you must take as a result—becomes clear. I like the
word *resolution,* by the way, and tend to use it in two of its several mean-
ings: a course of action decided upon, and an explanation or solution.
And *resolution* has a musical overtone that I like as well: the progression
of a dissonant chord to a consonant one.

On the subject of reflection, Barbara Corday said, "Unfortunately, too
often it's people's failures that get them to reflect on their experiences.
When you're going along and everything is working well, you don't sit
down and reflect. Which is exactly the moment when you should do it. If
you wait for a giant mistake before you reflect, two things happen. One,
since you're down, you don't get the most out of it, and two, you tend
only to see the mistake, instead of all the moments in which you've also
been correct."

It's true. Most of us are shaped more by negative experiences than by
positive ones. A thousand things happen in a week to each of us, but most
of us remember the few lapses rather than our triumphs, because we don't
reflect. We merely react. Playwright Athol Fugard said that he worked his
way out of a depression by starting every day thinking of ten things that
gave him pleasure. I've found thinking of the things in my life that bring
me pleasure a peaceful and positive way to start the morning, and I've
started doing it regularly. Thinking of the small pleasures around one—
the glow of the morning light on the ocean, the fresh-cut roses next to the
word processor, the tall café latte waiting at the end of a morning walk,
even the dog that wants to be fed—is a much better way to deal with a
perceived failure than to ruminate on it. When you're down, think of the
things you have to look forward to. When you are no longer in the grip
of the mishap, *then* you are ready to reflect on it.

In fact, mistakes contain potent lessons—but only if we think them
through calmly, see where we went wrong, mentally revise what we're
doing, and then act on the revisions. When a great batter strikes out, he

doesn't linger for a moment over the goof, but instead sets about to improve his stance or his swing. And great batters do strike out—Babe Ruth not only set a home run record, he set a strikeout record as well. Think what a great batting average is: .400—which means a great batter fails to get a hit more than half the time. Most of the rest of us, on the other hand, are paralyzed by our goofs. We're so haunted by them, so afraid that we're going to goof again, that we become fearful of doing anything. When jockeys are thrown, they get back on the horse, because they know if they don't, their fear may immobilize them. When an F–14 pilot has to eject, he or she goes up the next day in another plane. Most of us have lesser fears to face—but most of us have to cope with them through thought, before we act again. Reflection comes first, and then strategic action. As Roger Gould phrased it, reflection permits us to process our feelings, understand them, resolve our questions, and get on with our work. Wordsworth defined poetry as strong emotion recollected in tranquillity. That's the time to reflect, in tranquillity—and then to resolve.

The point is not to be the victims of our feelings, jerked this way and that by unresolved emotions, not to be used by our experiences, but to use them and to use them creatively. Just as writers turn experiences from their lives into novels and plays, we can each transform our experiences into grist for our mill. Isak Dinesen said, "Any sorrow can be borne if we can put it in a story." Your accumulated experience is the basis for the rest of your life, and that base is solid and sound to the degree that you have reflected on it, understood it, and arrived at a workable resolution.

Gloria Steinem, like many pioneers, has made a vocation of venturing into uncharted, untested waters. Her approach is direct: "I'm not very reflective. I work out whatever it is by acting or doing or saying it. It's the Midwest in me. In the Midwest, introspection is practically forbidden. As a result, I'm future oriented, which isn't great, because you can only live in the present, not the future. . . . There are learning moments. I think things happen over and over again, and we learn in a spiral, not a straight line . . . and then one day we get it. So I don't have the sensation of reflecting or examining. I have the sensation of, 'Oh, that's why.' If you've experienced the dynamic before, you sort of understand when it's happening again. There's a plateau for a long time, and then a sudden leap forward, and then another plateau. I think of those leaps as learning moments. But I think you often know things intellectually before you understand them emotionally. I wrote a piece about my mother that I can't read, because now I understand it, and it makes me too sad."

As both Steinem and Gould have said, too much intellectualizing tends to paralyze us. But true reflection inspires, informs, and ultimately demands resolution. Steinem leaps first and looks or reflects later. There is something to be said for that headlong approach, but only if you are able to see mistakes, failures, as a basic and vital part of life. Most of us, unfortunately, aren't that wise or that cool-headed. It is the pioneers like Steinem, the ones who head straight for the unmapped territory marked only by the legend "Here there be tygers," who believe so much in what they're doing that they accept the risks inherent in such undertakings as part of the job.

To do anything well requires knowing what it is that you're doing, and you can only know what you're really doing by making the process conscious—reflecting on yourself, reflecting on the task, and coming to a resolution.

As I mentioned in an earlier chapter, Erik Erikson sees our development as a series of resolved conflicts, one for each stage of life. He further postulates that until each conflict is resolved positively, we cannot move to the next stage or conflict.

These conflicts are so basic, and resolving them is so vital, that I've come to see them in much broader terms and a more general frame than Erikson's. We are subject to these conflicts all of our lives, and the way we resolve them determines how we will live. Here is how I would reframe them:

CONFLICTS	RESOLUTIONS
Blind trust vs. Suspicion	Hope
Independence vs. Dependence	Autonomy
Initiative vs. Imitation	Purpose
Industry vs. Inferiority	Competence
Identity vs. Confusion	Integrity
Intimacy vs. Isolation	Empathy
Generosity vs. Selfishness	Maturity
Illusion vs. Delusion	Wisdom

Physicist Niels Bohr said, "There are two kinds of truth, small truth and great truth. You can recognize a small truth because its opposite is a falsehood. The opposite of a great truth is another truth."

Our lives are made less of small truths and falsehoods than of great truths and the truths that are their opposites, which is why the resolution of these basic conflicts is so difficult sometimes. It's almost never a choice between a right and a wrong. For example, hope lies somewhere between blind trust and suspicion, but so does its opposite, despair. And wisdom usually follows illusion, delusion, and disillusion.

Once you have learned to reflect on your experiences until the resolution of your conflicts arises from within you, then you begin to develop your own perspective.

Perspective

John Sculley touched on the need for perspective: "It's important to change your perspective, maybe by living or traveling extensively abroad. Shifting your stance changes you. You take the same set of facts and shift the vantage point and everything looks different. One of the things leaders have to be good at is perspective. Leaders don't necessarily have to invent ideas, but they have to be able to put them in context and add perspective. . . . What I look for in people is the ability to transform their experience into ideas and to put those ideas in context."

What is your perspective? The following questions should give you some idea.

1. When you consider a new project, do you think first of its cost or its benefits?
2. Do you rank profit or progress first?
3. Would you rather be rich or famous?
4. If offered a promotion that required you to move to another city, would you discuss it with your family before accepting it?
5. Would you rather be a small fish in a big pond, or a big fish in a small pond?

There are, of course, no right or wrong answers to these questions, but your answers will tell you something about your perspective. If you think first of the cost of a project or rank profit higher than progress, then your perspective is short-term. A person who would rather be famous than rich is the more ambitious because—unless you're in show biz—fame requires more talent and originality than the making of a fortune. If you would discuss a promotion with your family before accepting it, you're more humane than ambitious. And if you'd rather be a big fish in a small pond, you may lack drive (or you may simply agree with Julius Caesar, who is reputed to have said, "I would rather be first in a small Iberian village than second in Rome").

Perspective is no more and no less than how you see things, your particular frame of reference. Without it, you're flying blind. But it's also your point of view, and as Marvin Minsky, a pioneer in artificial intelligence, said, point of view is worth 80 I.Q. points. Marty Kaplan told me, "I think one of the reasons for the fame or notoriety of this studio [Disney] is that the people who run it have a very strong point of view, which I guess I would add to leadership. . . . To the outside world we couch a rejection in subjective terms. 'Gosh, we just didn't like it.' But inside the company, a decision is not viewed as a kind of soft, mushy, relativistic thing. We have a viewpoint, and a project either works with our viewpoint or doesn't work with our viewpoint."

If you know what you think and what you want, you have a very real advantage. In this era of experts, when we have nutritionists to fine-tune our diets, turn family dogs over to professional trainers and even pet psychologists, and bring in consultants on any major decision, a point of view is not only rare, but valuable. Establishing a pattern that would survive his own demise, the late Morton Downey Jr., became rich and famous almost overnight by becoming the Archie Bunker of late–twentieth-century talk show hosts. It's not so much that people liked his biased, rude, macho act (although some obviously did), it's that they responded to the fact that he had a point of view and that he expressed it without apology. Like the steady stream of bigoted but confident radio and TV pundits that followed him, Downey was admired not so much for what he said, but that he said anything at all.

I am not for a moment suggesting that you emulate television and talk radio's narrow-minded big mouths. In fact, I'd rather you didn't—we have more than enough already. I am suggesting that anyone who wants to express him- or herself fully and truly must have a point of view. Leadership without perspective and point of view isn't leadership—and of course it must be your own perspective, your own point of view. You cannot borrow a point of view any more than you can borrow someone else's eyes. It must be authentic, and if it is, it will be original, because you are an original.

Once you master the arts of reflection, understanding, and resolution, perspective and point of view will follow. Your next task is to figure out what to do with all that.

Tests and Measures

Some people are born knowing what they want to do, and even how to do it. The rest of us aren't so lucky. We have to spend some time figuring out what to do with our lives. Vague goals, such as "I just want to be happy" or "I want to live well" or "I want to make the world a better place" or even "I want to be very, very rich," are nearly useless. But so are overly specific goals, such as "I want to be chairman of the XYZ Corporation" or "I want to be a nuclear physicist" or "I want to discover a cure for the common cold," because they leave out all the other values in life.

Jamie Raskin told me, "One of my heroes is a professor at Harvard Law School named Derek Bell. He told me that it's important not to have any specific ambitions or desires. It's more important to have ambitions in terms of the way you want to live your life, and then the other things will flow out of that."

What do you want? The majority of us go through life, often very success-fully, without ever asking, much less answering, this most basic question.

The most basic answer, of course, is that you want to express yourself fully, for that is the most basic human drive. As one friend put it, "We all want to learn how to use our own voices," and it has led some of us to the peaks and some of us to the depths.

How can *you* best express *you?*

The first test is knowing what you want, knowing your abilities and capacities, and recognizing the difference between the two.

Gloria Anderson said, "I always felt it wasn't right to be like everyone else. I thought I had to meet different standards and do different things." Journalism was an obvious choice of expression for her, because journal-ists, by definition, stand apart from other people. As reporters, they cover the action, rather than taking part in it, and as editors, they have the opportunity to speak out on issues they believe in.

Anne Bryant was first chosen by others. "In elementary school," she said, "I got awards for leadership activities, which always surprised me. In high school, I was asked to be a leader. Of course, I was taller than everyone else, so I sort of loomed over everyone, which may have helped. But I never ran for things. I do like taking charge of things. I always have." Since she likes "taking charge of things," it's not surprising that Bryant became an executive and led an organization, the American Asso-ciation of University Women, with 150,000 members and assets of over $47 million, whose goals include promoting equity for women, self-devel-opment, and positive social change.

Betty Friedan was always an organizer. "In fifth grade, we had a sub-stitute teacher who didn't like children, so I organized a club, the Baddy-Baddy Club, and at a signal from me, everybody dropped their books on the floor and did other things that would irritate the teacher. The princi-pal called me to his office and said, 'You have a great talent for leader-ship. You must use it for good, not evil.' . . . In my adult professional life, I'm theoretically a writer, but I spend much time on my political activity. I organized three of the key organizations of the women's movement and then bowed out of active leadership."

The second test is knowing what drives you, knowing what gives you satisfaction, and knowing the difference between the two.

Roger Gould said, "I remember dreaming every night about how I was going to save everyone, not just me, but everyone. I must have been 12 or 13 at the time." So Gould grew up to become a psychoanalyst, a kind of secular savior.

Mathilde Krim needed to be useful: "I spent three summers working on an isolated farm. It was horrible, but it gave me a fantastic feeling of self-confidence. I thought if I could do that, I could do anything. I did it because it was the right thing to do at the time, and I tried to do a good job of it, to be really useful, but it was very hard." This was a good start for someone who went on to become a scientist and was a pioneer in the fight to defeat AIDS. "I spend all my time on the AIDS issue now," she told me. "I'm incapable of doing anything else."

John Sculley's route was slightly more circuitous, although no less logical: "I've always had a sort of insatiable curiosity about things, everything, electronics for a while, then art, then art history and architecture, all sorts of stuff. When I get interested in something, I become totally absorbed by it, and I always run out of physical energy before my curiosity is satisfied. I never intended to become a businessman. That was the furthest thing from my mind. I thought I'd be an inventor or architect or designer. I was interested in visual things, and I was always interested in ideas and comfortable with them—in everything from calculus to architecture." It's hard to imagine a better background for heading an innovative, design-savvy technology firm such as Apple.

The point of the first two tests is that once you recognize, or admit, that your primary goal is to fully express yourself, you will find the means to achieve the rest of your goals—given your abilities and capacities, along with your interests and biases. On the other hand, if your primary aim is to prove yourself, you'll run into trouble sooner or later, as Ed, the lead character in the cautionary tale in chapter one, did. The man who follows his father into law or medicine in order to prove himself, or the woman who decides to be a stockbroker to show that she can make a lot of money, is playing the fool's game and will almost inevitably fail and/or be unhappy.

The third test is knowing what your values and priorities are, knowing what the values and priorities of your organization are, and measuring the difference between the two.

If you've found a way to express yourself fully and well, and are reasonably satisfied with your pace and performance, but you don't feel you'll get very far in your present position, it may be that you're in sync with yourself, but you're out of sync with your environment—your partner, company, or organization.

Herb Alpert said, "I used to record for a major company. And I didn't like the way I was being treated. I was sort of being fed through their computer. And it just seemed like they were on the wrong track. . . . I had this spark of an idea for Tijuana Brass, which involved overdubbing the trumpet, which I was experimenting with in my own little garage studio at home. They said it was impossible, that it violated union regulations, because I'd be putting some musician out of work. Well, they missed the point altogether. So I just decided that when I had my own company, the artist would be the heartbeat of the company and his needs would come first."

Alpert and Jerry Moss went on to found A&M Records, which is legendary for its fine treatment of artists, although their then partner Gil Friesen said, "A&M has a certain reputation for being artist oriented and having a sort of family atmosphere, but it's nothing we consciously do. It isn't calculated. . . . Actually, I think you do it by not doing it, by not managing very much."

Alpert's decision to start his own company in order to create the kind of environment he wanted to work in was as ultimately sensible as it was seemingly radical: he and A&M became major industry powers.

In the same spirit, Gloria Anderson founded her own newspaper. She said, "*Miami Today* was my first opportunity to do things my way, and I'm very proud of it. But when I realized that my partner didn't share my vision and never would, I decided to move on and do something on my own."

Anne Bryant, on the other hand, recommends walking more carefully. "Too often you come into a new job on a wave of fresh energy and, not by design, you tend to debunk what's been previously done. That's very hard on the people who've been with the organization for a while. It's better to try to put yourself in their shoes and acknowledge the good things that have been done and reinforce those things, before going forward with your own plans. If the existing personnel feel supported and are made to feel a part of the new plans, they're thrilled."

Being in sync with your organization is almost as important as being in sync with yourself, in other words. Some leaders are inevitably drawn to form their own organizations, while others, like Bryant, prefer the path of accommodation.

The fourth test is—having measured the differences between what you want and what you're able to do, and between what drives you and what satisfies you, and between what your values are and what the organization's values are—are you able and willing to overcome those differences?

In the first instance, the issues are fairly basic. Almost every one of us has, at one point in our lives, wanted to be an NFL quarterback or a movie star or a jazz singer, but we simply didn't have the requisite equipment. And although I've said—and believe—that you can learn anything you want to learn, certain occupations require gifts beyond learning. I know a highly successful radiologist who has always dreamed of being a singer, but he has no voice. Instead of abandoning his dream, he writes songs. A would-be quarterback who's fast and smart, but who weighs only 140 pounds, might well become a coach or manager. Or he might organize a Saturday afternoon touch-football league among his friends and co-workers.

Whatever it is you want to do, you shouldn't let fear get in your way. Fear, for most leaders, is less a crippler than a motivator. As Brooke Knapp said, "I started flying because I was afraid of it. If you give not 90 percent or 95 percent but 100 percent, you can make anything happen. The greatest opportunity for growth lies in overcoming things you're afraid of." She went on to become one of America's leading flyers.

In the second instance, the issue is more complex. We all know people who are driven to succeed, never mind at what or how, who are never satisfied, and who are often unhappy. It is entirely possible to succeed and satisfy yourself simultaneously, but only if you are wise enough and honest enough to admit what you want and recognize what you need.

For the third instance I'll refer again to that feckless fellow Ed. If he had thought more about what he wanted and what his company needed, he wouldn't have driven himself off the track. But he spent his energies doing and proving, not being. Some corporate cultures are so rigid that they require absolute obedience to the corporate line. Others are flexible, adjustable, and adaptable. By knowing the flex in yourself and the flex in the organization, you'll know whether you're a fit or not.

Desire

Brooke Knapp said, "Some people are lucky enough to be born with desire and the ability to make things happen. I've always had a desire to achieve. It's not calculated. It's as natural as eating to me."

Former CalFed CEO Robert Dockson was lucky, too. "I don't think you can be taught dedication, purpose, and a sense of vision," he said. "I don't know where that comes from."

If Knapp is right, and desire is as natural as eating, then it exists in all of us. And while Dockson may be right that it can't be taught, it can be activated. Virtually every one of us was born with a hunger for life itself, with what I call a passion for the promises of life, and that passion can take one to the heights. Unfortunately, in too many of us, it devolves into drive. Entrepreneur Larry Wilson defined *the difference between desire and drive as the difference between expressing yourself and proving yourself.*

In a perfect world, everyone would be encouraged to express, but not required to prove him- or herself. But neither the world nor we are perfect. In order to avoid booby-trapping ourselves, then, we must understand that drive is healthy only when married to desire.

Drive divorced from desire is often hazardous, sometimes lethal, while drive in the service of desire is often both productive and rewarding. Knapp, like the other leaders I spoke with, has that passion for the promises of life, and the drive to realize her passion. "I was raised with eight boys on my block," she said, "and I was stronger than all of them. I was the one with the energy and enthusiasm and drive and determination, so I became the leader."

Although she went through a docile period, her desire emerged intact some years later. "I'm an entrepreneur in spirit," she told me. "I see a window of opportunity and take advantage of it. Jet Airways [a company she founded that flies executives around the country] happened almost by accident. Deregulation had killed off a lot of small airlines, so corporations were having a tough time getting their people into small towns, and I wanted to buy a Lear Jet." Her desire to have her own plane and the need for cost-effective executive transportation were happily combined. Knapp remains restless and inventive. After founding Jet Airways, she managed a securities portfolio and became involved in the Florida citrus industry and with high-end real estate in southern California.

Barbara Corday credits her success partly to enthusiasm. "A corporation, or a show, is only as strong as the caring and enthusiasm that the people who are involved in it on a daily basis put into it. And I don't think you can expect caring and enthusiasm from people you, the leader, don't care about and are not conscious of. . . . I think my enthusiasm is catching. I think when I get on a project, if I love it, I can make you love it."

Jamie Raskin agreed that passion is infectious: "If you hold your ground and make your conviction known, people will come around. I'm committed to radical principles. As Oscar Wilde said, 'I'm on the left, which is the side of the heart, as opposed to the right, which is the side of the liver.'"

Gloria Anderson summed it up. "You can't make being a leader your principal goal, any more than you can make being happy your goal. In both cases, it has to be the result, not the cause."

Mastery

When I asked Marty Kaplan to describe the qualities of leadership, he said, "Competence, first. A true sense of mastery of the task at hand. Another is the ability to articulate, because if someone is a complete master of what they need to know, but is unable to explain why I should care about it, or want to help, then they can't get me to support them. And something I prefer to see in a leader, but isn't essential, is a level of human sensitivity, tact, compassion, and diplomacy. I've known leaders who have had none of it and nevertheless were leaders, but those who have had that quality have moved and inspired me more."

He's right. "A true sense of mastery of the task at hand." Leaders haven't simply practiced their vocation or profession. They've mastered it. They've learned everything there is to know about it, and then surrendered to it. For example, the late Fred Astaire mastered the choreography, and then surrendered to it. He became one with it, so it was impossible to say where he stopped and the routine began. He was the routine. Franklin Roosevelt mastered the presidency; Jimmy Carter was mastered by it.

Such mastery requires absolute concentration, the full deployment of oneself. Astaire had it. That's what got our attention before he did anything. Martin Luther King, Jr., galvanized America with a few words. He didn't simply have a dream, he was the dream, just as Magic Johnson was the Lakers and Bill Gates is Microsoft.

The Chinese practice something called *wushu,* which Mark Salzman, an American writer who has lived in China, describes as a means of achieving "perfect form and concentration. [One's] movements become instinctive and express a harmony of mind and body that the Chinese believe is crucial to spiritual as well as physical health. In classical *wushu* . . . the *wushujia* devotes most of his training time to the practice of *taolu,* or routines . . . choreographed sequences of movements, one to twenty minutes in length, that must be carried out according to strict esthetic, technical and conceptual guidelines. . . . An unbroken thread of intent must exist between the movements of a *taolu,* like the invisible line that passes through and connects the separate pieces of Chinese calligraphy."

Salzman quotes his instructor, Pan Qingfui, a master whose nickname is Iron Fist, as saying, "The eyes are the most important, because in them you can see a person's *yi* [will or intent]." Salzman goes on to say, "Chinese boxing depends on *yi* for its strength, so you have to train your eyes. . . . You must practice the *taolu* as if you had complete confidence in your strength, as if a single blow of your hand could destroy your opponent. . . . You must hit him with your eyes, your heart. Your hands will follow."

Author George Leonard writes of mastery, "Experienced pilots can tell a lot about how good another pilot is by the way he or she gets into the pilot's seat and straps on his or her safety harness. There are some people who are so obviously on that they give us a lift just by walking into the room. [Some people] can demonstrate mastery simply by the way [they] stand."

Leonard describes some other elements of mastery, too: "The path of mastery is built on unrelenting practice, but it's also a place of adventure. . . . Whether it's a sport or an art or some other work, those we call masters are shamelessly enthusiastic about their calling. . . . Those on the path of mastery are willing to take chances, play the fool. . . . The most powerful learning is that which is most like play. . . . The word *generous* comes from the same root as *genial, generative,* and *genius.* . . . [The genius] has the ability to give everything and hold nothing back. Perhaps, in fact, genius can be defined in terms of this givingness."

Barbara Corday said of a kind of self-mastery, "In my business, if you love something and want to make it happen, you can convince other people to go along with you. Personal style, personal belief, a tremendous desire to make something happen, tenacity, the ability to never give up, no matter how many people say no, are vital. I am in a business that is built on rejection, daily rejection. You have to be able to go beyond that, to simply turn a deaf ear to rejection, to keep moving forward, to build into your own psyche the ability to stay true to yourself and what you believe in. If you had a good idea yesterday, it's going to be a good idea tomorrow, and just because you haven't convinced anyone to go with it today doesn't mean you won't convince someone to go with it tomorrow."

Mastery, absolute competence, is mandatory for a leader. But it's also more fun than anything else you'll ever do. Jim Burke said, "It should be fun, the process ought to be exciting and fun. The person who's not having any fun is doing something wrong. Either his environment is stultifying or he's off base himself."

Roger Gould simply loves what he does. "I'd never known a psychiatrist and didn't really know what they did, but it seemed right for me. I like people and love talking to them on a deep level. I love being an analyst. I have a great feeling for people and like helping them. But at the core of it all is a profound curiosity about the thinking process. That's what drives me."

Strategic Thinking

There's an old saying: "Unless you're the lead dog, the scenery never changes." To extend that thought, for the leader the scenery is always changing. Everything is new. Because, by definition, each leader is unique, his or her circumstances are also unique.

Sydney Pollack, when asked if leadership could be taught, responded, "It's hard to teach anything that can't be broken down into repeatable and unchanging elements. Driving a car, flying an airplane—you can reduce those things to a series of maneuvers that are always executed in the same way. But with something like leadership, just as with art, you reinvent the wheel every single time you apply the principle."

Robert Dockson agreed: "Leaders aren't technicians."

Creativity is required, then, for the banker as well as the motion picture director. The creative process that underlies strategic thinking is infinitely complex, and as unexplainable finally as its inner mechanism, but there are basic steps in the process that can be identified. When you reduce something to its most elemental state, its nuclear core, you can generalize from there.

First, whether you're planning a novel or a corporate reorganization, you have to know where you're going to end up. Mountain climbers don't start climbing from the bottom of the mountain. They look at where they want to go, and work backward to where they're starting from. Like a mountain climber, once you have the summit in view, you figure out all the ways you might get there. Then you play with those—altering, connecting, comparing, reversing, and imagining—finally choosing one or two routes.

Second, you flesh out those routes, elaborate them, revise them, make a kind of map of them, complete with possible pitfalls and traps as well as rewards.

Third, you examine this map objectively, as if you were not its maker, locate all its soft spots, and eliminate them or change them.

Finally, when you have finished all that, you set out to climb your mountain.

Frances Hesselbein and her husband and their families were part of Johnstown, Pennsylvania, for four generations. They had a communications business, and she worked as a Girl Scout volunteer there, but she also did management training for Girl Scout Councils around the country. Asked to take over the CEO slot of the local council temporarily, she agreed. Six years later, although she hadn't applied for the job, she was made executive director of the Girl Scouts of the USA. She and her husband moved to New York City and set about reorganizing the Scouts, to reflect everything she had learned on her way up the ladder.

"The first thing we did," Hesselbein said, "was to develop a corporate planning system in which planning and management were synonymous. It was a common planning system for 335 local councils and the national organization. We developed a corporate planning monograph to mobilize the energy of 600,000 adult volunteers in order to carry out our mission to help young girls grow up and reach their highest potential as women. Today, our people feel we've achieved more unity and cohesion than anyone can remember.

"I just felt there was a compelling need to have a clear planning system that defined roles, differentiating between the volunteers, the operational staff, and the policy planners, one that permitted whatever was going on in the smallest troop—needs, trends, whatever—to flow through to the policy makers, so they had a clear idea of what was going on and what needed to go on. We have three million members, and we really listen to the girls and their parents, and we've devised ways to reach out to the girls wherever they are. We say, 'We have something of value to offer you, but you in return have something to offer us. We respect your values and culture, and if you open our handbooks, even if you're a minority, a Navajo, you're there.'

"I think we have the best staff anywhere. They're wonderful, and my job is to keep opening up the system and increase their freedom and scope. I can't stand to box people in. Everyone's in a circle. It's rather organic. If I'm in the center, then there are seven bubbles around me, and the next circle would be group directors, and then team directors, and so on. Nothing moves up or down, but rather laterally, across. It's so fluid and flexible that people who're used to a hierarchy have a bit of trouble adjusting, but it works. We sell it to outside groups.

"But the best thing about it is that every girl in America can look at the program and see herself."

There are risks to assume in making the results of your strategic thinking real. But as Carlos Castaneda said, "The basic difference between an ordinary man and a warrior is that a warrior takes everything as a challenge, while an ordinary man takes everything as a blessing or a curse."

Unless you are willing to take risks, you will suffer paralyzing inhibitions, and you will never do what you are capable of doing. Mistakes—missteps—are necessary for actualizing your vision, and necessary steps toward success.

Synthesis

Finally, the leader combines all the means of expression, in order to act effectively.

Little children are naturally creative, and so are the elderly. Novelist Carlos Fuentes said, "I really think youth is something you win from age. You are rather old and stupid when you are young. The youngest men I ever met in my life were Luis Buñuel, who made his greatest films between the ages of 60 and 80, and Arthur Rubinstein, a man who became a genius at 80, being able to strike a note by raising his hand to heaven and making it fall exactly as Beethoven and Chopin demanded. Pablo Picasso painted his most erotic and passionate works when in his 80s. These are men who earned their youth. It took them 80 years to become young."

I think what Fuentes was getting at was that, subject to all the usual peer, familial, and social pressures, we lose track of ourselves when we are adolescents. We become lost in the crowd, more connected and responsive to it than to ourselves, and so we lose our ability to create, because creation is the province of the individual, not the committee.

But leaders, having achieved self-possession, have long since recovered their creative powers too, and have continued to grow. We tend to think of growth in quantitative terms: heights and weights. When our bodies stop growing, our minds stop growing, or so we think. But, as the leaders I talked with have shown in their own lives, our intellectual and emotional growth doesn't have to stall, nor should it. Leaders differ from others in their constant appetite for knowledge and experience, and as their worlds widen and become more complex, so too do their means of understanding.

Dialectical thinking, a variation on the Socratic dialogue, is one such means. It presumes that reality is dynamic rather than static, and therefore seeks relationships between ideas, to aim at synthesis. You might find it useful to think of reflection and perspective as two horns, with synthesis balanced between them.

Frances Hesselbein demonstrates synthesis as she describes her approach to her work with the Girl Scouts: "First, you have to figure out how to organize your job, the management of time, what your responsibilities are. Second, you have to learn to lead, not contain. Third, you have to have a clear sense of who you are and a sense of mission, a clear understanding of it, and you must be sure that your principles are congruent with the organization's principles. Fourth, you have to demonstrate through your behavior all the things you believe a leader and a follower should do. Fifth, you need a great sense of freedom and scope so that you can free the people who work with you to live up to their potential. If you believe in the team approach, you must believe in people and their potential. And you must demand a great deal of them, but be consistent."

John Sculley saw synthesis as the difference between management and leadership. "Leadership is often confused with other things, specifically management. But management requires an entirely different set of skills. As I see it, leadership revolves around vision, ideas, direction, and has more to do with inspiring people as to direction and goals than with day-to-day implementation. . . . One can't lead unless he can leverage more than his own capabilities. . . . You have to be capable of inspiring other people to do things without actually sitting on top of them with a checklist—which is management, not leadership."

Robert Terry, formerly an executive at the Hubert H. Humphrey Institute of Public Affairs, defines leadership as "a fundamental and profound engagement with the world and the human condition."

Roger Gould demonstrated that engagement when he said, "Once you have a vision that you've tested over and over again, you've got the tiger by the tail. You almost can't stop leading, because that would mean being unfaithful to your vision of reality."

Betty Friedan concurred, saying, "When I see a need, I get people together to do something about it. My version of religion is 'You are responsible.'"

For all their particular talents, these leaders see themselves less as soloists than as collaborators.

Robert Dockson said, "The leader guides people, he doesn't force them, and he always treats them fairly. . . . Too many people claim that our only responsibility is to our shareholders. I believe we're responsible to them, but we're also responsible to our employees, our customers, and the community at large. There's something wrong with the private enterprise system if it doesn't recognize its responsibility to the community."

Former Red Cross director Richard Schubert, too, believes in relating well to others: "How you attract and motivate people determines how successful you'll be as a leader. Above all, the Golden Rule applies. Whether it's an employee or a customer or a senior vice president, the leader treats people the way he would like to be treated. Ninety-six percent of our people at disaster sites are volunteers. If we don't attract the right people and motivate them positively, we aren't going to make it."

Leaders who trust their co-workers are, in turn, trusted by them. Trust, of course, cannot be acquired, but can only be given. Leadership without mutual trust is a contradiction in terms. Trust resides squarely between faith and doubt. Leaders always have faith in themselves, their abilities, their co-workers, and their mutual possibilities. But leaders also have sufficient doubt to question, challenge, probe, and thereby progress. In the same way, his or her co-workers must believe in the leader, themselves, and their combined strength, but they must feel sufficiently confident to question, challenge, probe, and test, too. Maintaining that vital balance between faith and doubt, preserving that mutual trust, is a primary task for any leader.

Vision, inspiration, empathy, trustworthiness are manifestations of a leader's judgment and character. Former university president Alfred Gottschalk said, "Character is vital in a leader, the basis for everything else. Other qualities would include the ability to inspire trust, some entrepreneurial talent, imagination, perseverance, steadfastness of purpose. . . . Character, perseverance, and imagination are the sine qua non of leadership."

An Irish proverb is pertinent: "You've got to do your own growing, no matter how tall your grandfather is."

All of these leaders have consciously constructed their own lives and the contexts in which they live and work. Each is not just actor, but playwright, hammer and anvil, and each, in his or her own way, is altering the larger context.

The means of expression are the steps to leadership:

1. Reflection leading to resolution.
2. Resolution leading to perspective.
3. Perspective leading to point of view.
4. Point of view leading to tests and measures.
5. Tests and measures leading to desire.
6. Desire leading to mastery.
7. Mastery leading to strategic thinking.
8. Strategic thinking leading to full self-expression.
9. The synthesis of full self-expression = leadership.

Leadership is first being, then doing. Everything the leader does reflects what he or she is. So that is the next turn in our tale. . . .

JUDGMENT TRUMPS
EXPERIENCE (2007)

(coauthored by Noel Tichy)

AS THESE LATE NOVEMBER DAYS FADE away, the critical Iowa caucus looms ever closer—less than six weeks away. Which explains why the rhetoric of the two leading Democratic candidates is becoming more shrill but also more clarifying.

Hillary Clinton and Barack Obama have taken off their gloves. In one corner stands the champion of experience, with the best executive coach in the free world at her side and a dog-eared playbook of strategies that have won in the past. Standing in the opposite corner is a young contender, fairly new at the game, underweight and probably overmatched, but a natural, as they say. Mr. Obama and his handlers are putting their money on his judgment, disdaining the experience card as a stale rerun of earlier campaigns, skewering Mrs. Clinton's twisty judgments about Iraq, and subtly pushing the present over the legacy of the '60s, destiny over dynasty.

One newspaper article on Mrs. Clinton's latest TV ad noted that it mentioned her experience five times. Bloggers also highlight the themes of experience and judgment whenever they describe the ever more heated fight between the Democratic front-runners.

Where do we put our money? First, let us cite Ted Sorenson, one of John F. Kennedy's closest advisers and speechwriters. When asked about his former boss's judgment, Mr. Sorenson responded, "I cannot empha-

This article was originally published in the *Wall Street Journal*, November 29, 2007.

size how important that elusive quality is; far more important than organization, structure, procedures and machinery. These are all important, yes, but nothing compared to judgment."

After a five-year study of leadership covering virtually all sectors of American life, we came to the inescapable conclusion that judgment regularly trumps experience. Our central finding is that judgment is the core, the nucleus of exemplary leadership. With good judgment, little else matters. Without it, nothing else matters.

Take any leader, a U.S. president, a Fortune 100 CEO, a big-league coach, wartime general, you name it. Chances are you remember them for their best and worst calls. Can anyone forget that Harry Truman issued the order to drop the first atom bomb? Or Kennedy's handling of the Cuban missile crisis? When Nixon comes to mind, so does Watergate. The first George Bush: "Read my lips." Clinton? Monica. George W.? Iraq.

Leadership is, at its marrow, the chronicle of judgment calls. These will inevitably write the leader's legacy. Don't get us wrong. We are not discounting the importance of experience. Seminal and appropriate experiences must be drawn on and understood before judgments can be informed. But experience is no guarantee of good judgment. There is a huge difference between 20 years of experience that advances one's learning and one year of experience repeated 20 times.

In fact, there are numerous times when past experiences can prevent wise judgments. Barbara Tuchman long ago observed how generals tend to fight the last war, refusing to face new realities, almost always with disastrous consequences. And often, especially in today's dizzying world, we need to understand what Zen Buddhists call the "beginner's mind," which recognizes the value of fresh insight unfettered by experience. In this more contemporary view, the compelling idea is the novel one. Perhaps no one articulated the nature of the beginner's mind better than the composer Hector Berlioz when he said of his more popular rival Camille Saint-Saëns: "He knows everything. All he lacks is inexperience."

Judgment isn't quite an unnatural act, but it also doesn't come naturally. And speaking from decades of experience, we're not sure how to teach it. (We know it can be learned.) Wisely processed experience, reflection, valid sources of timely information, openness to the unbidden and character are critical components of judgment as well. As David McCullough reminds us over and over again, "Character counts in the presidency more than any other single quality."

Yes, Mrs. Clinton, experience is not without value. But judgment, fed by solid character, should determine the choice of our next president.

THE CRUCIBLES OF AUTHENTIC
LEADERSHIP (2004)

IT WAS THE PRACTICE OF RALPH WALDO EMERSON to ask old friends he had not seen in a while: "What's become clear to you since we last met?" As this volume makes clear, those engaged in the study of leadership have learned an enormous amount in the century or so since the enterprise began to evolve from the study of great men. The 20th century was marked by the emergence of some of the most powerful and disturbing leaders in human history. Millions died as a direct result of failed or evil leadership—in the death camps of the Third Reich but also in the Soviet Union and in famine-ravished China. The "butcher's bill" of the 20th century is a reminder of why we study leadership in the first place. Our very lives depend on it. That has never been more true than it is today, because one consequence of the extraordinary leadership of Franklin Delano Roosevelt was the creation of genuine weapons of mass destruction. I bring these matters up, not because any of you need a capsule history lesson, but because it is important to remember that the quality of all our lives is dependent on the quality of our leadership. The context in which we study leadership is very different from the context in which we study, say, astronomy. By definition, leaders wield power, and so we study them with the same self-interested intensity with which we study diabetes and other life-threatening diseases. Only when we understand leaders, will we be able to control them.

I would argue that context always counts when it comes to leadership, and, in the next few pages, I want to examine certain enduring issues and questions related to leadership in the context of today. I want to look at

This chapter was originally published in *The Nature of Leadership,* edited by John Antonakis, Anna T. Cianciolo, and Robert J. Sternberg (Sage, 2004).

how recent events and trends are reshaping contemporary ideas about leadership.

In the United States at least, leadership studies changed in some basic way on Sept. 11, 2001. As the nation watched, in horror, the television footage of people fleeing the World Trade Center and, in even greater horror, the collapse of the Twin Towers, I realized, as so many others did, that this was one of the transformational events of our time. One immediate consequence of the terrorist assaults on New York and the Pentagon was to make leadership a matter for public discussion in the United States in a way it has not been since World War II. Leadership became central to the public conversation—displacing the endless background noise about celebrity and pushing aside even worried talk about the sorry state of the economy. People in other parts of the world have been dealing with the ugly realities of international terrorism for decades, and, to them, the stunned horror of Americans must have seemed more than a little naïve. But the United States has long had the luxury of studying leadership with the leisurely detachment that only those in peaceful, prosperous nations can afford.

The assault on a non-military target in the paradigmatic American city was more stunning, in many ways, than Pearl Harbor. Not since the Civil War had ideologically motivated violence occurred on such a scale in a city in the United States. Americans are still sorting out the consequences of the attacks of 9/11 and will continue to do so for decades. But, with the collapse of the Twin Towers, came a new awareness that leadership is more than a matter of who looks best on television. Since 9/11, government officials have been scrutinized for evidence of leadership ability with an intensity usually seen only in wartime. And, indeed, in describing how then New York City Mayor Rudolph Giuliani and others responded to al Qaeda's assault, the media referred repeatedly to the larger-than-life leaders of World War II. The iconic leader du jour was unquestionably Winston Churchill. It was noted, for instance, that Karen Hughes, then special assistant to President George W. Bush, kept a plaque on her desk that bore Churchill's stirring line: "I was not the lion but it fell to me to give the lion's roar." The invocation of Churchill was a secular prayer for help, but it was also evidence of a shift in the very idea of leadership—a return to a more heroic, more inspirational definition than had been the fashion for decades. In the rubble of Ground Zero, people did not want a leader who could organize cross-functional teams; they longed for a leader for the ages, a sage and savior to lead them out of hell.

For those who have spent their lives studying leadership, 9/11 was a compelling reminder that war and other violent crises are inevitably crucibles from which leaders emerge. It was fascinating to watch how Rudy Giuliani was transformed in the days following the attacks from a lame-duck mayor with a reputation for mean-spiritedness into "Churchill in a baseball cap," as one phrasemaker dubbed him. Almost daily, CNN and the *New York Times* released first-draft case studies of leadership in action. Giuliani's performance was so full of lessons about leadership that he got a best-selling book on the subject out of it. And indeed his behavior in the wake of the attacks underscored many truisms about leadership, including how it can emerge in unlikely candidates and how it frequently endures only as long as the crisis itself. Giuliani, who served New York City tirelessly during those days, standing in for slain fathers of the bride and comforting both grieving relatives and the city as a whole, richly deserved to be named *Time* magazine's Person of the Year. But it remains to be seen whether he will again find himself in a position that allows his proven leadership ability to shine. History has a way of throwing leaders up and then covering them over, Ozymandias-style. After Churchill gave the lion's roar, he spent several decades as a Sunday painter, and Giuliani, too, may quietly disappear into a successful law practice.

Whatever else 9/11 meant, it was a vivid reminder that one of the sweeter uses of adversity continues to be its ability to bring leadership to the fore. What Abigail Adams wrote to son John Quincy Adams in the tumult of 1780 is still true today: "These are the times in which a genius would wish to live. It is not in the still calm of life, or in the repose of a pacific station, that great challenges are formed . . . great necessities call out great virtues." In 2001 and 2002, when Robert Thomas and I were doing the research for *Geeks & Geezers: How Era, Values, and Defining Moments Shape Leaders*, we interviewed almost 50 leaders—some 75 and older, the rest 35 and younger. In every case, we found that their leadership had emerged after some defining experience, or crucible, as we called it. These were often ordeals, and, among the older leaders, they often occurred in wartime. The crucibles of our leaders included such personal tragedies as television journalist Mike Wallace's discovery of the body of his son after an accident in Greece and global business pioneer Sidney Rittenberg's harrowing 16 years in Chinese prisons, much of it in solitary confinement, often in the dark. In a foreword to our book, David Gergen, head of the Center for Public Leadership at Harvard's John F. Kennedy School of Government, describes the crucible in which Truman discovered that he was a leader. We tend to think of Truman as the one-time haberdasher whose leadership emerged only after the death of Roosevelt. But, as Gergen recounts, Truman was tested during the Great War on the battlefields of France. The head of an artillery battery, he was in the Vosges

Mountains when his position was shelled by the Germans. His men panicked, and Truman's horse panicked as well, falling on him and almost killing him. But, as historian David McCullough writes in his prize-winning biography of Truman, the future president crawled out from under his horse and overcame his own fear, screaming profanities at his men until most of them returned to their posts. Truman's men never forgot that his courage under fire had saved their lives, and Truman discovered that he had a taste for leadership as well as a gift for it.

Again and again, we found that something magical happens in the crucible—an alchemy whereby fear and suffering are transformed into something glorious and redemptive. This process reveals, if it does not create, leadership, the ability to inspire and move others to action. We found intelligence, optimism, and other traits traditionally associated with leadership present in all our subjects, but those traits are no guarantee that the alchemy of leadership will take place. Countless gifted people are broken by suffering. But our leaders discovered themselves in their crucibles, for reasons we still do not fully understand. However searing the experience, our leaders were able to make sense of it or organize meaning around it—meaning that subsequently attracted followers. Instead of being defeated by their ordeal, each of our leaders saw it as a heroic journey. Whatever their age, these men and women created their own legends. Without being untruthful, they constructed new, improved versions of themselves. In many cases—as in Truman's—the ordeal and the leader's interpretation of it led others to follow the newly revealed leader.

In the model of leadership development that grew out of that research, successful individuals all evidenced four essential competencies—adaptive capacity, the ability to engage others through shared meaning, a distinctive voice, and integrity. Often, these abilities were evident to some degree before their ordeals, but they were intensified by the crucible experience. Of all these abilities, the most important was adaptive capacity. All our leaders had an extraordinary gift for coping with whatever life threw at them. I believe that adaptive capacity is essentially creativity—the ability to take disparate things and turn them into something new and useful. Indeed, it is no accident that there is a convergence between leadership studies and studies of creativity—a convergence that dates back to the first studies of Darwin, Einstein, and other geniuses, or thought leaders. When we speak of exemplary leadership, we are often talking about exemplary, creative problem solving—the discovery of new solutions to unprecedented problems.

But to return to the lessons of 9/11. During the 1950s, no one who heard Marshall McLuhan speak so confidently of the global village or the extent to which the medium is the message had any idea how truly prescient he was. But the terrorist attacks of 2001 underscored that ours is indeed one world, albeit a profoundly splintered one, and that television and more recent technologies are its primary mediators. Here were multinational terrorists dispatched by an individual holed up in an apartment, or a cave, in Afghanistan or elsewhere in the Middle East. Digital technology was used to advance a medieval ideology, with orders and money transferred in a nanosecond halfway across the planet. Globalization has created a host of new dangers that require a new kind of leadership—one that is, above all, collaborative. It was the inability of security agencies in the United States to work effectively together that allowed the 9/11 terrorists to enter and remain in the country and to learn how to fly a jet into a skyscraper at American flight schools. And global terrorism is only one contemporary threat that requires a multinational, collaborative response. Disease, poverty, and the oppression of minorities, women, and political dissidents are urgent international concerns. As the outbreak in 2003 of severe acute respiratory syndrome, or SARS, illustrated, the ability of almost anyone to jump on a plane and fly to some distant city has created the real possibility that future flights will spread deadly plagues with unprecedented ease and rapidity.

In the months that led up to the toppling of the regime of Iraq's Saddam Hussein in 2003, much was made in the media, and rightfully so, of President George W. Bush's failure to build a global coalition. The President's decision to enter Iraq with support from only a handful of nations (Great Britain, Australia, and Poland, among them) was widely seen as a leadership failure, despite the defeat of Hussein in record time. The critique of the president reflected more than political differences on whether American military action was appropriate only if legitimized by the United Nations. The criticism reflected an understanding that coalition building is one of the essential competencies of all leaders—in some ways, the defining one.

Among the committed coalition builders President Bush might have emulated was his father. Before the first Gulf War, President George Herbert Walker Bush doggedly wooed world leaders. When the president was not smiling over banquet tables himself, he dispatched his secretary of state, James Baker, on eight consensus-building trips abroad, trips that took Baker to 18 European capitals. The result was that the United States went to war as part of a genuine "coalition of the willing." We cannot know what father said to son in private conversation before the Iraqi conflict. But we do know what the older Bush counseled in a speech at Tufts University in February, 2003. "You've got to reach out to the other person," he said, describing what leaders in an interconnected world must do. "You've got to convince them that long-term friendship should trump short-term adversity." The senior Bush was articulating what democratic leaders have always known. In a society in which power must be given freely, not coerced, leaders make alliances by persuading others that their interests and fates are intertwined. As I write this in 2003, it is clear that the United States needs allies more than ever, as disorder continues in post-Hussein Iraq and a growing number of Iraqis perceive the forces of the United States and her handful of allies as occupiers, rather than liberators.

Coalition building is also an essential element of corporate leadership. Until American business was roiled by recent corporate scandals, we had long been guilty of treating CEOs and other business leaders as demigods whose success was a unilateral achievement resulting from their special genius. This tradition dates back at least as far as our deification of such business titans as Thomas Edison and Henry Ford, and it resurged during the late 1970s when Lee Iacocca was hailed as the savior of the American auto industry. In retrospect, the lionization of anyone connected with the battered U.S. auto industry seems like a cruel joke. But we forget, now that so many corporate heads have rolled, how recently CEOs were treated both as celebrities and as thought leaders whose public comments were scrutinized for hidden wisdom like tea leaves. In many ways, the rise of the celebrity CEO was a regression to the era when great institutions were thought to be the lengthened shadows of great men. The late 20th-century version of that durable myth differed only in conceding that a few great institutions—such as the Martha Stewart empire—were lengthened shadows of great women. But as Patricia Ward Biederman and I write in *Organizing Genius: The Secrets of Creative Collaboration,* one has almost always been too small a number for greatness. Whatever their sphere, authentic leaders know, even if they do not bruit it around, that their power is a consequence of their ability to recruit the talent of others to the collective enterprise. The Lone Ranger has never been as dead as he is today. In all but the simplest undertaking, great things are done by alliances, not by larger-than-life individuals, however powerful they may seem.

I doubt that the world was ever so simple that a single heroic leader, however capable, could solve its problems unilaterally. Even the Biblical tale of Noah underscores the importance of collaboration. But certainly today's world requires unprecedented coalition-building. The European Union may be the paradigmatic response to this changed reality. For those of us who experienced World War II first-hand, it is heartening to see such a high level of economic and political cooperation among nations that were so recently at one another's throats. And more and more coalitions, created and maintained by collaborative leaders, will be required in the years ahead. The pace of change is not slowing. It is accelerating as never before. Ever-changing problems require faster, smarter, more inventive solutions, solutions that can only be achieved collaboratively. In recent years, even the way leaders make decisions has changed. The day is all but over when a leader has the leisure to digest all the facts and then to act. As psychologist Karl Weick has pointed out, today's leaders are more often required to act first, assess the results of their actions, and then act again. Thanks to digital technology, facts can be collected and numbers crunched with unprecedented ease. In this new climate, information is always flooding in, and there is no final analysis, only constant evaluation and re-evaluation. Action becomes one more way to gather information, which becomes the basis for further action. As Weick so eloquently puts it, in such a world, leaders cannot depend on maps. They need compasses. And, as never before, they need allies.

The ability to form and maintain alliances is not just a political tool. The successful older leaders that Robert Thomas and I interviewed made it a point to seek out and befriend talented younger people. Forming these social alliances was a strategy the older leaders used to stay in touch with a rapidly changing world. These social alliances helped keep the older leaders vital in a way their less successful, more isolated peers were not. The younger leaders also benefited from relationships with more seasoned, older friends. And this strategy of forming alliances is not limited to humans. Stanford neurobiologist Robert Sapolsky, who lived, for a time, as part of a group of Serengeti baboons, found that the older males most likely to survive were those who were able to form strong bonds with younger males. Teamed with youthful allies, the senior males were able to compensate for the losses brought about by age. Mentoring is a variation on this primal theme, a way for the young and the old to pool their wisdom and energy to their mutual benefit.

Because leaders have power, the question of whether they use it for good or ill continues to be desperately important. We could argue forever over whether Hitler was an authentic leader, or whether leadership, by definition, implies a kind of virtue. Certainly, Hitler had many of the competencies of leadership—a vision, the ability to recruit others to it, insight into what his followers needed, if only in the most demonic parts of themselves. He had the unquenchable self-confidence that is associated with leadership, the ambition, the obsessive sense of purpose, the need to communicate it, and the oratorical gifts to do so. He even had a kind of twisted integrity, in that he was always what his followers knew him to be. My fear is that our concern over this question is a dead end. Like the problem, the solution may be a matter of semantics. Perhaps we should reserve the word *leader* for those whose leadership is morally neutral (if that is possible) or tilted toward the good. We might simply stop calling

Hitler an evil leader and refer to him as a despot or simply as a Fuhrer, the straightforward German word for leader until Hitler poisoned it.

To say that the problem of how to label bad leaders distracts us from more pressing concerns is not to say that morality and leadership are trivial matters. They are of the utmost importance, now and forever. As Harvard Business School scholar Lynn Sharp Paine says of morality and business, ethics does not always pay, but it always counts. Far more urgent than the issue of what to call bad leaders is the question of how to create a culture in which despots or even plain-vanilla corporate tyrants of the Al "Chainsaw" Dunlap sort cannot flourish. In truth, I think we do that by creating the same kind of climate in which talented people blossom and the very best work can be done. Fertile, liberating environments almost always have two components: able leaders who listen and capable followers who speak out. There is a memorable story about Nikita Khrushchev on this point. After the death of Stalin, the Soviet premier was at a public meeting at which he denounced Stalin's reign of terror. After Khrushchev spoke, someone in the audience confronted him. "You were a confidant of Stalin's," a voice called out from the crowd. "What were you doing when Stalin was slaughtering his own people?" "Who said that?" Khrushchev demanded to know. There was no answer. "Who said that?" he asked again, pounding the podium. And then Khrushchev explained: "*That's* what I was doing!"

By his silence, Khrushchev proved himself a bad follower (albeit a live one). This is one of those areas in which the lessons of leadership cry out for application in the workplace. The corporate scandals of the last few years have caused unprecedented havoc in the American economy, tumult that has rocked the linked economies of the world. And in nearly every case, those scandals resulted, not simply from crooked accounting and other crimes, but from the failure of corporate leadership to create a culture of candor. Enron is a perfect example. Long before the energy giant crashed and burned, key employees knew that the books were being manipulated in ways that were deceptive, if not illegal. Enron executive Sherron S. Watkins did the right thing and warned her bosses that "Enron could implode in a wave of accounting scandals." Naive but admirably concerned about the good of the organization, Watkins expected to be heard, if not rewarded. Instead, company CFO Andrew Fastow buried the evidence and immediately set out to get rid of Watkins. The problem at Enron, she said later, was that few were willing to speak truth to power. Employees, including management, knew better than to point out the increasingly obvious ethical lapses in the company's business practices. Critical talk was taboo at Enron. "You simply didn't want to discuss it in front of the water cooler," Watkins said.

It is one thing to remain silent when your life or that of your family is in danger. It is quite another to remain silent when other people's lives are at risk and the worst thing that can happen to you is losing your job. And yet many organizations implicitly demand silence and denial on the part of their employees, even at the cost of human lives. When the space shuttle *Challenger* exploded shortly after takeoff in 1986, killing all seven on board, the blame was ultimately put on the space shuttle's O-rings, which failed in the unseasonable cold the morning of the launch. Tragically, the potential flaw in the O-rings had been repeatedly noted by Roger Boisjoly, an engineer with NASA supplier Morton Thiokol. Only the day before, Boisjoly had made one more desperate attempt to warn his superiors that the crew was in danger. But the company suppressed the information. As for Boisjoly, the whistleblower got the reward annoying truth tellers so often receive. He lost his job, and indeed never worked again as an engineer. He now makes his living giving talks on organizational ethics. To an outsider, it is almost impossible to imagine that any organization would prefer silence to honest criticism that saves lives. But such deadly organizational quietism happens all the time. And one tragedy is often not enough to bring about change. In a report prepared after the shuttle *Columbia*'s deadly failure in 2003, investigators put part of the blame on "a flawed institutional culture that plays down problems," according to the *New York Times*. Just as Boisjoly had been ignored when he raised his concerns in 1986, a new generation of space-program managers had chosen to ignore signs of potential problems, including e-mails from employees warning of flaws in the system. The fiery failure of the *Columbia* killed seven astronauts, whose deaths are attributable, at least in part, to managers who closed their minds to vital but unwanted news. NASA created a system that rewarded silence before safety, and that is what it got.

Corporate enthusiasm for collective ignorance has launched a thousand Dilbert cartoons. Movie mogul Samuel Goldwyn, famous for his malapropisms as well as his autocratic rule, is said to have snarled at his underlings after a string of box-office flops, "I want you to tell me what's the matter with MGM even if it means losing your jobs." Too often, that is exactly what happens. More recently, Compaq CEO Eckhard Pfeiffer lost dominance of the computer market to Gateway and Dell, not because he lacked talent, but because he surrounded himself with an A-list of yes men and closed his office door to anyone who had the courage to tell him what he did not want to hear.

In the 2003 scandal at the *New York Times* that led to the resignations of executive editor Howell Raines and managing editor Gerald Boyd, insiders repeatedly told other media that the real problem was not the pathological behavior of rogue reporter Jayson Blair but a newsroom culture that rewarded a handful of favorites of questionable merit and marginalized everyone else. It was also a place where control was concentrated in the hands of a few, and dissent was unwelcome. Neither Raines nor Boyd listened when another editor warned that Blair must stop reporting for the *New York Times* immediately. Much has been made of Raines's role in the scandal, but the *Wall Street Journal* reported a disturbing example of Boyd's arrogant resistance to the truth as well. When the paper's national editor suggested a story to Boyd on the *Columbia* disaster, Boyd nixed it, saying it had already run that morning in *USA Today*. Investigations Editor Douglas Frantz subsequently brought Boyd a copy of *USA Today* to prove that the story had not appeared. Boyd, of course, should have acknowledged his mistake and ordered up the story. Instead, he told Frantz he should not embarrass his managing editor and handed Frantz a quarter to call his friend Dean Baquet, a former *Times* editor who had gone to the *Los Angeles Times*. In essence, Boyd told Frantz to hit the road. And like a number of other unhappy veterans of the *New York Times,* Frantz quit to go to Los Angeles.

Linda Greenhouse, who covers the Supreme Court for the *New York Times,* told *Journal* reporters Matthew Rose and Laurie Cohen: "There is an endemic cultural issue at the *Times* that is not a Howell creation, although it plays into his vulnerabilities as a manager, which is a top-down hierarchical structure. And it's a culture where speaking truth to power has never been particularly welcomed."

You would hope that leaders in any organization would have the ego strength to accept well-intentioned criticism from talented underlings. You would hope that leaders would be wise enough to know that what you do not want to hear is often the most valuable information you can get. You would think that tsar-like executive compensation packages would more than make up for any embarrassment corporate leaders feel when subordinates choose candor over ego massage. But such is rarely the case. Executive arrogance poisons the atmosphere in far too many organizations. It is especially deadly in idea-driven organizations (as more and more are) in which subordinates are often as talented as their leaders, or more so. In hard economic times, autocratic leaders may be able to retain talent. But as soon as the economy rebounds, talented people who do not respect the people they work for head for the door. At the height of the now battered New Economy, employers knew that talent was their treasure, and treated their employees with respect. In hard times, employers often become arrogant again, forgetting that good times will return and that the talent will again take flight.

The band-aid that *New York Times* Co. Chairman Arthur Sulzberger Jr. put on the paper's leadership problem was to name former Executive Editor Joseph Lelyveld, whom Raines had succeeded, as his interim replacement. (As I write this, Raines's permanent replacement has yet to be named.) Well-liked by reporters and editors, Lelyveld seemed to understand, as Raines did not, that the *New York Times* was about the work, not about the executive editor. Lelyveld had decentralized control, giving editors and reporters more autonomy and more discretion to work on longer, thoughtful stories appropriate to journalists at the top of their game (in contrast, Raines liked to dispatch masses of reporters to cover a breaking news story, a process he called "flooding the zone"). And, unlike Raines, who assigned reporters to execute his story ideas for the front page, Lelyveld joked that he had trouble getting his story ideas into the paper—an off-hand reminder to his staff that he did not confuse himself with god. Interestingly, Lelyveld was repeatedly described by those who worked with him as "aloof." He was not a charismatic leader, nor a warm, fuzzy one, just an able one, whom people respected. Lelyveld understood that smart, capable people should be treated with respect—not just because it is the right thing to do, but because it is good business. Lelyveld was also a reminder that leadership abilities are ultimately more important than leadership styles.

Future of Leadership Research

In reading the earlier chapters in this book, I was struck by how rich and varied the study of leadership has become over the last 20 years. My sense is that the field is now on the brink of the kind of major breakthroughs that revolutionized social psychology in the 1950s and '60s. Inspired by the earlier chapters, I will focus on two topics, among others, that seem to demand further study.

Leadership and Globalization

The GLOBE project, in which social scientists from more than 60 countries look at leadership from a cross-cultural perspective, is an important start. In a world made smaller by technology, it is more urgent than ever that we understand each other's symbols, values and mindsets. Only then can we hope to reach consensus on common goals, including how to ensure global peace and prosperity. In the last few years, Westerners have become acutely aware of how little they knew about Islamic cultures, including how to speak their languages. One subject that cries out for more scrutiny is tribalism, the force, powerful throughout the world, that undermines globalization at every turn. The private sector has long been aware of the importance of understanding its audiences and markets. Advertising agencies regularly recruit new Ph.D.s in cultural anthropology to study the customs and values of consumers. We need to turn even more experts on comparing cultures loose on such fundamental problems as what we mean when we use certain terms. This is essential, not just in order to understand those who oppose us, but to ensure the forging of effective alliances. As recounted in a recent issue of *Smithsonian,* British and American military had so much trouble communicating during World War II that the Allies asked anthropologist Margaret Mead to try to find out what the problem was. Writer Patrick Cooke explains: "Mead discovered that the two cultures possessed fundamentally different world views. One simple way to demonstrate this was to ask an Englishman and an American a single question: What's your favorite color?" The American would answer immediately with the color of his choice. The Englishman would answer with a question: "Favorite color for what? A flower? A necktie?" Cooke explains: "Mead concluded that Americans, raised in a melting pot, learned to seek a simple common denominator. To the British, this came across as unsophisticated. Conversely, the class-conscious British insisted on complex categories, each with its own set of values. Americans interpreted this tendency to subdivide as furtive." From our vantage point, Mead's conclusions seem a little simple-minded. But you cannot help admiring the unidentified leader who recognized the Allies' communication problem as cultural and, instead of assigning blame, chose an expert to study the problem dispassionately. Effective leadership will increasingly depend on being able to decipher what people really mean when they do and say things that baffle us.

Leadership and the Media

Leadership is and always has been a performance art. Rhetoric first developed as a tool of leadership, and leadership continues to involve both artifice and the perception of authenticity. There is a tendency to think of image consciousness on the part of leaders as a modern phenomenon. But as cultural historian Leo Braudy tells us, Alexander the Great facilitated the spread of his power by putting his image on the coins of his empire. We take as a given that television gave JFK an edge over Nixon during their debates because of the latter's five o'clock shadow and sour scowl. But do we yet know the real extent to which our public figures are created or undone by the media, and the nature of these processes? To understand leadership today it is essential to see how the competitive pressures of the media affect the reputations, and the behavior, of public officials. And you cannot get a handle on modern leaders without at least trying to gauge where spin begins and reality ends. When President Bush made his famous tailgate landing on the carrier *Abraham Lincoln*, associating himself with both the Great Emancipator and the pop-culture warriors of the movie "Top Gun," did he do something qualitatively different from Alexander the Great, who associated his exploits with those of the deities of his time? What impact does the public's knowledge that reality is being manipulated have on its trust in its leaders? And how does the Internet affect modern leadership, given its ability to create buzz about an individual or vilify him or her with a keystroke? These are things we need to know in an age when television cameras can create seeming character and instant polling allows leaders to change their positions in mid-speech.

Conclusion

Having studied leadership for the last six decades, I still find it remarkable how often leaders in talent-driven organizations (e.g., *New York Times*) forget what scholarship tells us about how to manage genius. They encourage competition among colleagues, instead of the more productive competition with outside organizations. They forget that most talented people chafe at bureaucracy and hierarchy. They forget that intrinsic rewards are the best motivators. They refuse to believe that work should feel like fun, or better than fun. In the gifted groups that Biederman and I studied, the most successful leaders were those who saw themselves, not as top dogs, but as facilitators. Although many had healthy egos, they were far more concerned with the project than with shows of deference on the part of their subordinates. Indeed they did not regard the others as subordinates, they saw them as colleagues or as fellow crusaders on a holy mission (whether that mission was creating the first personal computer or the first animated feature film). These leaders saw their primary responsibility as unleashing the talent of others so the collective vision could be realized. These leaders prided themselves on their ability to discover and cultivate talent and to recognize the best ideas that came across their desks. They concerned themselves with such issues as keeping the project moving forward, making sure everyone had the tools and information they needed, and protecting the group from outside interference. A spirited collegiality is the usual mood of these great groups. As head of the Manhattan Project, J. Robert Oppenheimer successfully fought the government's initial insistence on secrecy within the group. Oppenheimer understood that the free exchange of ideas was essential to the project's success because ideas ignite each other and create more ideas. At Los Alamos, candor within the group was so valued that no one was shocked when cheeky young Richard Feynman disagreed with legendary Nobelist Niels Bohr. If Los Alamos was not a genuine republic of ideas, Oppenheimer did all he could to make it feel like one. Inside the fence, he rewarded frankness and transparency as well as utter dedication to the urgent task at hand. The result was that the atomic bomb was built more quickly than anyone believed possible. The first mushroom cloud still hung in the air, when some of the scientists realized that they had unleashed a terrible force on the world. But most spoke admiringly of Oppenheimer's leadership for the rest of their lives.

Even though Oppenheimer's scientists were part of the Allied war effort, he treated them as if they were free agents. Oppenheimer realized that the most heroic effort is given freely, it cannot be coerced. He did not order. He inspired. Perhaps the best exchange on the limits of power is from Shakespeare's *Henry IV, Pt. II*. Glendower boasts to Hotspur: "I can call spirits from the vasty deep." And Hotspur responds: "Why, so can I, or so can any man; But will they come when you do call them?" Whatever the arena, genuine leaders find ways to make others want to come when they are called.

SUSAN NERO ON
"THE CRUCIBLES OF
AUTHENTIC LEADERSHIP"

I HAVE A LITTLE PERSONAL RUBRIC that I consult when I feel I need more clarity than I can muster: "What would WB say?" I am one of many who are always eager to know what Warren Bennis is thinking. I rely on Warren's realistic-but-never-cynical assessment of what is and what can be. In this essay he discusses his vision for what we need from our leaders as we look to the future. He sees leadership that excels in building coalitions, finding shared meaning, speaking truth to power, and, most poignantly, leadership that can discover redemption in hardship. This essay tells us what those who assume leadership need to do and it helps us believe in the promise of their success.

Written in 2003, the essay approaches leadership "in the context of today." The response to the events of 9/11, the invasion of Iraq, the *Columbia* disaster, the Enron collapse and *New York Times* scandals (specifically Howell Raines and Jayson Blair, as the Judith Miller saga was yet to surface) are the stories he mentions. It is six years later, and still Warren's clarity and insight continue to hold their truth and they look increasingly prescient of another era that begins now, in January 2009, with the inauguration of President Barack Obama.

Before discussing one of his insights, I'd like to take small exception to a particular topic in this richly layered and evocative essay: technology and the new media. Here is one place where the point of view could now be considered "dated," if only by six years. Since this short section appears near the end of the chapter, I'll assume it is a placeholder for Warren's continued thoughts on the subject. I hope so.

Warren questions, "What effect does modern media have on leadership, given its ability to create a buzz about an individual or vilify him or her with a keystroke?" This remains a timely concern. David Denby identifies the use of media for vilification and ridicule as "snark," and he documents its prevalence in a recent book of that title. It is clear snark is detrimental to the image and reputation of many people, as well as to the quality of public discourse. However, the increasing opportunities created as new technologies "mediate a splintered world" (Warren's words) are greater than most of us imagined in 2003. We have a blogosphere where news stories are broken by "nonprofessional" firsthand observers, and the most up-to-the-minute thoughts of experts are easily at hand—including Warren's own regular postings in a *Washington Post* blog. Anyone with an Internet connection can offer commentary on any subject, upload a video, or participate at will in any number of social networks or wiki enterprises. These recent technologies create an expanding sense of who we are, our shared world and our diversity.

The 2008 U.S. presidential election is perhaps the most dramatic demonstration of this technological sea change. A relatively unknown presidential candidate created enough buzz using Web 2.0 technology to mobilize a large grassroots organization, raise an unprecedented amount of money from four million online contributors, and campaign to victory. We then witnessed a president-elect exchange information with citizens daily. More than a half a million people sent in ideas for the Obama administration via the gov.org Web site in the ten weeks after the 2008 election. During his first in-office press conference, citizens e-mailed their own questions for the president. In such an immediate, interactive environment, the errant snarky keystroke does not seem quite as provocative as it might have a few years ago.

Now we have other questions to consider about the relationship between leadership and technology. What happens when skillful use of new media is coupled with presidential power? What is the effect when the president sends personal e-mails to his constituents? (I received four of them in the past week.) What will be the role of the traditional press? Warren offers us a vision of adaptive capacity, collaboration, transparency, and truthful exchange between leader and follower. Will these be enabled by the use of new media, or will it result in the same old spin in new packaging? I wonder how Warren assesses these new developments.

I don't want to lose sight of the gold in this chapter, more specifically the key idea that coalition-building is the most important skill for the leaders of our time. This deceptively simple assertion deserves more attention than it currently receives in leadership education and research. If we take this idea to heart, we have to learn to envision ourselves and others as partners and allies, and we need to teach this as a topic to current students and future leaders. With a new president who aspires to be coalition-builder, perhaps we have a better way to make this happen. We could be entering a time when our leaders will value the skills and knowledge of community organizers, and the ability to produce arenas where the discovery of shared values and interests can lead disparate groups to act in concert. Warren mentions the European Union as a model. The idea of creating unions has seemed an outdated or suspect undertaking. Yet here in Los Angeles there have been active successful coalitions between African Americans and Latinos, labor and government, churches and universities, all working to make a more progressive city. This essay gives us a nudge for redirecting our attention toward those activities and the people who lead them. It gives us a basis for feeling hopeful, even modestly idealistic about emerging leadership.

This is a descant of "yes, we can" in Warren's writing, a welcome and timely note in a moment of discouraging headlines, economic hardships, of personal and collective crucibles. Although any time is probably the right time for collaboration, coalition building, creating shared meaning, and acting with integrity, this essay seems especially on-target in January 2009. I will assign it to my management students, and I recommend it to you as a look into our possible future.

Susan Nero is a faculty member and chair of the master's program in organizational management at Antioch University Los Angeles. She has been an Antiochian for twenty-nine years and an Angeleno for thirty-nine years. Both continue to be more stimulating and rewarding than she had ever imagined.

THE ALCHEMY OF LEADERSHIP (2002)

(coauthored by Robert J. Thomas)

WHAT ALLOWED SIDNEY HARMAN to face a factory revolt and discover in it, not chaos, but a radically new way to empower workers? How did Tara Church, only 8 years old, find the inspiration for a thriving nonprofit in a downbeat discussion about paper plates?

In reviewing the videotapes of all our geeks and geezers, we found the answer to these questions again and again. In the previous chapter [not reprinted here], we talked about crucibles and the critical role they play in shaping leaders. All our leaders, whatever their age, brought to their crucibles four essential skills or competencies. These are the attributes that allow leaders to grow from their crucibles, instead of being destroyed by them. In every case, the quality most responsible for their successful navigation of these formative experiences was their adaptive capacity—an almost magical ability to transcend adversity, with all its attendant stresses, and to emerge stronger than before. Every one of our leaders had three other essential qualities as well: the ability to engage others in shared meaning, a distinctive and compelling voice, and a sense of integrity (including a strong set of values). In this chapter, we will talk more about each of these competencies and show how they contribute to the alchemy of leadership.

Some of our leaders had other gifts as well, such as technological virtuosity, but these four—adaptive capacity, the ability to engage others in

This chapter was originally published in *Geeks & Geezers* (Harvard Business Press, 2002).

a shared vision, a distinctive voice, and integrity—were the sine qua non of all our successful leaders. Once we identified these essential leadership qualities, we realized that these are the qualities of leaders in every culture and context. They are the attributes that sustain and define leaders, not just in our digital age, but in every era, every public arena, every business and boardroom.

Adaptive capacity is what allowed GE's Jack Welch to transform himself from staff-slashing Neutron Jack into Empowerment Jack as the needs of the corporation shifted. The ability to engage others through shared meaning is what allowed a mediocre tactician named George Washington to inspire the Continental Army to defeat the better equipped but less well led forces of King George. A fine physicist but previously undistinguished administrator named J. Robert Oppenheimer found his distinctive voice long enough to provide inspired leadership of the Manhattan Project, cajoling, counseling, and buoying his secret community of scientific geniuses as they raced to insure that the Nazis did not make the first atomic bomb. And all these leaders possessed a powerful moral compass of the same magnetism that inspired millions to follow Gandhi and Martin Luther King, Jr.— a quality we will refer to as integrity.

It became clear to us early on in our study that these qualities—the Big Four, as we came to think of them—were repeatedly underscored in the interviews with our geeks and geezers. They comprised their winning combination. In the elaborated model shown in [the figure], we illustrate each of the four basic competencies, plus related abilities.

In this chapter, we will show how these crucial attributes helped shape the leadership of our geeks and geezers and other leaders. We will underscore the importance of these qualities by looking at flawed leaders. And we will also talk more about the process that produces leaders—the alchemy of era, individual factors, and leadership competencies that allows leaders to emerge from the defining experiences we call crucibles.

It is important to note, however, that an individual may have the requisite qualities for leadership and little or no opportunity to use them. Who knows how many people with the necessary gifts for extraordinary leadership are stifled by class, racism, and other forms of discrimination, including the *burqa*. However gifted, great leaders emerge only when they can find the proper stage, a forum that allows them to exercise their gifts and skills. In the eighteenth century, Britain's restless American colonies produced half a dozen superb leaders as greatly talented individuals rose to a life-or-death challenge and grappled with a problem worthy of great minds—what form of government best suited a free people. Leadership guru Abigail Adams spoke of the importance of the crucible of history in

Our Complete Leadership Development Model

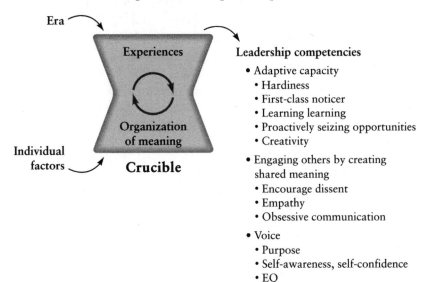

Leadership competencies

- Adaptive capacity
  - Hardiness
  - First-class noticer
  - Learning learning
  - Proactively seizing opportunities
  - Creativity

- Engaging others by creating shared meaning
  - Encourage dissent
  - Empathy
  - Obsessive communication

- Voice
  - Purpose
  - Self-awareness, self-confidence
  - EQ

- Integrity
  - Ambition
  - Competence
  - Moral compass

shaping leaders more than 200 years ago when she wrote to John Quincy Adams in 1780: "These are the hard times in which a genius would wish to live. Great necessities call forth great leaders."

Great Necessities, Great Leaders

The surprise terrorist attacks on the United States in 2001 seemed to call forth just that sort of greatness. In the months before September 11, Rudolph Giuliani was the lame duck mayor of New York, best known as the hard-liner who had cleaned up the city. It was a reputation off-putting to many, and somewhat tarnished by his nasty split from wife Donna Hanover. But in the crucible of the attacks on his city, Giuliani was transformed. As the *New York Times*'s Frank Rich wrote of Giuliani a few weeks later: "At ground zero, he projected comfort as well as authority, tenderness as well as steeliness. In the midst of performing round-the-clock triage on a grievously wounded city, he even found the time to honor a commitment to attend a wedding and serve as an honorary father of the bride, in a tux no less, to the sister of a New York fireman who had died on duty in August."[1] Giuliani was tireless throughout the ordeal, recognizing and dealing with issues as varied as deferring visits to the massive crime scene by former President Clinton and others to finding out whether canon law would allow missing Roman Catholics to be declared dead before seven years had passed (the answer was yes). But it was his palpable empathy and his ability to communicate this consoling message—that all New Yorkers, and indeed all decent people, had been grievously wronged but would endure—that revealed his unexpected stature as a leader, prompting some of the same journalists who had once damned him to write rapturous tributes.

Even more dramatic was how President George W. Bush seemed to be transformed in the same crucible. Snatched out of harm's way immediately after the assaults on the World Trade Center and the Pentagon, he did not get off to a distinguished start. "Where is the president?" people wondered, and understandably so. But in a matter of days a president with an uncertain mandate and a less-than-memorable oratorical style had found his voice. On September 20, Bush gave a half-hour speech to Congress and the nation that approached greatness.

Many observers were stunned. In a piece in the *Wall Street Journal,* longtime Democrat Gerald Posner described a new George Bush, one who suddenly emerged to meet the challenge the country faced. "Like Franklin Roosevelt or Winston Churchill," Posner wrote, "he rallied a country's spirit, had the courage to tell us the bad news that the upcoming battle would be neither swift nor easy, and declared that those who would destroy our culture and values would not prevail."[2] Posner had previously found Bush to be a stiff speaker, especially when delivering a prepared text. But on this occasion, Posner said, "he was infused with passion and outrage. His sincerity was heartfelt, and boosted almost all who listened to him. And precisely because we all know he is not a masterful orator, the power of his words and the forcefulness of his delivery carried even more impact. He rose to this most important occasion."

As we said earlier, the fact that we repeatedly see our leadership model at work in the world bolsters our confidence in its validity. The president's speech showed all four essential competencies of leadership. The adaptive capacity that allowed President Bush to turn even his usual verbal awkwardness into a strength. A newly found and compelling voice that allowed him to engage an entire nation and its allies through shared meaning and common purpose. Moral conviction that gave his condemnation of the attacks the force of something more than political expediency. Like Abigail Adams, Posner recognized crisis as a powerful catalyst. "More often than not," he wrote, "real leadership flourishes when faced with imminent threats and dangers."[3]

Bush was acutely aware of the seriousness of the moment and was determined to seize it, yet another ability evidenced by our geeks and geezers. As Leo Braudy tells us in his classic study of fame, *The Frenzy of Renown,* Alexander the Great associated himself with nothing less than the gods when forging his imperial image.[4] In conversations with friends, President Bush confided that he was inspired throughout the crisis by one of the deities of the modern leadership pantheon, Winston Churchill. (Mayor Giuliani was similarly inspired by the legendary communicator, who buoyed Britain during the prolonged terror of the Blitz.) Indeed, at one point in tweaking Bush's address, speechwriter Michael Gerson sat with presidential counselor Karen Hughes in front of a plaque that bore Churchill's stirring line: "I was not the lion, but it fell to me to give the lion's roar." Although echoes of Churchill were heard throughout the speech, Bush insisted that no quotes from great leaders be included. As Bush made clear to his writers and advisors, he saw the speech as an opportunity to lead, and he wanted his to be the words the world remembered. The speech was wildly effective, winning the praise of Ted Sorensen, Ted Kennedy, and other non-Republican connoisseurs of the language of leadership. More important, in the course of delivering its 2,988 well-chosen words, Bush seemed to change before the nation's eyes from a down-home, easy-to-dismiss Prince Hal into something more akin to a home-grown Henry V.

Leadership is one of the performing arts, and the leader always has to sell himself or herself to the audience. That is precisely what the president did. At the risk of committing psychobiography, he appeared, in the course of thirty minutes, to shed his previous role of Fortunate Son and to assume a leadership role based on models that included but transcended his father. In the crisis and its aftermath, the president seemed, for the first time, to recognize that he would be judged by history. Following the speech, Bush's approval rating shot to 90 percent, the highest in the history of presidential polling, with a record 72 percent of Democrats expressing their support for his crisis management.

Bush's transformation was reflected in his behavior as well as his speech. Fabled for his devotion to downtime before the attacks, he was now in the Oval Office at daybreak, studying briefing books with an unprecedented seriousness. He stepped up his physical fitness regimen as if in training, upping his daily time on the treadmill and trimming the fat in his diet. He even assumed a new formality in his dealings with the other members of his administration, calling Secretary of Defense Donald Rumsfeld "Mr. Secretary" instead of the usual pre-crisis "Rummy."

As the attacks recede in time, a far more subtle and complex presidential leadership will be required than the martial style that worked so well immediately afterward. We will need a leader who can balance protecting freedoms with protecting the lives of the citizenry, and it is not yet clear who that leader will be. The same president who moved us with his eloquence could falter badly in such critical areas as encouraging dissent, not a strength of his administration before the events. But while the ground was still smoldering after the assault, the president seemed worthy of his office even to many who had voted for other candidates.

In an "etymology" of the speech in the *New York Times Magazine,* writer D. T. Max wrote: "War had given the president a second chance to define himself, an accidental shot at rebirth."[5] War has been one of the most demanding and most dependable crucibles for leaders at least since David won his kingdom by defeating Goliath, and Bush recognized and seized the opportunity it presented. War's ancient association with leadership may be why military metaphors are irresistible to football coaches and CEOs. But war does have all the qualities of a genuine crucible—the mortal stakes, the terrible risks, the pressures that force one to decide what is truly important and how one wants to live, the need for intelligence and courage, the potential for obliteration, and the opportunities for greatness. The "great necessities" of September 11 seemed to call forth greatness in George Bush, Rudolph Giuliani, and countless others, just as World War II unleashed the leadership ability of so many of our geezers, from John Gardner to Mike Wallace. Whatever these post–September 11 leaders accomplish in the future will be achieved with the aid of insights and skills that they acquired in that horrifying, unexpected crucible. They will venture forth from a higher plateau, on firmer ground, as a result of that harsh education. At Ground Zero, as elsewhere, the competencies acquired in any one crucible prepare the individual for the next, in a great circle that allows higher and higher levels of learning and achievement.

Remarkable Adaptive Capacity

Although we talked about adaptive capacity at considerable length in the previous chapter, it is hard to overemphasize its importance in the creation of leaders. An exemplar in so many ways, Sidney Rittenberg outshone Houdini in his ability to overcome anything his captors threw at him. Rittenberg is hardiness incarnate, a remarkable embodiment of the ability to thrive in stressful situations so central to adaptive capacity. When years in isolation began to take an intellectual toll on him, he found inspiration in simple stories such as "The Little Engine That Could." Even more remarkable was the low-key way he dealt with his eventual release. He recalls his prison door suddenly opening in 1955, after his first six-year term in prison: "And here was a representative of the central government, telling me that I had been wronged, that the government was making a formal apology to me, that I was a good person and they had treated me wrongly, and that they would do everything possible to make restitution. He said, 'We'll give you money if you want to go back to the States and make a new start in something, we'll give you enough money. If you want to travel in Europe, we'll arrange that. If you want to stay here, we'll give you a nice villa somewhere and you can read and write and do whatever you like.' . . . I said, 'I want to go right back to doing the same job that I was doing on the day you came in that little jeep and arrested me.'"

People such as Rittenberg are models for Jeff Wilke, 34, who makes it a practice to seek out the hardy. "You know that Teddy Roosevelt quote about 'credit belongs to the one who is in the ring, whose face is marred by blood and sweat and knows the great passions and also knows the great failures,'" Wilke said. "I want to meet those people. I want to meet people who have thrown themselves into things and have something to say about it. And who have failed and have also triumphed while 'daring greatly.' . . . Those are the people I want to meet."

Perseverance is another component of hardiness and thus an aspect of adaptive capacity. Sky Dayton prides himself on being tough and says he psyches himself up to follow a course of action, however full of obstacles. "I can't tell you the number of people who told me I couldn't open a coffee house at 8205 Melrose," he recalls. "No way. Government guys with big stamps DECLINED, DISAPPROVED. My partner and I spent a week just pounding on the planning guy until we figured out a formula that was a loophole to the law that would allow us to do some really weird arcane thing, and the guy was scratching his head at the end, going, 'My God, you're right, I guess I have to approve you.' . . . Perseverance and toughness, it's really important."

How Not to Lead

As we have said before, bad leadership can be every bit as instructive as good. We have talked about the four competencies of leadership and some of the qualities and capacities that contribute to each of them. You can sometimes best see those qualities in their absence. Another reason for discussing bad leadership—failed leadership is a kinder term—is that there is so much of it. These are demanding times, and many gifted individuals falter in them. The most visible failures are the ones at the top. Once a sinecure, the job of CEO has become a revolving door in recent years. The remarkable twenty-year tenure of GE's Jack Welch is even more noteworthy when compared with those of most recent CEOs, who seem to fail faster than laptop batteries. According to a 2000 study by the consulting firm of Drake Beam Morin, chief executive officers named after 1985 were three times more likely to be fired than those appointed before that time.[6] According to the same study, 34 percent of Fortune 100 companies had replaced their CEOs since 1995. This churn at the top is universal, not confined to the United States or to a single industry. Worldwide, the average number of CEOs was 1.9 in ten years. And the trend is toward replacing unsatisfactory CEOs ever more quickly, a reflection perhaps of more vigilant boards and the staggering levels of compensation paid chief executives—now routinely 300 times that of ordinary workers. In recent years, Mattel, Lucent, Rubbermaid, Campbell Soup, Coca-Cola, and Covad have all replaced CEOs in thirty-seven months or less. Heads of Gillette, Procter & Gamble, Maytag, and Xerox have been ousted after less than a year and a half.

As we have said, Shakespeare's *Coriolanus* is a cautionary tale on how not to lead. Despite his integrity and other virtues, Coriolanus was fatally lacking in both adaptive capacity and the necessary gift of engaging others through shared meaning. Adaptive capacity always includes the ability to grasp context. But unlike Saul Bellow's alter ego in *Ravelstein,* Coriolanus was a fifth-rate noticer.[7] He failed to notice that Rome was changing from a patrician state to one where the plebeians also mattered. His mother, Volumnia, begged him to engage the crowd, to meet and communicate with his constituents. To do so, Coriolanus tragically believed, was to sacrifice his integrity in order to win over the mob. His bad leadership ultimately killed him.

Coca-Cola's Coriolanus

M. Douglas Ivester was the Coriolanus of Coca-Cola. Inheriting the chairmanship on the sudden death of its esteemed, longtime CEO, Roberto Goizueta, Ivester lasted just twenty-eight months. His grasp of context was woeful. Unlike his ethnically sensitive predecessor, Ivester failed to empathize with minority employees, so much so that he demoted the highest ranked African-American even as the company was losing a $200 million class-action suit brought by black employees. This in Atlanta, a city with a powerful African-American majority.

This lack of emotional intelligence was not Ivester's only flaw. He also failed to grasp the importance of his presiding over the European negotiations for Orangina and responding promptly and personally to the discovery of adulterated Coke in France. Worst of all, he didn't have the ego strength to acknowledge his interpersonal weaknesses and name a second in command with a defter touch, as his board repeatedly urged him to do.

Fortunately for Ivester, in this country, in this millennium, failed leaders get golden parachutes. They aren't struck down in the public square. His successor, Doug Daft, observed that the company had bungled its European alliances because it had on American blinders when it needed global vision. "You've got to be able to look at things through their eyes," Daft said.[8]

In fact, globalization has raised the stakes for leaders everywhere—the context they must grasp is no longer simply an institutional one or even a national one. Instead, today's leaders have to be able to respond nimbly to an avalanche of information from around the world and to grasp multiple contexts, some very different from the ones they grew up in. They can do so only with the help of other eyes, ears, and minds. Without damning his predecessor by name, Daft noted that Ivester ignored an invaluable source of information within the company—the loyal contrarians who disagreed with him. Ivester discouraged dissent, even though, as Daft correctly observed: "You need a network to prevent the danger that people will stop telling you things." Daft added, "I don't just want to hear good news."

The Flawed Logic of Yes-Men at Compaq

Compaq's former CEO Eckhard Pfeiffer shared many of Ivester's faults. He had an A list of executive yes-men and a B list of astute observers willing to speak truth to power, and he ignored the latter right out of a job. Pfeiffer refused the good counsel of those on his staff who realized Gateway and Dell were leaving Compaq in the dust by using the Internet to tailor their products to individual consumers and provide them with customer service in a keystroke. Pfeiffer not only failed to notice that other firms were gaining on his, he also failed to seize the opportunities created by the Internet as others had done. Like Coriolanus, he became isolated, unable or unwilling to reach out to all but a handful of colleagues and cut off from customers and their needs.

Cerner's Obsessive Communication

Every day we see examples of leadership gone awry. One of the most egregious cases in recent memory was that of Neal Patterson, head of the health care information technology firm Cerner. His is an almost textbook case of failure to engage others through shared meaning. Patterson is the CEO who dashed off the following blistering e-mail to his managers: "The parking lot is sparsely used at 8 AM; likewise at 5 PM. As managers, you either do not know what your EMPLOYEES are doing; or YOU do not

CARE . . . you have a problem and you will fix it or I will replace you. NEVER in my career have I allowed a team which worked for me to think they had a 40 hour job. I have allowed YOU to create a culture which is permitting this . . . if you are the problem, pack your bags. Folks, this is a management problem, not an EMPLOYEE problem. Congratulations, you are management . . . You have allowed this to get to this state. You have two weeks. Tick, tock."[9]

This is obsessive communication—a leadership skill—made poisonous. Had Patterson not been a founder of the company, the tick-tock he heard might have been the sound of his own tenure ending. It was bad enough that Patterson did the electronic equivalent of screeching at his executives with those contemptuous capital letters. It was bad enough that he patronized his managers and reminded them in the nastiest way possible that he was in charge, not them. Even worse, however, Patterson failed (or as he might have written, FAILED) to remember that in today's corporate world employees are not passive pawns, but intellectual capital. They are not just an asset, they are the asset, and they deserve to be treated well—not just because it the right thing to do, but because it is the only smart and fiscally responsible thing to do. Many things matter in today's highly competitive marketplace, but a full parking lot at seven o'clock in the morning is not one of them. That Patterson actually distributed such an e-mail, whose real message is that Patterson is an authoritarian executive with a tin ear and a blind eye, is the most remarkable aspect of the entire incident. It was the corporate equivalent of a suicide note. Within days, Cerner's stock price slipped 22 percent.

It is interesting to contrast Patterson's self-destructive behavior with that of Michael Klein, in his latest venture as a dot-com executive. Klein knows what Patterson failed or refused to see—that talented employees demand respect if only because they are invaluable. Klein told us he spends much of his time cheerleading in order to retain his essential knowledge workers. It isn't easy and it isn't always fun, Klein made clear, but it must be done. In a General Motors or other traditional business, he said, "Lots of people can walk out. They've still got a manufacturing plant. People go on strike, they'll still own all their assets. If we had a breakdown of key talent walking out the door, we would be lost." The reality that Klein has grasped is that his employees are greatly talented, intelligent, and fully cognizant of how much the company needs them. Moral issues aside, Klein would no more alienate his staff than his grandfather would have damaged his paint-manufacturing equipment. As a result, Klein spends much of his time "playing armchair psychologist and partner and coach." The job requires just as much adaptive capacity as did his more entrepreneurial enterprises. He was obviously surprised when a number of employees complained that the office was not sufficiently "fun." Instead of responding contemptuously, he took the complaint seriously and responded creatively. One result: a $40,000 employee party that featured such hip attractions as a rock-climbing wall and Sumo wrestlers as well as a band.

Creating Shared Meaning

Understanding context is rarely easy, and sometimes even talented leaders are destined to fail. Procter & Gamble has had a reputation for retaining CEOs more patiently than is the current norm in a world where CEO honeymoons tend to be painfully short. Former CEO Durk Jager was a man of considerable vision who saw the need to modernize the tradition-bound consumer-goods giant. Shortly after he took over in 1999, Jager announced a sweeping restructuring that he called Organization 2005. Jager planned nothing less than a cultural revolution for the huge firm. Its four regional business units would be replaced by seven global ones. Much of his plan hinged on getting the entire company, once notorious for its reliance on laboriously vetted one-page memos, wired for instant electronic communication. Fifty-four official change agents, all computer-savvy, were sent out to revolutionize its offices and plants throughout the world.

The result was Jager's precipitous and very public fall. Jager's was a classic fumble. He moved before he was able to get the rest of the company behind his innovative plan for change—before, in the language of our model, he had engaged others by creating shared meaning. Whether the plan was a good one or not, Jager never managed to communicate the urgency and superiority of his new vision for the company. His decision to eliminate 15,000 of the corporation's 110,000 jobs undoubtedly contributed to employee resistance. Employees were further alienated when they discovered that the company had tapped the phones of three staffers suspected of revealing insider information.

Jager also bungled external communications. He allowed the CFO to announce that profits would be up one quarter when they were actually down, triggering a plunge in the stock price. There were other career-ending moves as well. The company has long been dogged by public relations missteps and damaging rumors, the most persistent being the famous urban legend that the Procter & Gamble logo has satanic significance. Along with the embarrassing release of falsely optimistic earnings numbers, the company had another public relations crisis on Jager's watch. It pulled advertising from Dr. Laura Schlessinger's controversial radio and

TV programs because of her antigay stance, then was hit with a backlash from conservative consumers who thought the company's online apologia was too pro-gay. If all of P & G had been behind Jager, he might have weathered these brouhahas. But with the stock price down and the company getting unflattering media coverage, Jager was booted after only seventeen months in charge. In fact, many of the changes Jager made have stuck, including streamlining the product-development process (its innovative mop, the Swiffer, was brought to market in just eighteen months) and converting the company to instant communication worldwide. But Jager did not survive the turmoil he unleashed, in large part because he was unable to galvanize and inspire others. "In hindsight, it's clear we changed too much too fast," his successor, A. G. Lafley, told the press. Had Jager found a way to engage others, he might well have been hailed as a corporate hero.

Warnaco's Linda Wachner is an even more dramatic example of someone with vision who failed to engage others through shared meaning. Like Patterson, she was fatally deficient in emotional intelligence, particularly empathy. As one observer told the *New York Times* in 2000, as the company struggled to avoid bankruptcy: "She is the main reason why Warnaco has grown and the main reason it has fallen apart. There is some genius there, but she cannot run a $2 billion corporation by herself."[10]

No one can. Success can create enormous arrogance, especially when coupled with emotional tone-deafness. During Wachner's fifteen years as CEO (she was finally fired in 2001), she seemed to be increasingly insensitive to the contribution others made to the enterprise and to their feelings. According to the *Times,* she "developed a reputation for demoralizing employees by publicly dressing them down for missing sales and profit goals or for simply displeasing her. Often, many former employees said, the attacks were personal rather than professional." Former employees also reported that she used crude and racist language, a charge she denied. If true, however, that is the kind of insensitivity to cultural change—to put the kindest possible spin on it—that sinks executives, however talented in other ways (a dozen fallen bigwigs in professional sports come to mind). Such insensitivity represents not only a moral failure but also a colossal failure to understand context.

As a female leader, Wachner may have borne more burdens than her male counterparts, including being held to a higher standard, but she did seem to have an unusual propensity for undermining herself at every turn. Leaders of troubled corporations such as Warnaco cannot hope to reverse negative momentum by themselves. They must find ways to inspire and mobilize others in the organization in order to survive. Wachner struggled doggedly to keep her company alive, but, in the course of those struggles, she never managed to learn the essential lessons or acquire the necessary skills that would have equipped her for the next round of challenges— skills that our geeks and geezers have in abundance.

Every leader is a work in progress, however. Time will tell if Wachner's spectacular failure will prove to be the crucible in which she receives the priceless education that will equip her for successes in the future. William Butler Yeats wrote a marvelous little poem "To a Friend Whose Work Has Come to Nothing":

> Now all the truth is out, . . .
> Be secret and exult,
> Because of all things known
> That is most difficult.[11]

Failure is hard, yes, but instructive as well. If failed leaders are wise, and have developed the requisite adaptive capacity, they will look dispassionately at what went wrong and exploit that hardwon knowledge at the next opportunity. As Sidney Harman said: "The whole point of failure is to learn from it."

Having a vision and being able to sell it is an essential task of leadership. To a person, our geezers have become adept at galvanizing whatever organization they lead. They are able and obsessive communicators. Bob Crandall, former CEO of American Airlines, told us: "You simply cannot lead if you cannot tell the other guy what it is you want and expect." And, he added: "If you can't rouse the crowd, you cannot lead effectively." Business visionary Dee Hock, who founded Visa International, observed: "When you induce behavior, that's essential to leadership." Just as writers must find their voice, so leaders must find an individual and persuasive voice, an authentic version of themselves that engages and recruits others. As longtime Girl Scouts of America CEO Frances Hesselbein observed, "You lead by voice."

Leaders, Followers, and a Common Goal

Stripped to its essentials, leadership involves just three things—a leader, followers, and a common goal. Despite the relative inexperience of our geeks, many already know that their first and, in many ways, most important task is articulating their vision and making it their followers' own. Cofounder Young Shin says of his colleagues at Embark.com: "A lot of leading these people . . . is having them buy into the vision." Dan Cunningham, founder and CEO, or "Chief Chokolada," of Dan's Chocolates, uses the term "revolutionizing" to describe the process whereby he recruits employees to his vision. Teach For America's Wendy Kopp believes: "The essence of leadership is mobilizing people to achieve great things."

Effective leaders don't just impose their vision on others, they recruit others to a shared vision. Especially in our digital age, when power tends to coalesce around ideas, not position, leadership is a partnership, not a sinecure. Former military nurse Lingyun Shao told us that she believes "the essence of leadership is taking care of your subordinates." And she makes clear that she does not see this as a paternalistic relationship. Rather, she sees the leader as a steward, even a servant: "When you're a leader," she says, "you have to remember that you work for them, not the other way around." That advice applies in many settings, as Arthur Levitt describes in the sidebar that follows.

ARTHUR LEVITT, 70-year-old former head of the Securities and Exchange Commission, told us of a lesson he learned about engaging others through shared meaning from Senator Phil Gramm:

> When I came here, first thing I learned from my predecessor was he was not popular with the staff. He was very autocratic. And very formal and could be very nasty. So instead of spending my time with the Congress, instead of spending my time with the business community, I spent my time with the staff. At my own expense I had bagel parties for divisions, and I talked to them and I listened to them and I'd hear their complaints and I'd reach out to them.
>
> One act struck me as the most extraordinary since I've been here, dealing with a regal group of individuals who represent the Congress and the Senate of the United States, where you have to just kiss their ass morning, day, and night. It involved Phil Gramm. Phil Gramm had proposed a financial restructuring bill that was very important to him and to the country, and at one point in the negotiations where he wanted our support, I called him at six o'clock at night and said there were aspects of the bill I couldn't go along with. He said, "Where are you?" I said, "In my office." He said, "I'll be right over." And he came over himself.
>
> I learned a lesson there and I'm lusting for the opportunity to do the same thing in one of life's situations where it is most unlikely that I have to go to someone's office. That's just what I will do.

Sky Dayton shares the view that leaders must trust and empower followers, one way that leaders create shared meaning. "A very important part of leadership is the ability to trust other people and to hand them the reins and let them drive," Dayton says. When we pressed him to elaborate on that credo, he told us the following story, about returning from a ski trip with a candidate to succeed him as CEO of Earthlink:

> I had this car with big wide wheels that wouldn't take snow chains. We had to drive back on these really icy, snowy roads. And I never experienced driving in snow before, but he did, because he was from the East Coast. . . . So he talked me down the mountain. At one point I remember we did a whole 360 as we were driving. But he was really cool about it the whole way. And I don't know, we just clicked. There was something about that. I knew we were going to be in some pretty tough situations in the years ahead, and he was pretty cool under pressure.

Dayton was able to abandon his ego in order to unleash the talents of others, an important aspect of emotional intelligence. Moreover, he was able to craft a parable-like story around the event, one that vividly communicates his trust in his subordinates. It is a story that he can tell the people who work for and around him. And it has probably already become part of what management theorist Edgar Schein calls "the founder's tale"—the resonant, community-building stories that lie at the heart of so many vigorous organizational cultures.

Doing It Right

While we can learn a great deal from failure, it is even more illuminating to study exemplary leaders doing it right. Born in 1929, Frank Gehry has emerged in recent years as the most influential architect of the past half-century. His unique postmodern style combines technical virtuosity with a personal vision that results in buildings that float and undulate and make viewers fall hopelessly in love. "Frozen jazz," an admirer called Gehry's work. His Guggenheim Museum in Bilbao, Spain, is a unique phenomenon in the architecture of the last thirty years, drawing millions from around the world to an otherwise drab industrial town to see a structure, rather than a collection. Gehry is the only artist one associates with Bilbao. Although he has only 130 people working under him in his Santa Monica office, Gehry is a leader of the first order, a major shaper of the visual culture of our time.

Gehry exemplifies all four of the essential competencies of leadership. His adaptive capacity was evident as a teenager. At 18 he left his native

Toronto for Los Angeles, a city rarely thought of as an architectural mecca. Gehry liked that. As a first-class noticer, he realized that a city without a Chartres or other architectural icon was an empty canvas on which he could express himself. Cities like Toronto were not the future. They were centralized and authoritarian. Los Angeles was a huge pinball machine, a diverse jumble that energized him. Los Angeles was opportunity. "There was a great freedom in Los Angeles, because there wasn't the infrastructure like in Toronto, the European cities, or even New York," he says. "This was the Wild West. . . . And maybe this is wishful thinking, but it represents democracy to me."

When you design structures as unprecedented as Gehry's, you must be able to engage others through shared meaning or the projects will never be built. Gehry will accept a commission only if the ultimate decision makers are actively involved in the process. As he puts it, "I need Michael Eisner to play with me to do a building for him." Gehry does this for practical reasons, not ideological ones: "I insist on those relationships because the buildings look strange, and you've got to get into the logic system of why they are there. . . . Once you've been working with me and develop a relationship to whatever logic I bring to the project, then you realize it's not so from left field." When clients are engaged and share his vision for a project, he says, "They're in it, they get it." He gives the example of his most famous project to date. "Take Bilbao," he says. "Everybody gets Bilbao now. But you try to explain that up front. Whoa. Nobody got it."

Nobody except his clients. Gehry was able to explain the logic of the fluid titanium structure in ways that not only sold them on it, but gave them a sense of ownership. "They believed," he says. "The client group I worked with really believed that I could do it. And they supported it and they listened and I didn't sell them a pig in a poke." When Gehry can't create that kind of consensus, he walks away. He decided not to build a new home for the *New York Times* because he did not share the agendas of the commercial partners—even though he says the design was the best he has ever done.

Gehry also encourages dissent, another attribute of those who successfully engage others in a shared vision. Even the most junior members of Gehry's team, he says, "know that I'm not tender. They can talk about what they don't like." He says that "the senior guys" in the firm also tell him when an idea is over the top or not technically feasible. "I usually know I can't go there, but I test the waters a lot," he says. "Having them as the gatekeeper means that I can soar a little bit, and they'll pull me back. So I feel comfortable that they won't let me get out into outer space." Imagine how invested in the firm such partners are, how Gehry's willingness to hear them out both reflects genuine respect for them and helps cement their loyalty to the enterprise.

Voice and Character

Voice may seem an odd term to use in connection with Gehry, who works in a visual medium, but he clearly has a distinctive, confident one. He is obviously self-aware (a component of emotional intelligence), and says he learned more about himself and how he relates to other people as a result of group therapy. "As soon as I started listening to them and not sitting in judgment or sitting pissed off . . . and thinking they were wasting my time, it just changed," he says of his group experience. "I started listening and found myself involved with their lives and they became involved with mine."

A strong set of values and rules of conduct were common to all our leaders, independent of their theology, and Gehry is no exception. Unlike many architects, who have unpaid interns and other workers, Gehry insists on paying everyone on his staff. This was true even when he was starting out. From the beginning, he refused to do projects for free, as many architects do when trying to establish themselves. He told potential clients: "I'll only do it if I get paid because I can't do it without the help of people, and I'm not going to use people." He evidences the same sort of principles in his dealings with clients. We asked one of his former clients if, as Gehry says, he completes projects on time, on or under budget, and with the full partnership of his client. "Yes and yes and yes," the former client, a college president, replied.

Leadership is always about character, a formidable and protean word with twenty-six definitions in the *American Heritage Dictionary* (Fourth Edition). Our favorite comes from William James, who famously wrote, "I have often thought that the best way to define a man's character would be to seek out the particular mental or moral attitude in which, when it came upon him, he felt himself most deeply and intensively active and alive. At such moments, there is a voice inside which speaks and says, 'This is the real me.'"[12] Sometimes, as the next sidebar demonstrates, that voice can bring reason to a much larger audience.

What people respond to in leaders such as Gehry is not any espoused religion or philosophy, but their conviction, their powerful sense of justice, and their passionate desire to do the right thing. Our leaders include Protestants, Catholics, Jews, and atheists. Whatever they believe, they behave in ways that reflect their awareness of the value and rights of other people: None lives in a universe in which he or she is the sun. Like it or not, we are all post-Copernican. We know that millions of people have followed charismatic but evil men—that is the great tragedy of the twentieth century. But under normal circumstances, people prefer to give their allegiance to leaders of integrity. People know in their bones, or even their genes, it is the right thing to do.

A few of our leaders say that their lives are guided by a specific religious faith. John Gardner said his work was underpinned by his Protestant faith. Father Robert J. Drinan says: "For a convinced Catholic, he or she has a bedrock of convictions that bring peace and tranquility and direction in your life. And I think that when I deal with people, they understand that . . . I'm not seeking to impose it on them, but I have a whole range of bedrock convictions from which I can operate." Sky Dayton believes his training as a Scientologist set him on a moral path that includes the desire "to have a positive impact on the world."

We suspect that the religious practices of our leaders are largely irrelevant to those who follow them. The trust that Sidney Harman's factory workers put in him was not because of his religious beliefs, but because of his obvious personal integrity, the respect he showed them and his willingness to put his money into projects like piano lessons that enhanced their quality of life. Former Haverford president Jack Coleman (see sidebar) is admired, not because he is a member of the Society of Friends, but because of his willingness to walk in other people's shoes by working as a trash collector and living on the streets. Ed Guthman's Judaism may be of private importance to him, but it is his commitment to social justice that is relevant to his leadership. Whether Sidney Rittenberg was a Marxist or a Schumpeterian, he was concerned with every person's right to a full belly and freedom from fear. He has always practiced a kind of rational virtuousness in the cause of human betterment. Some of our leaders followed their moral compasses in directions their faiths of record would never have taken them. Former nun Elizabeth McCormack was on the board of Planned Parenthood even though she knew it might result in her excommunication. She was convinced that it was the right thing to do.

Some of our leaders have made tough moral choices that their followers probably know nothing about but that contribute to their moral authority. An example is supercoach John Wooden, who, early in his career, refused to participate in a national tournament that denied equal access to his black players.

A number of our leaders credited family members with their moral educations. Nonviolence activist Lorig Charkoudian told us that her grandparents were survivors of the Armenian genocide. "That shaped my view of the world and decisions about what I needed to do in the world," she explains. "There was a lot of hatred [in the world] and there was a lot of

JACK COLEMAN, 78-year-old former president of Haverford College, recalled a day etched in memory in which his values and his abilities as a leader were put to the test:

> There's one moment in my Haverford career that people talk about more than any other. It's because of the Quaker influence where there's very heavy emphasis on nonviolence. It's part of the tenet of the college and accepted by everybody there. And at one point when the Vietnam war was going particularly badly, the bombings at Cambodia and the killings at Kent State had taken place, word got to me that after our Tuesday morning collection, which is a gathering of all the students, a group of those most avidly working for peace led by a rather radical faculty member, were going to pull down the American flag and burn it. Word also got to me that we still had the survivors of what had once been our football team, a team now gone, and they were darn sure that wasn't going to happen at all. They were going to make sure it didn't. And any one of those football players could have taken on three of the peaceniks and handled it very nicely. And I knew this when I was sitting in collection, that this was going to happen. And absolutely baffled. What do you do about that? The possibility of violence, the flag being burned . . . [Coleman stopped for a moment]. I walked out at the end of the collection and there was a substantial gathering around the flagpole. I saw both factions there. And somewhere up above maybe, from somewhere a voice came to me, gave me a message. And I went to the peace faction and said, "Instead of burning the flag, why not get a bucket of Tide and soap and water? Wash the flag and put it back up." That's what happened. The troops dispersed. I don't know where that message came from, why. Certainly I didn't have it while I was sitting in [collection], but leadership there was luck I guess. That message came along. It was a wonderful moment.

pain, and all that had to be responded to." Dan Cunningham's moral inspiration was the steadfast refusal of his physician father to accept rewards from drug companies for prescribing their products. Cunningham recalls that his father always focused on what was best for his patients. "It was clear that money was not the motivating factor behind his work," Cunningham says. The lesson conveyed by both his parents: "The idea is basically what you can do for others and the community, and that's where your first thought should be."

The Integrity Tripod

Finally, let us turn to the fourth competence of leaders: integrity. We have to plead guilty to the charge that we've been using lots of words that are loosely related to integrity, and are more or less interchangeable; words and phrases such as moral compass, moral code, codes of conduct, values, ethics, character, voice, ideals, beliefs, ideology, principles, philosophy, and so forth. Many of these words were put into play in the preceding section, Voice and Character, and while they have some rough equivalence to integrity, we have to give integrity a more precise meaning. (We were even tempted to coin a neologism, "integritous," because that would be a convenient and shorthand way to describe all of our geeks and geezers. Fortunately, our aesthetic sensibilities prevailed and we dropped that vagrant thought.) It is high time we returned to the "I" word with a hope to refine its meaning.

The integrity of leaders is composed of three elements: ambition, competence, and moral compass. Think of these three as legs of a tripod that have to be kept in balance. By ambition, we mean the desire to achieve something, whether for personal gain or the good of the community or both. Competence includes expertise and mastery of specific skills. Moral compass comprises virtues that acknowledge the individual's membership in the larger human community as well as the capacity to distinguish between good and evil. In decent leaders, instead of merely successful ones, all three elements are in balance, forming a kind of tripod. But when any single element dominates the leader's behavior and the tripod becomes too wobbly, he or she is at risk of lacking integrity. Take ambition. Without it, there is no vision or engine for change. But unbridled ambition produces the worst sort of demagoguery. Ian McKellen's rendition of Richard III, bedecked with Nazi swastikas and a faux moustache, reminds us not only of Hitler and his scheme of world conquest, but of a danger that predated Hitler and survives him: the danger of giving power to people who can't live without it.

But it's not only in the political world that we see ambition run amok. Think of J. Albert Dunlap, who fudged his credentials and outright lied in order to advance his career. Long before the full extent of "Chainsaw Al's" dishonesty became public, some observers were appalled at his behavior and how he was widely lauded despite his ruthlessness. CEO David Friedson, of Sunbeam rival Windmere-Durable Holdings, described Dunlap as an individual with "no values, no honor, no loyalty, and no ethics. And yet he was held up as a corporate god in our culture. It greatly bothered me." With hindsight, we can see ethical lapses all along the road that make Dunlap's fall seem almost inevitable. The more recent and far more egregious collapse of Enron's ethically challenged leadership, accompanied by its Arthur Andersen "auditors," makes the Dunlap moral lapse look like small beer. Let's not mince words. Ambition, absent a moral compass, is naked destructiveness.

Let's turn to competence. If competence becomes mere virtuosity, it too can become monstrous. Many of the technocrats of e-business are examples of individuals whose leadership is undermined by their overreliance on technology and their failure to develop all the important skills unrelated to their beloved machines. At their worst, they become number-crunching, green-eye-shaded, statistical Vulcans, unable to respond to the many nontechnological needs of their organizations. Even during Harold Geneen's glory days at ITT, his leadership was undermined by a preternatural obsession with information, facts, numbers, charts, and all manner of technological fixes.

This is an extremely complicated issue and one not to be avoided or finessed, because it exposes the genius and the contradiction of our most successful human institutions, those wondrous behemoths Max Weber immortalized with the word "bureaucracy." The genius is what Weber characterized as their rationality. The contradiction is one that C. Wright Mills pointed out many years ago, the tension between rationality and reason.[13]

It is illuminating to examine that tension refracted through the prism of the recent GE/EPA controversy about dredging the Hudson River in order to clean up the PCBs dumped by a GE subsidiary over the course of many years. Jack Welch, one of the most celebrated CEOs of our time and one whom we personally admire, steadfastly opposed what he considered a stupid ruling by the EPA. From what we know of the case, he's probably right. GE's resistance to further perturbing the river's sediment was not at all irrational. But what GE's rational, cost/benefit analysis failed to take into account was the appropriate degree of sensitivity to the surrounding communities, to the environmentalists, and to the long and costly litigation, as well as the extremely negative PR problem GE's obstinately "right" decision would and did cost. The decision to contest the case was obviously rational. But was it reasonable? As our human institutions become more rationalized, leaders must be vigilantly aware of how technical/rational virtuosity, absent a moral compass (in the GE case being tone deaf to their noncorporate stakeholders), can lead to what Mills referred to as "crackpot rationality."

Whatever else a leader must do, he or she must know where to draw the line and find a way to keep these three elements—ambition, technical competence, and moral compass—in balance. One of the dangers of giddy immersion in a task characterizes many great organizations and their leaders—the lack of time for reflection on moral and ethical issues. It was only at the very end of the Manhattan Project, for example, after the bomb was close to completion, that some of the scientists stepped back from the technological race that obsessed them to consider the moral implications of what they were doing. The result was the realization by Niels Bohr and others that nuclear proliferation would be a human disaster, and steps had to be taken to prevent it. But that was well after the fact, because the smart group of gifted scientists, gathered around J. Robert Oppenheimer, simply couldn't resist the enormous challenge of building the bomb. It was irresistible catnip to them because, as Oppenheimer said when he agreed to lead the project, "It was too sweet a problem."[14]

We've talked about unbridled ambition and gifted competence absent a moral compass; what about moral compass absent ambition or competence? That's a more difficult and complex question and could deceive one to think it's of less consequence than the other two. After all, how many examples come to mind of individuals who have a powerful moral compass without competence and ambition? When we ask our students and friends this question, they often and incorrectly come up with names such as Jimmy Carter or Mother Theresa. Mother Theresa's competence and ambition were monumental, and whatever one thinks of Carter's success as president, he certainly had enough ambition and competence. The only clear example that comes quickly to mind is the enigmatic Shakespearean character, Hamlet. A strong moral compass, to be sure: to take sweet revenge on the killer of his father. He was highly principled but feckless, thrusting his sword in all the wrong places and killing off the innocents as well as the indifferent in equal numbers.

As we think about this question more, however, we do find such characters in real life, the likes of Father Charles Coughlin and Huey Long, who with their charismatic appeal and seductive ideas can trap people in false dreams and fatal folly. A strong moral compass, without competence or accountability, can be as dangerous as ambition without a moral compass. Such leaders can become, at their harmless best, objects of enchantment or, at worst, venomous pied pipers.

But let us return to our original task for this section, to refine the meaning of the word *integrity*. The word has taken on so many different connotations, has been casually finessed or used in so many disparate ways, that it helps to add one more critical distinction before we can move on: the difference between voice and character, which we discussed in the preceding section, and the key concept of this section, integrity.

Historian Arthur Schlesinger, Jr., once said that six individuals shaped the destiny of the twentieth century: Lenin, Hitler, Stalin, Roosevelt, Churchill, and Mao. All undeniably profoundly influential leaders. All certainly had clear, resonant, and strong voices. William James, using his own definition, would certainly have called them men of character.[15] Voice and character, big time, no question. We will argue that all were authentic and "real." They were all zealous believers in their ultimate goals. For example, Hitler's obsession with anti-Semitism wasn't just an act or a political move. It was a major aspect of his belief system. All these individuals had a reasonable degree of emotional intelligence. To call them "obsessive communicators" is an understatement. None of them lacked self-confidence. In fact, all six of these twentieth-century giants not only possessed all the major factors of voice that all our geeks and geezers embodied, but voice was indispensable for their success as leaders. But we now know, looking back through the shining ether of time, that four of the six (Lenin, Stalin, Hitler, and Mao), were responsible for the murder of some 80 million innocent souls. (Some twentieth-century historians put the figure closer to 120 million.) Their tripod of integrity was missing one leg, a moral compass. Integrity, in the most common dictionary usage, means wholeness and completeness. In their skewed vision of reality, their voices of evil were uncommonly effective and monstrously influential. All they lacked was the wholeness of integrity.

Although leaders rarely talk about it, those we most admire, from Abraham Lincoln to Nelson Mandela, have managed to keep the three legs of the integrity tripod in balance. Although most of our geeks have yet to have their integrity tested, it was heartening to see how important the whole issue of balance is to them. As a result, they may be better prepared than their elders were to keep one aspect of their lives from taking over.

At the outset of this chapter, we referred to the "Big Four" qualities of leadership: adaptive capacity, engaging others through shared meaning, a distinctive voice, and integrity. None of these four is especially new or unfamiliar to a reader versed in the literature on leadership. To a greater or lesser extent, they've been part of the leadership canon, but always singly. They've never been considered as a quartet of interrelated factors based on a theory of human development. This is the most thrilling discovery we made as we studied our geeks and geezers: that the factors that allow an individual to lead for a lifetime are indeed identical to the qualities of adult learning discussed in the previous chapter on crucibles. Moreover, they are the same factors that make a person a healthy, fully integrated human being.

Wonder and Neoteny

Inevitably, when we look at our geezers, we are struck anew by their capacity for wonder and other evidence of neoteny. A friend with whom we discussed our study suggested that the octogenarian zest that many of our older leaders radiate is the result of denial. Not at all. Our geezers were able to assess their abilities and limitations quite realistically. Indeed, at age 85 and again at age 90, urban activist Walter Sondheim wrote letters to respected friends imploring them to alert him to any evidence of diminished capacity. "The older you get, the less people are willing to tell you that your competence has begun to slip and it's time to hang it up," Sondheim explains. "And I was terribly afraid of [that], and I wanted each of them to have the opportunity to write me a letter and make it anonymous."

While our geezers do not deny their aging, they refuse to be defined by it. Each of them has a sense of being ripe with hard-won insight and ability and, at the same time, is eager for the next adventure. They are ready, as creative people always are, to leap into the unknown. A memorable passage from Henry James, written in midlife, expresses the eagerness we saw in our geezers: "I am in full possession of accumulated resources," he wrote. "I have only to use them, to insist, to persist, to do something more. . . . The way to do it—to affirm one's self *sur la fin*—is to strike as many notes, deep, full and rapid, as one can. All life is—at my age, with all one's artistic soul the record of it—in one's pocket, as it were. Go on, my boy, and strike hard. . . . Try everything, do everything, render everything—be an artist, be distinguished to the last."[16]

This is essentially the mantra of Tennyson's *Ulysses,* the sure and certain belief that "though much is taken, much abides" and the confidence that "some work of noble note may yet be done." Like Ulysses, every one of our geezers has "a hungry heart." They are focused on the future, not the past, and as addicted to life, as energized by it, as they ever were.

That is neoteny. We use the term, of course, as a metaphor, but let's look again at the scientific principle of neoteny. The retention of youthful characteristics in adulthood, neoteny is an evolutionary engine. It is the winning, puppyish quality of certain ancient wolves that allowed them to evolve into dogs. Over thousands of years, humans favored those wolves that were the friendliest, the most approachable, the most curious, the least likely to attack without warning, the ones that readily locked eyes with humans and seemed almost human in their eager response to people; the ones, in short, that stayed the most like puppies.

Neoteny's Power to Recruit

Recently, scientists studying perception have found that certain physical characteristics and qualities elicit a nurturing response in human adults. Those characteristics and behaviors are those evidenced by human infants—and by puppies. Babies have relatively large eyes that will lock onto those of adults without fear. Infants have relatively large foreheads and flat, nonprominent features except for those big eyes. When infants see an adult, they will often respond with a smile, a smile that begins small and grows slowly into a radiant grin that makes the adult feel that he or she is the center of the universe or, as they say in the South, "hangs the moon." Recent studies of bonding indicate that nursing and other intimate interactions with the infant cause the mother's system to be flooded with oxytocin, a calming, feel-good hormone that is a powerful antidote to cortisol, the hormone produced by stress. Oxytocin appears to be the glue that produces bonding. And the baby's distinctive look and behaviors are what causes oxytocin to be released in the fortunate adult. That appearance—the one that pulls an involuntary "aaah" out of us whenever we see a baby—and those oxytocin-inducing behaviors allow infants to recruit adults to be their nurturers, essential if such vulnerable and incompletely developed creatures are to survive.

The power of neoteny to recruit protectors and nurturers was vividly illustrated recently in the former Soviet Union. Forty years ago a Soviet scientist decided to start breeding silver foxes for neoteny at a Siberian fur farm. The goal was to create a new, tamer fox that would go with less fuss to slaughter than the typical silver fox. Only the least aggressive, most approachable animals were bred. The experiment continued for forty years, and today, after thirty-five generations, the farm is home to a new breed of tame foxes that look and act more like juvenile foxes and even dogs than like their wild forebears. The physical changes in the animals are remarkable (some have floppy, dog-like ears), but what is truly stunning is the change neoteny has wrought in the human response to them. Instead of taking advantage of the fact that these neotenic animals don't snap and snarl on the way to their deaths, their human keepers appear to have been recruited by their newly cute and endearing charges. The keepers and the foxes appear to have formed close bonds, so close that the keepers are trying to find ways to save the animals from slaughter.

A similar process may explain the form of bonding we call mentoring, a crucible common to so many leaders. The mentor sees in the prospective protégé a youthful energy and enthusiasm—we are tempted to call it "wide-eyed enthusiasm," to bolster the point—that triggers some primal desire to nurture, teach, and protect. However the mentor justifies his or her readiness to lavish time and other resources on the mentored (a desire to give back to the community; "she reminds me of myself at that age"), the real reason for the mentor's devotion may be as old as time and as inescapable as chemistry. It may be that the mentor benefits physiologically, in increased levels of oxytocin, just as he or she surely benefits socially, from camaraderie and from the opportunity to learn the often difficult-to-access realities of a generation younger than one's own. And there may be evolutionary benefits as well—a close relationship with a younger person may be advantageous to an aging individual whose strength and other physical powers are on the wane. There may even be an evolutionary payoff for the mentor in that he or she is being coached in neoteny, that most precious and life-enhancing of qualities, whether either party knows it or not.

It's worth remembering where the word *mentor* comes from. Mentor is the trusted friend Odysseus enlists to look after his son Telemachus when the hero sets out on his long journey. Created by Athena, Mentor embodies the wisdom of both genders. Transferring wisdom from one generation to another is central to the notion of mentoring. But these are always reciprocal relationships. There is a wonderful circularity about the mentoring process, whether it is the one Homer describes or such real-life examples as that of Helen Keller and Annie Sullivan. We all know that Sullivan was the gifted teacher who unlocked the intelligence of young, blind, and deaf Helen Keller. Less well known is that Keller taught her beloved teacher Braille when Sullivan finally lost her limited sight.

We suspect that what we call charisma—that never adequately defined quality that makes slavering devotees of us all—is actually neoteny. Charisma has the same essential element of recruitment, which so well serves the charismatic individual. The adored one receives not only adulation but countless other intangible benefits as well. Among these Matthew effects (a reference to the assurance in the Gospel According to Matthew that the rich get richer) are nonstop stimulation (so conducive to continued learning) and a dependable, external prop to self-esteem.

Whether it subsumes charisma or not, neoteny is a treasure. We are convinced it is the great secret shared by our geezers—the X factor that allows them to continue leading, learning, and feeling well, whatever their physical health.

Forever Young

As we said earlier, neoteny is a metaphor for all the youthful gifts the luckiest of us never lose. One of the Grant study men was asked what he had gotten out of his successful psychoanalysis. He answered that he had stopped biting his fingernails. And, he said: "I am more like I was at four than at seven." A good case can be made for nurturing your inner four-year-old. As Vaillant writes: "From four to five we are all romantics; we are all embryonic royalty, budding ballerinas, or intrepid astronauts; we are all fearless, open, affectionate, and beautiful."[17] Time, the loss of friends and loved ones, and a society that is often cruel in its denial of the worth of the old can take a terrible toll. But the person who remains a four-year-old—at least who retains the best qualities of one—has little time for mourning what is lost. In the now decidedly dated language of the human potential movement, four-year-olds live in the now. They also live outside themselves and in relation to other people. They do not spend a great deal of time in self-conscious contemplation. They have trouble to get into, trees to climb, frogs to find, mud pies to fashion. They have things to do. That quality of utter engagement with the world is as attractive in an 80-year-old as in a preschooler.

Neotenic Max Klein knew instinctively that he had things to learn from his grandson as well as to teach. In the course of our interviews, one leader told a wonderful story about writer Norman Corwin, whose 100-year-old father would call him every day and say, "Norman, are you keeping your mind active?" Neotenics keep their minds active as a matter of course. Our neotenic geezers tend to use their bodies with youthful brio as well. Near-octogenarian Bob Galvin windsurfs and takes pride in teaching the sport to others, including Sony founder Akio Morita. Former Securities and Exchange Commission chairman Arthur Levitt, Jr., likes to trek with Outward Bound. Frank Gehry and former Los Angeles mayor Richard Riordan play cutthroat ice hockey on local teams. A half-dozen of our geezers are enthusiastic tennis players, regularly defeating younger spouses. Bette Davis once famously said, "Old age is no place for sissies." Old age is one of the most predictable of crucibles, and eventually many of our most active geezers may have to put down their tennis rackets and find less physically demanding ways to test themselves. But adapting is what our leaders are all about—that, and discovering the best, most meaningful way to live now. Geeks and geezers alike, they still wake up every morning and fall in love with the world all over again.

HOWARD GARDNER ON
"THE ALCHEMY OF LEADERSHIP"

WARREN BENNIS CHOOSES HIS WORDS with care. We can therefore assume that, with his reference to alchemy, he means to remind us that the study of leadership is still in the medieval era. This characterization may be in fact true but it reminds me of something else. So much of our current understanding of leadership in the contemporary world comes from Warren that it is almost impossible to think of the field without drawing repeatedly on his ideas. And because so many of them have become part of the conventional wisdom, many persons, including me, find ourselves using them without attribution, sometimes even without awareness. It is therefore appropriate that this collection of his work be issued, so that we—like the innocent reader of Shakespeare—can recognize the source of so many ideas and phrases that we take for granted.

In reviewing these essays, I was struck by several points. Warren has a very broad view of leadership—he encompasses not only designated leaders but others throughout an organization and even creative types like architect Frank Gehry. The four factors of leadership have a timeless quality; yet whether they can aptly be applied to an individual depends so much on circumstances. For a brief span, Rudy Giuliani and George W. Bush seemed to be exemplary leaders, but neither of them springs to mind in that context anymore. On the other hand, had it not been for the second World War, Harry Truman would be unknown and Charles de Gaulle and Winston Churchill would be remembered as talented failures. The role of suffering, and the future leader's capacity to deal with it, is striking: in Edmund Wilson's famous phrase, only after receiving a wound can the archer perfectly bend the bow. Warren also reminds us of the conundrums built into the study of leadership: How can we study leadership without studying Adolf Hitler, and yet, do we want to apply this honorific term to someone who was so horrible? What happens to the word *integrity* when we realize, against every bone in our bodies, that it can in a certain sense be applied to Hitler?

In his instructions to the authors of these notes, Warren encouraged us to unleash our imaginations, to free associate, as if we had been presented a Bennis projective test. My thoughts wandered to an article that Warren and I had thought about writing but have not, as yet, put into words. The topic of that piece: "The Role of Listening in Leadership."

Nowadays, of course, it is a truism that leaders should listen to those about them; and any designated leaders worth their salt spend a fair amount of time speaking to those in the organization, be they peers, senior staff, or individuals in the trenches. Those running for public office almost always insist that they must go outside the Beltway and listen to the people. Listening is in.

But without Warren's explicit permission or endorsement, I am going to propose the *listening continuum*: from *hearing* to *listening* to *attending* to *reflecting*. Anyone with ears can hear; anyone who understands the language and can paraphrase what is heard may be said to be listening. At a far greater premium is the capacity to attend. I'll define *attending* as the capacity to go beyond what has been heard and paraphrased. Attending entails the ability to "listen with the third ear"—to go beyond what is actually said in so many words and to uncover what the individual would really mean, given an enviable memory, a rich vocabulary, a deep understanding of the audience, and the capacity to convey intentions fully in tone of voice, gesture, gait, what Warren terms the performing arts. Warren and I had many talks about the less-than-successful college presidency of Lawrence Summers; we had no doubt that Summers tried to listen, but he fell short in being able to attend to what was said and what was not said, but was meant.

One can attend deeply but in the end that is not sufficient for effective leaders. Such persons need not only retain the full messages but also think about how best to act on the basis of those messages. And that is because serious communication on the part of the speaker is not simply getting something off one's chest; in most cases, it is a call for an action, a reaction, that speaks to the deeper messages behind the superficial ones. Perhaps once they have attended, brilliant leaders know instinctively what action or reaction is called for. But in many, perhaps most cases, the shrewd leader attends widely and then reflects deeply on what needs to be done, what should be done, in full and proper response.

Of course, the listening continuum is not all that is needed. As Warren would be the first to suggest, an exemplary leader needs to listen to a wide range of people, including the team of rivals as well as the team of supporters; to know which messages to attend to and which to ignore; and, above all, to strive to make the right, the correct, the optimal response— one that preserves one's own values and conveys one's own integrity. Perhaps of the various arts involved in leadership, those having to do with listening have received too little attention.

Warren, however, is a master of the listening arts—he hears, listens, attends, reflects, and acts in accordance with his values. These are among the reasons that he is a very special person, one treasured by so many of us. And it is probably because of these skills that he has actually done more than any other person of our time to launch and guide the still emerging field of leadership studies. His listening has enabled right action. And if the field of leadership study has yet to mature, Warren has at least pointed us toward the Promised Land.

Howard Gardner is Hobbs Professor of Cognition and Education at the Harvard Graduate School of Education. He is the author of many books, including *Leading Minds* (Basic Books, 1995), *Changing Minds* (Harvard Business School Press, 2004), and *Multiple Intelligences* (Basic Books, 1993).

EPILOGUE TO THE TWENTIETH-ANNIVERSARY EDITION OF *ON BECOMING A LEADER* (2009)

WHEN I LAST REVISED *On Becoming a Leader* six years ago, the world was anxiously waiting to see if the United States would go to war with Iraq. Today we all know the tragic answer. The question that now torments the United States is when we will get out of Iraq, where we have been fighting longer than in World War II. That conflict has cost the lives of more than 4,000 American soldiers, left thousands more grievously wounded, and killed hundreds of thousands of Iraqi civilians. The war has also cost the United States almost a trillion dollars, money raised by borrowing from China and other nations because, for the first time in American history, we went to war without raising taxes to pay for it.

The United States was also suffering economically during the previous revision. In 2002 the nation was still reeling from a recession that saw the stock market tumble more than 40 percent. Today, as I write this, the country is in the midst of even deeper recession, one that is being compared to the Great Depression. In a pattern that has become distressingly familiar, the current economic downturn followed a bubble. This time around, houses, not tulips, were the object of the public's frenzied buying. After soaring to absurd heights, prices of American homes are now in free fall, with sale signs blighting entire neighborhoods. The prices of food and fuel have jumped, even as American jobs vanish by the hundreds of thousands. These problems were no act of God. They resulted from lack of leadership at every level, including failures by government officials and those heading the banking and financial services industries.

Crises reveal leadership as well as require it. The current financial mess elicited a relatively swift and concerted effort to address it. In the fall of 2008 lame-duck president George W. Bush urged Congress to pass a $700-billion rescue package. Action came after a false start or two, including treasury secretary Henry Paulson's initially using the toxic term *bailout* to describe the plan. Government intervention did not stop the stock market from going crazy in October, with the New York Stock Exchange plunging hundreds of points every day for a week, then surging a record 936 points in a single day. The market turbulence coincided with the end of the fiscal quarter, which meant millions of Americans received their 401(k) statements in the midst of it. Many were afraid to open them—with good reason, since the news inside the envelopes was dire. According to the Congressional Budget Office, Americans collectively lost $2 trillion in retirement money between July 31, 2007, and September 30, 2008. Many feared they would never be able to retire. Ever timely, the *New Yorker* spoke to the national mood with a pointed cartoon by Roz Chast. It offered this among three "Thanksgiving Recipes from the U.S. Treasury Department":

> Six sweet potatoes
>
> One can crushed pineapple
>
> Your retirement account
>
> Mix everything together.
>
> Bake until the account is completely melted.

In the past, an economic catastrophe could usually be contained within the nation's borders. But this economic emergency was especially scary because we are now all citizens of an interconnected world with a linked global economy. The crisis had been triggered by the freezing up of credit markets that had been caused by subprime mortgages that an underregulated financial industry bundled and sliced into complex new securities that plunged in value. The shaky new instruments were born in the United States. But when they suddenly lost value, investors in Brazil, Ireland, Bulgaria, South Africa, China, and Qatar also felt the pain.

The *New York Times* ran a map showing affected countries blotched with red under the headline "A Crash Heard Around the World." Tiny Iceland was hit especially hard. As it teetered on the edge of economic collapse, someone jokingly put the entire nation up for sale on eBay. In a column in the *New York Times,* Thomas L. Friedman asked: "Who knew that Iceland was just a hedge fund with glaciers?" The era when an economic event in one nation caused a far-off ripple was clearly over. As

Friedman so persuasively argues in two recent bestsellers, today's world is flat and its institutions and interests so intertwined that what happens in Iowa can hit Shanghai like a tsunami. With the economic dominoes stretched around the globe, greed and wrongdoing in one quarter can cause trouble anywhere. And so, when unscrupulous manufacturers in China contaminated milk with an industrial plastic, the first, most tragic victims were Chinese babies whose kidneys were damaged. But because the tainted dairy products were distributed worldwide, chocolate bunnies tainted with melamine were soon being pulled from Easter baskets in Europe and the United States.

In recent decades, Americans have rarely had to face such grim evidence that their leadership had failed. We were shocked at the fragility of the economy and shaken in our confidence that our leaders could fix the problem. The economic mess alone would explain why most of 2008 was an unusually pessimistic time in the world and especially in the United States. In the months before the landmark 2008 presidential election, many had a growing sense that the so-called American Century was fast coming to an end. Thoughtful people were not troubled by some jingoistic fear that the United States was losing its status as the world's sole superpower. Rather, many had an uneasy feeling that the country's best days were behind it. Those feelings were understandable. The dollar had become so weak against the euro that many U.S. citizens were forgoing European travel. Once a badge of honor, a U.S. passport no longer guaranteed a friendly welcome almost anywhere. And Americans were battered by nonstop criticism from European and other allies, most of it directed at policies of the Bush administration, but distressing nonetheless. The criticism surged as our meltdown proved contagious. In an op-ed piece in the *New York Times,* British writer Andrew O'Hagan wrote that "many a Londoner [is] seething at the subprime-mortgage disaster in America." To convey the quality of British anger at the Americans responsible, O'Hagan cited F. Scott Fitzgerald's description of the lethal disregard of *The Great Gatsby's* Tom and Daisy Buchanan: "They smashed up things and creatures and then retreated back into their money or their vast carelessness or whatever it was that kept them together, and let other people clean up the mess they made."

America's decline was evident on other fronts as well. Unimproved by the No Child Left Behind policy, our mediocre public schools have made the United States much less competitive, especially in math and science. A third of all American children and half of its minority children do not graduate from high school. And then there was the psychic wound of watching the city of New Orleans—the birthplace of that most American of art forms, jazz—all but destroyed by Hurricane Katrina and government incompetence. Even as this country grappled with uncharacteristic self-doubt, other nations were feeling newly empowered. No country is jacked up higher on its nascent sense of global clout than China. Every few weeks another of the highest skyscrapers in the world opens in Shanghai. China recently passed the United States in Internet users: 253 million Chinese are now on-line, compared to 220 million Americans. The point, of course, is not that China now holds the record for computer use, but that China is now embracing on a breathtaking scale the technology that defines our time. In a sense, the symbol of this shift away from American preeminence was the triumphant 2008 Olympic Games in Beijing. The most watched event in television history, the Beijing Olympics mesmerized 4.7 billion viewers worldwide.

Every decade or so I find myself writing that we need leaders now as never before. That seems especially true as I write this, observing the worried malaise that the country seems unable to shake off in the final months of the Bush administration. Others share my concern. A 2007 study of confidence in leadership found that 77 percent of participants felt the United States was in the midst of a leadership crisis. Slightly more (79 percent) thought the country would decline if it did not find better leaders. The 2008 survey, taken prior to the national election, showed results that were significantly worse. (The study was conducted by the Center for Public Leadership at Harvard's John F. Kennedy School of Government, and *U.S. News & World Report.*)

A major reason for this downbeat view was the spectacular failure of the presidency of George W. Bush (although nobody was very happy with Congress either). When I wrote the introduction to the previous edition, the new president had recently delivered his most eloquent speech—his 2001 address to Congress in the wake of the awful terrorist attacks on the World Trade Center and the Pentagon on 9/11. That speech, which inspired hope about Bush's ability to lead in difficult times, was the high point of his administration.

Unfortunately for the nation, failure followed failure during Bush's two long terms in office. Invading Iraq on questionable grounds and failing to plan for the postinvasion were among the most egregious. Others included the shockingly inadequate response to Hurricane Katrina, the erosion of the nation's moral stature in the world, the assault on the rights of American citizens, the economic catastrophe—the list goes on and on. Unfortunately, in large part because of the administration's reflexive lack of transparency, we still know very little about the mechanics of these failures. That lack of transparency constitutes a serious problem in itself.

Without knowing how things failed (in some cases, without knowing that things failed), the incoming administration will be seriously handicapped in its effort to change government for the better.

As president, Bush was an example of a particularly dangerous kind of leader—one with limited ability, great certainty, and enormous power. Indeed, no aspect of Bush's leadership was more striking than his assumption of unprecedented powers to the detriment of the legislative branch of government. A single example illustrates the imperial bent of the Bush presidency. While in office, Bush used so-called signing statements to change more than 1,100 sections of newly passed laws. In these signing statements Bush asserted that sections of the law should be ignored because they unconstitutionally constrained presidential power. How common is it for an American president to countermand the law of the land in this way? Rare indeed. According to the *New York Times,* all the previous presidents in U.S. history collectively made only 600 such changes.

Much of the credit or blame for the administration's extraordinary extension of presidential power goes to Bush's vice president, Dick Cheney. Francis Bacon wrote that "truth is the daughter of time." We will have to wait to know the actual role Cheney played in the Bush administration, but it appears that he quietly and assiduously transformed his office from one of legendary insignificance to a virtual shadow presidency. According to the U.S. Constitution, the vice president has only two responsibilities—to preside over the Senate and vote there in case of a tie, and to succeed the president should he or she die, become incapacitated, or be impeached and found guilty. That modest brief prompted Ben Franklin to label the vice president "his superfluous excellency." But John Adams, who actually served in the office, had a much shrewder sense of the paradox of the American vice presidency when he observed: "I am nothing but I may be everything."

The numbers bear Adams out. During the twentieth century, one in three U.S. presidents died or became incapacitated in office (or in the case of Richard M. Nixon, resigned on the cusp of impeachment). All but Woodrow Wilson, who remained president despite a debilitating illness whose seriousness was not made public, were succeeded by their seconds in command. But Cheney upgraded his job description without waiting for a change at the top. Like the Wizard of Oz, he toiled out of public view, tirelessly influencing such momentous decisions as the nation's oil-centric energy policy, going to war with Iraq, and adoption of such controversial policies as the use of "enhanced interrogation" techniques such as water-boarding. Many observers believe Cheney was a major architect of the Bush administration's exceptional lack of transparency (which in no way lessens the president's responsibility for it).

As I noted earlier, it will be years before we know the full truth about the Bush presidency. There are too few investigative journalists to go around in these days of shrinking newspapers. But we already have some meaningful measures of its unprecedented lack of transparency. Consider writer Graeme Wood's important 2007 piece on the subject in the *Atlantic* magazine. Wood compared and contrasted the approaches taken by the William J. Clinton and George W. Bush administrations in making government information public. According to Wood, Clinton's basic approach was, "When in doubt, let it out." His successor's antithetical approach was, "When in doubt, classify." As a result of this profound philosophical difference, 20.6 million documents were classified under Bush in 2006, more than six times the number classified during the entire Clinton presidency. As someone who has advocated candor and transparency for at least a half century now, I am convinced that opacity in government is the organizational equivalent of hardening of the arteries. Opacity blocks the free flow of information, the *sine qua non* of informed decision making and organizational health. Without candor and transparency, organizations sicken and fail.

As we know from one-time insiders in the Bush White House, the president valued loyalty above candor. There are few absolutes in the study of leadership, but there is at least one: No leader becomes truly great unless he or she accepts, even embraces, candor. Candor performs many invaluable functions within an organization. It keeps the leader from disappearing into an isolation booth of sorts, built and guarded by yes men. It forces the leader to listen to unpleasant truths and thus helps ensure that he or she has all the data needed to make informed decisions. We have a tendency to admire leaders who act decisively on the basis of gut instinct. Sometimes gut reactions are a wise, efficient response that takes into account many insights and pieces of data that are hard to articulate but are relevant nonetheless. But gut reactions are often nothing more than hasty choices based on too little information. My guess is that Bush's well-known confidence in his gut will give instinctive leadership a bad name, at least for a time. That should benefit us all.

As to candor, it is important to remember that it should be reciprocal. It needs to operate both up and down because followers also have a need to know. Leaders sometimes try to confine important information to the executive suite. They treat it as an executive perk, like the company jet. But whenever possible, information should be shared throughout the organization, whether it is a workplace or a nation. Obviously certain trade and national secrets must be kept. But most information is not sensitive, and sharing it allows followers to make informed decisions and act accordingly. Those who are given information are brought closer to the heart of the organization. Morale improves, often boosting performance. Alternatively, lack of candor lowers morale. The worst possible scenario is one in which people are given false information. In my experience, the follower who discovers he has been lied to is never the same. Thus are enemies born.

A vivid case in point is Scott McClellan, one-time press spokesman for George W. Bush. McClellan was a faithful, even avid supporter of the president. And then he discovered his superiors had lied to him about White House involvement in the politically motivated outing of CIA agent Valerie Plame. Their lack of candor caused McClellan to mislead, however unintentionally, the White House press corps and other media covering the Plame affair. Even more devastating for McClellan was the president's belated admission that he had green-lighted the selective leaking of classified information, after McClellan had been assured Bush had not done so. Once a reliable agent of opacity for the administration, McClellan was transformed by the president's revelation. When he published his 2008 confessional *What Happened: Inside the Bush White House and Washington's Culture of Deception,* some former Republican colleagues acted as if McClellan had lost his senses. But the former press liaison behaved as one would expect of a person who felt he had been betrayed by those he once trusted and admired. McClellan became an eleventh-hour convert to candor, with all the convert's zealous commitment to his new faith. He didn't just praise candor and transparency. In his book he argued that the White House needed a new post, a deputy chief of staff in charge of candor whose job would be to "make sure the president is open, forthright and working to transcend partisanship and achieve unity." In McClellan's plan the new deputy chief would have three assistants, including one whose sole mission was to promote and protect transparency. His or her responsibilities would include ensuring that information was classified for reasons that served the national interest, not simply "to protect the administration from revelations that are merely embarrassing or politically inconvenient."

Volumes will eventually be written on why and how the Bush presidency failed. But even now, it is important to scrutinize the former president, not to demonize him, but to learn from his negative example—to extract key lessons in how not to lead. One of Bush's major failings, I believe, was his overriding commitment to an ideology rather than to principled pragmatism. In foreign affairs, for example, Bush acted in the fervently held belief that democracy is universally desired and desirable and will ultimately triumph. That ideology proved particularly ill-adapted to the realities of the Middle East. Elections in Iraq resulted in a Shia government at odds with the country's once-powerful Sunni minority and our Sunni allies in the Middle East. Free elections in Gaza empowered Hamas, an anti-Western terrorist organization that seeks the destruction of Israel, our closest Middle Eastern ally. And, because of the administration's ideological disdain for government itself, one of the most destructive forces at work during the Bush years was the corrosive drip, drip, drip of privatization unchecked by effective oversight. It caused the outsourcing of much of the war in Iraq, inadequate oversight of the financial sector and other industries, and the stealthy semiprivatization of Medicare and other government programs. The administration's overt partisanship also harmed the Justice Department and other traditionally apolitical government departments that had proud histories of striving to be meritocracies. Moreover, by acting less like the president of the nation than of the conservative wing of the Republican Party, Bush further polarized an already badly divided country. There is a lesson here that transcends any single administration, Republican or Democratic. Ideologically charged approaches rarely solve complex problems. Great leaders do not try to impose an ideological template, right- or left-leaning, on problems. First-rate leaders know that every problem is thorny in its own way and inclusively and collaboratively find solutions that reflect the unique realities at hand.

In short, between my last introduction to *On Becoming a Leader* and this epilogue, the context that I urge every reader to master has changed dramatically. Optimism has been tested by a protracted war, economic pain, and a polarized citizenry. Given this new context, it is not surprising that the U.S. presidential election of 2008 was a riveting cliff-hanger. You didn't have to be a student of leadership to be fascinated by the race. It was as important a contest as any in American history. And it was addictive. As the seemingly endless campaign approached the election on November 4, the media ran stories on election junkies who spent so much time reading political blogs that their work suffered and relationships frayed. Candidates began to pop up in the dreams of those who watched too much political coverage on-line or on TV.

In many ways, the campaign was a microcosm of the most important cultural changes of the past decade. One major development has been the technology-driven emergence of alternative media that have transformed American society, including the electoral process. The most popular on-line newspapers, such as the Huffington Post, have as much clout as venerable opinion-shapers such as the *New York Times* and the *Wall Street Journal*. Cable television has edged out network TV as the go-to source for information, even though, or perhaps because, many cable TV personalities wore their politics on their sleeves. The pace of campaigning (like the pace of everything else) has also sped up to the point where the lag time between a candidate's remark and the appearance of a slick television ad countering it is a matter of hours. Thanks to Google, most of what the candidates have said in the past can be accessed in a nanosecond. In a sense, there is no past in the blogosphere. Anything that happens in front of a camera (and almost every cell phone is a camera) can be stored forever and retrieved and disseminated in an instant. As a result, what the candidates are saying on the campaign trail is paralleled by another campaign going on in the blogosphere. In this Internet campaign, truth and lies are mixed in unpredictable ways and may be hard to tell apart; Stephen Colbert's *truthiness* is the perfect coinage for this new reality. In contrast to the public campaign, the candidates don't necessarily control this shadow campaign, although they can influence it. And whether it is fact-based or steeped in bias or worse, this shadow campaign shapes attitudes and has a real though unpredictable affect on the outcome of the election.

Given the seriousness and complexity of the problems roiling the nation, it is no surprise that voters followed the 2008 presidential race with a nerve-wracking awareness that the stakes have rarely been higher. With no sitting president or vice president in contention, all the cards were in the air. The election season began unusually early in 2007 and was marked by the emergence of history-making rivals for the Democratic presidential nomination. New York senator and former first lady Hillary Rodham Clinton was the first woman to have a real shot at the Democratic nomination. She proved a formidable competitor in what quickly became a contest between her and the first serious African American contender, Illinois senator Barack Obama. First hailed as presidential material by Oprah Winfrey, Obama gave a reputation-making speech at the 2004 Democratic convention and distinguished himself from most Democratic political figures by his prescient opposition to the war in Iraq.

Obama was a phenomenon as well as a candidate, able to fill Yankee Stadium with his supporters, many of them voting for the first time. A sea of 100,000 people stretched before him at a campaign rally in St. Louis. When Obama went abroad to meet with world leaders, presidents and sheiks grinned like teenagers as they shook his hand. Perpetually poised and unflappable, Obama was endorsed early by Ted and Caroline Kennedy and later by former secretary of state Colin Powell. At the annual benefit dinner named for Al Smith, the first Catholic nominee for the presidency, Obama made fun of his cult-like following: "Contrary to the rumors you've heard, I wasn't born in a manger," he joked. For many, Obama embodied the promise of a postracial America in which candidates were judged "not by the color of their skin, but by the content of their character." But at the same benefit, Obama alluded with a light touch to the unknown effect on his chances of his Swahili and Arabic names, unprecedented for someone seeking the country's highest office. "I got my middle name [Hussein]," he explained, "from someone who obviously didn't think I'd ever run for president."

After a series of bruising debates, Clinton won an unprecedented 18 million votes in the 2008 primaries but ultimately lost the nomination to Obama. Although Clinton distinguished herself in the numerous Democratic debates, particularly in her mastery of the issues, Obama chose as his running mate Delaware senator Joseph Biden, who had also sought the presidential nomination.

The contest for the Democratic nomination was sometimes so contentious it seemed to call for net and trident. In contrast, the Republican contest was as dull as an infomercial. The Republican candidates were all mature white men, including 9/11 New York City mayor Rudolph Giuliani and former Massachusetts governor Mitt Romney. And their primary strategy seemed to consist of distancing themselves from President Bush without actually uttering his name and reminding voters that they were members of the president's party. Despite being counted out early in the contest, Vietnam War hero and Arizona senator John McCain eventually emerged as the Republican presidential candidate. A self-proclaimed maverick, McCain overcame such major obstacles as his unpopularity among hard-core conservatives and his age. If elected, he would become, at seventy-two, the oldest person to assume the office.

But the Republican campaign suddenly caught fire in the last days of August 2008 when McCain made the stunning announcement that his vice-presidential pick was not Democrat-turned-Independent Joe Lieberman or another of the relative moderates McCain was thought to favor. Instead McCain chose forty-four-year-old Sarah Palin, the young governor of Alaska little known outside of party circles. A former small-town mayor, beauty queen, and self-styled "hockey mom" of five, including an infant with Down Syndrome, Palin introduced herself to the nation in a mesmerizing speech that drew as many television viewers as Obama's convention address. In that speech, Palin—the first woman on the Republican ticket and thus a maker of history in her own right—made a bid for Hillary Clinton's many women supporters with a promise to assail the glass ceiling Clinton had cracked. As an opponent of abortion even in cases of rape and incest who believes creationism should be taught in the schools alongside evolution, Palin appealed strongly to evangelical Christians who helped elect President Bush and had little enthusiasm for McCain.

Initially the media fell hard for Palin, much as it had for Obama. Both were hailed as celebrities and rock stars, terms the Republicans had previously used to demean Obama. Palin proved to be a gifted campaigner with a sharp edge and a populist pitch (she often mentioned "Joe Six-Pack," apparently to capitalize on the belief that Bush had won, in part, because voters would rather have had a beer with him than with Al Gore or John Kerry). Palin had a folksy touch, smiling readily, winking, and dropping her final g's, but she also served as her party's attack dog. Without apparent qualms, she often roiled up conservative crowds by accusing Obama of "palling around with terrorists." Despite her initial appeal, she had a serious downside. With her paper-thin résumé, she undermined McCain's contention that Obama lacked the experience to be president. In my view, that had been a losing argument all along. History has shown over and over again that experience per se is no substitute for good judgment in determining the quality of a leader.

To an unusual degree, the lives of the four contenders were the stuff of biopics. As so often happens in our culture, where even brands of toothpaste are marketed via their own carefully honed "stories," the race became a battle of competing narratives. McCain, who took as his campaign slogan "Country First," embodied a tale of courage and patriotic sacrifice as a former navy pilot shot down over Vietnam who was tortured while a prisoner of war in the notorious Hanoi Hilton. Since then, he has earned a reputation as a maverick for bucking his party on such matters as immigration and cutting taxes for the wealthiest Americans (positions he later reversed). Born in 1961, Obama had a more exotic, more contemporary story, one that emphasized his ties with the rest of the world. He is the son of a black Kenyan father and a white mother from Kansas, who had struggled to raise him in Hawaii and Indonesia. All but abandoned by his father and briefly on food stamps as a child, Obama became the first African American editor of the *Harvard Law Review*. Instead of joining a four-star law firm after Harvard, he had begun his public life as a community organizer in Chicago. Obama, who acknowledged that he didn't look like the other men on American currency, ran on the promise of change.

Like McCain and Obama, Biden had experienced a life-changing event, a crucible that shaped his character and his leadership. Biden was twenty-nine in 1972 when he was elected to the Senate, the second youngest person in history to win the office. He was in Washington, getting ready to move into his new office, when a phone call revealed that his wife and infant daughter had died in an auto accident back in Delaware. Gravely injured, his two young sons were not expected to survive. The boys recovered; Biden was sworn in at their bedside. A popular senator and devoted single father, Biden remarried and is now the father of an adult daughter as well as a grandfather. A foreign-policy expert who opposed the appointment of conservative judge Robert Bork to the Supreme Court, Biden is also known for verbal gaffes and for taking the long train ride home to Delaware each night to be with his family.

Perhaps because Palin's was initially the least familiar tale, her narrative got the most media play. Her photogenic face appeared on one newsmagazine cover after another, often accompanying text that made her sound like a cross between Annie Oakley and Wonder Woman, able to shoot and dress a moose as well as change a diaper and do the state's business. Opponents saw her selection as a cynical bid to appease the Republican base and attract women (detractors dubbed her "Caribou Barbie"). The Republican campaign hailed her as a maverick in the McCain mold, who had fearlessly taken on her own party in Alaska. In a piece in *Newsweek*, Jeffrey Barthelot and Karen Breslau described how Palin fit into a time-honored American tale. They wrote: "Palin's personal story taps one of the great American myths—the hardy woman of the frontier, God-fearing and determined to succeed against the odds. Her story could be a Capra film, or a chick flick. But as with most political biographies (or Hollywood films), the rougher edges have been burnished. To her critics, she's also shallow, opportunistic and even corrupt herself." The last was an allusion to a bipartisan investigation by the Alaska legislature into whether Palin improperly fired a state official. In October, the investigative body determined that the governor Palin had violated state ethics laws and misused her power but had the legal right to replace the official.

The election season underscored the fact that ours is a culture in which entertainment and news have been transmogrified into a third category that marries the two, for better or for worse, often called *infotainment*. When polled, young voters routinely said they get their news from "The Daily Show with Jon Stewart" or "The Colbert Report," which are cable comedy shows, not news sources, to those who rely on the mainstream media. John McCain declared his intention to run for president on "Late Night with David Letterman" and returned to the show to ask Letterman's forgiveness after abruptly canceling an appearance. Cable TV pundits reported regularly on where the women of "The View" stood on the candidates. But the campaign became downright surrealistic after writer and performer Tina Fey began playing Sarah Palin on "Saturday Night Live." Sporting the candidate's signature glasses and often quoting her verbatim, Fey brilliantly caught Palin's *Fargo* accent, down-home mannerisms, and serpentine syntax. Palin later made her own appearance on the show, passing Fey in the studio and replacing her on the podium.

Like Palin, who trained for a career in television, Obama is richly endowed with charisma, the personal magnetism that allows an individual to captivate and sway audiences. It is the same kind of star power that allows certain actors to own a stage or a screen. Politics, too, is a performance art, as Orson Welles made clear when he first met President Franklin Delano Roosevelt. FDR graciously said to the already-legendary actor/director: "You know, Mr. Welles, you are the greatest actor in America." And Welles replied: "Oh, no, Mr. President. You are." Except for those rare occasions when candidates share the same physical space as those they hope to lead, they must have powerful enough rhetorical and acting skills to transcend the distorting effect of television and other media. They must be good enough performers to persuade the audience that they share the same dreams and interests. Such leaders have the ability to turn a crowd into a community—or a mob. Charisma is no small gift. FDR had it, JFK had it, Reagan had it, Clinton had it. Tragically, so did Hitler. But it is always part of the political equation, whether we like it or not.

More than ever since the advent of television, physical attractiveness is a constituent of charisma, albeit a controversial one. It has been noted so often it has become a cliché: virtually everyone who heard the landmark 1960 debate between Nixon and Kennedy on radio thought Nixon had won. It was only those who saw the close-up visuals—a frowning Nixon, with his five o'clock shadow, mopping flop sweat from his brow, versus a youthful, athletic-looking Kennedy, comfortable in his skin and flashing a ready smile—who knew that the victory belonged to JFK. Beauty is more than symmetrical features. It can be enhanced by behavior and our knowledge of the individual. But it is routinely a factor in the leaders we choose. Some leaders are so powerful they can rise above the way they look. Lincoln used humor to mock his strange appearance, once remarking to a rival who called him "two-faced": "Do you think if I had another face, I'd appear in public in this one?" But appearance matters to voters as well as prospective dates. An unkind but astute observer once remarked that Nixon had a face like a foot. Did that contribute to his disastrous debate? Likely it did. Certainly Sarah Palin's good looks are part of her appeal, as Republican conventioneers from Indiana crudely acknowledged with T-shirts that read: HOOSIERS FOR THE HOT CHICK. And it is a fair bet that Obama's athletic grace and easy smile attracted more voters than his Harvard law degree or his tax policy.

It is no secret that ours is a celebrity culture, and that routinely means that issues get short shrift in our public discourse. In the first weeks following Palin's debut, in the grip of Palimania, Americans heard about her seventeen-year-old daughter's untimely pregnancy and Palin's installation of a tanning bed in the governor's residence (an act hailed as a blow to the "the sun-scare industry" by the tanning lobby). In what could be called the *People* magazine phase of the race, the incidental drove out the substantial, in part, because the McCain campaign kept Palin, who performed best when scripted, away from traditional media. Cable TV filled its gaping news hole with such inconsequential questions as whether McCain looked less like the presidential candidate than Palin's second banana.

All that changed when giant investment banker Lehman Brothers announced it would seek bankruptcy protection on September 15; the Dow plummeted, and people began pulling their cash out of their banks. Suddenly the campaign focused with laser-like intensity on the battered economy and the pain it was causing voters. The resonant personal stories carefully constructed by the candidates and their handlers were put aside, and the public was able to compare and contrast the candidates' very different positions on matters of real weight. For a time, the carnival-like process of choosing a president and vice president was relinked to the next phase in the process—the one of paramount importance: how the president we choose will lead and, thus, shape our lives and those of our children and grandchildren. But just as the debate seemed finally to settle on the economy, with all its gravity, the politics of distraction reemerged. In the last of the three presidential debates, McCain repeatedly cited a voter in Toledo, Ohio, whom he called Joe the Plumber. Before the debate was over, Joe the Plumber was being alternately hailed and vilified in the blogosphere. He was a household name by the following day.

In the final weeks, the presidential race turned really ugly. At her rallies Palin continued to accuse Obama of terrorist associations, focusing on rehabilitated Weatherman Bill Ayers. Chants of "Kill him" directed at Obama were heard from some of the angry crowds. McCain bristled when civil rights leader John Lewis accused him of allowing a dangerous undercurrent of violence to develop at his campaign events. But anti-Obama innuendo, slurs, and distortions continued to mark the McCain campaign. Automated "robocalls" from the Republican Party warned anyone who picked up the phone away from Obama with charges of terrorist associations, involvement in voter fraud, and nefarious plans to redistribute the nation's wealth. Race was rarely mentioned during the campaign (until the Colin Powell endorsement was dismissed by some as an act of racial solidarity), but race was always close to the surface. Democrats feared the possible effect of an active on-line campaign that falsely but graphically presented Obama as a Moslem with ties to al-Qaeda. Supporters feared for Obama's life in a nation that has seen more than its share of politically and racially motivated assassinations. So did the U.S. government, which had assigned Obama Secret Service protection before any other candidate.

By mid-October Irish bookmakers were already paying off bettors who had put their money on Obama to win. But his supporters worried that polls that showed him ahead of McCain might be distorted by the Bradley Effect. That phenomenon was named for the late Tom Bradley, the first black mayor of Los Angeles, who ran for governor of California in the 1980s against George Deukmejian. Overwhelmingly, the polls showed Bradley in the lead. But he lost the election because, political scientists conjectured, voters feared being thought racist if they told pollsters they did not plan to vote for Bradley. Race was not the only emotionally charged issue in the 2008 campaign. Age was another. Obama, who fully exploited the Internet to raise funds, organize his supporters, and get out the vote, was the clear favorite of young, technologically hip voters. Obama even advertised on popular video games in the last weeks of the campaign. Although McCain argued that his age was evidence of his experience, many potential voters, including older ones, thought he was too old to serve as president. Their fears about his age were exacerbated by his history of malignant melanoma and by his choice of so green and controversial a running mate. McCain supporters accused the Obama campaign of exploiting such fears when they called McCain "erratic" in frequently changing his positions and tactics.

We now know who Americans wanted as their president. But it is interesting to look back at what qualities Americans *said* they were seeking in a president before the election. The national study on confidence in leadership that I alluded to earlier asked that question. Five qualities or traits were identified as extremely important by half or more of the respondents. The single most important trait was honesty and integrity, named by 66 percent. Next most important—intelligence. Ability to communicate was next, followed by willingness to work with people in both political parties and the ability to bring the American people together. The least important trait was having served in the military, which just 13 percent thought extremely important. Being likeable was the next lowest in importance (21 percent). Only 23 percent believed experience in Washington was extremely important. Two other responses are noteworthy. A strong belief in God was extremely important to 38 percent of those who responded. Having new ideas was extremely important to almost the same number (37 percent).

Those top five traits were perceived as extremely important across political or ideological lines. But the study reported significant differences between Republicans and Democrats on the value of other traits. Decisiveness, a strong belief in God, and military service were more important (in that order) to Republicans than Democrats. Democrats thought experience in foreign policy, having new ideas, understanding and sympathizing with others, experience in Washington, and being likeable were more important than Republicans did. The biggest gap between the parties was this: 14 percent or more Democrats than Republicans thought the following were extremely or very important—having new ideas, understanding and sympathy with others, and being likeable.

The study was published in November 2007, and it is fascinating to see which candidates were ascendant at that time. The top choice was Hillary Rodham Clinton—33 percent of respondents said they had a great deal of confidence she would be a good president. Barack Obama was second, with 22 percent reporting a great deal of confidence in his ability to lead. Next was Rudy Giuliani, chosen by 18 percent. John Edwards followed at 13 percent. Twelve percent said they had a great deal of confidence that John McCain would be a good president. Also worth noting is that 26 percent of respondents said they had no confidence ("none at all") that Clinton would make a good president. That was the largest no-confidence rating in the study. Nineteen percent had no confidence in Barack Obama, and 20 percent had no confidence in John McCain.

When retired general Colin Powell endorsed Barack Obama on "Meet the Press" on October 19, Powell described Obama as a "transformational figure" who was the right president for this moment in time. The long, contentious campaign had been a "final exam" for McCain and Obama, in Powell's view. Obama emerged as his choice because "he has both style and substance." The former Bush secretary of state said he thought the new president should address both the American people and the world at large to describe how his policies will be different from those of the past eight years. One of the most pressing challenges the new president will face, Powell said, is "to fix the reputation we've left with the rest of the world."

In the run-up to the election, historian Doris Kearns Goodwin noted that an even temperament characterized many of our best presidents. No matter what crisis Lincoln and FDR faced, they dealt with it in a calm, deliberative way. And great leaders are often able to rise above personal disappointments and hurts, even tragedies. Lincoln's political genius included his ability to assemble a brain trust of his former political opponents into a brilliant "team of rivals." "You can't let resentments poison you," Goodwin said.

It is clear that the new president will have to restore not just the broken economy, but the confidence of the nation. He will have to give the country its optimism back. The very fact of his election is a giant first step in that process. As Colin Powell predicted, Obama's election was a matter of pride not just for African Americans, but for all Americans. My guess is that Obama will conduct his new presidency with Lincoln, FDR and John F. Kennedy in mind (we know he read Doris Kearns Goodwin's *Team of Rivals: The Political Genius of Abraham Lincoln* during the campaign). There is a time-tested pattern for inspiring American citizens. Our greatest leaders have reminded us that we are all in this together, and that we will have to make hard choices, even sacrifices.

In the months ahead, the new administration will also have to begin discovering and undoing the worst machinations of the Bush years. None of that will be possible until the reflexive, even obsessive opacity of the previous administration is reversed and more transparent government restored.

Obama must also reach out to the rest of the world. It, too, needs reassuring. He will have to overcome the isolation of the United States that Bush's policies created. Many other nations seem eager to work with the new president. More than any president in our history, Obama looks like the rest of the world. That is an asset of incalculable value. Obama wasn't just the choice of American voters. He was the world's preferred candidate, in a campaign that was followed overseas as avidly as the world soccer finals. Just as international cooperation helped save far-flung banks and other financial institutions in 2008, we will need ongoing international collaboration to solve such enormous, shared problems as global warming, nuclear containment, and potentially explosive economic disparity throughout the world.

A classic purveyor of hope, Obama was able to energize young voters as never before. His appeal was even more palpable than John Kennedy's. Millions of older voters who had grown cynical about government and the electoral process were also galvanized. Those voters, young and old, whose passion was reignited now constitute a precious pool of talent excited by the possibilities of public service, including government. As a nation we pay a terrible price when we stop believing in the possibility of good government. In our disdain, we cede our country to the ideologues and the hacks. Those who worked for Obama's election know the joy of struggling for and achieving significant change. Now, while the crackle is still in the air, is the time to create twenty-first-century versions of the Peace Corps and dozens of other organizations that tap American energy and idealism.

In 2008, all eyes were on the men and the woman who sought the highest office in the land. But it is a mistake to focus only on leaders. Even if we rise to become president of the United States, we spend most of our lives as followers, not leaders. In the past we have tended to think of the distinction between the two hierarchically. But, in fact, as our workplaces and other organizations become flatter and more collegial, the terms become less and less meaningful. Leadership is a temporary assignment among Google engineers, who serve for a time, then pass the crown to another member of their small working groups. Even in more traditional organizations, a reciprocal relationship exists between leaders and followers. Leader and follower are partners in the same dance. It is our most important obligation as followers to speak truth to power. As hundreds of unemployed whistle blowers can tell you, candor is a more dangerous job than silence. Speaking truth to power always requires courage, and when the stakes are high enough, it demands true heroism. But the follower who boldly points out the elephant in the room or the flaw in the boss's preferred plan is transformed into what can only be called a leader—someone who assumes responsibility and acts in the best interest of the group. And it's not only the whistle blowers or the dissenters who need to be listened to, to be heard. We all do. A story about FDR comes to mind: crowded, grieving masses surged along Constitution Avenue in April 1945, waiting for his funeral cortege to pass by. As his hearse neared, a well-dressed, middle-aged man standing in the throng fell to his knees, sobbing desperately until finally regaining his composure. A stranger by his side asked, "Did you *know* the President?" The man could barely reply. "No . . . but he knew me."

As someone who remembers the Great Depression, I can assure you that the financial crisis of 2008 was an order of magnitude less serious. But it was a genuine crisis nonetheless, and they are always crucibles of leadership. Becoming a leader is not an orderly path. It is a fitful, often painful process that involves wrong turns and dead ends before great strides are made. Usually some transformative event or experience is central to finding one's voice, learning how to engage others through shared meaning, and acquiring the other skills of leadership. FDR's lifetime struggle with polio was most certainly his crucible of leadership. Instead of simply enduring hard times, we have to seize every opportunity for transformation they afford. In recent weeks, as the stock market rocked and rolled, I thought often of what Abigail Adams had written to John Quincy Adams

EPILOGUE TO *ON BECOMING A LEADER* 303

in the turbulent days of 1780: "These are the hard times in which a genius would wish to live. . . . Great necessities call forth great leaders."

It is significant, I think, that Adams chose the plural, *leaders*. Especially now that the United States has an exciting new president, it is easy to forget that we need more than one gifted leader at a time. At the founding of the United States, when our population was less than 4 million, we had six towering leaders: Washington, Jefferson, Hamilton, Madison, Franklin, and Adams. Now that we number more than 304 million people, we are surely capable of yielding at least 600 world-class leaders in this country alone.

Will you be one of them?

DAVID GERGEN ON
"EPILOGUE TO THE TWENTIETH-
ANNIVERSARY EDITION OF
ON BECOMING A LEADER"

WHEN I STARTED TEACHING IN A UNIVERSITY in the mid-'90s, I assumed that for most students, political history began with John Kennedy. I was wrong. Kennedy had already slipped into the mists of time, and their common point of reference was Ronald Reagan. By now, Reagan too seems almost ancient to young minds, and a quarter-century from now—who knows—even Barack Obama may seem a far-off memory. How quickly the recent past loses its grip on the imagination of rising generations.

And yet, some things do not change among students, among them the relevance of special books that speak to their hearts as well as their heads. In my classrooms, one book that has had enduring appeal is the classic by Warren Bennis, *On Becoming a Leader*, first published in 1989. Over the years, I have assigned it to a number of classes, and at the end of each semester, students report that it was one of the most helpful they read. Its messages are so timeless I can imagine that in their coming-of-age years, a young Pericles or Marcus Aurelius would have enjoyed an early version, too.

What draws the young into the book is the central insight in the introduction to the original edition: "The process of becoming a leader is much the same as the process of becoming an integrated human being. . . . No leader sets out be a leader per se, but rather to express him- or herself freely and fully. . . . Each of these individuals has continued to grow and develop throughout life." The text itself is an invaluable guide to living a life of integrity, passion, and authenticity. Such reflections are not usually found in a class on macroeconomics or political science, but they fly straight to the souls of young people setting out on a journey. And for Warren, leadership is all about a journey.

At first blush, it is discouraging to see one of the major themes of the original book reappear with even greater emphasis in this new epilogue, published two decades later—his lament about the sad state of leadership in the United States. When the Founders gathered in Philadelphia to write the Constitution, he pointed out in the first edition, America had a population of little more than 3 million people and yet had six world-class leaders (Washington, Jefferson, Hamilton, Madison, Franklin, and Adams). In 1989, we had a population of 288 million and, as Warren wrote then, were struggling to find a single world-class leader. Today, we have reached some 304 million and we are reeling from failures of leadership that have toppled our economy and left us weakened as a world power. As Warren argues in this epilogue, things have unraveled at a dizzying pace. From greed and egregious management in the private sector to incompetence and irresponsibility among political leaders, a sense is taking hold that our best days may be behind us. Three-quarters of Americans surveyed last fall told Harvard's Center for Leadership that we are suffering a crisis in leadership. Describing those who created these recent disasters and have since left the scene, Warren draws aptly from literature, in this case F. Scott Fitzgerald's description of Tom and Daisy Buchanan in *The Great Gatsby:* "They smashed up things and creatures and then retreated back into their money or their vast carelessness or whatever it was that kept them together, and let other people clean up the mess they made."

Yet this new epilogue, more than his earlier writings, also contains a sense of excitement that as we approach the second decade of the twenty-first century, perhaps the country can finally start to turn a corner. Warren has always been fond of a passage written to young John Quincy Adams by Abigail, his mother and a woman of considerable wisdom: "It is not in the still calm of life or the repose of a pacific station that great characters are formed. . . . The habits of a vigorous mind are formed in contending with difficulty. Great necessities call out great virtues." As with individuals, so it may be with nations. In his introduction to the revised edition of 2003, Warren predicted that 9/11 and the dot-com implosion (and by now, he would have added Iraq and an economic meltdown) "will be the crucibles that create a whole new generation of leaders. If so, we will have reason to celebrate as well as to mourn."

Now, in this epilogue to the 2009 twentieth-anniversary edition, Warren celebrates the coming to power of exactly that new generation, led by Barack Obama. In Obama, as Warren writes here, the country has elected a president who appears to have many of the traits we associate with successful leaders. He has impressed most Americans as a man of integrity and honesty, qualities highly valued by the public. He also has an even temperament—a preternatural calm—that was an enormous asset for Franklin Roosevelt during the Great Depression. His athletic grace and smile recall the charisma of John Kennedy. And if we are lucky, he will have the inner resolve of Lincoln. Still, as of this writing, it is far too early to tell whether this young, promising president will fulfill the hopes that America and the world have invested in him. The challenges he faces would overwhelm most presidents. We shall have to be patient.

Toward the end of this epilogue, Warren makes a larger point: as a people, we cannot rely upon a single individual, no matter how talented, to lead us to higher ground. The day of the single heroic figure, carrying the weight of an entire people upon his shoulders, is long gone—and indeed may never have really existed. We live in an age when not only the world has flattened, but when the hierarchy dividing leader and followers has largely flattened, too. A leader's role is to identify and encourage others to step forward and assume responsibility—to become a leader of leaders. Followers are participants in networks who must one day carry out directives and on another day must be willing to give them. "Leader and follower are partners in the same dance," writes Warren.

On Becoming a Leader is thus a book that, if anything, is more vitally relevant than when it was first published two decades ago. It has a message for each of us, especially the young. And it comes at a time when, as Warren writes, "we need leaders now as never before."

David Gergen is currently a professor of public service at Harvard's John F. Kennedy School of Government and director of its Center for Public Leadership. He is also editor-at-large for U.S. News & World Report and a senior political analyst for CNN. In earlier years, he served as a White House adviser to presidents Nixon, Ford, Reagan, and Clinton.

PART FOUR

LEADERSHIP
AS PERFORMANCE

ALTHOUGH I CAME OF AGE when psychoanalysis was a common rite of passage, I never felt that human behavior could be adequately explained by probing a single mind. To understand who we are we must look at how we behave in relation to others. During the 1940s and '50s, many of the brightest minds turned to anthropology for insights, much as many of today's best thinkers look to neuroscience. One of the landmarks of this interactive approach to understanding human behavior was Erving Goffman's 1959 *The Presentation of Self in Everyday Life*. Goffman borrowed the language of the theater to describe how we interact. He argued that we present ourselves to others much as actors create characters for an audience. For Goffman, human behavior is a series of performances. In Goffman's terms, leadership is a role, and a leader is one whose performance in that role wins his or her audience. No one understood this better than Shakespeare, an actor as well as a writer of singular genius. The role of king transforms Prince Hal into Henry V, not some psychological sea change. The role makes the monarch. I continue to be fascinated by leadership as performance, and in such related issues as how a leader can play that role and remain authentic. One of the ways that leaders captivate their audience—their followers—is through storytelling. No one who watched Barack Obama's extraordinary rise to the presidency has any doubt that crafting and sharing a resonant autobiographical story is key to becoming a leader.

THE SEVEN AGES OF
THE LEADER (2004)

MY INITIAL PLUNGE INTO LEADERSHIP came during World War II. I was a lieutenant in the infantry, 19 years old, and scared out of my wits. My orders were to assume command of a platoon on the front lines in Belgium. I arrived in the middle of the night, when most of the men were asleep. The platoon had taken up residence in a bombed out shell of a house. I was led into the kitchen by the platoon's runner, and he offered me a bench to sleep on. Instead, I put my sleeping bag on the floor, next to the rest of the men. Not that I slept. I lay awake all night, listening to the bombs explode. I was as green as can be and knew little about command—or the world, for that matter. When the others in the house began to stir, I heard one sergeant ask another, "Who's that?" "That's our new platoon leader," the man answered. And the sergeant said, "Good. We can use him."

Without realizing it, without having any idea what was the right thing to do, I had made a good first move. My entry had been low-key. I hadn't come in with my new commission blazing. In fact, I pretended to go to sleep on the floor. As a result, without drawing attention to myself, I learned something important about the men I would be leading. I learned that they needed me—or, at least, they needed the person they would subsequently teach me to be. And teach me they did. Over the next few weeks in Belgium, my men, who had already seen combat, kept me alive. They also taught me how to lead, often by example. The sergeant who had greeted my arrival with approval became my lifeline, quite literally, teaching me such essential skills as how to ride through a war zone without getting blown up.

This article was originally published in *Harvard Business Review,* January 2004.

While few business leaders need worry about being blown up, my experience in Belgium was in many ways typical of first leadership experiences anywhere. I was coming into an existing organization where emotions ran high, relationships had been established, and the members of the organization harbored expectations of me that I was not yet fully aware of. My new followers were watching me, to see if and how I would measure up. Every new leader faces the misgivings, misperceptions, and the personal needs and agendas of those who are to be led. To underestimate the importance of your first moves is to invite disaster. The critical entry is one of a number of passages—each of which has an element of personal crisis—that every leader must go through at some point in the course of a career. Business school doesn't prepare you for these crises, and they can be utterly wrenching. But they offer powerful lessons as well.

Shakespeare, who seems to have learned more every time I read him, spoke of the seven ages of man. A leader's life has seven ages as well, and, in many ways, they parallel those Shakespeare describes in *As You Like It:* to paraphrase, infant, schoolboy, lover, soldier, general, statesman, and sage. One way to learn about leadership is to look at each of these developmental stages and consider the issues and crises that are typical.

I can't offer advice on how to avoid these crises because many are inevitable. Nor would I necessarily recommend that you avoid them, since dealing with the challenges of each stage prepares you for the next. But knowing what to expect can help the leader survive and, with luck, come through stronger and more confident. And so first to the leader on the verge— Shakespeare's infant, "mewling . . . in the nurse's arms."

The Infant Executive

For the young man or woman on the brink of becoming a leader, the world that lies ahead is a mysterious, even frightening place. Few resort to mewling, but many wish they had the corporate equivalent of a nurse, someone to help them solve problems and ease the painful transition. Instead, the fortunate neophyte leader has a mentor, a concept that has its origins in Greek mythology. When Odysseus was about to go off to war, the goddess Athena created Mentor to watch over the hero's beloved son, Telemachus. The fact that Mentor had the attributes of both man and woman hints at the richness and complexity of the relationship, suggesting a deeper bond than that of teacher and student. In the real world, unfortunately, goddesses don't intervene and mentors seldom materialize on their own. While the popular view of mentors is that they seek out younger people to encourage and champion, in fact the reverse is more often true. The best mentors are usually recruited, and one mark of a future leader is the ability to identify, woo, and win the mentors who will change his or her life.

When Robert Thomas and I interviewed two generations of leaders for our book, *Geeks and Geezers,* we met a remarkable young real-estate and Internet entrepreneur, Michael Klein, who had recruited his first mentor when he was only four or five years old, as Robert and I wrote in our *Harvard Business Review* article, "Crucibles of Leadership" [presented earlier in this volume]. His guide was his grandfather, Max Klein, who was responsible for the paint-by-numbers craze that swept America in the 1950s and 1960s. The fad made Klein rich, but none of his children had the least interest in that business or any other. But little Michael did, and Max jumped at the chance to coach and counsel him, often in the course of long telephone conversations that continued until a few weeks before Max died. In effect, the older man served as a first-rate business school of one for his grandson, who became a multimillionaire while still in his teens.

It may feel strange to seek a mentor even before you have the job, but it's a good habit to develop early on. I was recruited as a mentor years ago while in the hospital for several weeks following a "coronary event." There, I had a remarkable nurse who seemed to anticipate my every need. We spent hours together, often talking late into the night. He told me of his ambition to become a doctor, although no one in his family in South Central Los Angeles had ever been to college. I was won over by his character and drive, as well as by the superb care he gave me. When he was ready to go to medical school, I did all I could to help, from putting him in touch with appropriate administrators to giving him a glowing recommendation. He had recruited me as skillfully as any executive headhunter and made me one of the first members of the team he needed to change his life. The message for the "infant executive"? Recruit a team to back you up; you may feel lonely in your first top job, but you won't be totally unsupported.

The Schoolboy, with Shining Face

The first leadership experience is an agonizing education. It's like parenting, in that nothing else in life fully prepares you to be responsible, to a greater or lesser degree, for other people's well-being. Worse, you have to learn how to do the job in public, subjected to unsettling scrutiny of your every word and act, a situation that's profoundly unnerving for all but that minority of people who truly crave the spotlight. Like it or not, as a new leader you are always on stage, and everything about you is fair game for comment, criticism, and interpretation (or misinterpretation). Your dress, spouse, table manners, diction, wit, friends, children, children's table manners—all will be inspected, dissected, and judged.

And nothing is more intense than the attention paid to your initial words and deeds, as any first-time presidential candidate can tell you. It's said of psychotherapy that the first ten minutes between doctor and patient are the most critical, and studies show that friendships formed by college students during orientation are the most enduring. Social psychologists have found that we base our judgments of people on extremely thin slices of behavior. We decide whether we are in sync or out of tune with another person in as little as two seconds.

So it is with leaders and organizations. Your first acts will win people over or they will turn people against you, sometimes permanently. And those initial acts may have a long-lasting effect on how the group performs. It is, therefore, almost always best for the novice to make a low-key entry. This buys you time to gather information and develop relationships wisely. It gives you an opportunity to learn the culture of the organization and benefit from the wisdom of those who are already there. A quiet entry allows the others in the group to demonstrate what they know. And it allows you to establish that you are open to the contributions of others. It shows them that you are a leader, not a dictator.

In retrospect, I realize that officer-candidate school had prepared me for my small triumph in that roofless house in Belgium. Even as the officers tried to cram all the survival skills we would need into four months of training, they told us again and again that the combat-seasoned men under our command would be our real teachers, at least at first. The same holds true in any organization. In the beginning, especially, your most talented, most seasoned, most decent followers will be the ones that keep you alive.

When Steve Sample became president of the University of Southern California in the early 1990s, he did a masterful job of easing in. He went to the campus incognito at least twice, and during one of those visits he attended a football game and spoke to faculty members and students who didn't know who he was. Those visits gave him a feel for the campus as it really was, not how the most assertive of his constituents wanted him to see it. And during his first six months, he did not make a single high-profile decision. He knew that the important things to be done could be deferred until the faculty, staff, and students were more comfortable with him and their relationships were more stable. Major changes in the first six months will inevitably be perceived as arbitrary, autocratic, and unfair, as much for their timing as for their content.

However, it is worth noting that, no matter what your first actions are, you can influence other people's image of you only to a limited extent. The people who will be working under your leadership will have formed an opinion about you by the time you walk into the office, even if they have never met you. They may love you, they may hate you, they may trust you or distrust you, but they've probably taken a stand, and their position may have very little to do with who you actually are. The leader often becomes a screen onto which followers project their own fantasies about power and relationships. To some degree, all leaders are created out of the needs, wants, fears, and longings of those who follow them. Events that predate your arrival will also shape followers' view of you. In an organization that's been through a crisis—several rounds of layoffs, say— people are liable to assume that you're there to clean house again and may respond with either open hostility or flattery in the hopes of keeping their jobs. Others may see you as their savior because of the bad leadership of your predecessor. Your first challenge is to try not to take your new followers' assessments too personally. The second—and far trickier—challenge is to embrace the fact that certain elements of their assessments may be accurate, even if they put you in an unflattering light.

The Lover, with a Woeful Ballad

Shakespeare described man in his third age "sighing like furnace," something many leaders find themselves doing as they struggle with the tsunami of problems every organization presents. For the leader who has come up through the ranks, one of the toughest is how to relate to former peers who now report to you.

Shakespeare painted a compelling portrait of the problem in *Henry IV, Part II*. Before Prince Hal becomes Henry V, his relationship with the aging rogue Falstaff is that of student and fellow hell-raiser. For all Falstaff's excesses, he is often Hal's wise teacher, helping the future king see beyond the cloistered, narrow education traditionally afforded a prince to glimpse what his future subjects feel, think, and need. But when it comes time for Hal to assume his royal responsibilities, he rejects Falstaff, despite their having shared a sea of ale and the sound of "the chimes at midnight." Henry doesn't invite Falstaff to his coronation, and he pointedly tells the ribald knight, "I know thee not, old man."

Today's leaders would instantly recognize the young king's predicament. It's difficult to set boundaries and fine-tune your working relationships with former cronies. Most organizations, with the exception of the military, maintain the fiction that they are at least semi-democracies, however auto-cratic they are in fact. As a modern leader, you don't have the option of telling the person with whom you once shared a pod and lunchtime con-fidences that you know her not. But relationships inevitably change when a person is promoted from within the ranks. You may no longer be able to speak openly as you once did, and your friends may feel awkward around you or resent you. They may perceive you as lording your posi-tion over them when you're just behaving as a leader should.

I know of a young executive, let's call her Marjorie, who was recently promoted from middle management to head of the marketing department at a pharmaceutical company. One of three internal candidates for the job, she was close friends with the other two. Marjorie had already dis-tinguished herself within the company, so it was no surprise that she got the promotion, even though she was the youngest and least experienced of the three. But the transition was much more difficult than she had anticipated. Her friends were envious. She would sometimes find herself in the awkward situation of attending an executive meeting at which one of her friends was criticized and then going straight to lunch with her. The new executive missed being able to share what she knew with her friends, and she missed their support. Her fellow executives had a more authori-tarian style than she did, and some even advised her to drop her old friends, which she had no intention of doing. Her compromise was to try to divide her time between her new peers and her old. The transition was still hard, but she made a good early move: she had frank conversations with her friends, during which she asked them how they were feeling and assured them their friendships were important to her and would continue.

However tough it was for Marjorie, she had the advantage of knowing the organization and its players. The challenge for the newcomer is know-ing who to listen to and who to trust. Leaders new to an organization are swamped with claims on their time and attention. Often, the person who makes the most noise is the neediest person in the group and the one you have to be most wary of, a lesson I learned more than 50 years ago from the renowned psychiatrist Wilfred Bion. At the time, Bion was doing pio-neering work in the new practice of group psychotherapy. He warned his students: focusing your attention on the most clamorous of your follow-ers will not only anger and alienate the healthier among them. It will dis-tract you from working with the entire group on what actually matters, accomplishing a common mission.

Knowing what to pay attention to is just as important and just as dif-ficult. In their efforts to effect change, leaders coming into new organiza-tions are often thwarted by an unconscious conspiracy to preserve the status quo. Problem after problem will be dumped in your lap—plenty of new ones and a bulging archive of issues left unresolved by previous administrations—and responding to them all ensures that you will never have time to pursue your own agenda. When I arrived at the University of Cincinnati as president I was totally unprepared for the volume of issues that found their way to my desk, starting with the 150 pieces of mail I typically had to respond to each day. The cumulative effect of handling each of these small matters was to keep me from addressing what was truly important: articulating a vision for the university and persuading the rest of the community to embrace it as their own. It is at this stage that an inability to delegate effectively can be disastrous.

Newcomer or not, almost all leaders find themselves at some point in the position of having to ask others to leave the organization—firing them, to put it bluntly. This is always a painful task, if only because it usually devastates the person being let go and because the timing is never opportune. Facing you across the desk always seems to be the employee who's just delivered triplets or bought an expensive house. There's little available to guide leaders on how to do this awful business in a humane way; only remember that you have people's emotional lives in your hands in such circumstances as surely as any surgeon or lover does.

The Bearded Soldier

Over time, leaders grow comfortable with the role. This comfort brings confidence and conviction, but it also can snap the connection between leader and followers. Two things can happen as a result: leaders may forget the true impact of their words and actions, and they may assume that what they are hearing from followers is what needs to be heard.

While the first words and actions of leaders are the most closely attended to, the scrutiny never really ends. Followers continue to pay close attention to even the most offhand remark, and the more effective the leader is the more careful he or she must be, because followers may implement an idea that was little more than a passing thought. Forget this and you may find yourself in some less dramatic version of the situation King Henry II did when he muttered, of Thomas à Becket, "Will no one rid me of this meddlesome priest?" and four of his nobles promptly went out and murdered the cleric. Many modern-day Henrys have mused along the lines of, "We should be looking at our technology strategy," only to be confronted a few months later with thick PowerPoint presentations and a hefty consulting bill.

Followers don't tell leaders everything. I know of an executive I'll call Christine who had a close working relationship with the rest of her group.

The department hummed along productively until the day one of her top performers, Joseph, showed up at her door, looking uncomfortable. He told her he'd been offered a job at another company and was planning to take it. The timing was terrible; the group was headed toward a major product launch. And Christine was stunned, because she and Joseph were friends and he had never expressed dissatisfaction with his position or the company. Why hadn't he told her he wanted a new opportunity? She would have created a job especially for him, and she told him as much. Unfortunately, it was too late. The fact is, however close Christine and Joseph were, she was still in charge, and few employees tell their bosses when they've talked to a headhunter. And because Christine and Joseph liked each other and had fun working together, she'd assumed he was satisfied.

A second challenge for leaders in their ascendancy is to nurture those people whose stars may shine as brightly as—or even brighter than—the leaders' own. In many ways, this is the real test of character for a leader. Many people cannot resist using a leadership position to thwart competition. I heard recently about an executive who had been well liked by his bosses and peers until he was promoted to head a division. Then those under him began to grumble about his management style, and it wasn't just sour grapes. His latest promotion had been a stretch, and he may have felt, for the first time in his career, vulnerable. Shortly thereafter, his employees began to notice that he was taking credit for their ideas and was badmouthing some of them behind their backs. When confronted about his behavior, he seemed genuinely surprised and protested that he was doing no such thing. Perhaps he was unconsciously trying to sabotage those under him to prop himself up. But those who reported to him began to leave, one by one. After a year, his reputation was such that nobody wanted to work with him, and he was asked to leave.

In contrast, authentic leaders are generous. They're human and may experience the occasional pang at watching someone accomplish something they cannot. But they are always willing—even anxious—to hire people who are better than they are, in part because they know that highly talented underlings can help them shine. Many of the greatest leaders of our times, including the Manhattan Project's Robert Oppenheimer, Xerox PARC's Bob Taylor, and even Walt Disney, had healthy enough egos to surround themselves with people who had the potential to steal their jobs.

The General, Full of Wise Saws

One of the greatest challenges a leader faces at the height of his or her career is not simply allowing people to speak the truth but actually being able to hear it. Once again, Shakespeare proves instructive. In *Julius Caesar*, that brilliant study of failed management, Caesar goes to the forum on the ides of March apparently unaware that he will die there. How could he not have known that something dreadful was going to happen on that inauspicious day? The soothsayer warns him to "beware the ides of March." There are signs of impending evil that any superstitious Roman would have been able to read, including an owl hooting during the day and a lion running through the streets. And then there is the awful dream that makes Calpurnia, Caesar's loving wife, beg him to stay home. She dreams that his statue gushed blood like a fountain with a hundred spouts. Shouldn't that have been clear enough for a military genius used to amassing and evaluating intelligence? If not, consider that Artemidorus, a teacher in Rome, actually writes down the names of the conspirators and tries three times to thrust the note of alarm into Caesar's hand, the last time seconds before Brutus and the gang fall upon him.

Caesar's deafness is caused as much by arrogance as anything else, and he is hardly the only leader to be so afflicted. Like many CEOs and other leaders, movie mogul Darryl F. Zanuck was notorious for his unwillingness to hear unpleasant truths. He was said to bark, "Don't say yes until I finish talking!" which no doubt stifled many a difference of opinion. A more current example can be seen in Howell Raines, the deposed executive editor of the *New York Times*. Among the many ways he blocked the flow of information upward was to limit the pool of people he championed and, thus, the number of people he listened to. Raines was notorious for having a small A-list of stars and a large B-list made up of everyone else. Even if Raines's division of the staff had been fair, which it certainly was not in the case of now-disgraced reporter Jayson Blair, the two-tier system was unwise and ultimately a career ender for Raines. He had so alienated the vast majority of people in the newsroom who knew what Blair was up to that they didn't even bother to warn him of the train wreck ahead, and he refused to believe the few who did speak up. The attitude of Raines and his managing editor, Gerald Boyd, was that their way was the only way. When a distinguished reporter dared to point out an error Boyd had made, Boyd literally handed him a coin and told him to call the *Los Angeles Times* about a job. The reporter promptly did, quitting the *New York Times* for the West Coast paper.

But the episode most clearly recalls Caesar's situation in that Raines seemed genuinely surprised when he was forced out in the summer of 2003. He had no doubt read Ken Auletta's lengthy profile of him that ran in the *New Yorker* in 2002, showing that Raines was widely perceived as arrogant. And he should have been a good enough newsman to be able to tell the difference between acceptance and angry silence on the part of those who worked for him. Arrogance kept Raines from building the alliances and coalitions that every leader needs. When Blair's journalistic crimes and misdemeanors came to light, there weren't enough people on the A-list to save Raines's professional life. Authentic leaders, by contrast, don't have what people in the Middle East called "tired ears." Their egos are not so fragile that they are unable to bear the truth, however harsh— not because they are saints but because it is the surest way to succeed and survive.

I've mentioned the wisdom of avoiding major change in the early months in a new position. At this stage, the challenge is different, because leaders further along in their careers are frequently brought in with a specific mandate to bring about change, and their actions have a direct and immediate impact on an organization's long-term fortunes. Hesitation can be disastrous. However, you still need to understand the mood and motivations of the people already in the company before taking action.

I wish I'd understood that when I arrived at the University of Cincinnati in 1971 with a mandate to transform the university from a local institution into a state one—a goal that was by no means widely shared among the faculty or, for that matter, the citizens of Cincinnati. One longtime university board member had warned me to keep a low profile until I had a better grasp of the conservative community and the people in it were more comfortable with me. I chose to ignore his wise counsel, believing that broad exposure of the university and, by extension, myself would benefit my cause. As a result, I accepted an invitation to host a weekly television show. Worse, the title of the show was *Bennis!* The exclamation point still makes me cringe. I might have been perceived as an arrogant outsider come to save the provinces under any circumstances, but *Bennis!* guaranteed that I would be viewed that way. That perception (all but indelible, as early perceptions tend to be) made it harder to realize my vision for the university.

The corporate world is filled with stories of leaders who failed to achieve greatness because they failed to understand the context they were working in or get the support of their underlings. Look at Durk Jager, who lasted less than a year and a half at Procter & Gamble. Critics accused him of trying to change the company too much, too fast. But what Jager couldn't do was sell his vision of a transformed P&G to its staff and other stakeholders. His very able successor, A. G. Lafley, seemed at first to back off from Jager's commitment to "stretch and speed" but in fact Lafley has been able to bring about change every bit as radical as any Jager spoke of, including going outside the company for new ideas, a reversal of P&G's traditional "invented here" philosophy. How did Lafley manage? "I didn't attack," he told *Business Week*. "I avoided saying P&G people are bad. . . . I preserved the core of the culture and pulled people where I wanted to go. I enrolled them in change. I didn't tell them."

The Statesman, with Spectacles on Nose

Shakespeare's sixth age covers the years in which a leader's power begins to wane. But far from being the buffoon suggested by Shakespeare's description of a "lean and slippered pantaloon," the leader in this stage is often hard at work preparing to pass on his or her wisdom in the interest of the organization. The leader may also be called upon to play important interim roles, bolstered by the knowledge and perception that come with age and experience and without the sometimes distracting ambition that characterizes an early career.

One of the gratifying roles that people in late career can play is the leadership equivalent of a pinch hitter. When *New York Times* publisher Arthur Sulzberger Jr. needed someone to stop the bleeding at the newspaper after the Blair debacle, he invited Howell Raines's predecessor, Joseph Lelyveld, to serve as interim editor. The widely respected journalist was an ideal choice, one who was immediately able to apply a career's worth of experience to the newspaper's crisis and whose tenure was unsullied by any desire to keep the job for the long term.

Consider, too, the head of a government agency who had chosen to retire from his leadership position because he had accomplished all his goals and was tired of the politics associated with his job. When an overseas office needed an interim leader, he was willing to step into the job and postpone retirement. He was able to perform an even better job than a younger person might have, not only because he brought a lifetime's worth of knowledge and experience but also because he didn't have to waste time engaging in the political machinations often needed to advance a career.

The Sage, Second Childishness

As I've pointed out, mentoring has tremendous value to a young executive. The value accrues to the mentor as well. Mentoring is one of the great joys of a mature career, the professional equivalent of having grandchildren. It is at this time that the drive to prepare the next generation for leadership becomes a palpable ache. I wrote earlier of my relationship with the young nurse who had ambitions to become a doctor. Clearly, the young man benefited from our relationship, but so did I. I learned about the true nature of mentoring, about its inevitable reciprocity and the fact that finding and cementing a relationship with a mentor is not a form of fawning but the initiation of a valuable relationship for both individuals.

When you mentor, you know that what you have achieved will not be lost, that you are leaving a professional legacy for future generations. Just as my nurse clearly stood to benefit from our relationship, entrepreneur Michael Klein was indebted to his grandfather, Max. But imagine the joy Max must have felt at being able to share the wisdom he acquired over a lifetime as a creative businessman. The reciprocal benefits of such bonds are profound, amounting to much more than warm feelings on both sides. Mentoring isn't a simple exchange of information. Neuroscientist Robert Sapolsky lived among wild baboons and found that alliances between old and young monkeys were an effective strategy for survival. The older males that affiliated with younger males lived longer, healthier lives than their unallied peers. Whether monkey or human, individuals in a mentoring relationship exchange invaluable, often subtle information. The elder partner stays plugged into an ever-changing world, while the younger partner can observe what does and doesn't work as the elder partner negotiates the tricky terrain of aging.

When we compared older and younger leaders for *Geeks and Geezers,* we found that the ruling quality of leaders, adaptive capacity, is what allows true leaders to make the nimble decisions that bring success. Adaptive capacity is also what allows some people to transcend the setbacks and losses that come with age and to reinvent themselves again and again. Shakespeare called the final age of man "second childishness." But for those fortunate enough to keep their health, and even for those not as fortunate, age today is neither end nor oblivion. Rather, it is the joyous rediscovery of childhood at its best. It is waking up each morning ready to devour the world, full of hope and promise. It lacks nothing but the tawdrier forms of ambition that make less sense as each day passes.

SIDNEY HARMAN ON
"THE SEVEN AGES OF THE LEADER"

IT IS FUN TO READ Warren Bennis's "Seven Ages" even as it is fun to read his twenty-five books on leadership. The fun arises because he has mastered the art of teaching without showing off. The reader comes away having learned a great deal but still rather liking the author. Of his "Seven Ages," I have six thoughts:

○ Warren's emphasis on mentors and mentoring is a good thing. I remind him of Horace Mann's marvelous metaphor: "The teacher and the student on a log." That notion of a horizontal relationship between the teacher and the student is the essence of serious mentoring. In the end, it becomes deliciously difficult to determine who is the mentor—who, the mentee. They have learned from each other.

○ As Warren reviews the roles of leaders, he omits one aspect he and I have talked about—the leader as catalyst. It is one thing—and a good thing—to chair a meeting in which good ideas are shared. It is a far better thing when, on occasion, prompted by the leader, a group produces an idea which represents a leap of imagination—a leap of creativity. Typically, the leader who can pull off that electric moment brings a combination of intellectual strength (grounded in a broad range of study) and the ability to subordinate himself or herself to the process.

○ I respect his urging that first steps are critical. My own practice in that respect (influenced in no small measure by Warren Bennis) has been to visit newly acquired firms and to direct my immediate attention to immediate needs—and then to address them. A typical example occurred years ago when acquiring a factory in the Midwest where employees were bedeviled by the fact that, whenever it rained, the parking lot became a morass. Parking and extricating their cars was a major nuisance. The very first thing we did was to pave that damned parking lot. The message was instantly clear. We understood and responded to their problems.

○ "Pay attention to the words," writes Dr. Bennis. That is no small thing. It is possible for one to lead without command of the language and the mechanism for delivering it, but it is an invaluable asset to be able to speak publicly and inspirationally. That, in turn, requires that the speaker (the employer of words) have something of substance to say. I have often declared, "Get me some poets as managers." It is not said merely to be provocative. Poets are our original systems thinkers. Poets have a unique facility to examine and contemplate the complex and the mysterious and to reduce them to the sublime.

○ My experience in business, government, and education persuades me that too many leaders think the way they manage—and manage the way they think—top down, linear, serial, sequential, synchronous. The need in the new digital world is for leaders who think and act horizontally, interactively, asynchronously. That is how poets think. It is how the poet-manager manages.

○ If many leaders think in analog fashion (top down, linear, synchronous, etc.), that style probably arises from an education focused on learning one special narrow discipline. That frequently leads to the fear: "I know my job, but I have no idea how the whole system—the whole company works. Somehow, it seems to have a life and a motion of its own—totally independent of me." That view promotes a life of silent terror. Such a leader simply cannot fathom the system. The poet/manager is the promising answer in a demanding new age.

Dr. Sidney Harman is founder and chairman emeritus of Harman International, as well as Judge Widney Professor of Business at the University of Southern California. He is also founder of the Program on Technology, Public Policy, and Human Development at the John F. Kennedy School of Government at Harvard, and author of *Starting with the People* (Houghton Mifflin, 1988) and *Mind Your Own Business* (Doubleday, 2003).

THE LEADER AS
STORYTELLER (1996)

WRITING ON LEADERSHIP has become a growth industry in recent years, with writers churning out thousands of articles and hundreds of books on the subject over the last two decades. Of the handful that seem likely to endure, two that immediately come to mind are James MacGregor Burns's still resonant *Leadership* (Harper & Row, 1978) and James O'Toole's *Leading Change: Overcoming the Ideology of Comfort and the Tyranny of Custom* (Jossey-Bass, 1995). These two have now been joined by a third, Howard Gardner's superb new book, *Leading Minds*.

Subtitled *An Anatomy of Leadership,* Gardner's book is extraordinarily ambitious. It attempts to do nothing less than create a cognitive framework for all that has been learned about leadership. Like Gardner's earlier *Frames of Mind* (Basic Books, 1983), *The Mind's New Science* (Basic Books, 1986), and *Creating Minds* (Basic Books, 1993), his new book is the product of his research into creativity and influence, undertaken at Harvard University's Graduate School of Education.

Because Gardner is a good teacher who knows that the most effective lessons are often couched in good stories, he does not just present his theory of leadership in a text full of the italicized terms and simplistic charts that have become as obligatory as page numbers in recent leadership books. Instead, he fleshes out his theoretical notions in lively minibiographies of 11 twentieth-century leaders, beginning with Margaret Mead and ending with Mahatma Gandhi. In the context Gardner creates, these condensed lives have the force of letters from some of the great leaders of the

This review of Howard Gardner's *Leading Minds: An Anatomy of Leadership* (Basic Books, 1995) was originally published in *Harvard Business Review,* January/ February 1996.

recent past—letters that tell us, if only in a fragmentary way, what these men and women learned about the conduct of public life during their remarkable careers. The brief biographies are a delight and an education, full of useful hints and signposts, if not answers.

Before analyzing Gardner's achievement in some detail, let me say why his book is so important. Around the globe, humanity currently faces three extraordinary threats: the threat of annihilation as a result of nuclear accident or war, the threat of a worldwide plague or ecological catastrophe, and a deepening leadership crisis in most of our institutions. Unlike the possibility of plague or nuclear holocaust, the leadership crisis will probably not become the basis for a best-seller or a blockbuster movie, but in many ways it is the most urgent and dangerous of the threats we face today, if only because it is insufficiently recognized and little understood.

The signs of a leadership crisis are alarming and pervasive. Witness the change in leadership at some of our most respected corporations—General Motors, IBM, and American Express. Gardner acknowledges the deterioration of leadership in our corporations when he compares the leadership capabilities of two of GM's former leaders, Alfred P. Sloan, Jr., and Roger Smith.

In politics, it is the same. No head of a developed, democratic nation has more than a tentative hold on his or her constituency. President Bill Clinton has an approval rating that threatens to dip below 40% and faces opposition from Congress unmatched in recent history. In Great Britain, John Major's Conservative government teeters. Italy and Japan must manage with interregnum governments. A recent survey taken in Canada shows that its Progressive Conservative Party, in office for a decade, has the support of only 3% of the population. The same poll indicates that twice as many respondents—6%—believe Elvis is still alive.

The leadership crisis appears to be spreading. In the United States, senators are resigning, some without encouragement of scandal. The mood of the populace is unsettled, angry, sometimes foul, and, in a few horrifying recent cases, even murderous. And those who ostensibly lead agree only that things are terrible and getting worse. Among the general population, cynicism is rampant. I don't recall such a widespread loss of faith in our major institutions even during the tumultuous 1960s. Indeed, I can't remember a time when so many of our leaders themselves were so vocally disenchanted with government, including their own political parties, as they are today. Vice President Al Gore recently told an apocryphal story that perfectly captures the tenor of the times. A government pollster, clipboard in hand, asks people whether they are more satisfied with government today. Five percent say they are more satisfied, 10% say less, and 85% refuse to answer because they think the question is part of a government plot.

It was with this crisis very much in mind, with "Where Have All the Leaders Gone?" playing in my head, that I read Gardner's book. And although *Leading Minds* offers no magic formula, no quick cure, it does provide a framework for thinking about leadership in clear, unemotional terms that is the necessary first step toward resolving the leadership crisis that faces us.

One of Gardner's central ideas is that effective leaders—the Hitlers as well as the Roosevelts—tell or embody stories that speak to other people. By leaders, Gardner does not mean only CEOs or heads of state. In his view, leaders are all those "persons who, by word and/or personal example, markedly influence the behaviors, thoughts, and/or feelings of a significant number of their fellow human beings." (Gardner prefers the term *audience* to *followers* for those who are influenced.) He describes a continuum of leadership that starts with indirect leadership, exerted through scholarly work or other symbolic communication, and progresses to direct leadership of the sort exercised by world leaders through speeches and other means.

Gardner also charts leadership in terms of its widening impact: from influence exercised within relatively narrow domains, such as academic specialties, to influence exercised over larger communities, such as the influence Pope John XXIII exerted over the Roman Catholic Church. In addition, he describes a hierarchy of leadership based on creativity, with smaller-scale leaders such as educator Robert Maynard Hutchins at the bottom and visionaries such as Gandhi at the top.

The four factors Gardner lists as essential for effective leadership are a tie to a community or audience, a rhythm of life that includes isolation and immersion, a relationship between the stories leaders tell and the traits they embody, and arrival at power through the choice of the people rather than through brute force. Readers may or may not agree with the theoretical framework that Gardner modestly describes as not a model of leadership but merely the ingredients for a model. Whether they agree or not, however, they will find his stories of actual leaders full of insights into the myriad ways leadership expresses itself. Gardner is never so committed to his cognitive theory that he limits his observations to what fits neatly within his paradigm. With remarkable economy, he gives us more, not less; he provides not only the abstract and theoretical but also the concrete and historical.

Gardner's attempt to analyze leadership systematically is courageous, given the vulnerability of any overarching explanation to critical assault.

But the magic of the book is this juxtaposition of the theoretical with the telling particulars. It is useful to learn that J. Robert Oppenheimer, head of the Manhattan Project and later a controversial spokesman for the responsible use of nuclear energy, began as an indirect leader within the relatively limited universe of theoretical physics. More interesting, however, is the idiosyncratic nature of Oppenheimer's leadership, vividly revealed in Gardner's account of Oppenheimer's career.

Gardner knows that the right anecdote can be worth a thousand theories, and he is best when he shows instead of tells. For example, rather than write at length on how Oppenheimer's leadership sometimes failed because of his arrogance, Gardner gives a single indelible example: Oppenheimer's icy dismissal of publisher Philip Graham for having failed to read some text in the original Sanskrit. In the same chapter, Gardner provides a glimpse of moral leadership when he recounts how President Lyndon Johnson (not one of Gardner's 11) ended Oppenheimer's unofficial banishment from public life by presenting him with the Enrico Fermi Award. Oppenheimer showed his profound understanding of the significance of Johnson's action when he said, "I think it is just possible, Mr. President, that it has taken some charity and some courage for you to make this award today. That would seem to me a good augury for all of our futures."

Again and again, Gardner gives us opportunities to think deeply about leadership by defining terms in which to do so and by describing and ordering the many forms that leadership takes. If this schematic approach sometimes gets a bit tedious, we know that in a page or two we will come to another illuminating moment, another small take-home lesson. This is the primary return on our investment of time. A secondary pleasure of the book is that it has us jotting notes to ourselves to find out more about leaders whom we might otherwise have overlooked, such as Angelo Giuseppe Roncalli, the future Pope John XXIII, who paused on his journey to the papacy to save Jews in the Balkans during World War II. Gardner's creativity, recognized with a MacArthur "genius" award, transforms what could have been a tedious slog through weighty subject matter into an intellectual thrill ride.

One of the great strengths of Gardner's book is that it avoids the false dichotomies that mar so much of the contemporary literature about leadership. However well intentioned, those who write about leadership have tended to become embroiled in one or more of the now familiar controversies on the subject. Three debates in particular have preoccupied those concerned with leaders and leadership.

The first of these debates is whether leaders are larger-than-life figures—heroes who can change the weather, as Winston Churchill said his ancestor John Churchill could—or whether they are simply vivid embodiments of forces greater than themselves. I think of this as a debate between Tolstoy and Carlyle. In Tolstoy's *War and Peace,* Napoleon and his Russian counterparts have very little to do with the ultimate outcome of the great battles with which they are identified. To use a metaphor that might have left Tolstoy tugging his beard in confusion, the leader in Tolstoy's view is just another surfer riding the waves of the zeitgeist, albeit the surfer with the biggest board. Carlyle, on the other hand, argues that every institution is the lengthened shadow of a great man. Had he been a Southern Californian, he might have written that great leaders don't just ride waves, they make them.

Instead of embracing either of these polarized views of leadership, Gardner is able to transcend them, even to reconcile them. Gardner never succumbs to the either/or thinking that is the province of what he describes as the five-year-old mind—five being the age Gardner chooses as representing the unschooled mind of the general public. In writing about General George C. Marshall, for instance, Gardner describes both the behavior of a hero—Marshall as a young officer who dares to confront General Pershing at their first meeting—and the career trajectory of a leader who sought to repair the economies of former enemies. If Gardner occasionally tips the scale in favor of Carlyle's view of leadership, who can blame him? After all, this is a book that recognizes the importance of stories in human affairs, and what stories are more compelling than those about heroes?

Gardner also rises above the persistent controversy over whether leaders are born or made. This debate is sufficiently widespread to have inspired a cartoon in which a nervous teenager presents a report card blackened with Fs to his CEO father and asks, "What do you think, Pop, genes or the environment?" Gardner acknowledges the controversy, which has occasioned raised voices in a thousand faculty clubs, but instead of choosing sides, he presents useful data from both as part of the matrix of what we know about leaders. He reports that leaders do seem to have certain experiences in common. A remarkable number of the prominent figures of our time, including President Clinton, suffered the early loss of a father. And leaders seem to have certain traits in common as well. As my own study of dozens of contemporary leaders has revealed, whether in the arts, the political arena, or the corporation, leaders are almost always risk takers. (They also tend to be curious, energetic, and gifted with an acute sense of humor.)

Gardner not only can examine the controversy over nature versus nurture equitably, he also can consider it without obsessing about it. His ability to juggle contradictory notions is a sign of his maturity. To argue over whether leaders are born or made is an indulgent diversion from the urgent matter of how best to develop the leadership ability that so many have and that we so desperately need. A Nobel Prize awaits the person who resolves the question of whether leaders are born or made. But until some unanticipated breakthrough occurs or compelling new data emerge, the argument leads nowhere. The need for leadership in every arena of public life has become so acute that we don't have the luxury of dwelling on the unresolvable.

The third of the false dichotomies that Gardner so artfully avoids is the perceived conflict between expedient and idealistic leadership. The literature on leadership uses several different terms to describe those leaders who seize the moment without regard for the impact of their actions on the quality of other people's lives. *Machiavellian* is the harshest of these terms. The gentler ones typically crop up in discussions of contingency theory and "situationalism." But Gardner wisely avoids labels, choosing instead to show us that leaders are often both pragmatists and idealists. He correctly characterizes Hutchins, for example, as a "pragmatically tinged idealist," and talks of Sloan's desire to serve the nation while making money for General Motors.

In four decades of studying leaders, I have repeatedly found them to be what I call pragmatic dreamers—men and women whose ability to get things done is often grounded in a vision that includes altruism. Thus when Steve Jobs was recruiting John Sculley, then head of PepsiCo, for Apple Computer, Jobs knew to appeal not just to Sculley's ambition but also to his desire to leave a legacy that would go beyond boosting profit margins. Jobs is said to have asked the man who was to become Apple's next president and CEO how many more years of his life he wanted to spend making flavored water.

Scholars tackle two kinds of subjects. Some, like dry-fly fishing and the iconography of sixteenth-century French poetry, can be plumbed to their depths. Others, like leadership, are so vast and complex that they can only be explored. The latter subjects are inevitably the more important ones. You may question a few of Gardner's specific choices. For example, you may wonder if his work would have been more applicable to corporate life if he had chosen not to focus almost exclusively on public leadership and its large-scale issues. But any such quibbles are only that, given the remarkable achievement of the book.

In the patterns of leadership that Gardner traces, several elements recur that have not been emphasized enough in earlier work on the subject. Travel, for instance, was even more important than formal education in shaping many of Gardner's leaders, including Roncalli and Gandhi. Gardner points out that nonauthoritarian leaders are more likely than authoritarian leaders to have traveled extensively abroad. Many leaders went on almost mythic interior journeys involving testing and rebirth. Gardner shows how Eleanor Roosevelt, who had to deal with both her husband's polio and his love for another woman, responded by reinventing herself as an increasingly independent advocate for the causes that were most important to her, notably women's rights and civil rights.

It is important, though, that we do not become too Carlylean in our view of leadership. Leadership is never exerted in a vacuum. It is always a transaction between the leader, his or her followers, and the goal or dream. A resonance exists between leaders and followers that makes them allies in support of a common cause. The leader's role in this process has been much analyzed. My studies show, for instance, that leaders are highly focused, that they are able to inspire trust, and that they are purveyors of hope. But followers are more essential to leadership than any of those individual attributes. As Garry Wills writes in *Certain Trumpets: The Call of Leaders* (Simon & Schuster, 1994), "The leader most needs followers. When those are lacking, the best ideas, the strongest will, the most wonderful smile have no effect."

Leaders are capable of deep listening: Gandhi demonstrated that when he traveled throughout India learning the heart of his people. But what distinguishes leaders from, say, psychotherapists or counselors is that they find a voice that allows them to articulate the common dream. Uncommon eloquence marks virtually every one of Gardner's leaders, but I have yet to see public speaking listed on a résumé. We seem to regard the ability to galvanize an audience as something almost tawdry, even dangerous. Yet it was the eloquence of Martin Luther King, Jr., grounded in the cadences of thousands of his father's sermons, that gave him the voice of a national, even international leader. That fact should be kept in mind by anyone trying to draw up a curriculum for future leaders.

Effective leaders put words to the formless longings and deeply felt needs of others. They create communities out of words. In *Leading Minds*, Gardner shows that he himself is just such a leader, able to articulate and clarify what many of us have been thinking on the subject for a long time.

PETER GUBER ON
"THE LEADER AS STORYTELLER"

MY ENCOUNTER OF THE FIRST KIND with Warren Bennis was through his participation in an event I had the privilege to recently host on the power of narrative. While the conclave engaged a formidable leadership group of renowned storytellers, business gurus, and academics, I couldn't help but be astonished by their reverence for Warren. When he spoke, more than listen, we practically inhaled his wisdom. One could not help but be touched by his generosity, enlightened by his knowledge, and moved by his spirit.

Conversing with the group in a powerful but gentle manner, Warren shared his conviction that if you dissected what made every great leader successful, you would find a collection of stories that fueled their dreams, which they converted into goals by igniting the passion of their audience. This obviously was not the first time Warren Bennis extolled the benefits of storytelling as a critical element of leadership success.

Nearly thirteen years ago, Bennis published an article titled "The Leader as Storyteller" in the *Harvard Business Review,* in which he reviewed Howard Gardner's book *Leading Minds: An Anatomy of Leadership.* This article shone the light on something our nation has experienced recently— a leadership crisis. Warren emphasized the author's focus on the leader needing to be an empowered storyteller—a tool that is often cited as soft stuff. But, when the chips are down, as they are today, it's the soft stuff that really counts.

Bennis adroitly noted the high value Gardner places on narrative in transforming theory into actionable prose. All stories are action-oriented. As Bennis appropriately underscored, leadership is always a transaction between the leaders, their followers, and the goal. I am an apostle of the proposition that it is only when the listeners take ownership of the leader's goal, and viral market the story and its mission that he is truly successful with his or her narrative.

As an executive, professor, writer, and artist, I have spent many career years analyzing what makes story so powerful. I've discovered the magic of story lies in the emotional connection between the storyteller, the story listener, and the content of the narrative itself. Storytelling encodes information that would on its own easily be meaningless and forgettable into this emotional experience, making it memorable, resonant, and actionable long after the story has been told. Listeners digest and repurpose the narrative with the critical information (dates, times, facts, or theories) as part of the story and become its viral advocates.

Storytelling clearly is one of the most effective and powerful tools in the leader's arsenal. Bennis quoted Gardner as defining leaders as all those "persons who, by word and/or personal example, markedly influence the behaviors, thoughts, and/or feelings of a significant number of their fellow human beings." He asserts that anyone who needs to convince or persuade an individual or a group of people to do something would greatly benefit by connecting to them through narrative. That is most often the mission of the business leader.

In his article, Warren Bennis cites the four factors Gardner describes as essential for effective leadership. These factors also comprise characteristics great business leadership must employ to become more effective storytellers and connected leaders.

A tie to a community or audience. I experienced firsthand that an effective storyteller must first disrupt the cacophony of noise that runs rampant in an audience's minds to focus their attention. This is best accomplished by being interested in them, not just interesting. Do your research and then aim at their hearts before asking them to open their wallets. Gardner prefers the term *audience* to *followers* for those who are influenced. My life has been dedicated to shaping the decision and actions of the "audience" rather than interacting with people as a customer, patron, or client. Audiences expect experiences, not information. If you think of your listeners as an audience, you'll want to render an experience, not regurgitate information. You will find in return that your audience will be less protective of their time and money and more receptive to your offering.

A rhythm of life that includes isolation and immersion. The most effective and compelling leaders must first find their intention, their internal motivation, before they externally motivate others through their stories. Discovering your intention requires isolation from the often chaotic stimuli of the organization. I encourage leaders to first put themselves in "state" by sitting quietly and calming the breath. Much like the athlete who visualizes a ski run and then competes, this state simulates what it feels like to be completely and empathetically heard, regardless of whether the audience heeds the call to action. It is only when leaders have achieved this state and found their unconditional intention that they are truly emotionally, physically, and spiritually ready to tell their story and have it be heard. Great leaders infuse their narratives with their intention and then motivate others to become as passionate. At the same time, leaders and their stories are only credible when the leaders are immersed in all facets of their business and are open to being curious rather than critical of information—including the good, the bad, and the ugly.

A relationship between the stories leaders tell and the traits they embody. Leaders must be genuine and authentic to motivate others. If the leaders' tongue, feet and wallet are going in opposite directions, so, too, will their listeners. Authenticity cannot be faked in an attempt to convince, persuade, or motivate others. The leaders' stories must demonstrate that they have skin in the game, that they are congruent with their story's mission, and are willing to share the risk.

Arrival at power through the choice of the people rather than through brute force. I have discovered through my own storytelling and coaching experience that the hardest thing for the storyteller to do is to surrender control of the story. We are not in control of anyone else. That's an illusion; don't make it a delusion. More important, no one wants to be controlled, sold, or manipulated. The only thing the storyteller is absolutely in control of is the telling of the story. Regardless of the outcome, the storyteller is successful with the story if it is well told and empathetically heard. The storyteller must step back, creating a gap for the listeners to willingly choose to cross. It is only when the listener takes this step forward, in essence taking ownership of the story, that the listener will not only embrace your goal but begin to virally market it as their own.

Peter Guber is chairman and CEO of Mandalay Entertainment Group, a multimedia venture spanning motion pictures, television, sports entertainment, and new media. Among the films he personally produced are *Batman, Rain Man, Gorillas in the Mist, Midnight Express,* and *Flashdance.* Peter Guber is also a full professor at the UCLA School of Theater, Film and Television.

LEADERSHIP AS A PERFORMING ART (2002)

WHATEVER ELSE IT IS, LEADERSHIP IS A ROLE, a part that a person plays. And so we are not surprised that the writer, who seems to have known the most about leadership, as indeed he knew the most about everything, was also a man of the theater. William Shakespeare was acutely aware of the leader as actor, both in the sense of a person who acts or is expected to act and in the sense of a performer on stage. Shakespeare understood that there was nothing like a play about power—its achievement, its use and misuse, its loss, and the way it changes the person who has it—to hypnotize his audience, be they groundlings or nobility. One way or another, all of Shakespeare's tragedies, all his history plays and even a number of his comedies are about the rise and fall of leaders. Indeed the link between leadership and drama was recognized long before the highly theatrical Age of Elizabeth. Aeschylus, Sophocles and other ancient playwrights knew intuitively that audiences would be riveted by plays about legitimacy, succession and other leadership matters—perhaps because the playwrights understood that the power that leaders have over the rest of us means that their lives are inextricably bound up with our own. Some men may, in fact, be islands, but no leader ever is. Palpable in ancient Greece and Elizabethan England, the link between leadership and performance is even more obvious today in a nation where at least one president—Ronald Reagan—was earlier both a member and a leader of the Screen Actors Guild.

A word about method here. This essay will be more post-modern in spirit than Aristotelian: instead of having a beginning, middle and end, it will be a work of bricolage. It will consist of a string of observations based

This previously unpublished essay was written in the winter of 2002.

on notes I've written to myself over the years on the convergence of leadership and performance. Occasioned by everything from movies I've been struck by to conversations with insightful friends, including my actor daughter, Kate, and other entertainment industry professionals, these notes have been fattening one of my accordion files for years.

Let me reach into that file and start with an anecdote about an encounter between Orson Welles and Franklin Delano Roosevelt. The first time FDR met Welles, the President graciously said to the fabled young actor: "You know, Mr. Welles, you are the greatest actor in America." "Oh, no, Mr. President," Welles replied. "You are."

That story is true even if it is apocryphal. Just as theater and religion have been linked since ancient times, so have theater and leadership. Look at all the actorly attributes the two great men shared. They were both masters of the relatively new medium of radio—Roosevelt paternalistically reassured the nation during his weekly Fireside Chats; Welles scared the same nation out of its wits with his apocryphal description of a Martian invasion in the infamous "War of the Worlds" broadcast. Both men skillfully used theatrical dress and props—Welles, his rakish hats, FDR, his signature cape and cigarette holder—to create dashing images for themselves despite significant physical imperfections.

In his fascinating short study *On Politics and the Art of Acting,* playwright Arthur Miller talks about the star quality that great actors, including Welles and FDR, have in abundance. Miller writes about seeing Marlon Brando on stage for the first time in an otherwise forgettable play by Maxwell Anderson. Brando made his entrance and said absolutely nothing for what seemed like a long time. The audience was mesmerized. "Without a word spoken, this actor had opened up in the audience a whole range of emotional possibilities, including, oddly enough, a little fear," Miller recalled. When Brando finally spoke his first line—"Anybody here?"—the relief was palpable that no violence had been done, Miller writes.

Miller then makes a brilliant observation, equally true of great actors and great leaders: "Here was Napoleon, here was Caesar, here was Roosevelt. Brando had not asked the members of the audience to merely love him; that is only charm. He had made them wish that he would deign to love them. That is a star. Onstage or off, that is power, no different in its essence than the power that can lead nations."

The star power that FDR had is an example of what is sometimes called charismatic leadership, a fuzzy but irresistible term. Miller incisively homes in on the intensity and intimacy of the emotion that such leaders arouse in us. For reasons that no one has satisfactorily explained, such magnetic individuals—such stars of leadership—cause us to care deeply about them. Without needing to share the same physical space, they induce in us a response that normally requires the presence of powerful pheromones.

Gifted director Peter Brook once observed that "one actor can stand motionless on the stage and rivet our attention while another one does not interest us at all. What is the difference? Where chemically, physically, psychically does it lie?" Brook argues that this question is "the starting point of our whole [dramatic] art?" It is also, I would argue, the starting point of the whole art of leadership, at least of all of true leadership, which is to say all leadership that is not purely situational. The poet W. H. Auden observed something comparable when he said a great actor can break your heart at 50 feet.

We tend to describe a star's power in personal terms—to say, for instance, that he or she has "presence." But such terms miss an important point about both being a star and being a leader. I'll come back to this subject a bit later, but for now, let me just say that what both great actors and great leaders do is make us—the audience—part of the performance. They engage us. However self-obsessed the star may be, he or she is only successful when the audience is engaged. As actors will tell you, the audience is essential too, perhaps even determinative of, a great performance. Similarly, no matter how soaring his or her agenda, a leader is truly successful only to the extent that his or her followers share that vision. Leadership is always a transaction between leader and follower and always involves reciprocity.

Shakespeare, of course, has something to say on this point. In *Henry IV, Part I,* we encounter Glendower, trying to impress Hotspur. "I can call spirits from the vasty deep," Glendower boasts. And Hotspur, in a hilarious outbreak of candor, replies: "Why so can I, or so can any man, but will they come when you do call for them?" Genuine leadership requires more than putting on the trappings of power. It requires the ability, as Miller observes, "to find the magnetic core that will draw together a fragmented public"—not just to call the spirits but to make them come when they are called. In essence, the leader is able to create community. Former President Clinton did this brilliantly in his speech accepting his party's first nomination when he spoke so movingly of there being "no them, only us." A content analysis of great political speeches would reveal a wealth of skillfully brandished plural personal pronouns—the one that pops immediately to mind is Churchill's prediction that "this will be our finest hour."

One of the great lingering questions of the leadership literature is whether leaders are born or made. Once again, I defer to the leadership guru from Stratford-on-Avon on this. In *Twelfth Night,* Malvolio, tangled up in his cross-garters, pronounces: "Some are born great, some achieve greatness, and some have greatness thrust upon them." Like so many comic moments, this one is packed with truth. The only misleading aspect of Malvolio's statement is the relative equality his syntax gives to these three paths to greatness. Few are born leaders—although we tend to rewrite the biographies of the great after the fact in ways that suggest they were found in a basket on the doorstep of history, already fully formed and armed with the skills of diplomacy and war. Knowing Harry Truman's remarkable performance as president, it is easy to forget that he was once regarded as little more than a smalltime politician who got lucky. FDR had so little respect for his vice president that he never fully confided in him—Truman wasn't told the true nature of the Manhattan Project until after Roosevelt's death. Indeed Truman was so ill-regarded early in his presidency that Washington wags joked: "To err is Truman."

Most leaders acquire greatness, and they do so as a result of having a role requiring greatness thrust upon them. Abigail Adams, a superb presidential advisor and shrewd analyst of leadership, was acutely aware of the role that crisis plays in forming leaders. Look at the stature and number of leaders who were forged in the relatively peaceful revolution that produced the United States—Washington, Jefferson, Adams, Franklin, Madison and Hamilton come immediately to mind. "These are the hard times in which a genius would wish to live," Abigail Adams wrote to her son John Quincy Adams in 1780. "Great necessities call forth great leaders."

The American Revolution was a crucible in which great leaders were formed, an experience that revealed and forged greatness. To use a term favored by the writer/producers of episodic television, the story of each of the founding fathers is an arc—Washington, Jefferson and the others are transformed by the war with Great Britain and the responsibilities of defining a nation into individuals quite different from the men they were before. Such transformations, which often take place in demanding times, or eras, are a consequence of the roles these leaders assume or create for themselves.

In the course of doing research for a new book on the alchemy of leadership called *Geeks & Geezers,* coauthor Bob Thomas and I interviewed the late John Gardner. The only Republican in Lyndon Johnson's cabinet (Gardner headed what was then called the Department of Health, Education and Welfare), Gardner was a reticent, even shy man who nonetheless helped create such innovative and durable organizations for the public good as Common Cause. Much to his surprise, Gardner told us, he discovered during World War II that he was a gifted manager. He had never thought of himself in those terms—he didn't even respect managers—but once cast in that role by his government superiors, he thrived in it. Gardner explained with unusual precision how role and talent sometimes converge to produce greatness. His management gifts were evident almost at once because, he theorized, "some qualities were there waiting for life to pull those things out of me." There are unknown numbers of people with the qualities necessary for leadership who never become leaders because life does not present them with the roles that will pull greatness out of them.

The plays in which Shakespeare dealt most directly with the alchemy of leadership are those that show the transformation of hell-raising Prince Hal into a heroic Tudor king. Monarchies reveal leadership at its most theatrical. A school child can list the ways in which kings and queens are like great stars of theater. They have the most lavish costumes, they wield props (throne and scepter among them) that allow even the people in the cheap seats to know who's in charge, they are at the center of the action and almost always in the spotlight—the list goes on and on. But political leaders are not simply like actors. They *are* actors. It's no accident that the time-honored education of the prince that Hal undergoes has, as its denouement, his acceptance of his royal role and all that goes with it. What turns him into a true king is not his performance in battle but his recognition that he both is and must act like a king. Although he has resisted royal responsibility mightily, he now accepts that he will always be on stage and always under scrutiny. And he knows that the script he must follow in the future is not about whim and self-indulgence but about what is best for the kingdom. When Hal says to Falstaff, "I know thee not, old man," the prince is denouncing the lay-about life of the ale house and the brothel as well as rejecting his no-longer seemly mentor. The moment would be heartbreaking if it were not, in effect, the moment that Henry accepts the mace and crown.

Great necessities call forth great leaders. In our own time, the terrorist attacks of September 11th, 2001, seemed to trigger just such a transformation in President George W. Bush. Whatever the President knew and whenever he knew it, the attacks revealed a newly serious leader in the White House. Before the suicide bombings of the World Trade Center and the Pentagon, Bush had an uncertain mandate and something of an aging frat-boy image. But he clearly recognized that the unexpected assault on the United States presented an opportunity to reveal himself as a world-class leader. He did so in an overtly theatrical way, with a speech to Congress and the nation broadcast on September 20. Whether history will declare Bush to have been a great president, for 30 minutes, in the course of that speech, he acted like one. Observers, including many Democrats, were stunned. Among them was Gerald Posner, who wrote of the speech in the *Wall Street Journal*: "Like Franklin Roosevelt or Winston Churchill, he rallied a country's spirit, had the courage to tell us the bad news that the upcoming battle would be neither swift nor easy, and declared that those who would destroy our culture and values would not prevail." In short, Posner observed: "He rose to this most important occasion."

In a fascinating behind-the-scenes look at how the speech evolved, D. T. Max wrote in the *New York Times Magazine* that Bush was very conscious of such historical models of exemplary leadership as Winston Churchill. (Churchill was another whose leadership flowered in mid-life, much to the surprise of his contemporaries. One of his biographers said of Churchill that he jaywalked through life until he was 66.) As Bush advisor Karen Hughes helped tweak Bush's speech, she had a plaque on her White House desk bearing Churchill's ringing declaration: "I was not the lion, but it fell to me to give the lion's roar." But Bush had no intention of sharing the stage with great presences from the past. He insisted that the speech contain no lines, however memorable, attributable to anyone else. This was his chance to dominate the world stage, and he knew it. It's fair to say that when the press began comparing his metamorphosis to that of Prince Hal, Bush was not the least surprised, despite his non-intellectual, good-ol'-boy persona. The headline in the *New York Times Magazine* described the speech as "2,988 words that changed a presidency." Put in appropriately theatrical terms, Bush's performance was a smash.

In his book, Miller notes that the kind of acting that modern media require is the less-is-more kind, not the grand, florid style that flourished before the microphone and the close-up. It would be fascinating to know what the expectations were of the crowd that gathered for the Lincoln-Douglas debates and what kind of actors the two men were. Today we know that the camera, and the voting public, tend to favor the candidate who acts as if the camera isn't there. Nixon's palpable dread of the camera during his televised match with John F. Kennedy would have doomed him even if it had been broadcast without sound. As Miller points out, Al Gore's inability to act relaxed on camera cost him far more than George W. Bush's verbal confusion, which never seemed to unnerve him or dim his easy smile. Joe Klein calls his latest book about Bill Clinton *The Natural*, and that's what we expect our leaders to be—even if they have to fake it. Whether real or feigned, their apparent ease makes us comfortable with them. Miller argues that such ease, however studied, makes an audience receptive, rather than defensive.

Acting ability is an aspect of leadership in every arena, from the playground to the board room. But it is absolutely key in national politics, where the only contact the average person has with the candidate or office holder is mediated by an entertainment medium. Even when we know our politicians by their written words, we inevitably read those words with media-generated images in mind. No wonder our prospective leaders call in experts to vet the color and cut of their suits and spend hours practicing their speeches and critiquing videotapes of those practice sessions. For modern leaders not to do so would be as foolish as it would have been for Greek and Roman leaders not to master the arts of rhetoric. And, in fact, those same arts of rhetoric and other time-honored dramatic techniques still matter—perhaps more now than ever. In May 2002, the *New Yorker* ran a Washington letter on "Democratic rising star" North Carolina Senator John Edwards, which amusingly but seriously described the entertainment values of a recent Democratic party conference in Florida. Writer Nicholas Lemann might have been a drama critic, not a political commentator, as he described "the dramatic buildup" culminating in keynote speaker Al Gore's appearance and parsed the speech Gore gave as "an art form with a lot of rules," from thanking "your introducer for that generous introduction" to finally basking "in the glow of the audience's applause, raising your arms above your head, palms forward, in a gesture that expresses something of triumph and self-effacement." We tend to think of ourselves, even our political selves, as spontaneous souls, but our conventions, state-of-the-union addresses and other political performances reveal that we practice a form of political theater as highly conventionalized as Kabuki.

Some years ago, in the course of writing an earlier book on leadership, I interviewed the distinguished director Sydney Pollack, whose work includes the Oscar-winning films *Tootsie* and *Out of Africa*. Pollack began his career as an actor—and he continues to take roles in films from time to time. In the course of that interview, Pollack talked about his first directorial experience. He told me that he had no idea how to direct a film, so he fell back on the skills he had developed as an actor and acted like a director. "That's the only thing I knew how to do, because I didn't know anything about directing," he told me. His "acting as if" (a favorite strategy of the Human Potential Movement, you'll recall) included costuming himself as a director and surrounding himself with the props he associated with the profession. "I had images of directors from working with them," Pollack said, "and I even tried to dress like a director—clothes that were kind of outdoorsy. I didn't put on puttees, or anything like that. But if there had been a megaphone around, I would have grabbed it."

I have included that anecdote because it raises a crucial question about leadership and acting. Can a leader be authentic, or do the masks of command (as John Keegan so aptly called them) force the leader to be something other than his or her true self? Can a leader both act and be real?

These are terribly important questions with no easy answers. Let's look at Pollack again. When he was acting as if he was a director, was he faking it or not? My belief is that he was not faking it—he was a real director, albeit an inexperienced one—even if, in his own mind, he was only acting as if he was one. The feeling of not being up to the job—the belief that the role is too big and important for one to play—is an emotion that every leader with the potential for greatness feels at one time or another. It is evidence that the role is greater than the individual and, thus, worth taking on. By putting on his outdoorsy clothes and grabbing his metaphorical megaphone, the nascent director in Pollack had already made the leader's requisite leap into the unknown, boldly accepting the risk of failure that is the essential first step in becoming a leader.

In the new book I mentioned earlier, *Geeks & Geezers*, my coauthor and I found that adaptive capacity is the single most important attribute in determining who will become a leader. Adaptive capacity is also the defining characteristic of successful actors. Being able to project yourself into someone else's skin—called empathy both in and outside the theater—is a skill every great leader has mastered. Rushmorean figures such as FDR and Churchill seemed to have known our fears better than we did and were able to address them even before we had fully articulated them.

Actors have a sense, often lacking in non-actors, of alternative selves—they know, as Shakespeare wrote, "That each man in his time plays many parts." They have an image of themselves as malleable, a consciousness of their potential for change. This sense that they can inhabit roles other than the one most of us think of as self is essential to leadership as well. Like stage performers, leaders can act as if, without losing track of who they are. Shakespeare—who else?—was perhaps the first person to show his audience a leader in the midst of doing one thing while thinking another. I refer, of course, to the scene in *Richard III* when Richard turns to the audience, in the first great aside in English theater, and reveals to the audience his plan to win Lady Anne, despite her contempt and his murder of her brother. Among other things, this may be the first theatrical acknowledgement of the unsettling truth that transparency is a luxury that not every leader can afford. I am not arguing here in favor of executive duplicity—we have seen far too many CEOs in recent years whose scheming and double-dealing would make Richard III blush. But, as Shakespeare is wont to do, here again he adds to the essential literature of leadership when he describes the kind of dilemma that explains why "heavy lies the head that wears the crown."

As we who do not lead countries know mostly from the media, whether they are the plays of Shakespeare or weekly installments of *The West*

Wing, leaders are routinely required to keep secrets and to balance conflicting values (the public's right to know and the need for national security are the two we hear most about these days). Virtuous leaders are faced with this dilemma as surely as wicked ones are. Can a leader be less than forthcoming and still be real? Was FDR a fraud when he ran against Wendell Wilkie as an isolationist, even as he secretly prepared the United States to enter the war? Not necessarily. Was Roosevelt's lack of candor justified by the millions of lives that were saved because the United States joined the fight against the Axis powers? I don't know, and, in a sense, I don't have to know. These are the big, hard questions leaders must grapple with. Indeed the most problematic aspect of leadership may be that it forces the leader to make moral decisions the rest of us don't have to make. At such times, the leader must improvise without any models conveniently at hand. Leadership forces people into situations in which character is not a straightforward matter of conformity to some widely accepted code. Instead, in such circumstances character may more fairly be defined as William James proposes when he suggests that the way to determine an individual's character "would be to seek out the particular mental or moral attitude in which, when it came upon him, he felt himself most deeply and intensively active and alive. At such moments, there is a voice inside which speaks and says, 'This is the real me.'" In the absence of the psychopathology that creates a Hitler or other monster, the ability to hear that interior voice and act upon it may be the only kind of authenticity a leader needs.

Earlier, I alluded to the interdependence of leaders and followers, of the leader and his or her audience. Like great actors, great leaders create and sell us on an alternative vision of the world, a better world of which we are an essential part. Isaiah Berlin wrote about Churchill that he idealized his countrymen with such intensity that in the end they approached his ideal. Gandhi, it has been said, made India proud of herself. Washington and the other founding brothers also had that great leader's gift of making people believe they could be part—that they *were* part—of a great nation. Martin Luther King (who was also a speaker of rare power) had that same genius. When you consider such towering and theatrical leaders, you realize that leadership is not just a performing art, it may be the greatest performing art of all—the only one that creates institutions of lasting value, institutions that can endure long after the stars that envisioned them have left the theater.

GLENN CLOSE ON "LEADERSHIP AS A PERFORMING ART"

AFTER READING (and re-reading . . . many times) Warren's intriguing essay "Leadership as a Performing Art," one thing keeps sticking in my actor's brain. It's this: Like all great actors, great leaders are skilled craftsmen and, like actors, they use their craft to actively engage whatever audience they are playing to. They can sense who their audience is and, with them, set up a palpable energy exchange. A great leader's charisma, like a great actor's, makes us all into believers. But where does the truth lie between the personas that a leader presents to us and the one we are never privy to—except, of course, in the rare moments when a microphone picks up something not intended for our ears or a camera catches an unguarded, telling look. How do we know—in this world of paid political handlers, polls, and focus groups—what is artifice and what is authentic? Can a leader be truly great if the face he presents to the public is not who he really is? Does it matter?

An actor doesn't have to worry about that because he knows when he is playing a character and when he is not. When he leaves the set or exits the stage, his job is done. I take off my costume, wipe the make-up off my face, put my wig back on its stand, put on my jeans and go home, leaving the character behind. And I have been lucky enough to play many different characters. I would like to think that I could be anyone I am asked to be. That is my craft.

The irony is that great acting is all about truth even though one could say that the actor is just pretending. It is impossible to grab the heart of an audience and give them an unforgettable emotional experience unless the performance is based on truth. An actor has no other agenda but to be truthful and that truth is all about finding a point of nonjudgmental common humanity with the character to be portrayed; a common humanity between an imagined character and a very real actor. When that point is found, it enables the actor to infuse his performance with an authenticity that comes from self-knowledge. That authenticity has a subliminal resonance with the audience, compelling them to care, to pay attention. It enables them to relate to the character, intellectually and emotionally, giving them an experience that is real and unforgettable. As Kevin Kline says in Harold Guskin's wonderful book *How to Stop Acting*, "Good acting is when it is a truth that is intellectually and absolutely inspired— something personal and transcendent that moves you. It is truth that is important to you—the truth that is personal in a profound way."

So even though an actor is usually not at all like the character he plays and leaves the character behind at the end of the day, without innate integrity, without a deeply informed understanding of human behavior, without an authentic ability to empathize, that actor would not move his audience and would not be considered great.

I am certainly not an expert on great leadership or great acting, but after thinking about it, I suppose great leadership really is no different than great acting. Except that a great leader can't shed an imagined persona at the end of the day or when the door to his limo is closed. Therefore, who he is in public should *not* differ from who he is privately . . . if he is *truly* great. And yes, it matters. He must be authentic in his integrity, in his understanding of, his connection to, and his empathy with the people he leads. It is impossible otherwise. If he is not authentic, there will always be that unexpected live microphone or that unguarded moment of scary spontaneity. As they say, it's impossible to fool all the people all of the time. We've grown cynical about our leaders. We are waiting to be fooled. I guess that is why great leaders do not come our way very often, but then again, neither do great actors. When they do, we know it.

Glenn Close works on stage, television, and film, and has been known to sing the national anthem for the New York Mets.

PART FIVE

CULTIVATING THE LEADER IN OTHERS

IT STRUCK ME LONG AGO that we make an exaggerated distinction between leaders and followers. The ability to attract and inspire followers is part of the very definition of leadership, and leaders without followers quickly fade away, however exciting their vision. In 1989 I made a case for the importance of followers in an editorial in the *New York Times* titled "Followers Make Good Leaders Good." In the years since, I have been heartened to see followership emerge as an area of study in its own right. Such study is apt given that all of us are followers at some point in our lives, whatever heights we achieve. The single most important responsibility of the follower is essentially a moral one—to speak truth to power. Organizations often resist hearing necessary truths, and so followers need every bit as much courage as leaders—perhaps more. Followers also need to master the art of persuasion, just as leaders do. In fact, persuasion is a more valuable skill for followers, given that others may not automatically listen to them with the rapt attention the designated leader commands. In today's flatter, more collegial organizations, leadership is increasingly a temporary role, passed from one follower to another. In such organizations, leadership and followership converge into an as yet nameless role in which responsibility is shared. For decades now, we have depended on our business schools to teach leadership skills. As an educator, I have been increasingly distressed by the growing irrelevance of much of the management school curriculum. In the essay "How Business Schools Lost Their Way," Jim O'Toole and I call for a reevaluation of the practice of hiring business-school faculty largely on the basis of quantitative research that often offers students very little that helps them in their professional lives.

THE CHALLENGES
OF LEADERSHIP IN THE
MODERN WORLD (2007)

IN THE BEST OF TIMES, we tend to forget how urgent the study of leadership is. But leadership always matters, and it has never mattered more than it does now. If the United States presidential election of 2004 taught us anything, it was that half the nation has a radically different notion of leadership than the other half. It is almost a cliché of the leadership literature that a single definition of leadership is lacking. But how likely is it that a consensus will be reached on something as straightforward as how to define leadership when, less than two years ago, it became clear that half the electorate saw its candidate as the embodiment of a strong leader while close to the same number saw him as poorly qualified at best, and dangerous at worst? Why allude to current political leadership in an academic journal? Because leadership is never purely academic. It is not a matter such as, say, string theory that can be contemplated from afar with the dispassion that we reserve for things with little obvious impact on our daily lives. Leadership affects the quality of our lives as much as our in-laws or our blood pressure. In bad times, which have been plentiful over the millennia, twisted leaders have been the leading cause of death, more virulent than plague. Even in relatively tranquil times, national leaders determine whether we struggle through our final years, whether our drugs are safe, and whether our courts protect the rights of minorities and the powerless. Our national leaders can send our children into battle and determine whether our grandchildren live in a world in which, somewhere, tigers still stalk their prey and glaciers are more than a memory. Corporate leaders have almost as much power to shape our lives, for good

This article was originally published in *American Psychologist,* January 2007.

or ill. The corrupt executives at Enron, WorldCom, and Tyco—plus the other "usual suspects"—were not mere symbols of corporate greed and malfeasance. Bad leadership at Enron alone impoverished thousands of employees, stealing their livelihoods, gutting their retirement accounts, and tearing them apart with stress. (I was informed recently that the total dollar cost to investors and pensioners was over $80 billion.) There are, no doubt, people who took their own lives because of what was done at Enron by its lavishly compensated bad leaders.

It is easy to forget this context when one is describing leadership in the cool, clear, invaluable language of academic discourse. As students of leadership, it is important for us to distinguish between what we can and cannot say with authority on the subject—that is the essential first step in developing a grand unifying theory of leadership. But we must remember that the subject is vast, amorphous, slippery, and, above all, desperately important. As Robert Sternberg points out in his discussion of cognitive-systems models of leadership, creativity is an essential characteristic of leaders.[1] As leaders, those in the forefront of the analysis of leadership must make creative choices about what aspects of this sweeping subject to study. Even as we examine those aspects that are amenable to the methodologies now at hand, some analysts must be willing to look at leadership in all its complexity, which may mean looking at elements that cannot be nailed down in the laboratory. Psychologists should do so if only to identify those aspects of leadership that seem most pressing and most overlooked and those that hold out promise for changing for the better the way leadership is studied and practiced. We have to use our creativity to identify and reframe the truly important questions.

In the bad old days, leadership was taught mainly by means of the biographies of great men. I predict that one quality of a genuine discipline of leadership studies—once such an animal exists—will be its inclusiveness. No matter how many mathematical models the discipline produces, it should always have room for inspirational stories about wonderful leaders as well as grim cautionary tales about bad ones. At least since Joan of Arc miraculously recruited French soldiers to follow her into battle, people have submitted to the will of outsized, charismatic leaders. Although heroic leaders may have commanded a disproportionate amount of people's attention in the past, psychology still does not know enough about how they develop and how they recruit and maintain their avid followers. Heroic or charismatic leadership is still an essential, unsolved part of the puzzle. I was recently reminded of this by David Gergen, a frequent advisor to U.S. presidents and an astute student of leadership. He tells how, in December 1931, while on a visit to New York, a middle-aged

Briton was struck by a car while crossing Fifth Avenue. Badly hurt, but not so badly that he didn't send the British press his own account of the accident, the English visitor left the hospital as soon as possible to recuperate at the Waldorf Astoria. Now try to imagine what World War II would have been like without the galvanizing rhetoric of the leader almost done in by a New York driver—the visitor was, of course, Winston Churchill. Or imagine how different the United States, and indeed the world, would be today if, in Miami in 1933, Guiseppe Zangora had not fatally shot Chicago Mayor Anton Cermak instead of killing his intended victim, President-Elect Franklin Delano Roosevelt. No wonder people have tried to understand leadership by attempting a kind of reverse engineering of outstanding public figures. To this day, psychologists have not sorted out which traits define leaders or whether leadership exists outside of specific situations, and yet we know with absolute certainty that a handful of people have changed millions of lives and reshaped the world.

One healthy development in the recent study of leadership is a new appreciation for the lessons taught by bad leadership. Barbara Kellerman, research director at the Center for Public Leadership at Harvard's Kennedy School of Government, and Jean Lipman-Blumen, professor at Claremont Graduate University's School of Management, have both recently taken on the daunting task of analyzing what makes bad leaders tick. Kellerman's *Bad Leadership* distinguishes between incompetent leaders and corrupt ones, for example, a valuable reminder that there are many ways for leaders to fail.[2] And in Lipman-Blumen's book, *The Allure of Toxic Leaders,* she reminds us that, most of the time, we choose our bad leaders, they do not kidnap us.[3] She argues that the main reason we are attracted to bad leaders is that they soothe our fears—surely a hypothesis worthy of further study in the laboratory. And both authors raise the important issue of the havoc that can be wreaked by effective leaders with a perverse agenda.

As these writers suggest, leadership is always, in some sense, a matter of values. In talking about leadership, we must ask ourselves, "Leadership for what?" Every leader has an agenda, and analysis of that aim, that intent, often fits uneasily with the objectivity that psychologists rightfully strive for in scholarly research. Sternberg describes a relatively small group of leaders who are characterized by wisdom, which includes an awareness of "the common good."[4] Such terms are too rare in the leadership literature, as is the word "justice." One of the greatest challenges for students of leadership is to find an academically respectable way to deal with the value-laden nature of the subject. No matter how much psychologists might like to avoid grappling with the values issue, we ultimately cannot. Values are part of the very fabric of the phenomenon. How we confront this without compromising our commitment to objectivity is another of our creative challenges. Perhaps we will have to invent new scholarly forms, new formats that allow us to be both expansive and rigorous. One question begging to be answered by scholars is how the simple invocation of the term "values" can attract or repel followers, as it did in the last presidential election.

As Bruce Avolio and others importantly point out in this special issue, psychologists still tend to see leadership as an individual phenomenon.[5] But, in fact, the only person who practices leadership alone in a room is the psychotic. When speaking on the subject, I often show a slide that includes dozens of names, from Sitting Bull and Susan B. Anthony to Kofi Annan and Carly Fiorina, and I ask the audience what these leaders have in common. In fact, the single commonality among these men and women is that all of them have or had willing followers. If we have learned anything in the decades psychologists have now devoted to the study of leadership, it is that leaders do not exist in a vacuum. Shakespeare, perhaps the greatest of all students of leadership, debunked the so-called "great man" theory of leadership before it was even articulated. In *Henry IV, Part I*, Glendower boasts to Hotspur, "I can call spirits from the vasty deep." And Hotspur shoots back, "Why, so can I, or so can any man; But will they come when you do call them?" Any person can aspire to lead. But leadership exists only with the consensus of followers. As the late psychologist Alex Bavelas frequently reminded his students at MIT, "You can't tickle yourself." Leadership is grounded in a relationship. In its simplest form, it is a tripod—a leader or leaders, followers, and the common goal they want to achieve. None of those three elements can survive without the others.

Given the enormous surge in interest in leadership following the terrorist attacks on the United States in 2001, I am hopeful that psychology is on the verge of making great strides in leadership studies. I do not know that we will ever have an all-encompassing theory of leadership any more than we have a genuine theory of medicine. But I do think forces are converging—a sense of urgency, a critical mass of committed scholars with highly developed skills—for the field to make a great evolutionary leap. In their contributions, all of the authors in this issue note the breakthroughs in leadership studies in the mid-20th century, when the subject was reimagined and a whole new way of thinking about it emerged. During that fertile period, the charismatic leader was deemphasized, as was trait-based leadership. The emphasis shifted to followers, groups, and systems. Those changes were brought about both by political leaders and intellectual leaders trying to make sense of the horror that a series of horrifically bad leaders had wrought. One of the leaders of that new way of looking at leading was the great Kurt Lewin, a refugee from Hitler's Germany, grateful almost to the point of giddiness to be in the democratic United States, who realized that the best minds to have survived in his generation needed to address the most urgent social problems. In 1936, at the meeting of the American Psychological Association at Dartmouth College, he founded the Society for the Psychological Study of Social Issues to apply the tools of psychology to such terrible conundrums as the rise of fascism, racial injustice, and other societal problems. The groundbreaking work of Solomon Asch, Muzafir Sherif, Irving Janis and, later, Stanley Milgram on peer pressure surely follows in spirit the path that Lewin and other public-minded scholars helped create. This new zeitgeist was informed by a hunger to understand why the world had gone mad, and it was led by scholars who felt empowered by such new tools as systems theory and a willingness to collaborate across traditional disciplinary lines.

Although we do not yet know what a theory of leadership would look like, we do know it will be interdisciplinary, a collaboration among cognitive scientists, social psychologists, sociologists, neuroscientists, anthropologists, biologists, ethicists, political scientists, historians, sociobiologists, and others. Before we can achieve a comprehensive theory, we need to fill the gaps in our knowledge. We desperately need, for instance, longitudinal studies of both leaders and followers.

The study of leadership will be increasingly collaborative because it is precisely the kind of complex problem—like the genome—that can only be solved by many fine minds working together. (Leadership itself is likely to become increasingly collaborative. We already have a few examples in the corporate world of successful power sharing—the triumvirate at the top of the search engine Google is a good example. And other shared-power models will surely develop as the most creative organizations deal with the issue of leading groups in which the ostensible leader is neither more gifted nor less gifted than the led.)

Among the existing disciplines that must contribute if modern leadership is to be understood are those related to communication. One aspect of leadership that is routinely overlooked is the extent to which it is a performance art. Because leaders must have a vision that they are able to convey and share with their followers, rhetoric is part of the equation. Although President George W. Bush is not universally admired for his spoken presentation of self, he is occasionally masterful in this regard. When crafting the memorable address he gave to Congress following 9/11, for example, he eliminated from preliminary drafts all quotable lines from the towering leaders of history, including Churchill. The president's apparent reasoning was flawless: If powerful language stuck in the memory of listeners, he wanted to make sure it was his. Perhaps because the idea offends our somewhat puritanical notions of authenticity, we tend to forget that leadership often involves acting as if one were a leader. It was Churchill who uttered during the darkest days of World War II that though he was not a lion, he would have to learn to roar like one. Centuries before, Queen Elizabeth I, who was a master of performance, once remarked, "We princes are set on stages in the sight and view of all the world." So those who understand the dramatic arts should be among our collaborators in the search for the nature of leadership.

The other experts who must be part of the collaboration are students of media and communication. Today public leaders rarely, if ever, interact with their followers directly. They are always filtered through the media. Those media are growing in number and constantly changing, and people who understand how these new media work and shape the perceptions of followers are essential to plumbing the field. Is a leader whose message is accessed on a Blackberry different in kind from one whose message is read in the pages of the *New York Times?* Is a politician's vision described in the news pages perceived differently from the same vision presented on the op-ed page? Do viewers of the *Daily Show* have a different relationship to the political candidates they favor than listeners to public radio or talk radio? Does the stature of an interviewer change the perception of the candidate? If Matthew Brady helped create our heroic notion of Lincoln, what role do today's news photographers play in our choice of leaders? Recently, I have been thinking about the role that costume plays in our perception of public figures. What message does a trimly cut jacket simultaneously suggestive of Eisenhower and *Star Wars'* Han Solo send? Can a candidate ever rise above the message of foolishness projected by a pair of floral, knee-length swim trunks? And do young followers, inundated with more visual images than any generation in history, react differently to visual imagery than those of us who have spent only half our lives with television? In his essay Sternberg insightfully discusses the importance of stories in leadership effectiveness.[6] The modern media are a key element in the creation and distribution of those stories, and to understand modern leadership we must have a much deeper understanding of those media, in all their power and with all their biases. We must also think more and more about leadership in the context of globalization and instant communication. The world has so shrunk because of the new media that dissidents can now climb electronically over the walls imposed on them by repressive regimes. And yet while we have instant global communication, we have no guarantee of understanding. It is safe to assume that leadership and followership, like cuisine, have distinctive flavors from one culture to another. Psychologists have to begin to master those different ways of perceiving leadership.

After studying leadership for six decades, I am struck by how small is the body of knowledge of which I am sure. I do believe that leaders develop by a process we do not fully understand, from a crucible experience—a rich trauma like Sidney Rittenberg's 16 years in Chinese prisons—that somehow educates and empowers the individual. I believe adaptive capacity or resilience is the single most important quality in a leader, or in anyone else for that matter who hopes to lead a healthy, meaningful life. Rittenberg is a perfect example. Now in his 80s, he emerged from prison not embittered, but more convinced than ever of the need for the United States, including American enterprise, to collaborate with modern China. And I believe all exemplary leaders have six competencies: They create a sense of mission, they motivate others to join them on that mission, they create an adaptive social architecture for their followers, they generate trust and optimism, they develop other leaders, and they get results.

After reading the contributions of the five leadership scholars in this issue and rereading them a few more times, and then having the time to reflect on them, I am convinced more than ever of two things: The first is that we are learning more and more every day about this most important and urgent subject. The second is my heartfelt conviction that the four most important threats facing the world today are: (a) a nuclear or biological catastrophe, whether deliberate or accidental; (b) a world-wide epidemic; (c) tribalism and its cruel offspring, assimilation (all three of these are more likely than they were a decade ago); and finally, (d) the leadership of our human institutions. Without exemplary leadership, solving the first three problems will be impossible. With it, we will have a better chance. The noble hope of advancing the empirical and theoretical foundation of leadership—after all, we are all Pelagians at heart—could influence the course of leadership and, eventually, the quality and health of our lives.

BILL GEORGE ON "THE CHALLENGES OF LEADERSHIP IN THE MODERN WORLD"

FOR DECADES LEADERSHIP SCHOLARS have attempted with limited success to define the essence of leadership. Warren Bennis's ground-breaking article "The Challenges of Leadership in the Modern World" (*American Psychologist*, January 2007) explains why this is the case and what twenty-first-century leaders must do to succeed in today's environment. While decrying the possibility of developing a unifying theory of leadership, Bennis's prophetic piece brings us much closer to that goal.

To those who question leaders' impact, or challenge whether one can correlate leadership with institutional success, Bennis states unequivocally, "Leadership always matters, and it has never mattered more than it does now." Written prior to the leadership failures that led to the 2008 economic crisis, Bennis's article carries even greater urgency today.

In recent decades many leadership scholars have adopted the reductionist model used in medicine to correlate the traits, characteristics, styles, and competencies of leaders with their organizations' financial outcomes. It hasn't worked. More than a thousand studies have been unable to produce definitive results, and we are no closer to the "holy grail." As Bennis notes, "Leadership cannot be nailed down in a laboratory."

By now, the reasons for this should be evident: a definitive list of the ideal leader's characteristics does not exist, nor will it. Ironically, many leaders who possess the most desired characteristics fail to sustain their leadership. Conversely, many successful leaders lack basic characteristics that scholars have identified as prerequisites to success. For example, when he was selected as CEO of General Electric in 1981, Jack Welch demonstrated glaring omissions in his traits and style, yet he became "CEO of the twentieth century."

Bennis asserts that "leadership is never purely academic." The essence of leadership is not developing a set of discrete competencies that can be examined under a microscope. Rather, it is the capacity to integrate complex ideas, concepts, and practical realities into a holistic approach that aligns people around a common mission and values that they readily buy into. To quote Bennis again, "Leadership is always, in some sense, a matter of values. In talking about leadership, we must ask ourselves, 'Leadership for what [purpose]?'"

Most important of all is the alignment of individual leaders with their authentic selves. Of the leaders I have studied who were ultimately unsuccessful, all failed to lead themselves, rather than failing to lead others.

Among the 125 successful and authentic leaders interviewed for my book, *True North*, none suggested their traits, characteristics, or competencies led to their success. Instead, most said their life stories and experiences provided the passion, purpose, and values by which they lead. Over three-quarters identified a specific transformative experience, which Bennis terms a *crucible*, as the most important factor in their success. It was through the crucible—or through reframing it years later—that they discovered the authentic leadership that enabled them to become fully integrated leaders.

The essence of leadership is the relationship between leaders and their colleagues, and how leaders and their organizations both grow from interacting with each other. Bennis says the key to successful twenty-first-century leadership will be the ability to collaborate—within the organization, with customers and suppliers, and even with competitors. Progressive CEOs like IBM's Sam Palmisano have already converted their huge organizations from dense hierarchical structures to collaborating teams of empowered people.

Collaboration is underpinned by the ability of authentic leaders to align people around a common mission and values and to empower them to step up and lead. This type of leadership was apparent in President Obama's campaign organization. It is also evident in organizations like Johnson & Johnson that sustain success around a credo. Kroger CEO David Dillon provides meaning to employees' work by turning it "into a dignified, proud profession that makes customers' lives better by little touches of human kindness."

The leaders of these organizations recognize they are not all-powerful, nor do they have all the competencies required for success. Hence, they must rely on colleagues who possess capabilities they lack. When I joined

Medtronic in 1989, I had twenty-five years of experience in high-technology businesses, but no medical experience. Hence I teamed up with Vice Chairman Glen Nelson, M.D., who coached me on all decisions involving medicine. Glen was an invaluable partner and a primary reason for Medtronic's success.

Bennis cites adaptive capacity, or resilience, in leaders who master changes in their organizations' context. This capacity comes from the ability to get their organizations to face reality. As former Herman Miller CEO Max De Pree writes in *Leadership Is an Art*, "The leader's first job is to define reality." It's too bad that generations of General Motors leaders never followed that advice.

The importance of the global context in decision making is also highlighted by Bennis. The essential quality of leaders operating in a global world is embracing all types of diversity. Differences in personal experience, national origin, culture, religion, gender, and sexual identity must be viewed as strengths rather than barriers. Integration of people with diverse life experiences into decision-making processes leads to better decisions and increased use of the organization's capabilities.

Finally, Bennis cites the importance of mastering the world of instant communication resulting from new electronic media. The essence of this mastery is embracing transparency as a way of life, both organizationally and personally. For the authentic leader, being open, admitting mistakes, and being vulnerable are the essential strengths that enable leaders to bond deeply with their colleagues and establish mutual trust. As one Harvard student noted, "Being vulnerable to others enables you to take control of the situation." Conversely, a lack of transparency can ultimately lead to the leader's downfall.

As a result of these findings and those of other leading scholars, leadership development is undergoing a radical transformation. Attempts to use computer models of leaders to determine which individuals will be successful leaders, and programs to inculcate styles, traits, and characteristics into their behaviors, are being abandoned for the development of the inner leader.

By exploring their life stories and crucibles, leaders learn to operate as fully integrated and authentic human beings. The best method for this exploration is through ongoing interactions with a small group of committed individuals, combined with introspection and honest feedback. For more than twenty-five years I have been a member of two small groups that meet on a regular basis. My Harvard students have half of their classes in six-person groups, where they discuss openly intimate subjects ranging from their crucibles to ways they can become fully integrated leaders.

These new authentic leaders will enable their organizations to thrive in the twenty-first century, precisely because empowering their people will provide the competitive advantage that sustains their long-term success. Nothing is more important to the success of our institutions, and to solving the world's greatest problems, than developing a new generation of authentic leaders.

BENNIS: REQUIREMENTS FOR LEADERS	LEADERS' CHARACTERISTICS
1. Alignment around mission	Shared values
2. Collaboration/shared power	Empowering/team-based
3. Adaptive capacity/resilience	Facing reality
4. Mastering global context	Embracing diversity of all kinds
5. Instant communications	Transparency:
	Openness
	Being Vulnerable
	Admitting Mistakes

Bill George is professor of management practice and Henry B. Arthur Fellow of Ethics at Harvard Business School. He is author of *Authentic Leadership* (Jossey-Bass, 2003) and *True North* (Jossey-Bass, 2007). Formerly, he was chairman and CEO of Medtronic Inc.

HOW BUSINESS SCHOOLS
LOST THEIR WAY (2005)

(coauthored by James O'Toole)

BUSINESS SCHOOLS ARE ON THE WRONG TRACK. For many years, MBA programs enjoyed rising respectability in academia and growing prestige in the business world. Their admissions were ever more selective, the pay packages of graduates ever more dazzling. Today, however, MBA programs face intense criticism for failing to impart useful skills, failing to prepare leaders, failing to instill norms of ethical behavior—and even failing to lead graduates to good corporate jobs. These criticisms come not just from students, employers, and the media but also from deans of some of America's most prestigious business schools, including Dipak Jain at Northwestern University's top-ranked Kellogg School of Management. One outspoken critic, McGill University professor Henry Mintzberg, says that the main culprit is a less-than-relevant MBA curriculum. If the number of reform efforts under way is any indication, many deans seem to agree with this charge. But genuine reform of the MBA curriculum remains elusive. We believe that is because the curriculum is the effect, not the cause, of what ails the modern business school.

The actual cause of today's crisis in management education is far broader in scope and can be traced to a dramatic shift in the culture of business schools. During the past several decades, many leading B schools have quietly adopted an inappropriate—and ultimately self-defeating—model of academic excellence. Instead of measuring themselves in terms

This article was originally published in *Harvard Business Review,* May 2005.

of the competence of their graduates, or by how well their faculties understand important drivers of business performance, they measure themselves
almost solely by the rigor of their scientific research. They have adopted a
model of science that uses abstract financial and economic analysis, statistical multiple regressions, and laboratory psychology. Some of the research
produced is excellent, but because so little of it is grounded in actual business practices, the focus of graduate business education has become increasingly circumscribed—and less and less relevant to practitioners.

This *scientific model,* as we call it, is predicated on the faulty assumption that business is an academic discipline like chemistry or geology. In
fact, business is a profession, akin to medicine and the law, and business
schools are professional schools—or should be. Like other professions,
business calls upon the work of many academic disciplines. For medicine,
those disciplines include biology, chemistry, and psychology; for business,
they include mathematics, economics, psychology, philosophy, and sociology. The distinction between a profession and an academic discipline is
crucial. In our view, no curricular reforms will work until the scientific
model is replaced by a more appropriate model rooted in the special
requirements of a profession.

Before asking how business education should change, we need to examine its evolution. Most business schools claim a dual mission: to educate
practitioners and to create knowledge through research. Historically, business schools have emphasized the former at the expense of the latter. In
fact, for the first half of the twentieth century, B schools were more akin to
trade schools; most professors were good ole boys dispensing war stories,
cracker-barrel wisdom, and the occasional practical pointer. We remember when MIT's Sloan School of Management was known as MIT School
of Industrial Management and its production class was taught by the
manager of a nearby General Motors assembly plant. That was a useful,
but hardly comprehensive and professional, education.

Then, in 1959, prompted at least in part by the enormous demand for
professional managers in a booming postwar economy, the Ford and Carnegie foundations issued devastating reports on the woeful state of business
school research and theory. Both foundations recommended ways to give
B schools respectable academic underpinnings and offered grant money
toward achieving that end. Driven by conscience and cash, top-tier universities began to treat their business schools almost as seriously as law schools.
By the end of the twentieth century, nearly all the nation's leading business
schools—the two dozen or so elite MBA-granting institutions and another
dozen schools fighting to join the highest echelon—offered a curriculum of
academic distinction. But, in the process, their focus switched, and now the

objective of most B schools is to conduct scientific research. Going back to the trade school paradigm would be a disaster. Still, we believe it is necessary to strike a new balance between scientific rigor and practical relevance.

The Scientific Model

Virtually none of today's top-ranked business schools would hire, let alone promote, a tenure-track professor whose primary qualification is managing an assembly plant, no matter how distinguished his or her performance. Nor would they hire professors who write articles only for practitioner reviews, like this one. Instead, the best B schools aspire to the same standards of academic excellence that hard disciplines embrace—an approach sometimes waggishly referred to as "physics envy." In departments such as physics and economics, top faculty members have few responsibilities other than to attend to their disciplines. They are not required to train practitioners or to demonstrate practical uses of their work; and they are free to do whatever research they choose and to produce subsequent, even more focused, generations of scholars. In this scientific model, the university exists primarily to support the scholar's interests. For the most part, universities accept this arrangement and the intellectual premise on which it rests: namely, that universities help society advance by supporting scientists who push back the boundaries of knowledge. They leave the practical implications to others.

It's very different in schools of law and medicine, which deliberately engage with the outside world. Law schools expect faculty members to be first-rate scholars; in fact, articles published in law reviews are often cited in trials. But these institutions also value professors' ability to teach. Similarly, medical schools carry on advanced biological research, but most members of the teaching faculty are also practicing doctors.

Why have business schools embraced the scientific model of physicists and economists rather than the professional model of doctors and lawyers? Although few B school faculty members would admit it, professors like it that way. This model gives scientific respectability to the research they enjoy doing and eliminates the vocational stigma that business school professors once bore. In short, the model advances the careers and satisfies the egos of the professoriat. And, frankly, it makes things easier: Though scientific research techniques may require considerable skill in statistics or experimental design, they call for little insight into complex social and human factors and minimal time in the field discovering the actual problems facing managers.

Business school professors using the scientific approach often begin with data that they use to test a hypothesis by applying such tools as regression analysis. Instead of entering the world of business, professors set up simulations (hypothetical portfolios of R&D projects, for instance) to see how people might behave in what amounts to a laboratory experiment. In some instances those methods are useful, necessary, and enlightening. But because they are at arm's length from actual practice, they often fail to reflect the way business works in real life.

When applied to business—essentially a human activity in which judgments are made with messy, incomplete, and incoherent data—statistical and methodological wizardry can blind rather than illuminate. Consider some of the most difficult questions facing managers: How does a culture of celebrity affect leadership? How should a CEO be compensated? How does one design global operations so they are at once effective and equitable? What is the purpose of a corporation beyond the creation of shareholder value? Such broad, multifaceted questions do not easily lend themselves to scientific experiment or validation.

Another consequence of the scientific model is that professors' evaluations are influenced by the number of articles they publish in A-list business research journals. Submissions to these discipline-based publications are refereed by anonymous panels of scholars who assess research findings based on objective, scientific standards. Those safeguards, de rigueur for A-list journals, help ensure that published research passes scientific muster. Indeed, the system works fairly well in the hard business disciplines, such as economics and finance, to which mathematical modeling can be easily applied. Even in finance, however, the system creates pressure on scholars to publish articles on narrow subjects chiefly of interest to other academics, not practitioners.

To be fair, some of what is published in A-list journals is excellent, imaginative, and valuable. But much is not. A renowned CEO doubtless speaks for many when he labels academic publishing a "vast wasteland" from the point of view of business practitioners. In fact, relevance is often systematically expunged from these journals. For instance, a leading management journal recently reviewed the results of a promising study of the behavior of several thousand leaders in global corporations. The initial research results showed that certain indicators of leadership misbehavior could be monitored to identify ethical problems before a crisis occurs. Unfortunately, that finding could not be proved in a strictly scientific sense. As a result, the version of the article that was finally published focused not on developing practical methods to reduce organizational risk but, instead, on questioning a minor detail in a previous study on a different subject. The article was factual, but it was neither interesting nor useful.

Scholars, in their own defense, argue that the gradual accumulation of tiny facts will one day accrete to a larger and more general scientific understanding of organizational behavior. Practitioners who have to make real decisions, however, must meanwhile look elsewhere for guidance, notably to the business press and to the best-seller list—now home to fewer and fewer books by faculty members.

Most issues facing business leaders are, in the final analysis, questions of judgment. What looks like a straightforward financial decision—say, to cut costs by relocating a service center—often has implications for marketing, sales, manufacturing, and morale that can't be shoe-horned into an equation. Strategic decisions, especially, are likely to go awry when based purely on quantitative factors, as Robert McNamara—the developer of many such techniques at Ford and, later, the U.S. Department of Defense—ruefully admits. In what amounts to a major mea culpa, he now argues that hard analysis often leads to overweighting the value of the knowledge you have. Of course, this bias affects everyone, not just scientists, but the aura of quantification masks the fact that social scientists often assume that the variables not included in their equations are insignificant. In business research, however, the things routinely ignored by academics on the grounds that they cannot be measured—most human factors and all matters relating to judgment, ethics, and morality—are exactly what make the difference between good business decisions and bad ones.

As McNamara's Vietnam War–era experience painfully demonstrates, leaders tend to get into trouble not by fouling up the numbers but by failing to give the correct weight to all the quantitative and qualitative factors that should figure in their decisions. The greatest risks they run are the by-products of their trained tendency to define problems in terms of what they know and then to fall back on past behavior when faced with a new challenge. As McNamara concedes, "We see what we want to believe." That is not surprising; most of us wear the concrete shoes of our earlier successes. But in a rapidly changing global economy, business education should help students learn to recognize their conditioned reflexes. However reassuring the halo of science, it can also lull us into a false sense of confidence that we are making objective decisions.

By allowing the scientific research model to drive out all others, business schools are institutionalizing their own irrelevance. We fear that this will be a difficult problem to correct because many business professors lack enough confidence in the legitimacy of their enterprise to define their own agenda. For example, business economics journals today are practically indistinguishable from traditional economics journals. And, not to be "outscienced," management researchers now focus on technical issues that have the look and feel of topics studied by their peers in the harder disciplines.

Business scholars could take a lesson from their colleagues in the discipline of psychology, which was stifling under the scientific model three or four decades ago. Psychological research then was dominated by rigorous, but ultimately unproductive, studies of reaction time. As long as psychology professors labored within that small area, they learned little that was of value to anyone. It was only after they began to apply their imaginations—and rigor—to much broader problems that psychology began to make enormous strides. Not until respected psychologists dared to ask questions that mattered, whether or not they could be quantified in traditional ways, were groundbreaking studies undertaken, such as the Nobel Prize–winning work of Daniel Kahneman and the late Amos Tversky on how people make financial decisions. Unfortunately, most B school professors still limit their sights to what they can measure readily—a kind of "methodolatry"—instead of searching for new ways to study what is important. In fact, management professors seem to have an almost morbid fear of being damned as popularizers. Do they believe that the regard of their peers is more important than studying what really matters to executives who can put their ideas into practice? Apparently so.

Who Gets Tenure

This new emphasis on scientific research in business schools remains, for the most part, unspoken. Indeed, most deans publicly deny it exists, claiming that their schools remain focused on practice, albeit with an increasing awareness of the value of rigorous research. Here we must watch what leaders do, not what they say. At elite business schools, and at the wannabes emulating their practices, the shift toward the centrality of scientific research is evidenced almost everywhere.

Just look at the hiring and tenure processes. Deans may say they want practitioner-oriented research, but their schools reward scientific research designed to please academics. By recruiting and promoting those who publish in discipline-based journals, business schools are creating faculties filled with individuals whose main professional aspiration is a career devoted to science. Today it is possible to find tenured professors of management who have never set foot inside a real business, except as customers.

At many schools, the road to tenure does not run through field work in businesses. Among young academics and their advisers, this understanding is explicit. Junior scholars are urged to avoid too much work with practitioners and to concentrate their research on narrow, scientific subjects, at least until late in their quest for tenure. (While many conscientious researchers take it upon themselves to learn about the practice of business after they are tenured, there are few incentives for them to do so.) To be sure, there is merit in suggesting that fledgling faculty members try their wings before attempting arduous intellectual journeys, but B school research is becoming too narrow even for academics. One traditional factor in tenure decisions is how often a candidate's work is cited by other scholars. Paradoxically, deans and tenure committees tell us that the number of citations of articles written by candidates is dramatically lower than it was a decade ago—evidence that researchers' work doesn't matter even to their peers.

Nevertheless, a management professor who publishes rigorously executed studies in the highly quantitative *Administrative Science Quarterly* is considered a star, while an academic whose articles appear in the accessible pages of a professional review—which is much more likely to influence business practices—risks being denied tenure. We know of no scholar at a first-rate business school with a good publishing record who has been denied tenure or promotion for being a poor teacher or for being unable to teach effectively in executive education programs, where teachers must have real-world business experience. But we do know of a professor of finance who was denied promotion when his department decided he was not a serious scholar. The damning evidence against him included seven articles in this publication and the highest teaching ratings in his department. In short, the stated end of business education may remain the same: to educate practitioners and to create knowledge through research. But the means make that end impossible to achieve because rewards are directed elsewhere.

What Gets Taught

What professors study, and the way they study it, directly affects the education of MBA candidates. As research-oriented business professors come to dominate B school faculties, they assume responsibility for setting the MBA curriculum. Not surprisingly, they tend to teach what they know, which often translates into first-class instruction on methodology and scientifically oriented research. These professors are brilliant fact collectors; but despite their high level of competence, they are too often uncomfortable dealing with multidisciplinary issues in the classroom. They are ill at ease subjectively analyzing multifaceted questions of policy and strategy, or examining cases that require judgment based on wisdom and experience in addition to—and sometimes opposed to—isolated facts. As a result, these messy issues, no matter how pressing, receive less attention in MBA courses. The trend away from using the case method corroborates this point and is accelerated by greater emphasis on mathematical and quantitative skills in the revised Graduate Management Admission Test, the first filter of future managers.

Business professors too often forget that executive decision makers are not fact collectors; they are fact users and integrators. Thus, what they need from educators is help in understanding how to interpret facts and guidance from experienced teachers in making decisions in the absence of clear facts. After all any low-level administrator can make sound decisions when all the facts are in; having the courage to take a shot in the dark is one of the hallmarks of leadership. If the purpose of graduate business education is to develop executives—leaders—then the faculty must have expertise in more than just fact collection. The best classroom experiences are those in which professors with broad perspectives and diverse skills analyze cases that have seemingly straightforward technical challenges and then gradually peel away the layers to reveal hidden strategic, economic, competitive, human, and political complexities—all of which must be plumbed to reach truly effective business decisions. We all can name great practitioners of this style of business education; unfortunately, given the narrowing of the intellectual paradigm over the past two decades, chances are good that not one of them would be hired—or tenured—at a top business school today. Columnist David Brooks laments that " . . . our universities operate too much like a guild system, throwing plenty of people with dissertations at students, not enough with practical knowledge. Why aren't there more scholars . . . who teach students to be generalists, to see the great connections?"

In that regard, conditions at business schools have worsened dramatically since the mid-1980s. During the 1970s and early 1980s, the best business schools were arguably the most intellectually exciting places in academia. In many universities, B schools were the primary loci of multidisciplinary research. That intellectual ferment and cross-pollination helped make business schools the hugely popular institutions they are today. At one point, the faculty in our department at the University of Southern California's Marshall School of Business included individuals with advanced degrees in mathematics, anthropology, sociology, engineering, decision sciences, economics, and psychology. Recruitment committees actively sought out scholars who were conducting innovative research and, at the same time, were committed to making a difference in organizations. Those scholars published regularly, but few appeared in what today are regarded as the "right" journals. During the past 15 years, however, hiring almost everywhere, including at the Marshall School, has focused on narrowly trained specialists, particularly those holding discipline-based doctorates from other business schools. One unfortunate result of this trend has been that many B schools have to hire adjunct professors to teach required MBA courses.

Worse, the integration of discipline-based knowledge with the requirements of business practice is left to the student. A few years back, the curriculum committee of a highly regarded B school considered a proposal for a multidisciplinary first-semester MBA course based on the current challenges of a well-known global corporation. The committee rejected the proposal—but not because it was poorly designed or pedagogically flawed; in fact, the committee said it would be an advance over the existing program. The problem, in the words of one faculty member, was that "we are not qualified to teach it."

The impact of this loss extends far beyond the classroom. Businesspeople are starting to sense that individuals in the academy are not engaged in the same profession they practice. Employers are noticing that freshly minted MBAs, even those from the best schools—in some cases, *especially* those from the best schools—lack skills their organizations need. At first, employers were confused about the source of this problem, but they seem to be realizing that the people who taught their new hires had spent little time in organizations as managers or consultants and that younger faculty members may not even know many businesspeople. Today, business practitioners are discovering that B school professors know more about academic publishing than about the problems of the workplace. It's no wonder there's been such a marked increase in the number of in-house corporate universities and for-profit management education organizations.

Regaining Relevance

In a 1927 address to the American Association of the Collegiate Schools of Business, the philosopher and mathematician Alfred North Whitehead spoke prophetic words:

> Imagination is not to be divorced from the facts: It is a way of illuminating the facts. . . . The tragedy of the world is that those who are imaginative have but slight experience, and those who are experienced have feeble imaginations.

Today, Whitehead's observation is more fitting than ever. If business schools are to regain their relevance, they must come to grips with the reality that business management is not a scientific discipline but a profession, and they must deal with what a professional education requires. Harvard Business School associate professor Rakesh Khurana has pointed out that professions have at least four key elements: an accepted body of knowledge, a system for certifying that individuals have mastered that body of knowledge before they are allowed to practice, a commitment to the public good, and an enforceable code of ethics. Professions thus are oriented toward practice and focused on client needs. Above all, professions integrate knowledge and practice. We do not propose making management a gated profession requiring credentialing and licensing. Nonetheless, we believe a useful step toward acknowledging that business is a profession would be to recognize that both imagination and experience are vital—and ought, therefore, to be central to business education. With an eye toward integrating knowledge and practice, Polaroid's Edwin Land suggested 50 years ago that every business school should run its own business. Why shouldn't business schools operate ventures that function like the equivalent of medical-school teaching hospitals? Cornell University's S.C. Johnson Graduate School of Management has recently responded to this long-ignored challenge by establishing the Cayuga MBA fund, run by students at the Parker Center for Investment Research.

By whatever means they choose—running businesses, offering internships, encouraging action research, consulting, and so forth—business school faculties simply must rediscover the practice of business. We cannot imagine a professor of surgery who has never seen a patient, or a piano teacher who doesn't play the instrument, and yet today's business schools are packed with intelligent, highly skilled faculty with little or no managerial experience. As a result, they can't identify the most important problems facing executives and don't know how to analyze the indirect and long-term implications of complex business decisions. In this way, they shortchange their students and, ultimately, society. Things won't improve until professors see that they have as much responsibility for educating professionals to make practical decisions as they do for advancing the state of scientific knowledge.

The strongest potential force for change is the business community, but, unfortunately, most corporate employers have been sending mixed signals. They complain that B schools aren't producing potential leaders, but then they hire MBAs with narrow specialties. What's more, business leaders have been unstinting in their support of business schools, often giving large sums of money, typically without strings. This support is interpreted as a vote of confidence. After all, when a donor gives $30 million to put his name on the outside of a school, one can't blame faculty members for assuming that donor is pleased with what they do inside. In our view, business leaders have not demanded enough from the educational institutions purporting to serve them. But until the business community clearly articulates its needs, deans will continue to respond to calls from the faculty for more of the same.

If prestigious organizations like the Business Roundtable or the World Economic Forum were to undertake a study of the quality and utility of business education, the findings would likely garner a level of attention among faculty and administrators similar to that generated by the 1959 Ford and Carnegie reports. We don't think it is healthy for corporate philanthropists to micromanage the policies of educational institutions; but in the case of professional schools, practitioners must adopt a governance role. The first step in this process is for corporate leaders to educate themselves about the current practices of the schools producing their future managers. They might start by picking up a copy of an A-list business journal and asking themselves if the articles in it say anything their managers need to hear.

At the risk of sounding repetitive, let us be clear: We are not advocating a return to the days when business schools were glorified trade schools. In every business, decision making requires amassing and analyzing objective facts, so B schools must continue to teach quantitative skills. The challenge is to restore balance to the curriculum and the faculty: We need rigor *and* relevance. The dirty little secret at most of today's best business schools is that they chiefly serve the faculty's research interests and career goals, with too little regard for the needs of other stakeholders. Serving the business community by educating practitioners and generating knowledge they can use may exist as secondary functions at those institutions, but such objectives are honored mainly in speeches made by deans seeking donations.

The Professional Model

To balance the goals of faculty members with the needs of other constituencies, business schools might look to their sister professional schools in medicine, dentistry, and law for guidance. Dental education is an apt model to the extent that it prepares students to deliver a service requiring sophisticated skills and to manage hands-on enterprises. Research is critical to dental education, but it plays a secondary role to the task of educating competent and ethical practitioners. Isn't that also the right balance for business education?

Ultimately, however, we believe business schools would reap the greatest benefit from emulating the most innovative law schools. The law is a broad-based activity drawing upon many of the same disciplines relevant to business: economics, psychology, accounting, politics, philosophy, history, sociology, language, literature, and so on. Law schools, however, have not succumbed to physics envy and the scientism it spawns. Instead, they tend to reward excellence in teaching and in pragmatic writing. Research is an important component of legal practice and education, but most of it is applied research, and its validity is not equated with the presence of a scientific patina. Law schools recognize that a well-written book or a well-documented article published in a serious, practitioner-oriented review is as valuable as a quantitative article published in a journal read only by cutting-edge researchers. Nevertheless, scientific publications are certainly valued in law school performance assessments. A law school professor who uses the scientific method to demonstrate that a commonly held belief is wrong, or to quantify an insight that is counterintuitive, will be rewarded. When assessing the work of law school faculty members, evaluators ask questions such as: Is the research important? Is it useful? Is it interesting or original? Is it well thought-out, well argued, and well designed? All of these queries seem more appropriate as standards for appraising the work of business school faculties than the narrowly defined standard of scientific rigor.

Of course, not all business schools suffer from the attenuated focus we find so alarming. Deans and faculties at a few top-tier institutions are conscientiously struggling to find ways to conduct rigorous research without abandoning their professional missions. At Harvard Business School, for instance, continued emphasis on case studies makes practitioners an integral part of the educational process. And Harvard helps ensure that its curriculum will keep evolving by making course development a consideration in tenure and promotion decisions. Similarly, Tom Campbell, dean of the Haas School of Business at the University of California, Berkeley, has made a public commitment to teaching and research in the broader and softer areas of business that are the focus of his school's influential—but unrefereed—*California Management Review.*

Many second-tier B schools, especially those not housed in large research-oriented universities, have also retained their professional focus. (Unfortunately, the quality of education offered at some of those institutions harkens back to trade school days.) We are impressed with the University of Dallas's recognition that an overly narrow approach to business education may have been a factor in the Tyco, Arthur Andersen, World-Com, and Enron scandals. As Thomas Lindsay, the university's former provost, explains:

> [B]usiness education in this country is devoted overwhelmingly to tech-
> nical training. This is ironic, because even before Enron, studies
> showed that executives who fail—financially as well as morally—
> rarely do so from a lack of expertise. Rather, they fail because they
> lack interpersonal skills and practical wisdom; what Aristotle called
> prudence.
>
> Aristotle taught that genuine leadership consisted in the ability to
> identify and serve the common good. To do so requires much more than
> technical training. It requires an education in moral reasoning, which
> must include history, philosophy, literature, theology, and logic. . . .

Lindsay estimates that, before the recent scandals, business students
spent "95% of their time learning how to calculate with a view to maxi-
mizing wealth. Just 5% of their time . . . is spent developing their moral
capacities." To right that balance, the Dallas business school introduced
liberal studies into the curriculum and initiated a series of intellectual and
ethical exercises.

Looking Ahead

Traditionally, business schools have lacked offerings in the humanities.
That is a serious shortcoming. As teachers of leadership, we doubt that our
topic can be understood properly without solid grounding in the humanities. When the hard-nosed behavioral scientist James March taught his
famous course at Stanford using *War and Peace* and other novels as texts,
he emphatically was not teaching a literature course. He was drawing on
works of imaginative literature to exemplify and explain the behavior of
people in business organizations in a way that was richer and more realistic than any journal article or textbook. Similarly, when executives are
given excerpts from the classics of political economy and philosophy in
seminars at the Aspen Institute, the intent is not to turn them into experts
on Plato and Locke but to illuminate the profound recesses of leadership
that scientifically oriented texts either overlook or oversimplify.

Naturally, reforming business education means more than adding
courses in the humanities. The entire MBA curriculum must be infused
with multidisciplinary, practical, and ethical questions and analyses reflecting the complex challenges business leaders face. We are encouraged on
this score that the freshly appointed dean of the Marshall School has
courageously gone on record as advocating a major rebalancing of our
MBA program in order to link hard and soft skills. We certainly do not
advocate that business schools, in revising MBA curricula, abandon science. Rather, they should encourage and reward research that illuminates

the mysteries and ambiguities of today's business practices. Oddly, despite B schools' scientific emphasis, they do little in the areas of contemporary science that probably hold the greatest promise for business education: cognitive science and neuroscience. In those fields, pioneering researchers use magnetic resonance imaging technology to study how the brain behaves while making economic decisions, taking into account such factors as gender differences and the role of trust.

The problem is not that business schools have embraced scientific rigor but that they have forsaken other forms of knowledge. It isn't a case of either-or. Not every professor needs to be a switch-hitter, however. In practice, business schools need a diverse faculty populated with professors who, collectively, hold a variety of skills and interests that cover territory as broad and as deep as business itself. As the late Sumantra Ghoshal wrote in a shrewd analysis of the problems with management education today, "The task is not one of delegitimizing existing research approaches, but one of relegitimizing pluralism."

Rebalancing runs against the perceived self-interest of many professors, not to mention the seemingly unstoppable trend in academia toward specialization. We believe the most effective levers for overcoming this resistance are personnel policies related to recruitment, promotion, tenure, and other academic rewards. Instead of blindly following the paths forged by trade schools or traditional academic departments, business schools must create their own standards of excellence. However, many business school leaders now say their universities are forcing them to adopt the same standards for hiring and promotion used by graduate departments in the hard sciences. In our view, this is often an excuse for maintaining a dysfunctional (but comfortable) system. Other professional schools have carved out standards that are appropriate for their various professions; now business schools must have the courage to do the same.

JOEL M. PODOLNY ON
"HOW BUSINESS SCHOOLS
LOST THEIR WAY"

ONE MEASURE OF AN ARTICLE'S REACH is the number of persons opining on an article relative to the number who have actually read the article. As the former exceeds the latter, the author should take comfort that the article has clearly had an impact. Based on my interactions with colleagues from academia over the past several years, Bennis and O'Toole should not only take comfort; they should rejoice. There are a large number in the academy who have reacted strongly to this article, though invariably in a negative fashion and, of course, invariably without reading the article.

It is not surprising that the reaction of so many would be strongly negative. The article is a powerful challenge to the way things are, and as the authors themselves point out, a significant majority in the academy have—at least in the short term—a strong vested interest in preserving a system that is aligned more with their own worldview of how the challenges of business should be understood, framed, and approached than with the worldview of those who actually have to go out and practice.

However, it is unfortunate that so many are willing to opine so strongly without actually reading the article. It is a sign that so much of the conversation about the state of affairs in business schools is bogged down in reification and dichotomies, such as "theoretical" versus "applied," "hard" versus "soft," or "rigorous" versus "relevant." Such abstractions are misleading. A good theory can be more broadly applicable than an observation that derives from observing a few selected contexts, and individual managers can be extremely analytical in the way in which they approach "soft" topics like managing groups and teams or providing developmental feedback for their employees. Such abstractions foster the factionalization of business school faculty, with individual faculty members feeling obligated to choose the label with which they would wish to be associated.

As I write these words, I have just recently stepped down as dean at the Yale School of Management. During my tenure there, I worked with the faculty to move beyond such dichotomies. Indeed, in my first year there, the faculty embarked on a thorough reexamination of the curriculum. The faculty in charge of the reform consulted a variety of overlapping constituencies from the world of practice—recruiters, alumni, and leaders from all industries and sectors. The feedback from these groups was consistent, pointing to the current disjuncture between how problems and opportunities arise in organizations and how the disciplines frame problems. To paraphrase Sharon Oster, one of my former colleagues and the person who succeeded me as dean, there is no problem in an organization that is *just* a finance problem or *just* an organizational behavior problem. The problems that arise in organizations require insights from all the disciplines.

For example, if the organization is poorly regarded by its customers, the issue may be one of marketing, which is the discipline within business schools that focuses most on the customer. However, it may be a problem of organization design, typically the purview of organizational behavior. Or it may be a problem with the CRM system, a topic that can often fall through the cracks of the marketing, accounting, and operations disciplines. A problem of customer perceptions could have originated from countless sources, and the different disciplines within the business school all have something to contribute to understanding the problem. Indeed, as Bennis and O'Toole argue, there are disciplines outside the boundaries of traditional business schools that could also make meaningful contributions to understanding the challenges and opportunities that will confront MBAs as they embark upon their careers.

In short, in the traditional MBA curriculum, the world of business is presented to students in disciplinary silos, but in "the real world," the problems and opportunities do not respect these same boundaries. Notably, this disconnect between discipline-based education and the true nature of managerial challenges cannot simply be solved with a more applied emphasis. Even cases can be siloed by discipline, as faculty members often bring their disciplinary frame to the cases on which they write.

So what is the solution to the problem? I suspect that there are a number of different ones, but I will focus on the solution pursued at Yale. The faculty put in place an interdisciplinary curriculum where the core courses were no longer structured by disciplinary silos, but by the key constituencies or perspectives that a manager needs to engage to be effective. So, instead of a course in marketing, they created a course on the customer perspective. Instead of a course in organizational behavior, they put in place a course on the employee perspective. Instead of a course in finance, they created a course on the investor perspective, and so on. There are a total of eight perspective courses in the core; each is team taught by faculty from multiple disciplines.

I have heard a number of colleagues characterize the Bennis and O'Toole piece as hostile to discipline-based education. Even a cursory reading of the article reveals that this is not the case. Bennis and O'Toole point to the example of various leading law schools, where scholars draw on disciplinary tool kits to help inform legal questions that are broader than any particular discipline's purview. Bennis and O'Toole are simply arguing that disciplinary knowledge should not be presented in a way that obscures the fundamental challenges of management and leadership. The disciplines should not impose their own frame on managerial problems; rather, they should be contributors to a holistic, integrated understanding of those problems.

I regard the curriculum reform at Yale as one attempt at changing MBA education in a way that is consistent with what Bennis and O'Toole advocate; however, I am most encouraged by the fact that a number of other schools—for example, Stanford, Darden, and Fuqua—are also pursuing more integrated, interdisciplinary approaches to business education. As these schools do pursue such reforms, the field will hopefully move past the polemical response that greeted this article when it first appeared.

I still worry that even as individual schools pursue these changes, there is a broader context that may impose limits on how much change can actually occur. There are at least two features of that broader context that are troubling, the tenure system at the leading universities and the increasing attention being paid to student services as the key determinant of an MBA program's quality. Bennis and O'Toole discuss the first of these in their article. Under the current criteria for tenure at the leading universities, a junior faculty member receives little to no credit for actions that contribute to greater interdisciplinary integration in research or teaching. In fact, since the most important determinant of an individual's tenure chances is the evaluation of leading scholars from the individual's own discipline, there may indeed be some considerable opportunity cost associated with junior faculty reaching across disciplinary lines. Unfortunately, even if business school faculty and deans could agree that there should be a change, they do not control their destiny. In almost all leading universities, the ultimate decision to award tenure is made by the president or provost, usually with a committee of disciplinary scholars from the arts and sciences providing guidance. In my experience, the scholars who sit on these committees know and care little about the unique demands and obligations associated with being a professional school. They know and care only about the quality of research, which they judge from their own disciplinary vantage. Unless business schools are granted more control over their own tenure criteria, I think it will be difficult for business schools to build the human capital on their faculty that will, in turn, foster greater interdisciplinary integration.

The second feature of that broader context that undercuts integration is the increasing focus on providing services to students—services that are only indirectly connected to the curriculum itself. In using the term *services*, I am referring to everything from the career development office to support infrastructure for student clubs to dedicated athletic facilities for the MBAs. There are significant scale economies associated with the provision of such services. Accordingly, as these services become more important to the students, business schools are forced to grow their programs to be able to compete. The problem is that increasing scale makes integration more difficult. If one looks at the schools that have been most aggressive in pursuing an integrated, holistic MBA, they have invariably been the smaller schools. I certainly know that as dean of Yale, I regarded it as a tremendous advantage that we had a small faculty. It was much easier to pursue intergroup integration when one did not need to devote much time and energy to intragroup integration. However, as the scale of a school increases, the department structure becomes increasingly salient, and more and more faculty time is just devoted to maintaining coordination within a department and therefore discipline. I could discuss some other factors that work against multidisciplinary integration, but consideration of these two factors makes the point that there remain forces against change.

Based on my experience at Yale and my knowledge of the faculty at other schools, I do believe there is a strong desire on the part of faculty at a number of leading schools to "find their way again." Therefore, even with the worries and concerns that I have about the broader context and even with the large number of faculty whose thinking about these issues is still ensnared in the false dichotomies, I am sanguine about the future of MBA education. This piece by Bennis and O'Toole played an important role in fostering the conversation that, in turn, has already prompted some important initiatives and changes.

Joel M. Podolny is vice president and dean of Apple University and author of *Status Signals* (Princeton University Press, 2005) and *Strategic Management* (Wiley, 2005). Previously, he was dean of the Yale School of Management and professor and director of research at Harvard Business School.

THE END OF LEADERSHIP (1999)

I'VE NEVER FULLY APPROVED of formal debates. The very premise of a debate, where issues are egregiously over-simplified, can't help but lose the subtly-nuanced distinctions we academics relish and thrive on. So when I was asked not long ago to participate in this kind of foolishness, I was naturally resistant to participate. Especially when the "resolution before the house" was phrased as follows: "All successful organizational change must originate at the top." To make matters worse, the organizers of the debate insisted that I take the opposite position of the "resolution of the house," casting me "against type," so to speak. I would have felt far more comfortable being on the side of strong leadership, a position more compatible with most of my recent writing. I did agree, however, despite my strong reservations primarily because the organizers were colleagues and I wanted an expense paid trip to the East Coast. In accepting, I was reminded of an old *New Yorker* cartoon showing Charles Dickens in his publisher's office, being told rather sternly by his editor: "Well, Mr. Dickens, it's either the best of times OR the worst of times. It can't be both."

What I discovered was that getting impaled on the horns of a false dichotomy was rather more fun than I anticipated. More importantly in preparing for the debate, I arrived at an unexpected conclusion, close to an epiphanic event. I came to the unmistakable realization that TOPdown leadership was not only wrong, unrealistic and maladaptive but also, given the report of history, dangerous. And given certain changes taking place in the organizational landscape, this obsolete form of leadership will erode competitive advantage and destroy the aspirations of any organization that aims to be in the phone book beyond the year 2002.

I think it is now possible to talk about the end of leadership without the risk of hyperbole. Some of this change is organic and inevitable. But

This article was originally published in *Organizational Dynamics*, Summer 1999.

much of it is the legacy of our times ignited by that dynamic duo: globalization and relentlessly disruptive technology.

The Encompassing Tendency

The idea of traditional TOPdown leadership is based on the myth of the triumphant individual. It is a myth deeply ingrained in the American psyche and unfortunately fostered and celebrated in the daily press, business magazines, and much of academic and popular writing. My own work, at times, has also suffered from this deification of the icons of American business: the Welches, the Barneviks, the Gateses—fill in your own hero. Whether it is midnight rider Paul Revere or basketball's Michael Jordan or, more recently, Mark McGwire, we are a nation enamored of heroes—rugged self-starters who meet challenges and overcome adversity. Our contemporary views of leadership are entwined with our notions of heroism, so much so that the distinction between "leader" and "hero" (or "celebrity," for that matter) often becomes blurred.

In our society leadership is too often seen as an inherently individual phenomenon. It's Oprah and Michael (Jordan or Eisner) and Bill (Clinton or Gates) and Larry and Hillary and Monica. We are all victims or witnesses to what Leo Braudy calls the "frenzy of renown," the "peoplification" of society. Think of it: Can you imagine a best-selling magazine as popular as *People* called *System?*

And yet we do understand the significance of systems. After all, it is systems that encourage collaboration and systems which makes change not only effective but possible. A shrinking world in which technological and political complexity increase at an accelerating rate offers fewer and fewer arenas in which individual action, TOPdown leadership, suffices. And here is the troubling disconnect. Despite the rhetoric of collaboration, we continue to live in a "by-line" culture where recognition and status are conferred on individuals, not *teams of people* who make change possible.

But even as the lone hero continues to gallop through our imaginations, shattering obstacles with silver bullets, leaping tall buildings in a single bound, we know that that's a falsely lulling fantasy and that is not the way real change, enduring change, takes place. We know there is an alternative reality.

What's surprising is that this should surprise us. In a society as complex and technologically sophisticated as ours, the most urgent projects require the coordinated contributions of many talented people working together. Whether the task is building a global business or discovering the mysteries of the human brain, it doesn't happen at the top; TOPdown leadership can't hope to accomplish it, however gifted the person at the TOP is. There are simply too many problems to be identified and solved, too many connections to be made. So we cling to the myth of the Lone Ranger that great things are accomplished by a larger-than-life individual shouting commands, giving direction, inspiring the troops, sounding the tocsin, decreeing the compelling vision, leading the way and changing paradigms with brio and shimmer.

This *encompassing tendency* is dysfunctional in today's world of blurring, spastic, hyper-turbulent change, and will get us into unspeakable troubles unless we understand that the search engine, the main stem winder for effective change, is the workforce and their creative alliance with top leadership.

A personal case in point. My colleague David Heenan and I wrote a book about the role of Number Twos in organizations, how they work and don't work. We thought it an original idea, one that was significant and astonishingly neglected in the literature. We entitled the book *Second Banana* and had chapters on some of the most famous and successful partnerships between Ones and Twos in corporate life; for example, the fabled relationship between Warren Buffett and his Number Two, Charles Munger, known for containing Buffett's enthusiasm about investments and referred to by Buffett as the "Abominable No Man." And there was a chapter called "Banana Splits," on infamously unsuccessful partnerships such as the widely publicized split between Michael Eisner and Michael Ovitz. All twelve of the publishers who reviewed the book declined. One put it rather nicely. He said, "Warren, no one in America wants to be Number Two." He also quoted Leonard Bernstein who once proclaimed that "The hardest instrument to play in a symphony orchestra is second fiddle."

So David and I changed the title to *Co-Leaders* and added a subtitle, *The Power of Great Partnerships*. With that new title and a shift in emphasis away from being Number Two, it was published this year by John Wiley.

I give this example not to plug the book but to illustrate the power of this encompassing tendency of the Great Man which dominates our thinking and perverts our understanding of organizational life and how leading change really works.

The Argument

I will present my argument in an unorthodox way by drawing on sources a little out of the ordinary for management scholars: examples and analogies from poetry, history and theater, as well as the more traditional sources of experimental studies and business anecdotes. I'll start with an excerpt from a poem by Berthold Brecht, the Marxist playwright.

QUESTIONS FROM A WORKER

Who built the town of Thebes of Seven Gates?
The names of kings are written in the books.
Was it the kings who dragged the slab of rock?
And Babylon, so many times destroyed,
Who built her up again so many times?
Young Alexander conquered India.
All by himself?
Caesar beat the Gauls.
Not even a cook to help him with his meals?
Philip of Spain wept aloud when his Armada
Went down. Did no one else weep?
Frederick the Great won the Seven Years War. Who
Else was the winner?
On every page a triumph.
Who baked the victory cake?
In every decade a great man. Who picked up the check?
So many reports.
So many questions.

"In every decade a great man." That encompassing tendency again. And it shows up throughout history. In Plutarch's great biography of Cato the Elder, he wrote: "Rome showed itself to be truly great, and hence worthy of great leaders." What we tend to forget is that greatness lies within nations and organizations themselves as much, if not more, than their leaders. Could Gandhi achieve his greatness without staying close to the people and representing their greatness of spirit? So many questions. . . .

Now for a contemporary business example—I wrote an article in which I quoted one of my favorite management philosophers, The Great One, Wayne Gretzky, saying:

> It's not where the puck is, it's where the puck will be." Soon after I received a rather sour letter from the Chairman and CEO of one of our largest Fortune 100 companies who wrote: "I was particularly interested in what you characterize as the Gretzky factor. I think I know where the puck is going to be—the problem is, we've got thousands and thousands of folk who don't want the puck to go there, would rather that it wasn't going there, and in the event that it is going there, aren't going to let us position ourselves to meet it until after we've skated past. *In plain English, we've got a bunch of people who want the world to be the way it used to be—and are very disinclined to accept any alternative forecast of the future.* (Emphasis mine.)

Now what's interesting about this "leader" is that (a) he was regarded as one of the most innovative and creative CEOs in his industrial sector and (b) his unquestionable "genius" was totally useless because he lacked a critical mass of willing followers. And he had no followers because he was unable to generate and sustain a minimum degree of trust with his workforce, widely known to be resistant to and—no exaggeration—*dyspeptic* with his pre-Copernican ego and macho style.

If there is one generalization we make about leadership and change, it is this: No change can occur without willing and committed followers.

Let us turn now to social movements and how they are led and mobilized. Mohandas Gandhi's singular American apostle was Dr. Martin Luther King, Jr., who was introduced to his teachings as a graduate student in Boston University's Divinity School in the early 1950s. I had gone to college with Coretta Scott and got acquainted with her future husband while she attended the New England Conservatory of Music and I was in graduate school at M.I.T. Recently, upon reading John Lewis's book, *Walking with the Wind,* I recalled how back then, light years ago, Coretta seemed the charismatic one and Martin shy and bashful. Lewis, one of King's acolytes in the Civil Rights Movement of the '60s, now a Congressman from Atlanta and one of the most respected African-American leaders, tells us in his book how much of the movement was a team effort, a "band of brothers and sisters," and how Dr. King "often joined demonstrations late or ducked out early." (I should add that Lewis was and is a devoted admirer of King.) Garry Wills writes that "he tried to lift others up and found himself lifted up in the process. *He literally talked himself into useful kinds of trouble.* King's oratory urged others on to heroic tasks and where they went he had to follow. Reluctant to go to jail, he was shamed into going—after so many young people responded to his speeches and found themselves in danger." (Emphasis mine.)

Don't be misled here. I'm not just reiterating one of those well-worn bromides about leadership; you know, where leaders carefully watch where their followers are going and then follow them. I'm saying something quite different. I'm saying that exemplary leadership and organizational change are impossible without the full inclusion, initiatives and cooperation of followers.

I mentioned earlier on that TOPdown leadership tendency is also *maladaptive* and I think it's time to return to that now. It's become something of a cliché to discuss the extraordinary complexity and ambiguity and uncertainties of our current business environment. As one of my CEO friends put it, "If you're not confused, you don't know what's going on." At the risk of oversimplifying his important work on leadership, Ron Heifetz asserts that with relatively simple, "technical problems," leadership is relatively "easy";

i.e., TOPdown leadership can solve them. But with "adaptive" problems, complex and messy problems, like dealing with a seriously ill cancer patient or cleaning up an ecological hazard, many stakeholders must be involved and mobilized. The truth is that adaptive problems require complex and diverse alliances. Decrees, orders, etc., *do not work*.

An elegant experiment dreamed up by one of the most imaginative, and least acknowledged social psychologists of his day, Alex Bavelas, dramatizes, if not proves, this point. Imagine a simple wooden circular dining room table, about 10 feet in diameter with plywood partitions walling off the five participants from visible sight of each other. The table is constructed so that subjects can communicate only by passing messages written on 3 × 5 cards through narrow slots in the partitions. The cards are all color coded so that you can count how many messages were sent to whom and by whom. Also, the table was constructed so that different organizational forms can be simulated. For example, you can create a rough example of a typical bureaucratic, command-and-control organization by restricting the flow of messages to only one central person. We used three kinds of organizational models, the Wheel, which more or less resembles the typical organizational pyramid, the Chain, a slight modification of the Wheel, and the Circle, where everyone could communicate to the two participants adjacent to them. Not quite a completely connected network, but one of equality.

The problem to be solved was relatively simple. Each subject was given a pill box which contained six different colored marbles. They were what we used to call "puries," pure white, pure blue, pure green, red, etc., and easily identifiable. For each experimental trial, there was only one color that each subject had in common. On one trial, for example, it was the red, on another it was the green, and so on, randomly varied. There were 15 trials. As soon as the subject thought he had the correct color, he would drop the marble down a rubber tube in the table so that the experimenter could not only measure the accuracy for the group but also how long it took for all five subject to deposit the marble. Our predictions were not surprising and they were confirmed. The Wheel, the form most like the TOPdown leadership model was the most accurate and the most efficient; they were very, very quick. We did notice that in our post-experiment questionnaire, the central person reported having the highest morale and was wildly enthusiastic about his role while the other group members were, to be polite, pissed.

Expectable and not particularly exciting results. So we decided to change the task to a more "adaptive" problem and substituted for the primary colors, the so-called "puries," ambiguously colored marbles: cat's eyes, ginger ale-ish, bluish-green or greenish blue, all sorts of dappled colored marbles. . . .

Again, our predictions were confirmed. Now, under ambiguous and changing conditions, the Circle was the most efficient and accurate and all members claimed relatively high morale. On only one occasion, and we repeated this particular experiment about 50 times, did the Wheel perform better. In this one case, the central person was an exceptionally gifted artist and writer. She was also taking a minor in art history. Genius happens. Once in a blue moon.

The connection between that antediluvian experiment and the messy, changing business environment barely needs stating. But it dramatically illustrates my point that none of us is as smart of all of us, that the TOPdown model, in the present business context, is dysfunctional, maladaptive and, as I'll get to now, dangerous.

The dangers of TOPdown leadership, vivid examples of colossal folly and disaster, are so numerous that one doesn't know where to begin. Stalin's communal farms? Niemeyer's Brasilia? Hitler's Holocaust? Chainsaw Al's follies? Napoleon's Russian campaign? LBJ's Vietnam? Mao's Cultural Revolution? Maggie Thatcher's poll tax? Perhaps the best source to turn to in this respect is Barbara Tuchman's *March of Folly*, an ignored treasure for students of organizational behavior.

She argues that folly occurs when a governmental leader pursues policies contrary to the self-interest of the nation. But to be real folly, the policy must have been perceived as counter-productive *in its own time*, not merely by hindsight. Secondly, there are always feasible alternative means that were available. She takes her notion of folly and refracts it through the prism of four major epochal events: the Trojan Horse escorted through the gates of Troy, led innocently (and stupidly) by Priam's own warriors (who had heard from Cassandra, among others, that it was probably a Greek ploy); the Renaissance Popes and how their actions brought about the Protestant Reformation; George III and the loss of the "colonies"; and LBJ and the Vietnam War. Tuchman writes: "Woodenheadedness, the source of self-deception, is a factor that plays a remarkable role in individuals. It consists in assessing a situation in terms of preconceived fixed notions while ignoring or rejecting any contrary signs. It is acting according to wish while not allowing oneself to be deflected by the facts. It is epitomized in a historian's statement about Philip II of Spain, the surpassing wooden-head of all sovereigns: 'No experience of the failure of the policy could shake his belief in its essential excellence.'"

The New Leadership

So where does all of this lead us in terms of the current organizational context? What should be clear by now is that post-bureaucratic organization requires a new kind of alliance between leaders and the led. Today's organizations are evolving into federations, networks, clusters, cross-functional teams, temporary systems, ad hoc task forces, lattices, modules, matrices—almost anything but pyramids with their obsolete TOPdown leadership. The new leader will encourage healthy dissent and values those followers courageous enough to say no. It will go to the leader who exults in cultural differences and knows that diversity is the best hope for long-term survival and success. The title of this article was deliberately provocative but, I hope, not too misleading. It's not quite the *end* of leadership, actually, but it clearly points the way to a new, far more subtle and indirect form of influence for leaders to be effective. The new reality is that intellectual capital, brain power, know-how, human imagination has supplanted capital as the critical success factor and leaders will have to learn an entirely new set of skills that are not understood, not taught in our business schools, and, for all of those reasons, rarely practiced. I am going to suggest that there are four competencies that will determine the success of the New Leadership.

1. *The New Leader understands and practices the Power of Appreciation. They are connoisseurs of talent, more curators than creators.* We all pay lip service to acknowledgement and appreciation. To generalize just a tad, most organizations are woefully neglectful of bestowing either. And it is one of the most powerful motivators, especially for knowledge workers. To take only one example out of numberless cases, many years ago, I sent my first book to the Dean and, in turn, received a perfunctory, dictated note saying that he would take the book on his next plane trip and read it then. That was it. That was the last word I ever heard from him about something I had spent over three years working on. Not very motivating or energizing, to say the least.

What I'm also getting at is that the leader is rarely the best or the brightest in the new organizations. The New Leader has a smell for talent, an imaginative Rolodex, unafraid of hiring people better than they are and are often more a curator than a creator. In my book, *Organizing Genius,* I looked at the leadership of Great Groups and in most cases, the leader was rarely the cleverest or the sharpest. Peter Schneider, president of Disney's colossally successful Feature Animation studio, leads a group of 1,200 animators. He can't draw to save his life. Bob Taylor, former head of the Palo Alto Research Center, where the first commercial PC was invented, wasn't a computer scientist. J. Robert Oppenheimer, head of the befabled Manhattan Project which produced the first nuclear device, while a brilliant physicist, never matched the accomplishments of the future Nobel Laureates working for him at Los Alamos. It goes on and on. Perhaps a story about two of Britain's most famous 19th-century Prime Ministers illustrates this point. It was said about William Ewart Gladstone that when you had dinner with Mr. Gladstone, you felt that he was the world's most brilliant and provocative, the most intelligent and wittiest conversationalist you have ever met. But when you were dining with Mr. Disraeli, you felt that *you* were the world's most brilliant and provocative, the most. . . .

Max De Pree put it best when he said that good leaders "abandon their ego to the talents of others."

2. *The New Leader keeps reminding people of what's important.* Organizations drift into entropy and the bureaucratization of imagination when they forget what's important. Simple to say, but that one sentence is one of the few pieces of advice I suggest to leaders: Remind your people of what's important. Even in my profession of teaching I will occasionally hear a colleague say, usually in half-jest, that the university would be a great place to work if only there weren't students around. What else is there but helping students to become successful at life? What can be more ennobling?

A powerful enough vision can transform what would otherwise be routine and drudgery into collectively focused energy—even sacrifice. Witness again the Manhattan Project. The scientists there were willing to put their careers on hold and to undertake what was, in essence, a massive engineering feat because they believed the free world depended on their doing so. Reminiscing about Los Alamos, Richard Feynman, the irreverent future Nobel Laureate, told a story that illustrates how reminding people of "what's important" can give meaning and value to work. The U.S. Army had recruited talented engineers from all over the United States for special duty on the project. They were assigned to work on the primitive computers of the period (1943–45), doing energy calculations and other tedious jobs. But the Army, obsessed with security, refused to tell them anything specific about the project. They didn't know that they were building a weapon that could end the war or even what their calculations meant. They were simply expected to do the work, which they did slowly and not very well. Feynman, who supervised the technicians, prevailed on his superiors to tell the recruits what they were doing and why. Permission was granted to lift the veil of secrecy, and Oppenheimer gave them a special lecture on the nature of the project and their own contribution.

"*Complete* transformation," Feynman recalled. "*They* began to invent ways of doing it better. They improved the scheme. They worked at night. They didn't need supervising in the night; they didn't need anything. They understood everything; they invented several of the programs we used." Ever the scientist, Feynman calculated that the work was done "nearly ten times as fast" after it had meaning.

Meaning. Charles Handy has it right in his book *The Hungry Spirit.* We are all hungry spirits craving purpose and meaning at work, to contribute something beyond ourselves and leaders can never forget to stop reminding people of what's important.

3. *The New Leader generates and sustains trust.* We're all aware that the terms of the new social contract of work have changed. No one can depend on life-long loyalty or commitment to any organization. Since 1985, 25% of the American workforce has been laid off at least once. That's about a half-million on average each year. In 1998, when the unemployment rate was the lowest in 30 years, roughly 110,000 workers were down-sized. At a time when the new social contract makes the ties between organizations and their knowledge workers tenuous, trust becomes the emotional glue that can bond people to an organization. Trust is a small word with powerful connotations and is a hugely complex factor. The ingredients are a combination of competence, constancy, caring, fairness, candor and authenticity. Most of all the latter. And that is achieved by the New Leaders when they can balance successfully the tripod of forces working on and in most of us: ambition, competence and integrity. Authenticity, as Groucho joked, cannot be faked. To be redundant, it's real. The current cliché is "walk your talk." But it's far more than that. The best and perhaps the only way I know of to illustrate (as opposed to define) authenticity is to quote from Robert Bolt's Preface to his play, *A Man for All Seasons:*

> At any rate, Thomas More, as I wrote about him, became for me a man with an adamantine sense of his own self. He knew where he began and left off, what area of himself he could yield to the encroachments of his enemies, and what to the encroachments of those he loved. It was a substantial area in both cases, for he had a proper sense of fear and was a busy lover. Since he was a clever man and a great lawyer, he was able to retire from those areas in wonderfully good order, but at length he was asked to retreat from that final area where he located his self. And there this supple, humorous, unassuming and sophisticated person set like metal, was overtaken by an absolutely primitive rigor, and could no more be budged than a cliff.

4. *The New Leader and the Led are intimate allies.* Earlier I referred to how Dr. King's followers shamed him into going to jail because so many young people responded to his speeches and found themselves in danger. They were the unsung heroes. People you've never heard of: James Bevel, Diane Nash, Otis Moss and many others. All heroes. John Lewis tells us in his book how much of the Civil Rights Movement was a heroic team effort, referring to *Henry V*'s "band of brothers."

It's not too much of a stretch to consider Jakob Schindler, the protagonist of an epochal story immortalized in the film *Schindler's List*. The power of Spielberg's film is the transformation of Schindler from a sleazy, down-at-the-heels small-time con-man who moves to Poland in order to harness cheap Jewish labor to make munitions which he can then sell to the Germans at low cost. His transformation is the singular compelling narrative of the film. And it comes about over a period of time where Schindler interacts with his Jewish workers, most of all the accountant, Levin, but also frequent and achingly painful moments where he confronts the evil of the war, of the Holocaust, of the suffering, of the injustice. In the penultimate scene, when the war is over and the Nazis have evacuated the factory, but before the American troops arrive, the prisoners give him a ring, made for him, from the precious metals used by the workers. As he tries to put the ring on, he begins crying, "Why, why are you doing this? With this metal, we could have saved three, maybe four, maybe five more Jews." And he drives off in tears.

I find it hard to be objective about a scene that tears at my soul, but I want to argue that though this was a unique, singular event, it portrays what New Leadership is all about: the great leaders are made by great groups and by organizations that create the social architecture of respect and dignity. And, through some kind of weird alchemy, some ineffable symbiosis, great leadership brings that about. Without each other, the leader and the led are culturally impoverished. Only a poet could sum up the majesty of this alchemy:

> We are all angels with only one wing.
> We can only fly while embracing each other.

These New Leaders will not have the loudest voice, but the most attentive ear. Instead of pyramids, these post-bureaucratic organizations will be structures built of energy and ideas, led by people who find their joy in the task at hand, while embracing each other—and not worrying about leaving monuments behind.

Selected Bibliography

There are several books I referred to in the article that would more likely be found on the book shelf of a history or English professor than a management scholar or practitioner but two of them, *Frenzy of Renown* by Leo Braudy (Oxford, 1986), and Barbara Tuchman's *March of Folly* (Alfred Knopf, 1984), deserve to be. They are just terrific books on leadership. Braudy's is the first and only history of celebrity and is brilliantly written as might be expected but often found lacking in academic treatises. I've said enough about Tuchman in the text. I use it in my undergraduate leadership class and it's very useful. What historian Tuchman refers to as folly or wooden-headedness, we might refer to as cognitive dissonance. John Lewis's book, *Walking with the Wind* (Simon & Schuster, 1998) is a splendid personal memoir of the civil rights movement, written by one of the most important African-American leaders. In Jim O'Toole's *Leading Change* (Jossey-Bass, 1995), the frontispiece of that book underlines, with great wit and clarity, the basic premise of this important work; i.e., leaders better learn how to enroll willing followers. It could have also been written by a humanities professor, which he basically is, except with brio and a deep philosophical lens, he has written one of the most provocative and important books on leadership. Ronald Heifetz's book, *Leadership Without Easy Answers* (Belknap, 1994), more than lives up to its name and is not an easy read, as the title suggests. But it is deep and complex and goes way beyond the domain of Corporate America, though he doesn't exclude that, into areas of community leadership, doctor/patient relationships among others. Garry Wills's book *Certain Trumpets* (Simon & Schuster, 1994) is already a classic. It has a lot in common with Howard Gardner's *Leading Minds* (Basic Books, 1995) which I should have referenced as well. Wills goes at leadership as a political scientist cum historian would, while Gardner is a cognitive psychologist. They both rely on fascinating narratives, but their choices of leaders, at the margins anyway, give away their world view, their range, and their informed biases. So while Wills chooses to focus on Cesare Borgia or King David, Gardner will take up Robert Maynard Hutchins or Jean Monet. At the same time, they often choose the same icon, like Martha Graham, Gandhi, Eleanor Roosevelt and Pope John XXIII. Two recent books I co-authored, one with Patricia Ward Biederman, *Organizing Genius* (Perseus, 1997) and one with David Heenan, *Co-Leaders* (Wiley, 1999) provided some of the conceptual background for this article but try to put the spotlight not so much on leadership but on Great Groups and Partnerships.

I'll end this bibliographic narrative with Berthold Brecht who always liked to have the last word anyway. He was incapable of collaboration or partnership except for his brilliantly wicked and bittersweet lyrics to Kurt Weill's *Threepenny Opera*. The poem I used came from Georg Tabori's book, *The World of Brecht* (Samuel French, 1964).

INTRODUCTION TO *THE ART OF FOLLOWERSHIP* (2008)

WHO IS NOT FASCINATED by the dance between leaders and followers, who depend upon each other as surely as animals and air. But until recently followers have been largely neglected in the study of leadership, an omission famously addressed by Robert Kelley [a contributor to *The Art of Followership*] in his 1988 *Harvard Business Review* piece "In Praise of Followers." Now, almost 20 years later, we have this welcome book, a long overdue effort to explore leadership's underappreciated complement in all its complexity, as role, relationship, and process. It is no surprise that books on leadership, promising to reveal the secrets of countless football coaches and historical figures as disparate as Jesus and Attila the Hun, outnumber those on followership several thousand to one. After all, leadership is the prize that ambitious men and women have struggled and even died for at least since Alexander the Great. Whether their field is politics, business, science or the arts, leaders are at the center of the action, the envied if not enviable stars whose lives seem to burn a little brighter than our own. We aspire to their power and its perquisites even as we take unseemly pleasure when one of them stumbles and falls. Indeed the moment when each of us realizes he or she is mostly a follower, not a leader, is a genuine developmental milestone; who forgets that painful leap over the line of demarcation between the boundless fantasies of childhood and the sober reality of an adulthood in which we will never quite become the god we hoped to be.

Reading the diverse essays that make up this valuable book, I was reminded how hollow the label of leadership sometimes is and how heroic

---

This chapter was originally published in *The Art of Followership*, edited by Ronald E. Riggio, Ira Chaleff, and Jean Lipman-Blumen (Jossey-Bass, 2008).

followership can be. As editor Jean Lipman-Blumen and other contributors point out, followers play an especially vital role in the presence of "toxic leaders," those malignant wielders of power who have made the last century the bloodiest in all of humanity's decidedly sanguinary history. When evil leaders emerge, followers have no moral choice but to try to wrest power from them. Such behavior is usually termed resistance, but it is, in fact, a heroic form of action. Moreover, this honorable rebellion reflects an underappreciated underlying truth. Yes, leaders have enormous power, but so do those who follow them. Without their followers, tyrants can accomplish little. Even toxic leaders sleep and are subject to other human constraints, and so they depend upon their followers to wield the gas, the guns and the machetes. For better or for ill, followers do the heavy lifting of any successful enterprise. No matter who is memorialized as founder, no nation or organization is built without the collective effort of a group of able, energetic, unsung followers. Moreover, followers bear the brunt of the horrors toxic leaders make. Many of the most notorious political leaders of recent times peacefully ended their days sleeping on Frette sheets in comfortable exile, sad to say.

In organizational life, the consequences of toxic leadership are less obvious but no less dire. In recent years, we have seen more and more examples of courageous followership as nameless, faceless shareholders rebelled against arrogant, underperforming executives when their corporate boards failed to do so. The last couple of decades have served as a corrective to the once widespread view of the CEO as demigod. Our recent disillusionment with much corporate leadership is the cumulative effective of too many insider-stock trades, too much executive venality, too many $6,000 shower curtains. As executive compensation packages began to approach the size of the budgets of some countries, observers began to wonder if they had not given too much of their own power over to those at the top. The cult of the celebrity CEO gave way to a renewed appreciation of the leader as steward of the collective treasure of his or her followers.

A gathering of research such as this not only reminds us of the importance of followers, it underlines how blurred the line is between leaders and those they lead. When followers check the power of their leaders, they clearly function as leaders themselves, albeit less well-paid ones. And whether by augmenting the actions of their leaders or conscientiously challenging them, followers both advance the collective enterprise and polish their own leadership skills, a fact neatly reflected in the title of Roger Adair's chapter, "Developing Great Leadership, One Follower at a Time."

One of the most important—and potentially perilous—arenas for follower action is within the organization. We tend to value the leader who acts decisively, whether right or wrong, but followers are expected to behave with more restraint. Too often a follower who dares to poke holes in a leader's plan is seen as a maverick at best, more often as a dissident, even a lunatic. But such internal critics are invaluable, the people most likely to save the organization from investing time and resources in a doomed product or project. Historians tell us that George Washington routinely solicited the advice of subordinates before going into battle, unlike his status-conscious British counterparts. And in order to elicit candid feedback from his men, Washington did not tell them that a particular plan under consideration was his own. Washington had an intuitive understanding of what good followers bring to the table. Sadly such understanding is rare. Most of us can tick off the attributes of a great leader, but the nature and functions of a great follower are little understood and almost never articulated. Too often, followers are expected to be acquiescent and are rewarded for being so, when in fact followers who practice knee-jerk obedience are of little value and often dangerous.

If I had to reduce the responsibilities of a good follower to a single rule it would be to speak truth to power. We know that toxic followers can put even good leaders on a disastrous path—Shakespeare's Iago comes immediately to mind. But heroic followers can also save leaders from their worst follies, especially leaders so isolated the only voice they listen to is their own. When the leader cannot be persuaded, the follower is sometimes forced to break the collective rules and become a whistleblower, a kind of rogue leader who wrests power from those in charge and often pays a terrible personal price for doing so. But the most effective followers are those who possess or acquire the skills that allow them to make their case and effect change without destroying the organization. One important function of a book like this is to get more people thinking about how to create and become great followers, especially in light of the fact that we spend much of our lives in that capacity, whatever exalted titles we may hold. The tools of great followership are not so different from those of leadership, including the ability to persuade. In fact, given that followers usually lack the power to order and insist, they are wise to acquire a quiver of diplomatic tools, including an expansive knowledge of the psychology of human behavior and mastery of such neglected persuasive arts as rhetoric and acting.

In many ways, great followership is harder than leadership. It has more dangers and fewer rewards and it must routinely be exercised with much more subtlety. But great followership has never been more important, if only because of the seriousness of the global problems we face and the fact that they must be solved collaboratively, not by leaders alone but by leaders working in tandem with able and dedicated followers. No single leader, however charismatic, however brilliant, can solve the problem of climate change. It can only be addressed by millions of creative, dedicated individuals who know they must act, no matter what their leaders tell them.

In fact, I will go out on a limb and predict that a decade from now the terms leader and follower will seem as dated as bell bottoms and Nehru jackets. The world is changing with dizzying speed and, among those changes, is an erosion of traditional notions of leadership. What does leadership mean in a world in which anonymous bloggers can choose presidents and bring down regimes? When John F. Kennedy ran against Nixon, his biggest challenge was mastering the relatively new medium of television in order to win the presidency. But the days are gone when a leader's rise to power is linear and relatively orderly. Today power is being democratized by new media that spread ideas virally and can topple the established order without revolution or manifesto. In this strange new world, a teenager with a camera phone may be more powerful than a politician who spends decades acquiring his or her position. Not traditional leaders but people whose fingers are on the send key rule this brave new world. Agendas are being set, sometimes with murderous seriousness, sometimes whimsically, by global networks of people who effect change without meeting anywhere except in cyberspace. Recently, a virtual journalist interviewed a virtual U.S. Congressman on a computer-generated set in Second Life, the electronic playground where real fortunes are being made. Whatever else transpires in the next ten years, it is safe to say that we will have very different notions of leadership and followership if only because each of us will be able to peek into and expose any corner of an increasingly wired world, upending any current notion of what constitutes the status quo.

Let me make one more prediction. One of the pleasures of this book is its references to the discoveries about how humans influence each other (the beating heart of leadership) made by such pioneering social scientists as Solomon Asch, Stanley Milgram, and others. Each age has its paradigmatic science and none is more important today than neuroscience. I am sure that generously supported researchers are even now using functional magnetic resonance imaging to explore how leaders and followers think. The best of that work will be a worthy addition to the insights offered by these authors.

FOLLOWERS MAKE GOOD
LEADERS GOOD (1989)

IT IS PROBABLY INEVITABLE that a society as star-struck as ours should focus on leaders in analyzing why organizations succeed or fail. As a long-time student and teacher of management, I, too, have tended to look to the men and women at the top for clues on how organizations achieve and maintain institutional health. But the longer I study effective leaders, the more I am persuaded of the under-appreciated importance of effective followers.

What makes a good follower? The single most important characteristic may well be a willingness to tell the truth. In a world of growing complexity, leaders are increasingly dependent on their subordinates for good information whether the leaders want to hear it or not. Followers who tell the truth, and leaders who listen to it, are an unbeatable combination.

Movie mogul Samuel Goldwyn seems to have had a gut-level awareness of the importance of what I call "effective backtalk" from subordinates. After a string of box-office flops, Mr. Goldwyn called his staff together and told them: "I want you to tell me exactly what's wrong with me and M.G.M. even if it means losing your job."

Although Mr. Goldwyn wasn't personally ready to give up the ego-massaging presence of "yes men," in his own gloriously garbled way he acknowledged the company's greater need for a staff that speaks the truth.

Like portfolios, organizations benefit from diversity. Effective leaders resist the urge to people their staffs only with others who look or sound or think just like themselves, what I call the doppleganger, or ghostly-double, effect. They look for good people from many molds, and then they encourage them to speak out, even to disagree. Aware of the pitfalls of

This article was originally published in the *New York Times*, December 31, 1989.

institutional unanimity, some leaders wisely build dissent into the decision-making process.

Organizations that encourage thoughtful dissent gain much more than a heightened air of collegiality. They make better decisions. In a recent study, Rebecca A. Henry, a psychology professor at Purdue University, found that groups were generally more effective than individuals in making forecasts of sales and other financial data. And the greater the initial disagreement among group members, the more accurate the results. "With more disagreement, people are forced to look at a wider range of possibilities," Ms. Henry said.

Like good leaders, good followers understand the importance of speaking out. More important, they do it. Almost 30 years ago, when Nikita Khrushchev came to America, he met with reporters at the Washington Press Club. The first written question he received was: "Today you talked about the hideous rule of your predecessor, Stalin. You were one of his closest aides and colleagues during those years. What were you doing all that time?" Khrushchev's face grew red. "Who asked that?" he roared. No one answered. "Who asked that?" he insisted. Again, silence. "That's what I was doing," Mr. Khrushchev said.

Even in democracies where the only gulag is the threat of a pink slip, it is hard to disagree with the person in charge. Several years ago TV's John Chancellor asked former Presidential aides how they behaved on those occasions when the most powerful person in the world came up with a damned fool idea. Several of the aides admitted doing nothing. Ted Sorenson revealed that John F. Kennedy could usually be brought to his senses by being told, "That sounds like the kind of idea Nixon would have."

Quietism, as a more pious age called the sin of silence, often costs organizations—and their leaders—dearly. Former President Ronald Reagan suffered far more at the hands of so-called friends who refused to tell him unattractive truths than from his ostensible enemies.

Nancy Reagan, in her recent memoir, *My Turn*, recalls chiding then-Vice President George Bush when he approached her, not the President, with grave reservations about White House chief of staff Donald Regan.

"I wish you'd tell my husband," the First Lady said. "I can't be the only one who's saying this to him." According to Mrs. Reagan, Mr. Bush responded, "Nancy, that's not my role."

"That's exactly your role," she snapped. Nancy Reagan was right. It is the good follower's obligation to share his or her best counsel with the person in charge. And silence—not dissent—is the one answer that leaders should refuse to accept. History contains dozens of cautionary tales on the subject, none more vivid than the account of the murder of Thomas à Becket. "Will no one rid me of this meddlesome priest?" Henry II is said to have muttered, after a contest of wills with his former friend.

The four barons who then murdered Becket in his cathedral were the antithesis of the good followers they thought themselves to be. At the risk of being irreverent, the right answer to Henry's question—the one that would have served his administration best—was "No," or at least, "Let's talk about it."

Like modern-day subordinates who testify under oath that they were only doing what they thought their leader wanted them to do, the barons were guilty of remarkable chutzpah. Henry failed by not making his position clear and by creating an atmosphere in which his followers would rather kill than disagree with him. The barons failed by not making the proper case against the king's decision.

Effective leaders reward dissent, as well as encourage it. They understand that whatever momentary discomfort they experience as a result of being told from time to time that they are wrong is more than offset by the fact that reflective backtalk increases a leader's ability to make good decisions.

Executive compensation should go far toward salving the pricked ego of the leader whose followers speak their minds. But what's in it for the follower? The good follower may indeed have to put his or her job on the line in the course of speaking up. But consider the price he or she pays for silence. What job is worth the enormous psychic cost of following a leader who values loyalty in the narrowest sense?

Perhaps the ultimate irony is that the follower who is willing to speak out shows precisely the kind of initiative that leadership is made of.

JEAN LIPMAN-BLUMEN ON "INTRODUCTION TO *THE ART OF FOLLOWERSHIP*" AND "FOLLOWERS MAKE GOOD LEADERS GOOD"

IN HIS CHARACTERISTICALLY ELOQUENT introduction to *The Art of Followership*, Warren Bennis articulates the irresistible attractions of leadership: power, perquisites, and a place at the center of action. Garbed in these vestments, the leader projects a godlike persona. Consequently, we endow leaders with an exceptionalism that invites extraordinary action, action that sometimes leads to noble enterprises, yet at other times spirals into toxic devastation. Festooned with such powerful magnets, leadership roles frequently attract candidates more driven by the tyranny of their ego and drawn by the nectar of privilege than by a dedication to the critical needs of the larger community.

The title *follower* holds no such obvious blandishments, although its downsides are clearer. The dictionary describes a follower as someone who "is in the service of another," "one that follows the opinions or teachings of another," "one that imitates another."[1] If we hark back to the archaic definition, we find that a follower is "one who chases." Hardly a recipe for daring, heroic action! In fact, Bennis poignantly describes that epiphanal "moment when each of us realizes he or she is mostly a follower, not a leader" as "that painful leap over the line of demarcation between the boundless fantasies of childhood and the sober reality of an adulthood in which we will never quite become the god we hoped to be."[2]

Nonetheless, as recent efforts to rethink followership have suggested, followers remain irreducibly indispensable to leaders. Without followers, social movements die abirthing, innovations remain unadopted, new insights lie fallow, and noble intentions shrivel into naught. More generally, without followers, leaders rarely have the muscle to implement their vision. Lacking the immense collective effort of followers, President Barack Obama could not have turned his challenge, "Yes, you can" into a groundswell of "Yes, *we* can." That army of energized followers swept Obama into the White House, creating a historical moment fraught with national hope and renewed confidence.

Another far more important and subtle aspect of followership frequently falls below our angle of vision. I call that "the franchise of followership." Again, the dictionary draws us back to essentials: A franchise invokes "freedom or immunity from burden or restriction vested in a person or group."[3] A franchise is a "constitutional or statutory right or privilege, especially the right to vote." We begin to glimpse the strength and the latitude of followership, a strength waiting to be seized, a latitude begging to be stretched.

If we take the "franchise of followership" seriously, we can begin to appreciate the concern that Bennis sounds in his introduction to *The Art of Followership*. There, he talks about the obligation of followers in the face of toxic leaders: "Followers have no moral choice but to try to wrest power from them." Bennis reminds us that such action on the part of followers is "usually termed resistance, but it is, in fact, a heroic form of action . . . an honorable rebellion."

To exercise the franchise of followership, followers need not wait until they encounter a full-blown toxic leader, whose "grand illusions often masquerade as noble visions."[4] Bennis reminds us of the followers' obligation to "speak truth to power." That franchise is not meant simply to rein in the occasional toxic leader. Instead, it is embedded in the quotidian interaction between all leaders and followers to ensure that the leader's vision is no longer a burning bush witnessed by a solitary Moses.

In that daily engagement of leader and followers, followers help to reframe the leader's vision. By chipping away at the marble block of the leader's intentions, followers not only exercise their "freedom from restriction" but ultimately help to reveal the essential contours of the leader's vision. Thus followers play a central role in refining and perfecting the leader's vision, so often skewed and endangered by the leader's ego and thirst for power.

The late Joseph Rost, whose intellectual contributions to the field of leadership were legion, railed against the term "follower." In his landmark book,[5] *Leadership for the Twenty-First Century,* as well as in his last published work (a chapter in *The Art of Followership*),[6] Rost argued that the term "follower" was an "outmoded concept." He saw it as a leftover from the Industrial Era, "a consequence of industrial assumptions and actions based on top-down management and the Great Person view of leadership."[7]

Instead, Rost focused on the *collaborative relationship* between leaders and followers and argued that "collaborative leadership is an influence relationship among leaders and collaborators who intend significant changes that reflect their mutual interests."[8] Indeed, in this postindustrialized, technology-driven world, structured by the contradictory demands of diversity and interdependence, a deeper understanding of collaboration is more needed than ever before.[9]

This is hardly the place for an extended semantic discussion; however, proposing another term, such as *constituent* (favored by leadership thinker John Gardner),[10] draws our attention to other dimensions of the follower's role. The term *constituent* reminds us of an individual's contribution as a full-fledged co-founder or co-establisher. As one who helps to create or establish a process, an event, an idea, or an entity, we remain completely engaged. We maintain an ongoing ownership and responsibility. That is why the "franchise of followership," which prompts followers or constituents to invoke their own special power and obligations, is a useful lens through which to view this bedeviling stumbling block to fruitful leadership discussions.

What results from the interaction of leaders and followers, perchance constituents (or whatever better term we might devise), is the creation of our collaboration, the product of our partnership with other constituents, as well as with the leader. It is as much ours, the constituents', as the leader's. Through that partnership, we inherit a serious obligation to protect both the process and the outcome from degradation by anyone, including a toxic leader (be the leader's toxicity intentional or inadvertent). This courageous followership is not simply confined to rebellion in the face of a full-blown toxic leader. Rather, it infuses the daily interaction of leaders and constituents that guides nontoxic leaders along a constructive path and protects them from stepping over the toxic line.[11]

Opening this discussion—which is all that we can hope to accomplish here—allows us to acknowledge the growing awareness among leadership scholars that a new vessel of leadership and followership is slowly sailing into view. The flurry of books with titles such as *Inclusive Leadership, Shared Leadership, Connective Leadership,* and *Collaborative Leadership*[12] testifies to the new leadership paradigm struggling to click into place, as Thomas S. Kuhn described.[13]

The emerging paradigm portrays a more connective enterprise, one born of the complementary interaction of diverse but interdependent equals: leaders and followers or constituents. This more complex paradigm integrates the contradictory tensions within which the contemporary world lives and both leaders and followers or constituents must work. Let us hope that the many who must live and work together—and that inevitably includes us all—can find renewed, ennobling possibilities through the franchise of followership.

Jean Lipman-Blumen is Thornton F. Bradshaw Professor of Public Policy, professor of organizational behavior, and co-founding director of the Institute for Advanced Studies in Leadership at The Drucker School, Claremont Graduate University. She is author of *The Connective Edge* (Jossey-Bass, 1996), *Hot Groups* (Oxford University Press, 1999), and *The Allure of Toxic Leaders* (Oxford University Press, 2004).

PART SIX

LEADERSHIP
AND THE MEDIA

LEADERS HAVE LIVED AND DIED by the media since the media were the ancient singers of heroic deeds. Political leaders depend on the media to communicate their messages to all those potential followers whose hands they can't shake or whose babies they can't dandle in person. FDR (and Hitler) had radio; JFK had television, which temporarily derailed Richard Nixon in the first televised presidential debate in 1959; Barack Obama had Facebook. Given the long symbiotic relationship between the media and political leaders, it will be fascinating to see what new media rise up to take the place of the embattled mainstream variety, especially print, now horribly reduced and struggling to survive. In the past, much of the material disseminated by the mainstream media was vetted by professionals committed to maintaining high standards of fairness and accuracy. That is less so in the digital age, which leaves the task of separating facts from opinion (or spleen or propaganda) to the consumer. The essay "The New Transparency" is a look at how the blog, the online newspaper, and other new media are democratizing power. In this new electronic universe, reputations can be made or shattered in an instant. Since nothing ever disappears from the electronic landfill, would-be leaders can't be sure an embarrassing lapse, caught on a cell-phone camera, won't come back to undo them.

But there is an invaluable upside to the new transparency as well. Under repressive regimes, the electronic media are doing what traditional reformers often could not do: allowing the voices of dissidents to ring out, while their governments struggle, with less and less success, to silence them. In today's wired world, transparency is inevitable.

THE AGE OF UNREALITY (1989)

IF AMERICA HAS ANY POINT AT ALL NOW, and I am by no means convinced that it does, it is to avoid reality. It is as if the entire nation had decided to stop facing facts. As he abruptly left the 1988 presidential race, Gary Hart suggested, quite sincerely, that he was too good for us. Defrocked minister Jim Bakker insisted that he had had an affair with secretary Jessica Hahn in order to save his marriage. Hahn countered by saying that it wasn't an affair, it was rape, took more than $200,000 to keep silent, and then not only talked but did a *Playboy* interview and posed for the usual *Playboy* centerfold shots. This, she said, proved not only that was she a free person but that God was on her side. Ronald Reagan, having said initially that he knew nothing about the gun runs to the Nicaraguan Contras, later said that not only had he known about it, but it had been his idea.

In the same vein, Ollie North's secretary, Fawn Hall, declared, by way of justifying breaking the law, that sometimes you have to obey "a higher law." And North himself admitted that he had not only lied but destroyed evidence—but told Congress that he was telling it the truth. Presidential candidate Joe Biden not only lied about his academic achievements and borrowed passages from other people without crediting them, he borrowed the life of an English politician, claiming that he was the first Biden in "a thousand generations" to go to college.

Meanwhile, Wall Street traders became victims of their own practical jokes, TV minister Oral Roberts went up in a tower and said that God would strike him dead if people didn't immediately send him lots of money, and TV minister turned presidential candidate Pat Robertson went to Bedford-Stuyvesant, one of New York's most ravaged sections, to announce his candidacy, because he had once briefly been a minister there. This was news to area residents, who protested his presence as, at the very least, exploitative.

This chapter was originally published in *Why Leaders Can't Lead* (Jossey-Bass, 1989).

Football great Rosey Grier, who once served Bobby Kennedy and after Kennedy's assassination drifted steadily to the right politically, sort of summed up our general confusion by introducing Robertson and his wife as "Mr. and Mrs. Robinson."

Rather than protesting all this doubletalk, the American people seem not only to accept it but to understand it. This, then, is the Age of Unreality.

Of course, reality has never been our strong suit. "Oh, beautiful for spacious skies, for amber waves of grain, for purple mountains' majesty above the fruited plain. . . ." By 1893, when Katherine Lee Bates wrote "America the Beautiful," once-pastoral America had become a vast blast furnace, and more Americans sang about spacious skies, amber waves of grain, and fruited plains than ever saw them, but never mind. They were out there somewhere, and, if we got rich enough or brave enough, we could go and see them for ourselves.

But if we were vague and dreamy in 1893, today we are only semiconscious, real people living in an imaginary landscape. In Thoreau's phrase, we have become the tools of our tools. We invented a whole range of amazing machines, and now they are reinventing us. Ironically, the more sophisticated they become, the more primitive we become, and the more active they are, the more passive we are. And the real world has receded and receded.

The majority of us now live in cities and suburbs, vast, shapeless megamixes of shopping centers, fast-food parlors, supermarkets, freeways, and the occasional lawn, which by now may be Astroturf. But this is all merely a backdrop, the setting for the action. And there's plenty of action—advertising, radio, TV, movies, rock 'n' roll, fashion, evangelism, and journalism, a twenty-four-hours-a-day, seven-days-a-week, fifty-two-weeks-a-year whirlwind of sound, images, ideas, faces. Everything is in motion, but nothing is happening. We have become extras in this perpetual national drama. At parties, people talk about whoever is in the headlines at the moment. The hostess at a recent dinner party explained that several invited guests had called to cancel. They were staying home to watch the season finale of the television show *Dallas*. She seemed to think it was perfectly reasonable that these highly sophisticated, educated people (who presumably had VCRs) had opted to spend the evening with the Ewings rather than with friends.

But, of course, the Ewings—J. R., Bobby, Miss Ellie, Pam, and the rest—*are* friends, and television is not just entertainment, it's life. It's bigger than all of us, and it's miraculous. It can bring the entire world into our bedroom. It's there, busy, pumping away all day, all night, every day, every night. It never sleeps. You wake up at three in the morning, turn on the

TV, and there's Charley Rose talking to Alexander Haig. Of course, it isn't really three in the morning where they are. It's six in the morning, but they probably taped the interview at four o'clock the afternoon of the previous day. They're in Washington. We know that, because an announcer tells us so. Sometimes, you can see the Washington Monument over Charley's shoulder. But maybe it isn't the monument, maybe it's a giant photo.

So here we are, at three in the morning, in Los Angeles, watching two men who say they're in Washington, where it's 6 AM, only they're probably in bed, maybe in Washington, maybe someplace else, because we're really watching a tape. Maybe. It should be confusing, but it isn't, because we're very advanced. We understand this stuff. We understand that the TV, the box, the instrument, the appliance, is our world now, our landscape, our context. Everything that really matters happens on the box. Gary Hart withdraws, Jim Bakker confesses, Oral Roberts commands, J. R. Ewing dies (maybe), the Carringtons are kidnapped. And, for God's sake, there's a fire on Hill Street.

Hill Street Blues is over, of course. Not because of the fire, but because people got bored and the ratings declined. Actually, it's not really over. It'll be around in reruns until the year 2000. That's one of the amazing things about the box. It can contain *everything*, everything that matters, anyway, no matter how much everything there is. The box's capacity is infinite. Ads, rock 'n' roll, wars, peace, cities, people, moments, murders, dancers, everything is in the box. It forgets nothing. Dial around enough, you'll even find spacious skies, amber waves of grain, and fruited plains in there. The new context, then, is no context, is everything and nothing, fact and fiction, history and right now.

And here's the amazing thing: everything is equal. The assassination of John Kennedy and David Letterman's stupid dog tricks are absolutely equal. TV is the ultimate democracy, the great leveler. In this new context of no context, which *New Yorker* writer George W. S. Trow first identified in 1978, everything has the same weight, and nothing is ever over. Jim Bakker, *Wheel of Fortune,* and *Miami Vice* get not merely equal but precisely the same treatment.

Everything is in living color (which is an oxymoron, but in the Age of Unreality, everything is an oxymoron), and in two dimensions, but without the size (on my set, Ted Koppel's head is about two inches high; on your larger set, it may be life-size, but neither of us can see his feet). We see parts of everything—people, places, and things. We have no sense of space or distance, because TV can go from Nashville to New York to your bedroom in a wink. That's comforting, of course. We're all just one big happy family. Here I am, in my bedroom, and here the entire world is, in my bedroom, too, and I know Letterman and Johnny Carson better than I know my neighbors. Carson has told us all about his divorces. I have no idea whether any of my neighbors have ever been divorced, or whether they're married to the people they're living with now, or whether, indeed, they're living with anyone. There is a kind of intimacy about TV—actors and musicians talking about drug problems, marital difficulties, deals gone bad, "sharing" everything. I don't mind. They get it off their chests, but I don't have to do anything about it. I don't even have to worry about it, and I can talk about it at parties, because it's not a secret. There are no secrets now.

This, then, is the best sort of intimacy. We know everything, but we don't have to do anything. Gary Hart doesn't want to say whether he has committed adultery or not, but he's the exception here. Almost everyone else—from Shelley Winters to Jimmy Swaggart—has already confessed.

In ABC Sports' immortal phrase, everything "is up close and personal," but it is, of course, also very far away. Surely, in the Age of Unreality, this is the best of all possible arrangements. We're in on everything, but unscathed by it, untouched; involved but not responsible.

TV is the dominant medium. Everything else looks more and more like TV. *Us* and *People* magazines are print versions. David Salle's paintings are paint versions. Top-forty radio stations are audio versions. Some clothing stores now use closed-circuit TV to show you the clothes that are on the racks. More people look at the clothes on TV than on the racks. In the same way, audiences at tapings of TV shows are more comfortable watching the TV monitors than watching the actual actors on actual sets. No wonder. TV has shown itself to be far more trustworthy than the real world. Husbands, wives, friends, presidents come and go, but TV is always there. We move; it moves along with us. TV prefers movement and pictures to stillness and words. Now we all do. While we enjoy hearing rock stars or all the legions of unhappy, even warped people who pass by Donahue's cameras telling their secrets to us, we don't much enjoy people talking about issues, people just sitting there, looking at us, discussing foreign policy or religion or literature. From TV, we have learned to handle images, avalanches of them, blizzards of them, but ideas are so, well, dull. If you can't see them, how can you understand them?

When Ronald Reagan talks to us on TV, we understand everything, but when he talks to us on the radio, when we can hear him but not see him, we don't understand. He sounds old, raspy, cranky, like the old man in the hardware store who's always mad about something. It was just the opposite with Richard Nixon. He used to sound pretty reasonable on the radio, but when we saw him, he seemed quite mad. We incline toward attractive people, pretty images. Ideas are often neither attractive nor pretty, and they're demanding, they require us to work. The new content then is no content. Just show us everything; we'll think about it later.

Given our belief in image, the ascension of actor Ronald Reagan to the White House was not only fitting, it was inevitable. You want a leader who understands what's going on, and what's going on is TV. So what if he didn't know much about politics. He knew all about TV, knew the value of a wink and a smile, knew how to look right through the camera into our hearts. He was perfect, until the Iran-Contra scandal. Suddenly, he began trying to explain things, and we hate it when that happens. Now he's like the guest who overstays his welcome. We want him to go home.

The Democrats haven't been able to get our attention because there hasn't been a Democrat since John Kennedy who really understood the new context and was comfortable in it. It's as if they have a death wish. Lyndon Johnson, Hubert Humphrey, George McGovern, Jimmy Carter, and Walter Mondale all had awful, grating voices; none but McGovern was good-looking, and he was balding. These were not men you wanted in your house on anything like a regular basis. Gary Hart wasn't bad-looking, and he has plenty of hair and a nice speaking voice, calm, deep, unshrill, but then he began to behave like J. R. Ewing. Now, we love J. R., but we wouldn't choose him to be president.

As for Michael Dukakis, the nicest thing that was said about him was that if George Bush reminded every woman of her first husband, Michael Dukakis reminded every woman of her second. He seemed to possess ample character and judgment, but all told, he was more of an effective manager than a bold leader. If the Democrats had any sense at all, they would draft a real TV veteran—Jim Garner, for instance. He's good-looking, we all know him and like him, and he's mastered TV, handles it as well as or better than anyone else. We're a whole lot more comfortable with stars than with leaders. Leaders not only are unreliable, they're demanding. John Kennedy said, "Ask not what your country can do for you—ask what you can do for your country." Stars are entertaining and undemanding. Even when they fall from grace, and end up at the Betty Ford Center, they're entertaining. We love confessions, ours and other people's, the franker the better now, and the line between stars' lives and roles is virtually invisible. *Moonlighting* star Bruce Willis is a scamp on and off the box, as his scuffle with Los Angeles cops proved. Jimmy Smits of *L.A. Law* is now in trouble with the law. Maybe Smits the TV lawyer will end up winning an acquittal for Smits the citizen. There's a kind of wonderful symmetry about all this. Elizabeth Taylor portrays alcoholics and becomes an alcoholic herself. She marries Richard Burton on screen and off. She marries and divorces other men, off and on screen, until finally it all sort of melts together, and we can't separate real life from reel life.

In addition to being attractive, interesting, rich, and entertaining, stars know all the stories we like, and we do like stories; some, in fact, we love. As described by Robert Reich (1987) in *Tales of a New America,* there are four we especially like: "The Mob at the Gates," "The Triumphant Individual," "The Benevolent Community," and "The Rot at the Top." We live by them, and TV lives on them. These are not merely our central morality tales, the core of American mythology; they are the bases for virtually all of our TV and film diversions—the basic plots. TV and film don't merely imitate life now, they are life.

In "The Mob at the Gates," it's America versus foreigners and foreign influences. The Russians, the Cubans, the Iranians, the Nicaraguans, the Japanese, the Germans are all out there, waiting to pounce on us. But we are alert, courageous, and proud and will not succumb—not as long as we have Charlton Heston and Clint Eastwood and Sylvester Stallone and Chuck Norris out there defending us.

In "The Triumphant Individual," the little guy wins—again and again, by himself, unassisted, powered by grit and guts. Goldie Hawn beats the system in Washington, Eddie Murphy wins in Philadelphia and Beverly Hills, Steve Martin gets the girl, even if he has a grotesque nose. We can win, too, any time we want to. That's one of the glories of America.

Another glory is demonstrated in "The Benevolent Community," the good-neighbor syndrome. When someone's in trouble, we rally around, pitch right in, and help out. We're the most generous, the kindest people on earth. Everyone knows that.

There are villains, of course. There are always villains. They, of course, are "The Rot at the Top," the big businessmen, such as Burl Ives and Ned Beatty, the political bosses, such as Broderick Crawford, and the Mafia dons, such as De Niro and Pacino and Brando. They have their ways with us—but, of course, we're on to them, so they never get very far. TV and movies tell us these stories so often and so well and blend fact and fiction so smoothly that we believe this is it: America in the box, in our heads. It's all we know and all we need to know.

Octavio Paz (1962) wrote, in *Labyrinth of Solitude,* "Would it be more accurate to say that the North American wants to use reality rather than to know it?" Yes. We have used it, and we do not merely use it but manhandle it now. TV, in particular, has permitted us to do what we have always wanted to do: rewrite, rearrange, reshape, and box reality to suit us. In the Age of Unreality, all of the people fool themselves all of the time.

The question is, then, who did it? Have we done it to ourselves? Was it done to us? Or did it just happen? Social critics are divided. The more cynical say we did it to ourselves, that we are a childlike species with a low tolerance level for reality. We can take only so much at a time, and virtually none now. Less cynical critics say it was done to us, that media moguls have conspired to hypnotize the nation. Why would they do that? To sell us things, say the critics.

I think they're all wrong. I think it just happened. We've always been mechanical wizards, perhaps because America is far more a product of the Industrial Revolution than the American Revolution, and so we just kept inventing machines to improve our lives, and we have improved ourselves right into this pleasant oblivion. Since we aren't fond of reality anyway, we were particularly susceptible to our own sleight of hand, so it's worked out nicely. Now that we're here, we're quite happy. Life is easy, entertaining, and undemanding. Isn't that what we always wanted—the good life? I think so.

Technologically, we're very advanced. We've always had a gift for thinking of and then making highly sophisticated machines. Psychologically, however, we're babes in the woods. We don't understand ourselves or anyone else very well. So, again and again, we've made machines that, in turn, have remade us. This makes social critics crazy, but it doesn't seem to bother us at all.

NEWS ANALYSIS:
IT'S THE CULTURE (2003)

JAYSON BLAIR. WHAT AN UNLIKELY change agent. And yet the notorious young fiction writer and plagiarist has brought one of the world's great newspapers to its knees. Blair did what dozens of his honest colleagues at the *New York Times* could not do. He toppled one of the least popular executive teams in the paper's 107-year history. On June 5, only a year after the world's most esteemed newspaper won a record seven Pulitzer prizes, executive editor Howell Raines and managing editor Gerald Boyd stepped down. *Times* publisher Arthur Ochs Sulzberger Jr., who tapped Raines for the job, was one of the few who managed to look sorry.

On the surface, the tumult at the *Times* was about Blair's brazen dishonesty and his failure to obey the first law of journalism: Thou shalt report faithfully what you see and hear. But it soon became clear that the story was really about the cruel and unusual management that Raines had practiced in the course of garnering all of those prized Pulitzers.

Part of the problem was Raines himself. For all of Raines's liberal politics and Southern gentility, he was an ego-driven autocrat who ruled by fear, played favorites, had an idiosyncratic news judgment (witness his Augusta National Golf Club obsession), and loathed hearing unwanted truths. Again and again, he gave Blair plum assignments despite warnings from other editors that the hyperactive, erratic rookie reporter was a disaster in the making. Everyone who has ever met Raines seems to have a colorful story about him, often an anecdote that hints at his resemblance to one of the more volatile Roman emperors, albeit one in a Panama hat. But Raines's problems preceded him. Linda Greenhouse, the distinguished reporter who covers the Supreme Court for the paper, told the *Wall Street*

This article was originally published in *Fast Company,* August 2003.

Journal: "There is an endemic cultural issue at the *Times* that is not a Howell creation, although it plays into his vulnerabilities as a manager, which is a top-down hierarchical structure." Greenhouse points to the real villain in the *New York Times* scandal and avoids simply demonizing Raines. To paraphrase Greenhouse: "It's the culture, stupid."

Organizational cultures are not like breaking-news stories. They don't happen suddenly. They evolve slowly, imperceptibly, over years, if not decades. Unlike mission statements, they are never written down. But they are the soul of an organization and determine much of what happens within it. "It's the way things are done around here," one CEO told me, in defining his corporation's culture. Such cultures are collections of unspoken rules and traditions. They determine which offices are sacrosanct, whether the men wear ties, and who speaks to whom and in what tone of voice—the red, amber, and green lights that aren't visible but that operate 24 hours a day and determine the quality of organizational life.

In the 19 months under Raines, the newsroom culture at the *New York Times* became more and more unhappy. Veteran journalists were routinely pushed aside, and green, malleable reporters were promoted beyond their talent or experience. Many of the seasoned writers went elsewhere—something that has rarely happened at the *Times,* since it truly is the ultimate gig in journalism. Moreover, the newsroom values shifted. Hustle came to be rewarded above all. The long-accepted pattern had been for experienced reporters to spend much of their time on thoughtful, in-depth pieces. Now these same writers were expected to be plugged into their pagers at all times, so they could join 100 of their colleagues at a moment's notice to "flood the zone" on a breaking news story. It was clear that a reporter's family life was to be secondary to his or her uncritical willingness to go wherever the editors wanted.

Like all big-time newspapers, the *New York Times* is a pressure cooker in the best of times. It has had its share of hard-driving, insensitive managers. When Raines stepped down, former executive editor Abe Rosenthal told the media, "The management of Howell Raines won the paper seven Pulitzer awards in one year. If that reflects a poor management style, they should patent it and sell it all over the world." No wonder Rosenthal liked Raines's style. Rosenthal, too, was a newsroom tsar who controlled by fear. Just as Raines had an implicit family-last policy, Rosenthal once screeched at a favorite reporter who balked at reassignment because his wife had a good job in town: "If you're married, you don't belong in journalism!"

Forget the numbers game. Whether it's 7 or 15 Pulitzers, it doesn't matter how many prizes you win if you damage your real prize—your talent—in the process.

Rosenthal needn't worry about patenting Raines's managerial style. It's already practiced in countless corporations, including most of those that have imploded in scandal in recent years. Is Raines's failure so different from Ken Lay's failure at Enron? Both failed to create cultures of candor—organizations where employees know they can deliver bad news and their bosses will listen even if they don't like what they are hearing. The *Times* even had its version of Enron whistle-blower Sherron Watkins. At least one person, metropolitan editor Jonathan Landman, delivered the bad news, told the truth, and tried to expose Blair. Raines, it turned out, just wasn't much of a truth listener. If he was, how long would Blair have lasted before one of his disaffected colleagues—or a half-dozen of them—had exposed him to Raines? Speaking truth to power is essential, but it's only half of the equation. Cultures in which power welcomes truth tend to solve their problems internally. They discover and deal with their Jayson Blairs before their Jayson Blairs make headlines. A culture of candor isn't just some warm, fuzzy way to cosset employees. It's good business.

Whoever follows Raines at the *Times,* he or she must have the strength of character to invite thoughtful criticism, from whatever quarter. Whenever leaders waver in their willingness to hear the truth, however distasteful, they should remind themselves of the fate of those who have covered their ears, from Julius Caesar to such latter-day casualties as former Compaq CEO Eckhard Pfeiffer. Under Pfeiffer, Compaq fell farther and farther behind its competitors because he listened only to his A list of yes men and ignored his truth-telling B list, who repeatedly tried to warn him that Dell was gaining ground, and fast.

Let me be frank. For all of its flaws, the *New York Times* is a national treasure. No matter where I am, I begin my day by reading it from the first page to last. In fact, I still call it *The Times,* to the consternation of my friends at my hometown paper, the *Los Angeles Times.* So I want to end with three pieces of advice for Arthur Sulzberger Jr. and the others who must now find a replacement for Raines.

1. Forget the numbers game.

Whether it's 7 or 15 Pulitzers, it doesn't matter how many prizes you win if you damage your real prize—your talent—in the process. Uncaring, arrogant leadership that values accolades at any cost is always inappropriate, but it is especially ill-suited to idea-driven organizations such as the *Times.* Whatever their titles or official positions, talented people have their own power. They have the power to walk. They will not stay in an organization that treats them like cattle, even if the name on the building is as august as the *New York Times.* Raines and his more imperious predecessors polarized their staffs and made them compete with each other for newsroom resources, including the favor of the executive editor. Such intramural competition ends up making people less creative, not more creative.

2. Talented people need appreciation.

We all pay lip service to the importance of acknowledging the good work of others, but most organizations can't bring themselves to do it. Like everyone else, gifted people want someone to notice a heroic effort or a distinguished piece of work. Instead of keeping his staff off balance, Raines should have devoted more of his time to praising them for the stories that won seven Pulitzers and for all the others that might have. So many otherwise able managers act as if compliments come out of their bank accounts. Had Raines sat down every morning and sent an email of praise to those responsible for the paper's 10 best stories, we would be writing about his superb management instead of analyzing what went wrong.

3. The new executive editor must have a genius for forging newsroom alliances and creating the sense that we are all in this grand game together.

Whoever is in charge, the *New York Times* is so rich with talent that it will survive. But if it had a truly creative, collaborative person at the top, the *Times* could become the envy of the information economy and a thriving, happy workplace. Do that, and the Pulitzers will follow.

GENEVA OVERHOLSER
ON "NEWS ANALYSIS:
IT'S THE CULTURE"

WHEN WARREN BENNIS EXAMINED the Jayson Blair scandal as a case study in flawed management, he nailed a problem that is all too prevalent in newsrooms: The know-it-all, can't-hear-anything-contrary-to-my-views kind of editor. What's clear now—though it wasn't so evident in 2003 when the piece was published—is that the top-down approach of Howard Raines as executive editor wasn't just an *internal* problem for the *New York Times* and other newsrooms. Looked at from these perilous times, the hubris and rigid thinking behind the Raines saga goes a long way toward explaining how it is that traditional media got into the fix they are in today.

As Bennis notes, while Raines's particular personality exacerbated the situation, the editor-as-supreme-being culture had been around for a long time, at the *Times* and at other top newspapers. So prevalent was the model in both film and reality that, when I took Abe Rosenthal to lunch to pick his brain before I left the *Times* to become editor of the *Des Moines Register*, I remember wishing I could ask the famously mercurial Abe if one could even *be* a successful editor without being a tyrant.

I didn't ask, of course. But when I took the helm at the *Register*, with a very different style in mind, I found my own newsroom so accustomed to the tradition (my predecessor had been very much of this mode) that hard-bitten sportswriters could not feel comfortable unless they were calling me "chief." It must have seemed strange to address someone much younger—and a woman, for crying out loud—in such a way. But it would have seemed stranger still, apparently, to give up on the notion of leadership as they knew it.

Cultures die hard—which is a big piece of the traditional media's problem in these days of fast-paced change. The public has now shown itself to be firmly against the father-knows-best delivery method for information. People want to be part of the decisions—about what makes a good story, about what topics ought to be covered. They'll choose what they want to read, thank you very much. Many of them would, by the way, like to contribute to the report, as well. And they want different voices and viewpoints to be heard. None of this exclusive, down-from-on-high style so comfortable for the predominantly white males long accustomed to power.

No wonder then that, in an era when participatory information opportunities from social networking to blogs abound, our hidebound legacy newsrooms have had a hard time adjusting. When you're pretty sure you know everything there is to know, and you don't brook opposing viewpoints, change doesn't come easily. Nor was this viewpoint limited to top editors; it had a way of sifting down to the merely aspiring. I remember, as ombudsman of the *Washington Post,* having reporters look at me in amazement that I'd actually be *listening* to the readers who were calling and e-mailing me. Worrying about what the readers thought of our work was just not in the model we legacy newspaper people grew up with.

Now those readers want to do a lot more than comment—if newspapers are lucky enough still to be attracting them. As for thinking about how the work was paid for—it would be wildly insufficient to say that this was simply not done. It was positively forbidden, for reasons that seemed at the time to make sense. Yet now that the old economic model of advertising supporting the journalism is broken, this is the (unaccustomed) number one concern on many a journalist's mind. But we are so unused to thinking in these new ways that many observers believe the needed changes cannot come from "old media," no matter how important their journalism continues to be for democracy.

What we saw in Raines's case, as Bennis so artfully shows, is that an editor can be doomed by thinking he knows all there is to know and keeping his mind closed to information that might help him see otherwise. What we are confronted with now is the unsettling possibility that this kind of thinking can doom not only individual editors. It may be that it has doomed as well the newsrooms they have been running.

Geneva Overholser is director of the School of Journalism at the USC Annenberg School for Communication. Previously, she held the Curtis B. Hurley Chair in Public Affairs Reporting for the Missouri School of Journalism, and was a Pulitzer Prize–winning editor of the *Des Moines Register.* She has also worked at the *New York Times,* the *Washington Post,* and the *Colorado Springs Sun.*

THE NEW TRANSPARENCY (2008)

THE DEFINITION OF *TRANSPARENT* is simple enough. It means, in addition to the literal "capable of being seen through," "without guile or concealment; open; frank; candid." But in the last few years, *transparency* has acquired new implications. As a headline writer for *Fast Company* joked, "Transparency: It's Not Just for Shrink Wrap Anymore." Once largely reserved for international trade negotiations, it has surged in popularity. Now it seems that no American president, CEO, mayor, school official, or police chief can make a public pronouncement without using the word, usually with the implicit promise that his or her statement is true and motives pure. As a culture, we obviously long for our public institutions, our corporations, and our other organizations to be open and honest about their dealings. We want to be confident that our leaders are telling us the truth, the whole truth, and nothing but the truth in matters that involve our national security, the safety of the products we use, and the state of our economy. We want to believe that our government agencies are transparent and honorable, without secret prisons or secret agendas that reflect special interests rather than the public weal. We want to believe that, but we often do not. Despite the promise of transparency on so many lips, we often have the sinking feeling that we are not being told all that we need to know or have the right to know.

But at the same time, a countervailing force is making transparency less and less dependent on the will of those who run our institutions. The digital revolution has made transparency inevitable, not just in this country but worldwide. The Internet, camera-equipped cell phones, and the emergence over the last decade of the blogosphere have democratized power, shifting it inexorably away from the high-profile few to the technology-

This chapter was originally published in *Transparency* (Jossey-Bass, 2008).

equipped many. Historians of the phenomenon say this new digital transparency was born barely a decade ago (in 1998) when online columnist Matt Drudge revealed that the *Washington Post* had quashed a story about then President Bill Clinton's dalliance with a White House intern.[1] Blogs began to multiply with the launch in 1999 of San Francisco–based blogger.com, a free site that helped users create their own online forums. Since then millions of blogs have sprung up around the world, and their collective clout has transformed politics, the mainstream media, indeed the public and private lives of people everywhere.

In the past, we often had to wait until a courageous whistleblower came along before we learned an institution's secrets. Now a company's most incendiary internal memos may be disclosed by an anonymous blogger, without ties to any newspaper or television station but with inside knowledge, who can reach thousands, even millions of readers. The proliferation of networked computers has finally created the Global Village that Marshall McLuhan predicted more than a half-century ago. Now anyone with Internet access can take on the most powerful institutions on earth, without making any significant financial investment and often with little or no fear of reprisals.

The history of the U.S. Navy's swastika-shaped building complex illustrates how digital technology increasingly drives transparency.[2] In 1967 the Navy broke ground on a cluster of four L-shaped buildings on its Coronado Naval Base in San Diego. Not long afterward, someone pointed out that the buildings had the unfortunate characteristic of looking like a giant swastika when viewed from the air. Since the complex was in a civilian no-fly zone, Navy brass decided the best thing to do about the potential embarrassment was to keep quiet about it. Almost four decades later, however, some wired individual spotted the swastika-shaped complex among the satellite images available on Google Earth. In 2006 word of the inaptly shaped building leaped from the blogosphere to talk radio, then, in quick succession, to the leadership of the San Diego branch of the Anti-Defamation League, the city's Democratic Congresswoman Susan Davis, and *Los Angeles Times* reporter Tony Perry. At first, the Defense Department said it had no plans to change the complex. But in September 2007, the Navy announced it would spend more than $600,000 to obscure the complex's problematic shape with landscaping and modifications to its rooftops. As a spokeswoman for the base said, "We don't want to offend anyone, and we don't want to be associated with the [Nazi] symbol." And she explained, "You have to realize back in the 1960s we did not have the Internet."

Global Transparency

To begin to understand how digital technology is creating greater transparency worldwide, it is useful to look first at the Opacity Index, launched in 2001. As its creator Joel Kurtzman explains in his 2007 book *Global Edge,* the index was developed in response to a question posed by former PriceWaterhouseCoopers CEO James Schiro, who wondered if a nation's transparency could be measured.[3] Kurtzman and his colleagues reasoned that opacity—the lack of transparency—could be measured even if transparency itself could not.

The resultant index gauges the economic cost to some fifty nations of their lack of transparency. Each country is evaluated in five areas of concern: corruption in business and government, ineffectiveness of its legal system, negative aspects of its economic policy, inadequacy of its accounting and governance practices, and detrimental aspects of its regulatory structures. The countries receive a numeric score in each area as well as an overall opacity rating. The higher the number, the less open the country. In the most recent index, in 2005, the United States was one of the five most transparent nations. Its overall opacity score of 21 trailed the United Kingdom, which had the best score of 14, Finland, and Hong Kong, and edged out Denmark, with an overall score of 22. At the other end of the transparency spectrum was Nigeria, which was the most opaque with a score of 60. Slightly more transparent were Lebanon, Indonesia, and Saudi Arabia, all with scores over 50. China's overall score was a fairly opaque 48.

Kurtzman and his colleagues argue that bribery, fraud, unenforceable contracts, and other opacity-related risks "represent the real costs to [global] business."[4] In their view, these frequent small-scale risks ultimately cause more economic harm than such rarer high-profile risks as natural disasters and terrorism. "These [opacity-related] risks interfere with commerce, add to costs, slow growth and make the future even more difficult to predict," the authors write. "They also deter investment." In the 2004 report, Matt Feshbach, chief investment officer of a Florida hedge fund, observes: "The key to any good investment relationship is clarity—the ability to see and even be in communication with what's really going on. It's the same whether it's a company, a country or a region."

It is useful to have a country's opacity score in mind when evaluating news about it, especially news relating to transparency. Consider China, for example. Despite its Communist government's continuing attempts to control the flow of information within China and between it and other nations, China is moving toward greater technology-driven openness. By 2008, China had 210 million Internet users and 47 million bloggers. And while the Chinese government diligently polices the Internet—limiting what people can access on Google, for instance—citizens are using the Internet to expose some of the most disturbing aspects of Chinese life.

Favoritism and bribing officials have long been scourges of life in China. In the 2005 Opacity Index China's corruption score was a considerable 65, high enough to put it among the ten most corrupt nations studied, along with Saudi Arabia, Indonesia, Pakistan, Russia, and, topping the list, Lebanon. But such time-honored Chinese practices as buying the silence of police are crumbling under the collective power of ordinary citizens with computer access. In June 2007, for example, the *Wall Street Journal* reported that parents went online to protest the kidnapping of children forced into slave labor in coal mines and brick factories in Henan and Shanxi provinces.[5] In part because of the parents' digital crusade, the government sent more than 45,000 police into the area, rescuing more than 500 people, and making more than 150 arrests. Before the parents took to their computers, some had tried to get local officials to find their children, some of them handicapped. But as one parent told the *Wall Street Journal,* "We contacted the local police, but they are protecting the brick-kiln owners. They wouldn't help us."

The rising power of China's new digerati hasn't turned every Chinese official into a champion of sunshine, any more than scrutiny from the blogosphere has loosed the lips of all American officials. The Chinese government still tries to keep a lid on its embarrassing secrets, including, recently, the number of citizens dying prematurely from pollution-related illnesses (more than 750,000 a year) and the outbreak of an Ebola-like disease in pigs. China's own mainstream media are kept on a tight leash, and foreign media are closely monitored. Besides digital pressure, other forces are making China more open, notably its desire to favorably impress the West at the 2008 Olympic Games in Beijing and an international expo in Shanghai in 2010. The West is also calling for greater transparency in the wake of lead-tainted toys, exploding tires, poison toothpaste, counterfeit diabetic testing strips, and other dangerous Chinese exports.

But the potential power of a billion Chinese citizens with Internet access and cell phone cameras cannot be ignored, even by a government that has a long history of holding information close. In April 2007, China issued new Regulations on Open Government Information that require the posting online of data about land use, public health investigations, and other official activities, starting May 1, 2008. For the first time, citizens will be able to request information from government agencies with the expectation of a response within fifteen days. Still off-limits to the public will be information that threatens "state security, public safety, normal economic operations, and social stability" as well as individuals' personal information, according to the *Wall Street Journal*.[6] In classic Chinese fashion, the content of the new regulations was kept secret until they were announced in April. But inside observers think the new rules represent a genuine shift in the direction of openness. As a media expert from the University of Hong Kong told the *Wall Street Journal* in March 2007, "This legislation is important in the sense that it changes presumptions about information in China, making release of information the rule rather than the exception."[7]

India is another vast nation where digital technology is boosting transparency. Deemed fairly corrupt by the Opacity Index (its corruption score was 57 in 2005), India is also undergoing profound technology-driven social change. In a 2004 article called "The Digital Village," *Business Week* reported on the impact computerization of more than 20 million land records has had on poor farmers in villages surrounding the high-tech capital of Bangalore.[8] In the past the farmers had access to their deeds only through village accountants who sometimes conspired with large landowners to cheat uneducated, lower-caste farmers out of their property. Now when small farmers need copies of their deeds to get bank loans for seed and other supplies, they can access the deeds at government-owned computer kiosks. The farmers can even print out the documents for 30 cents apiece, down from the $2 to $22 they paid to an accountant under the old system.

India has a relatively modest number of Internet users, an estimated 60 million in early 2008. But the government's high-tech kiosks are teaching the poor farmers an indelible lesson: digital technology changes the rules of the game and thus can transform their lives. Explains the Indian official who oversaw the computerization project: "With equal access to information, a lower-caste person now has the same privileges as an upper-caste person." That no doubt overstates the case. But the new transparency has given the villagers a new set of expectations. They dream of acquiring computers of their own and of sending their children off to study computer science, *Business Week* reports. In short, the villagers know that digital technology is the ladder that will let them climb out of the well to which poverty, social class, and tradition have consigned them.

The ability to access sympathetic Web sites and to blog is especially liberating in countries with repressive governments that can clamp down on newspapers and television stations far more readily than on the ethereal Internet. In such places, blogs can be tantamount to a digital resistance movement. A compelling posting on a blog can recruit thousands of readers to its point of view; each of those readers can send the message to thousands more, and soon the cry is heard around the world. Iran, for example, has an estimated 100,000 bloggers among its 5 million Internet users, including controversial blogger-in-chief President Mahmoud Ahmadinejad. Government pressure on Iranian bloggers varies from day to day. Once ignored by digitally illiterate religious authorities, bloggers now risk arrest. But pressure on them is less intense than it might be, given the country's fundamentalist climate, because "the government wants to look like a democracy," Iranian blogger Hossein Derakhshan told *Wired*'s Jeff Howe in June 2005.

Political blogs helped make the 2005 election "the most open and transparent . . . Iran has ever seen," according to *The Nation*. Before the election, in a piece called "Bloggers of Iran," the magazine speculated on how Iran's bloggers could reshape the Islamic republic: "While Iran remains a closed society, a fierce debate about the country's future is underway in the blogs. The coming election might not bring about much, if any, change in Iranians' lives, but the blogs could help open up that society, permitting the free flow of information and ideas like never before."[9]

Fear of transparency was the main reason for the digital crackdown on protesters by Myanmar's ruling military junta in the autumn of 2007. In contrast to past demonstrations, the anti-government protests that began in Myanmar in August were conducted in cyberspace as well as on the streets. When thousands of saffron-robed Buddhist monks gathered in the former capital city of Yangon, they were surreptitiously photographed by video and cell phone cameras and the images distributed worldwide via the Internet. Sympathy for the protesters was fueled by such disturbing images as that of a Japanese photojournalist shot by government soldiers who continued taking pictures as he died in the street. Vividly documenting the cyber-revolt in the *New York Times,* Seth Mydans reports that protesters sent e-mail and instant messages, blogged, and posted updates on Facebook and Wikipedia.[10] For weeks, they evaded local authorities by sending reports electronically to online sympathizers in Thailand and elsewhere. In addition, Mydans writes, the dissidents "used Internet versions of 'pigeons'—the couriers that reporters used in the past to carry out film and reports—handing their material to embassies or non-government organizations with satellite connections."

But finally, Mydans writes, "the generals who run Myanmar simply switched off the Internet." That meant shutting down the country's two Internet providers. Just as the authorities seized cameras to stop the flow of images, they disrupted international telephone service to silence the protesters. The editor of a Thailand-based magazine for Burmese exiles recounted the last telephone call he got from one of his most reliable activist sources inside Myanmar: "We can no longer move around . . . we

cannot do anything any more. We are down. We are hunted by soldiers—
we are down."

At the time Mydans's piece was published, little news of dissent was
trickling out of fear-filled Myanmar, a nation so opaque that outsiders
who track transparency lack the data to evaluate it accurately. But
Mydans quoted New York University professor Mitchell Stevens on the
likelihood of the truth emerging eventually in the new era of the technol-
ogy-empowered citizen journalist: "There are always ways people find of
getting information out, and authorities always have to struggle with
them. . . . There are fewer and fewer events that we don't have film images
of; the world is filled with Zapruders" (alluding to Abraham Zapruder,
the businessman who filmed John F. Kennedy's 1963 assassination).

The Role of Blogs

Because of the blogosphere's ability to expose secrets to outsiders, George
Washington University professor Michael Cornfield has described it as "half
forensic lab and half tavern."[11] Web logs, as blogs are properly called, are
also strange hybrids that combine multiple functions. Currently the most
popular facilitator of Web logs, Google gave the trademarked name Blogger
to the free application that allows users to set up their own sites. Google
explains at Blogger.com: "A blog is a personal diary. A daily pulpit. A collaborative space. A political soapbox. A breaking-news outlet. A collection of links. Your own private thoughts. Memos to the world."

A blog is, in short, a tool. And as Steward Brand, one of the counterculture creators of the wired world, understood when he chose the phrase
as the subtitle of his *Last Whole Earth Catalogue,* those who have "access
to tools" have access to power. One notable denizen of the blogosphere
is the corporate blogger. A handful of top executives have made names
for themselves as bloggers, including General Motors' vice president and
car guru Robert Lutz, who describes himself as "at the wheel of FastLane
blog." But the most effective corporate bloggers are often nonmanagers
who allow outsiders to peek inside their companies and project a David-
unafraid-of-the-corporate-Goliath persona despite collecting a paycheck.
Fortune magazine featured a popular employee blogger from Microsoft,
Robert Scoble, in a story on the pervasiveness of blogs.[12] Scoble's most
notable achievement appears to be lessening the hostility routinely directed
at his employer, so often treated as the Great Satan by the digital elite.
Chairman Bill Gates told *Fortune* that Scoble's and other blogs by
Microsoft staff have enhanced the company's image: "It's all about openness," Gates said. "People see them as a reflection of an open, commu-
nicative culture that isn't afraid to be self-critical."

By their nature, blogs challenge hierarchies, introducing an outsider's or non-elitist voice into the conversation at hand. When those voices are wise or even simply contrarian, they benefit the organization by challenging its dominant assumptions, preventing tunnel vision, and reminding the powers that be that they don't have a lock on all useful truths. Because the technology behind blogs includes creation of an index, the opinions and information they contain are relatively easy to access—a real plus in a world in which we are always at risk of being swamped by a tsunami of undifferentiated data.

Network pioneer John Patrick, former longtime vice president of Internet technology at IBM, offered a compelling vision of how blogs can aid companies and other organizations when he talked to *CIO Insight*'s Marcia Stepanek in 2003: "It's a way to energize the expertise from the bottom—in other words, to allow people who want to share, who are good at sharing, who know who the experts are, who talk to the experts or who may, in fact, be one of the experts, to participate more fully. We all know somebody in our organization who knows everything that's going on. 'Just ask Sally. She'll know.' There's always a Sally, and those are the people who become bloggers."[13]

The Winning Circle

Energizing *all* the talent in an organization, not just that at the top or that of the chosen, increases productivity and value, and not just value resulting from better morale because of greater inclusiveness—no small thing in itself. I learned this firsthand more than sixty years ago when I was a graduate student at Massachusetts Institute of Technology. A group of social psychologists at MIT (I was among the most junior) conducted an elegant experiment that demonstrated that collaboration leads to better outcomes when solving complex problems—as virtually all our problems, beyond which tie to wear, are today. For the experiment, five subjects sat at a round table, hidden from each other by partitions.[14] Each subject received a box that contained six colored marbles. The participants were asked to choose the single one of their six marbles that was the same color as just one of each of the others' marbles. The subjects couldn't talk to each other, but they could share information by passing messages on index cards through slots in the partitions.

With the round table, we were able to simulate the flow of information in three kinds of organizations. We simulated the pyramidal bureaucracy that still persists in many organizations with what we called the Wheel. In that arrangement, all the messages went to a single person, the unseen leader. The Circle was the most collegial configuration. In it, each subject could pass messages to both immediate neighbors. We also had a config-uration we called the Chain in which all the index cards were passed in one direction.

As soon as a subject felt sure which marble matched one of all the other subjects' marbles, that marble was dropped down a rubber tube in the table. The experimenter at the other end of the tube was able to measure the speed and accuracy with which the subjects chose their matching mar-bles. When the data were subsequently analyzed, the result was a land-mark finding—solid empirical evidence that collaboration beats top-down control in complex decision making.[15]

I say *complex decision making* because when the task was easy—that is, when the marbles were all readily identified bright, single colors (called "puries" by aficionados)—the top-down Wheel was the most efficient configuration. But as soon as the task was made more difficult, by using mottled, ambiguously colored marbles such as cat's eyes, the democratic Circle was fastest and most accurate. Because the experiment was care-fully controlled, the reason for the Circle's superiority was clearly its democratic flow of information. And there was a bonus to the Circle. When the Wheel proved superior at its simple task, only the leader felt good. The non-leaders experienced no rush of satisfaction. But when the Circle beat the other configurations on its more demanding task, higher morale was reported all around.

The Internet was only a dream when that experiment was first done. But its findings are confirmed again and again in today's wired, networked world. Several years ago, I participated in a forum on leadership in the twenty-first century. Fellow speaker Meredith Belbin, an expert on teams, offered a compelling insight. He speculated that the traditional idea of the alpha male leader may be natural to us as primates. But, he argued, this century's ever-increasing interconnectedness calls for new models, notably the "sophisticated interdependent systems of social insects."[16] Informa-tion does not just circulate within today's organizations. Because of digi-tal technology, information increasingly flows between organizations and such outside entities as their clients and suppliers. As Belbin observed: "Information is coming in from the side instead of from the top down. Such a switch in information supply is creating pressure on the top. By losing its likely monopoly on leadership, the top can survive with credi-bility only by empowering the most suitable individuals and teams."

Knowledge is still power. But as knowledge becomes more widely dis-tributed, so does the power it generates. The very idea of leadership is beginning to change as power is democratized. At such influential work-places as Google, leadership rotates within small groups of engineers. As greater openness demystifies what leaders do, we are likely to see less time and money spent on costly, time-consuming executive searches. Leadership may come to be seen as a role that moves from one able individual in an organization to another as projects come and go. Soon the CEO may have to share responsibilities, at least for a time, with John Patrick's Sally, the one who knows everything. And should leadership become a transitory role, one likely and welcome result will be a drop in stratospheric executive compensation, one of the most corrosive facets of corporate life today.

Collegial collaboration enhances transparency, which in turn enhances success. Lack of transparency erodes trust and discourages collaboration. One place to see the transformative effect of transparency is at companies that practice so-called open-book management. As Joe Nocera explains in a 2006 column in the *New York Times,* that term, first used by a writer at *Inc.* magazine almost two decades ago, refers to the sharing of financial information with everyone in a company.[17] But effective proponents do more than throw numbers at their staff, Nocera notes. They explain what the financial information means and how employees contribute to the group's success. As evidence of the effectiveness of open-book management, Nocera reports that a 2005 survey conducted by *Inc.* found that 40 percent of the firms on its yearly list of the five hundred fastest-growing private companies employed the practice in some fashion—far more than in the business community as a whole. And it has recently been instituted at *Inc.* by Mansueto Ventures, the private firm that bought the magazine in 2006. Again and again, studies show that companies that rate high in transparency tend to outperform more opaque ones. In a global study of corporate transparency conducted in 2005, for example, the twenty-seven U.S. firms that appeared among the thirty-four most transparent companies beat the S&P 500 by 11.3 percent between February 2004 and February 2005.

More and more companies are choosing transparency for two reasons: they have less and less choice—and it works. Don Tapscott talked about its many benefits shortly after publication of his 2003 book, *The Naked Corporation: How the Age of Transparency Will Revolutionize Business.* "This isn't simply New Age stuff," he told *CIO Insight* magazine.[18] "It's about money and efficiency. When you have openness and candor, you drop transaction costs, you reduce office politics and game playing, you increase employee loyalty, you increase the effectiveness of collaboration and so on." That said, it is important to remember that, like democracy, transparency isn't easy. It requires courage and patience on the part of leaders and followers alike. It also requires a considerable investment of time, if only to share information with a larger group of people.

Transparency's Woes

But there is a downside to the instantaneous access to all kinds of information that is making organizations more transparent. The same forces are fast making privacy a thing of the past. Consider one mundane example. The digital technology that allows supermarkets to manage inventory as never before, stocking only the goods they currently need, also allows Big Brother to peer into the shopping cart of every patron who signs up for an electronic discount card. Thus, somewhere in the computer files of Supermarket Central is a record of how many bottles of bourbon Mrs. X purchased this week, the brand of hair dye she uses, and the fact that she recently bought a year's supply of roach poison—all information that Mrs. X might prefer to keep to herself. The grocery chain stores the specifics of every trip to the supermarket Mrs. X makes, along with records of all its other electronically linked customers, in its computer files. That information will probably remain there forever, given the indelible nature of most digital information. And there is no guarantee that the stored data about Mrs. X's shopping habits will not be hacked or misused. Look at the millions of customers of the discount shoe chain DSW whose social security numbers and other credit-card data now float through cyberspace, accessible to anyone with the computer skills of a bright fifth grader. As more and more of our personal records go online, our ability to keep our information confidential will continue to diminish, no matter how conscientiously privacy advocates strive to protect it. At the same time, the ubiquity of cell phone cameras makes each of us the potential target of amateur paparazzi, as anyone knows who's turned up on the Bad Drivers Web site.

The lack of privacy that results from transparency can be annoying, embarrassing, and infuriating. It can also be dangerous. Public access to electronic court records has given rise to such controversial Web sites as Whosearat.com. Here the public can find the names and other information about individuals who have agreed to testify against others, usually as part of plea agreements. According to the *New York Times,* the Justice Department is scrambling to get this information removed from public view, although most experts agree its publication is protected by the First Amendment.[19] The concern is that the individuals named on the site for giving evidence against accomplices and others may be subjected to "witness intimidation, retaliation and harassment." Transparency would not be a problem in a world in which everyone is decent and fair-minded. In the real world, thugs and predators have computers, too.

If the new transparency changes our expectations of privacy in ways that can be problematical, the digital technology that drives it also has an invaluable upside. One of its remarkable strengths is its ability to tap into the wisdom of crowds, in writer James Surowiecki's resonant phrase. We can access collective intelligence as never before, making primitive forms of tapping opinion, such as focus groups, obsolete. We can also benefit from the wisdom of the group in such modest but valuable forms as the aggregate restaurant ratings in the popular Zagat guides and the collective recommendations that send many consumers to angieslist.com to find roofers and other service providers. Typically, we ease into relationships with electronic advisers. We take a chance on one of their referrals, and if we like the meal or the paint job, we feel confident using the resource again. Trust is important when you don't really know the people whose collective counsel you are taking. The blogger is a powerful but problematic presence in this vast electronic neighborhood. The blogosphere is filled with millions of voices—some brilliant, some boorish, some bigoted, some crazy. We sift through them and choose the ones that make sense to us. Those bloggers who attract large numbers of regular readers acquire enormous clout, reflected in the willingness of advertisers to buy space on their blogs.

The popular blogger has the power of an ancient Roman to turn a digital thumb up or down and determine the fate of a business or product, all at the speed of light. Commerce has already been altered by this force. Manhattan restaurant owner Paul Grieco recently told the *New York Times* how bloggers have upped the pressure on him to please those he greets at his eatery Insieme.[20] "It used to be that if something went wrong, you might lose a circle of family or friends," Grieco said. "Now, half our reservations come from the Internet, and a negative experience on a blog can affect thousands of potential customers."

The problem here, of course, is that what looks like transparency may not be. The blogger who slams a restaurant may not be a run-of-the-mill diner. He may be the unscrupulous owner of a rival restaurant who decides to whack the competition electronically, a despicable sock puppet. The digital realm is wild and minimally policed, an electronic Deadwood where things are not always what they appear to be. Any number of commentators on the difficulty of establishing identity online cite a *New Yorker* cartoon that has been taped on thousands of computers: "On the Internet nobody knows you're a dog." Genuine transparency is impossible as long as we cannot be sure that those online are who they say they are.

Although digital technology may not be the sole cause of the problem, the United States is in the throes of an expertise crisis. Because the Internet is open to everyone, it tends to be a great leveler. But when all voices have the same force, it is harder and harder to identify those who have the training, experience, and wisdom that make them truly worth listening to. Television today is full of self-appointed experts who make assured pronouncements on current events and other matters and yet have no credentials beyond a good haircut and an even better agent. The mainstream media have accelerated this devaluing of authentic expertise by treating ordinary viewers and readers as the equals of those with genuine insight and experience. Thus, CNN devotes some time that could be spent hearing expert analysis to asking viewers what they think about American immigration policy and other issues of the day. Such public involvement may massage viewers' egos and increase loyalty to the station, but, arguably, it does little to advance the audience's understanding of important, often complex issues.

This devaluing of expertise is of great concern to everyone who fears that the blogosphere may be the fatal blow to the world's great and beleaguered newspapers. Information in reputable papers is vetted by experienced journalists striving for the truth and committed to fairness. Bloggers may be committed to nothing more than making themselves heard. Former Gawker blogger and mainstream journalist Choire Sicha articulated his fears in 2006, in a far-ranging critique of blogging by Trevor Butterworth in London's *Financial Times*.[21] Blogs are a substitute for professional journalism only if you are willing to forgo much of what we receive from good newspapers today, Sicha argued. "Where is the reporting?" he asked. "Where is the reliability? The blogosphere crowd are apparently ready to live in a world without war reporting, without investigative reporting, without nearly any of the things we depend on newspapers for. The world of blogs is like an entire newspaper composed of op-eds and letters and wire service feeds." Many of us feel that blogs will be an adequate substitute for great newspapers only when they go beyond repackaging content to generate comprehensive content of their own and when they commit to high standards of accuracy, fairness, and conduct.

Truth and Transparency

On the Internet the ideas of truth and authenticity do not mean the same thing to everyone. It is a cliché of e-marketing that the public will excuse anything but hypocrisy. Candor is all, we are repeatedly told. But since who you are online is not always clear, transparency and truth may be relative. In the fall of 2007, one of the biggest stories in the business press was a possible bid by Microsoft to buy a stake in the wildly popular social-networking site Facebook. In the *Wall Street Journal*, the story was cast as a "battle of the titans between Microsoft Corp. and Google Inc." Microsoft ultimately won the right to invest $240 million in Facebook Inc., a phenomenon even by the hyperbolic standards of the Web. Founded by twenty-three-year-old Mark Zuckerberg in his Harvard dormitory room in 2004, the company has been valued at as much as $15 billion. Once open only to the invited, Facebook is now accessible to everyone. It already has 40 million users and is adding a remarkable 200,000 new participants a day.

What differentiates Facebook from other social networking sites such as MySpace, besides a residual air of exclusivity, is its transparency. On Facebook, you have to use your real name. As a result, David Kirkpatrick wrote recently in *Fortune*, "a culture of authentic identity became part of Facebook's DNA."[22] Interactions on Facebook are organized around circles of friends who keep each other informed about whom and what they are seeing, the books by their bedside, their favorite presidential candidate, and the like. Much of Facebook's magic is based on the assumption that you can trust friends and your friends' friends in ways that you can not trust the rest of the universe, wired or not.

Kirkpatrick foresees a future for Facebook in which transparency reaches new heights as new applications facilitate easier communication. This hyper-transparency could be bad for some, he predicts, especially marketers whose products are slammed by users. But it is likely that the growing millions who frequent Facebook will set their own limits on how freely on-site information is shared. Late in 2007, some 50,000 Facebook users protested the site's decision to notify their circles of friends about their online purchases. The protestors let Zuckerberg know they felt their Internet use was their own business—a vote for privacy over involuntary transparency. The company finally agreed to get permission before revealing users' purchases.

While Kirkpatrick and other card-carrying adults see Facebook as an island of authenticity in a sea of Internet uncertainty, some early adopters say "Not so fast." In a hilarious op-ed piece in the *New York Times*, recent Dartmouth graduate Alice Mathias notes that "in no time at all, the Web site has convinced its rapidly assembling adult population that it is a forum for genuine personal and professional connections."[23] Not for her cohort, it isn't. Instead, Mathias writes, "It's all comedy: making one another laugh matters more than providing useful updates about ourselves, which is why entirely phony profiles were all the rage before the grown-ups signed in. One friend announced her status as In a Relationship with Chinese Food, whose profile picture was a carry-out box." Users her age turn to Facebook for escapism, she writes: "I've always thought of [it] as on-line community theater."

Even as the value of Facebook is pushed into the stratosphere by its perceived authenticity, genuine or not, a very different notion of what is real coexists online. That is the world of Second Life, a platform or game or obsession in which people gleefully create inauthentic versions of them-selves, called avatars, and spend hours at their keyboards selling virtual real estate and setting up digital shops that sell real products and even having virtual affairs with the avatars of real people other than their spouses. This would seem to give the lie to the notion that authenticity is what people want on the Internet. My sense of this brave new world (that has such avatars in it!) is that there are those who want reality and those who want role-playing and fantasy. Some people undoubtedly want both. There is a real generational difference at work here, I believe. People of my generation who suddenly have the urge to play online in the persona of an intergalactic princess reach for the telephone to call their therapists. A mostly younger generation wonders where to buy their avatar a virtual ball gown and tiara. It isn't clear to me whether spending long periods of time in Second Life will eventually change participants' ideas of what is true and what is not. We will have to see. But Second Life is a reminder that the Internet is many things to many people, and that authenticity is not the goal of everyone who goes online (ask Ms. Mathias). Niche mar-keting is all.

One thing I am certain of. The new technology-driven transparency will only accelerate. It has already changed our lives in countless ways and will continue to reshape us. The ubiquity of cell phones has turned public life in every major city into an odd, alienating experience in which people walk around, phone to ear, utterly engaged in a relationship with someone other than you. The new technology has also democratized power in a way that must come as a dreadful shock to those who previously monopolized it in the traditional manner. Editor and writer Harold Evans was on the mark when he observed in the *Wall Street Journal*'s 2007 Blogiversary feature that all bloggers have "a megaphone to the world."[24] However eccentric, shallow, even banal the blogger's message is, it has the ability to shape pub-lic opinion and thus to have a significant impact on the world—a far cry from the fleeting impact ordinary individuals could expect when the only outlet for their opinion was a letter to the editor of a major newspaper. And because bloggers have power, organizations are forced to react to them, whether they want to or not. Not to respond is to abdicate control of your reputation and that of your organization to someone who is far less likely to serve you well.

The lack of privacy is perhaps the most unsettling aspect of the new transparency, as we are reminded daily. We have no real expectation of privacy except when we are alone in a locked, windowless room. As Thomas L. Friedman writes in "The Whole World Is Watching," his *New York Times* column of June 27, 2007: "We're all public figures now." As a result, anyone has the ability to embarrass us, should they tilt their cell phone camera in our direction and catch us squabbling with a sales clerk or being rude to a spouse. Every day has the potential to turn into a real-life episode of *Candid Camera,* the classic, cringe-inducing television show from the 1950s on which hapless individuals were filmed without their knowledge, then had their awkward behavior broadcast for all the viewing public to see. This is a downside of transparency most of us never in our worst nightmares expected to face. It is the sort of glass-house exposure that Brad Pitt and other celebrities have had to cope with for years, although they are at least paid handsomely for the discomfort of being public figures.

The new electronic transparency has other characteristics that both organizations and individuals are just now coming to terms with. Negative information can be spread much more rapidly than in the past, and, once it is committed to the Internet, it is there forever. Performances such as Michael Richards's racist rant in a Los Angeles comedy club will run on YouTube and its successors in perpetuity. You can hire someone to spin what comes up when you Google your name or that of your organization, but you can't really make it go away. Damaging information will be in the ether longer than a plastic bag in a landfill. You can't do anything about what others say about you, but you can at least be careful about not harming your own reputation. Indeed, we have already had to add the warning "Remember that the Internet is forever, so don't put anything on MySpace that will come back to haunt you" to the long list of things we teach our children, along with "Don't talk with your mouth full" and "Don't run with scissors."

There is another major problem with the new transparency besides its tendency to catch and preserve experience like some vast digital La Brea tar pit. That is the troubling fact that what is exposed usually seems true. Harold Evans was again on the money when he said that the information on blogs, true or false, is marked by the "spurious authenticity of electronic delivery." In a world in which organizational and personal secrets are revealed round the clock at blog speed, we have a greater responsibility than ever to vet and verify what we see. Lies, urban legends, and distortions are as much a part of the mix as authentic revelations. Moreover, it is often impossible to determine the actual source of a nugget of information on the Web; we recently learned, for example, that companies often add to their Wikipedia entries or delete information from them without leaving tell-tale fingerprints. On the Internet propaganda often masquerades as fact. A classic example: that all Jews were warned away from the World Trade Center on 9/11, a cruel racist fabrication that appeared on many Islamist Web sites. The Internet is a dispassionate delivery system; it doesn't care whether it trades in enlightenment or lies.

As a result, governments, other institutions, and individuals must find ways to authenticate online information, much as they earlier had to devise methods to determine the authenticity of signatures and $100 bills. South Korea had to grapple with these issues in 2007 after electronic tipsters exposed prominent citizens who had claimed academic credentials they had not earned, egregious behavior in a country that worships degrees from prestigious universities. Among the cheats: a noted art historian, a famous chef, and even a celebrated Buddhist monk.[25] A South Korean prosecutor involved in the effort to prevent such fraud in the future told the *New York Times* in September 2007: "Before we struggled more with fake luxury goods. Now that we have entered the knowledge-based society, we have to deal with an overflow of fake knowledge."

The new transparency is no doubt changing us in unanticipated ways we don't yet recognize. With its millions of intrusive cameras, its constant potential for trumpeting past indiscretions through cyberspace, and its other discontents, the new reality will force us to adapt or go mad. Eventually, a new etiquette will evolve that will allow us to live more comfortably with the round-the-clock possibility of surveillance by anyone who happens to pass by. Some new method will emerge that quiets the cacophony of ever-present cell phones and lessens the pain of being "flamed" online by any malcontent who decides to go after us. Until then, we will have to be more wary, and we'll have to develop thicker skins. And since the cameras aren't going away anytime soon, we'll have to find a way to lower the blinds in our glass houses, if only in our minds.

GEOFF COWAN ON
"THE NEW TRANSPARENCY"

IN THE WORLD OF THE NEW TRANSPARENCY, what role is there for the mainstream media and traditional journalists? Have they been superseded or eclipsed by technology and history? Or have they become more important than ever? The unsatisfying and perhaps untenable answer is: probably both. They have simultaneously become less and more important.

The new media have certainly brought about a revolution in reporting about politics and government. When Joshua Marshall won the 2008 George Polk Award for legal reporting, bloggers and traditional media all took note that a new day had dawned. So did former Attorney General Alberto Gonzalez. The Justice Department's decision to fire eight U.S. Attorneys for political reasons was one of the biggest news stories of the year, filling some 1 percent of the news hole in the mainstream press. Marshall, his colleagues, and the readers and contributors to his Web site, Talking Points Memo (www.talkingpointsmemo.com), led the investigation. "Noting a similarity between firings in Arkansas and California," the Polk citation said, "Marshall and his staff connected the dots and found a pattern of federal prosecutors being forced from office for failing to do the Bush Administration's bidding. Marshall's tenacious investigative reporting sparked interest by the traditional news media and led to the resignation of Attorney General Alberto Gonzales."

A new media watchdog had helped to strip away the government's veil of secrecy. Without the work of Marshall and his network of reporters, interns, and readers, the extent of the Justice Department's politically motivated campaign might never have come to light. But for those concerned with government transparency, their success carries two other important lessons. First, the mainstream media were not throwing adequate reportorial resources into one of the most important stories of the

year, a story of historic importance since it represented a perhaps unprecedented effort to politicize the Justice Department's frontline prosecutors.
Second, the story would probably not have achieved maximum impact
without the validating role and still greater megaphone of what some refer
to as the legacy media.

The legacy media may have an even more important role in covering
and commenting on business. While the research cited by Warren Bennis
provides overwhelming evidence of the benefits of transparency, the current economic crisis offers plenty of evidence that not everyone in government or the economic community wants to accept that message. Under
the circumstances, journalists, both old and new, are indispensable.

The bailout plan originally proposed by Treasury Secretary Henry Paulson in mid-September 2008 lacked any level of transparency or accountability; indeed, the draft text said that Paulson's decisions would be
"non-reviewable" by Congress, the courts, or any administrative agency.
When the final bill was passed, the government's actions remained largely
opaque. In mid-December, 2008, ABC News posed a fairly straightforward question to executives at sixteen of the banks that had received
money from the Treasury Department's $700 billion Troubled Asset Relief
Program. ABC asked: how has your financial institution used the money?
Only one bank pointed to a specific loan that it had made—a $17 billion
loan by Morgan Stanley to Verizon Wireless. Wells Fargo, which had been
given $25 billion, said that it "cannot provide any forward-looking guid-
ance." More typically, ABC reported, the Bank of New York Mellon
vaguely explained that it was "using the $3 billion to provide liquidity to
the credit markets." Although Paulson's original document said that the
entire program was designed "to purchase mortgage-related assets,"
apparently very little of the money was being used for that purpose.

The Madoff case shows even more systematic failures of transparency.
Bernard Madoff's Ponzi scheme apparently cost investors $50 billion. But
no one seemed to want to know how his money was invested—not auditors,
not business schools, not investment advisers—not even the SEC. Secrecy,
rather than transparency, was the hallmark of his work. Investors paid handsome fees to investment advisers who simply gave Madoff their money to
invest. Whatever the market's fluctuations, Madoff's funds turned a profit.
But if anyone wondered how that was possible, or where his money was
being invested, they failed to make their concerns widely known.

Some commentators blame the regulators for looking the other way—
or for advocating and accepting laws that don't require them to look at
all. Others argue that investors have been lulled into a false—and dangerous—sense of security by hedge fund managers who have produced

such extraordinary returns that they have been allowed to conduct much of their business in secrecy. Now, though it is a bit late, they are all beginning to think anew about the importance of transparency, and about new rules to govern the markets.

But we also need to ask, where were the bloggers, where was the mainstream press—and what are the lessons for the media in the years ahead? During the past decade, during what may one day be seen as an era of economic denial, both new and old media had an indispensable role to play. There were countless opportunities for what Bennis calls "digital transparency," and some business journalism operations were growing rapidly, including CNBC, Bloomberg, Reuters, and any number of online and specialized services. Maybe there was a Joshua Marshall in the mix. But no such voice was heard above the go-go din.

Sadly, the world of legacy journalism is having its own financial crisis, with bureaus closing and layoffs the order of the day. But as Warren Bennis shows so persuasively, we all have a vital stake in transparency. Hopefully we won't let this teachable moment pass without finding a way to make sure that we have a thriving and fiercely honest marketplace of information and ideas.

Geoff Cowan is university professor and holder of the Annenberg Family Chair in Communication Leadership at the USC Annenberg School for Communication, as well as former dean. He has also been a founding director of UCLA's Center for Communication Policy, director of the Voice of America, and an Emmy Award–winning television producer.

NOTES

AN INVENTED LIFE: SHOE POLISH, MILLI VANILLI,
AND SAPIENTIAL CIRCLES

1. I am indebted to Abraham Zaleznik for this idea.

THE BERKELEY OF THE EAST AND WHAT WENT WRONG

1. Barbara Probst Solomon, who taught during 1967–68 in Buffalo's English
   department, wrote in an article "Life in the Yellow Submarine: Buffalo's
   SUNY" (*Harper's,* 1968, p. 98): "I've always been fond of paranoia as a
   lifestyle, but paranoia on a grand scale, preferably in some major European
   capital with good restaurants to plot in. Of course, for paranoia to work,
   I've always believed you have to have a lot of spare time; with the new small
   teaching loads (average of two courses a week), the placing of sixty-five
   assorted geniuses, poets, writers (Lionel Abel, Robert Creeley, John Logan,
   Leslie Fiedler, John Barth among them), the scholars looking nervously at
   writers, writers feeling sullen among all those Ph.D. types, all crammed
   together in a cinder-block Stalag 17 office, additionally huddled together
   because the university has no connection with the town of Buffalo—and
   even more intensely huddled together because the Life of the Mind is being
   carried on in brutal weather and with an ugliness of surroundings that took
   imagination to produce—one is often overwhelmed by the sheer weight of
   the paranoia."
2. Personal communication from writer.
3. "The Empty-Headed Blues: Black Rebellion and White Reaction," *The
   Public Interest,* Spring 1968, pp. 3–16.
4. This was a good beginning but only that. Ratification occurred only two
   months after Meyerson arrived and almost a year before the plan was
   implemented. The senate that ratified the plan was not truly representative,
   and the plan itself was barely understood. Basically it was a "paper plan"
   with virtually no commitment except to a vague and poetic vision.
5. This was true of university-community relations in 1970. From all I have
   heard about Ketter's administration, the current UB president has worked

hard and successfully at reviving sympathy and support for the university among the Buffalo community.

SEARCHING FOR THE "PERFECT" UNIVERSITY PRESIDENT

1. Booz, Allen had actually created the presidential vacancy, it seems. It was Booz, Allen that recommended that Miller be moved up from president to chancellor as part of an administrative reorganization plan commissioned earlier by the Northwestern board.
2. A survey reveals that in 1939, faculty were consulted in the selection of 29 percent of the college presidents then in office. By 1955, that figure had risen to 47 percent. By 1965, faculty were formally represented by a committee to advise the board in 65 percent of the cases.
3. Confidentiality was actually poor, I've learned since. A member of the search committee told me that he was amazed at the number of Northwestern faculty who could recount the details of any meeting of the committee. Alumni talked even more openly. An alumnus broke the story of a three-way race to the *Daily Northwestern*.

DEMOCRACY IS INEVITABLE

1. The original essay appeared in the March-April 1965 issue of the *Harvard Business Review*.
2. W. G. Bennis. *On Becoming a Leader*. New York: Addison-Wesley, 1989.
3. P. Slater. *A Dream Deferred*. Boston: Beacon Press, 1991.
4. J. Sniezek and R. Henry. "Accuracy and Confidence in Group Judgment." *Organizational Behavior and Human Decision Process Journal*, 1989, pp. 1–28.
5. F. Capra. *The Web of Life*. New York: Anchor, 1996.
6. M. Rosenblum. "Growing Prosperity, Hope Changes the Face of Africa." Associated Press, Nov. 31, 1997.
7. R. T. Eisler. *The Chalice and the Blade*. New York: Harper & Row, 1987; *Sacred Pleasure*. San Francisco: Harper San Francisco, 1996.
8. M. Gimbutas. *The Goddesses and Gods of Old Europe*. Berkeley: University of California Press, 1974; J. Mellaart, *Catal Huyuk*, New York: McGraw-Hill, 1967; J. Mellaart, *The Neolithic of the Near East*, New York: Scribners, 1975; N. Platon, *Crete*, Geneva: Nagel Publishers, 1996.
9. R. T. Eisler. *Sacred Pleasure*. San Francisco: Harper San Francisco, 1996.
10. P. Slater. *A Dream Deferred*. Boston: Beacon Press, 1991.
11. E. E. Lawler. *From the Ground Up*. San Francisco: Jossey-Bass, 1996.
12. W. Adams and J. W. Brock. *The Bigness Complex*. New York: Pantheon, 1986.

13. For a complete review of this work see W. G. Bennis, "Effecting Organizational Change: A New Role for the Behavioral Scientist," *Administrative Science Quarterly,* September, 1963; and C. Argyris, "T-Groups for Organizational Effectiveness," *Harvard Business Review,* March-April, 1964.

14. W. G. Bennis, "Toward a 'Truly' Scientific Management: The Concept of Organizational Health," *General Systems Yearbook,* 1962, p. 273.

15. It would be a mistake to ignore the fact that there are many tasks for which the military-bureaucratic model is best suited, but it is precisely these tasks which are most vulnerable to automation.

16. N. Sanford, "Social Science and Social Reform," Presidential Address for SPSSI, Washington, D.C., August 28, 1958.

17. J. R. Oppenheimer, "On Science and Culture," *Encounter,* October, 1962, p. 5.

18. J. R. Killian, Jr., "The Crisis in Research," *The Atlantic Monthly,* March, 1963, p. 71.

19. M. Gardner, *Relativity for the Million,* New York: Macmillan, 1962, p. 11.

20. For a fuller discussion of this trend, see T. Levitt, "Marketing Myopia," *Harvard Business Review,* July-August, 1960, p. 45.

21. M. McLuhan, *Understanding the Media,* New York: McGraw-Hill, 1964, p. 251.

22. I. Edman (ed.), *The Philosophy of Santayana,* New York: Random House, 1936.

23. Cf. O. Handlin, *The Uprooted,* Boston: Little, Brown, 1952, pp. 252–253; and K. Geiger, "Changing Political Attitudes in Totalitarian Society: A Case Study of the Role of the Family," *World Politics,* January, 1956, pp. 187–205.

THE COMING DEATH OF BUREAUCRACY

1. Let me propose an hypothesis to explain this tendency. It rests on the assumption that man has a basic need for transcendental experiences, somewhat like the psychological rewards which William James claimed religion provided—"an assurance of safety and a temper of peace, and in relation to others, a preponderance of living affections." Can it be that as religion has become secularized, less transcendental, men search for substitutes such as close interpersonal relationships, psychoanalysis—even the release provided by drugs such as LSD?

COMMENTARY ON "THE END OF THE GREAT MAN"

1. J. R. Hackman & R. E. Walton, "Leading Groups in Organizations," in *Designing Effective Workgroups,* edited by P. S. Goodman et al. (San Francisco:

Jossey-Bass, 1986), p. 75; quoting J. E. McGrath, *Leadership Behavior: Some Requirements for Leadership Training* (Washington, D.C.: U.S. Civil Service Commission, 1962), p. 5.

2. L. Hill, "Leadership as Collective Genius," in *Management 21C: New Visions for the New Millennium,* edited by Subir Chowdry (New York: Financial Times Publishing, 1999).

WHEN TO RESIGN

1. Written by Barbara Garson, this political satire from 1967 conflates Shakespeare's *Macbeth* and the LBJ presidency. The play was a bicoastal hit, with such characters as the Earl of Warren and the Egg of Head.

2. For many reasons, notably my decision to retain another administrative position while resigning the acting post. The distinction between the positions was clear only to other members of the administration, and the public generally interpreted my equivocal exit as a halfhearted protest.

THE ALCHEMY OF LEADERSHIP

1. Frank Rich, "The Father Figure," *New York Times Magazine,* 30 September 2001.

2. Gerald Posner, "I Was Wrong About Bush," *Wall Street Journal,* 25 September 2001.

3. Ibid.

4. Leo Braudy, *The Frenzy of Renown: Fame and Its History* (New York: Vintage, 1997).

5. D. T. Max, "The Making of the Speech," *New York Times Magazine,* 2 October 2001, 32ff.

6. Drake Beam Morin Consulting Co., Inc., "CEO Turnover and Job Security: A Special Research Report" (Boston: Drake Beam Morin, 1999), 6.

7. Saul Bellow, *Ravelstein* (New York: Penguin, 2001).

8. "New Formula: To Fix Coca-Cola, Daft Sets Out To Get Relationships Right," *Wall Street Journal,* 23 June 2001, 1.

9. "The Year in Business," *Fortune,* 24 December 2001, 142.

10. Leslie Kaufman, "Question of Style in Warnaco's Fall," *New York Times,* 6 May 2001.

11. Richard Finneran (ed.), *The Collected Poems of W.B. Yeats* (New York: Scribner, 1996).

12. William James, *The Letters of William James,* Volume 1 (New York: Longmans Green, 1878).

13. C. Wright Mills, *The Sociological Imagination* (New York: Oxford University Press, 1959), 165–194.

14. Derived from Warren Bennis and Patricia Ward Biederman, *Organizing Genius* (Reading, MA: Addison-Wesley, 1997), 172.
15. William James, *The Letters of William James*.
16. F. O. Mathiessen and K. B. Murdock, *Notebooks of Henry James* (New York: Oxford University Press, 1961).
17. George E. Vaillant, *Adaptation to Life* (Cambridge, MA: Harvard University Press, 1995), 120.

THE CHALLENGES OF LEADERSHIP IN THE MODERN WORLD

1. R. J. Sternberg, "A Systems Model of Leadership: WICS," *American Psychologist* 62 (2007): 34–42.
2. B. Kellerman, *Bad Leadership: What It Is, How It Happens, Why It Matters* (Boston: Harvard Business Press, 2007).
3. J. Lipman-Blumen, *The Allure of Toxic Leaders: Why We Follow Destructive Bosses and Corrupt Politicians—and How We Can Survive Them* (New York: Oxford University Press, 2006).
4. Sternberg, "A Systems Model of Leadership."
5. B. J. Avolio, "Promoting More Integrative Strategies for Leadership Theory Building," *American Psychologist* 62 (2007): 25–33.
6. Sternberg, "A Systems Model of Leadership."

COMMENTARY ON "INTRODUCTION TO *THE ART OF FOLLOWERSHIP*" AND "FOLLOWERS MAKE GOOD LEADERS GOOD"

1. *Merriam-Webster's Collegiate Dictionary*, 11th ed., s.v. "follower."
2. Warren Bennis, "Introduction," in *The Art of Followership: How Great Followers Create Great Leaders and Organizations*, edited by Ronald Riggio, Ira Chaleff, and Jean Lipman-Blumen (San Francisco: Jossey-Bass, 2008), pp. xxiii–xxvii.
3. *Merriam-Webster's Collegiate Dictionary*, 11th ed., s.v. "franchise."
4. Jean Lipman-Blumen, "Toxic Leadership: When Grand Illusions Masquerade as Noble Visions," *Leader to Leader* no. 36 (Spring 2005): 29–36. See also Jean Lipman-Blumen, *The Allure of Toxic Leaders: Why We Follow Destructive Bosses and Corrupt Politicians—and How We Can Survive Them* (New York: Oxford University Press, 2005).
5. Joseph Rost, *Leadership for the Twenty-First Century* (Westport, Conn.: Praeger, 1993).
6. Joseph Rost, "Followership: An Outmoded Concept," in Riggio, Chaleff, and Lipman-Blumen, *The Art of Followership*, p. 57.
7. Rost, "Followership," p. 56.

8. Rost, "Followership," p. 57.

9. Jean Lipman-Blumen, *The Connective Edge: Leading in an Interdependent World* (San Francisco: Jossey-Bass, 1996).

10. John Gardner, *On Leadership* (Boston: Harvard Business Press, 1990).

11. Ira Chaleff, *The Courageous Follower* (San Francisco: Berrett-Koehler, 2003). (originally published 1995.)

12. Edwin Hollander, *Inclusive Leadership: The Essential Leader-Follower Relationship* (Florence, Ky.: Routledge, 2008); Lipman-Blumen, *The Connective Edge;* Craig L. Pearce and Jay A. Conger, Eds., *Shared Leadership: Reframing the Hows and Whys of Leadership* (Thousand Oaks, Calif.; Sage, 2003); Rost, *Leadership for the Twenty-First Century.*

13. Thomas S. Kuhn, *The Structure of Scientific Revolutions* (Chicago: University of Chicago Press, 1996).

THE NEW TRANSPARENCY

1. James Taranto, editor of OpinionJournal.com, calls Drudge's a "proto-blog" in Tunku Varadarajan's "Happy Blogiversary," *Wall Street Journal,* July 14–15, 2007.

2. Tony Perry, "Navy to Mask Coronado's Swastika-Shaped Barracks," latimes.com, September 26, 2007, and "Swastika Shaped Building Oops," ker-plunk.blogspot.com, September 28, 2007.

3. Joel Kurtzman and Glenn Yago, *Global Edge: Using the Opacity Index to Manage the Risks of Cross-Border Business* (Boston: Harvard Business School Press, 2007), p. ix.

4. Joel Kurtzman, Glenn Yago, and Triphon Phumiwasana, "The Opacity Index 2004" (Cambridge, Mass.: MIT Sloan Management Review, October 2004). Available online: www.opacityindex.com/opacity_index.pdf. Access date: December 29, 2007.

5. Gordon Fairclough, "China Rescues 'Slave' Workers," *Wall Street Journal,* June 16–17, 2007.

6. Geoffrey Fowler and Juying Qin, "China Moves to Boost Transparency, but Much Is Kept Hidden," *Wall Street Journal,* April 25, 2007.

7. Geoffrey Fowler and Juying Qin, "China Pushes Openness," *Wall Street Journal,* March 1, 2007.

8. *Business Week* article in *Chindia: How China and India Are Revolutionizing Global Business,* edited by Pete Engardio (New York: McGraw-Hill, 2007).

9. Katrina vanden Heuvel, "Editor's Cut: Bloggers of Iran," May 30, 2005. Available online: www.thenation.com/blogs/edcut?bid=7&pid=2947. Access date: December 28, 2007.

10. Seth Mydans, "Monks Are Silenced, and for Now, the Web Is, Too," *New York Times,* October 4, 2007.

11. Michael Cornfield quoted in Tom Zeller, "Are Bloggers Setting the Agenda? It Depends on the Scandal," *New York Times,* May 23, 2005.

12. David Kirkpatrick and Daniel Roth, "There's No Escaping the Blog," *Fortune,* January 10, 2005.

13. Marcia Stepanek, "Expert Voice: John Patrick on Weblogs," *CIO Insight,* November 1, 2003.

14. I described this experiment earlier in "Share the Power," *CIO Insight,* March 1, 2004.

15. The late Harold J. Leavitt, author, management expert, and friend, wrote an influential dissertation on the experiment.

16. Also described in "Share the Power."

17. Joe Nocera, "Want to Rally the Troops? Try Candor," *New York Times,* February 11, 2006.

18. Stepanek, "Expert Voice."

19. Adam Liptak, "Web Sites Expose Informants and Justice Dept. Raises Flag," *New York Times,* May 22, 2007.

20. Joe Drape, "Out in Front but Often Overlooked," *New York Times,* September 26, 2007.

21. Trevor Butterworth, "Blogged Off," *Financial Times,* February 18–19, 2006.

22. David Kirkpatrick, "Facebook's Plan to Hook Up the World," *Fortune,* June 11, 2007.

23. Alice Mathias, "The Fakebook Generation," *New York Times,* October 6, 2007.

24. Harold Evans, "A Spurious Megaphone" in Tunku Varadarajan's "Happy Blogiversary."

25. Su Hyun Lee, "Revelations of False Credentials Shake South Korea," *New York Times,* September 1, 2007.

ABOUT THE AUTHORS

Warren Bennis is the founding chairman of USC's Leadership Institute, distinguished professor of business administration at the USC Marshall School of Business, and advisory board chairman of the Center for Public Leadership at Harvard's Kennedy School. One of the world's foremost experts on leadership, Bennis has written thirty books and numerous articles on leadership, change, and creative collaboration. His book *Leaders* was designated by the *Financial Times* as one of the top fifty business books of all time, and he received a Pulitzer Prize nomination for *An Invented Life. Geeks & Geezers*, coauthored with Bob Thomas and republished in paperback as *Leading for a Lifetime* (2007), examines the differences and similarities between leaders of seventy and older and thirty-two and younger. In 2005, HarperCollins published his series of conversations with the late Bob Townsend, *Reinventing Leadership*. His best-selling book *On Becoming a Leader*, republished in 2009 on the occasion of its twentieth anniversary, has been named one of the one hundred best business books of all times and considered the top leadership book.

Prior to his tenure at USC, Bennis spent eleven years as a university administrator, first as provost at SUNY-Buffalo and then as president of the University of Cincinnati. He has consulted for many Fortune 500 companies and has served as an adviser to five U.S. presidents. In May 2000, the *Financial Times* referred to Bennis as "the professor who established leadership as a respectable academic field." *Forbes Magazine* referred to him as the "dean of leadership gurus." In 2007, *Business Week* named Bennis as one of the top ten most influential thought leaders. In World War II, at the age of nineteen, he led an infantry platoon in Germany. He received his Ph.D. from the Massachusetts Institute of Technology and his bachelor of arts in psychology and business from Antioch College.

Patricia Ward Biederman, a former staff writer at the *Los Angeles Times* and the *Atlanta Journal Constitution*, is a prize-winning reporter and columnist. A long-time collaborator with Warren Bennis, she coauthored the national best seller *Organizing Genius: The Secrets of Creative Collaboration*.

The authors are grateful for the contributions of:

Marie Dolittle, Warren's administrative assistant, for her intelligence, generosity of spirit, and remarkable patience when confronted with the phrase, "Oh, and one more thing. . . . "

and

Eric Paul Biederman, for his insightful editing, thoughtful research, and deep understanding of the utility of humor, in both writing and the collaborative process. Laughter makes everything easier . . . even deadlines.

INDEX

CREDITS

GRATEFUL ACKNOWLEDGMENT IS MADE to the following for permission to reprint previously published materials.

"An Invented Life" is from *An Invented Life: Reflections on Leadership and Change,* by Warren Bennis. Copyright © 1993 by Warren Bennis Inc. Reprinted by permission of Basic Books, a member of Perseus Books Group.

"The Berkeley of the East" and "What Went Wrong" are from *The Leaning Ivory Tower,* by Warren Bennis, with Patricia Ward Biederman. Copyright © 1973 by Jossey-Bass, Inc., Publishers, an imprint of John Wiley & Sons. Reprinted with permission.

"Searching for the 'Perfect' University President," by Warren Bennis, with Patricia Ward Biederman, is from *Atlantic Monthly,* April 1971. Reprinted by permission of the author.

"Foreword to *The Age of Heretics*" is from *The Age of Heretics: A History of the Radical Thinkers Who Reinvented Corporate Management,* by Art Kleiner. Copyright © 2008 by Art Kleiner. Published by Jossey-Bass Inc., Publishers, an imprint of John Wiley & Sons. Reprinted with permission.

"Democracy Is Inevitable," by Warren G. Bennis and Philip Slater, is reprinted by permission of *Harvard Business Review* from the September/October 1990 issue. Copyright © 1990 by the Harvard Business Publishing Corporation; all rights reserved.

"Death of Bureaucracy" is from *Managing the Dream: Reflections on Leadership and Change,* by Warren G. Bennis. Copyright © 2000 by Warren Bennis Inc. Reprinted by permission of Basic Books, a member of Perseus Books Group.

"The End of the Great Man" is from *Organizing Genius: The Secrets of Creative Collaboration,* by Warren Bennis and Patricia Ward Biederman. Copyright © 1997 by Warren Bennis and Patricia Ward Biederman. Reprinted by permission of Basic Books, a member of Perseus Books Group.

"The Pornography of Everyday Life" is from the *New York Times,* November 28, 1976. Reprinted by permission of the author.

"Winning and Losing" first appeared in the journal *Executive Excellence,* July, 1988. It was included in the collection *Managing People Is

Like Herding Cats by Warren Bennis (Executive Excellence Books, 2000). Reprinted with permission of Executive Excellence Publishing. Visit www.LeaderExcel.com.

"Lessons from Larry" is from *Business Week,* March 6, 2006. Reprinted by permission of the author.

"A Corporate Fear of Too Much Truth" is from the *New York Times,* February 17, 2002. Reprinted by permission of the author.

"When to Resign" is from *Esquire* magazine, June 1972, adapted from *The Leaning Ivory Tower,* by Warren Bennis, with Patricia Ward Biederman. Copyright © 1973 by Jossey-Bass, Inc., Publishers. Reprinted by permission of the author.

"March of Folly Redux: Iraq" is printed here by permission of the author.

"Learning Some Basic Truisms About Leadership" is from *Why Leaders Can't Lead,* by Warren Bennis. Copyright © 1989 by Warren Bennis, Inc. Published by Jossey-Bass Inc., Publishers, an imprint of John Wiley & Sons. Reprinted by permission of the author.

"Understanding the Basics" is from *On Becoming a Leader,* by Warren Bennis. Copyright © 2003 by Warren Bennis, Inc. Reprinted by permission of Basic Books, a member of Perseus Books Group.

"Deploying Yourself: Strike Hard, Try Everything" is from *On Becoming a Leader,* by Warren Bennis. Copyright © 2003 by Warren Bennis, Inc. Reprinted by permission of Basic Books, a member of Perseus Books Group.

"Judgment Trumps Experience," by Warren Bennis and Noel Tichy, is from the *Wall Street Journal,* November 29, 2007, p. A19. Copyright © 2007 by Dow Jones & Company, Inc. Reproduced with permission of Dow Jones & Company, Inc. via the Copyright Clearance Center.

"The Crucibles of Authentic Leadership" is from *The Nature of Leadership,* edited by Robert Sternberg, John Antonakis, and Anna T. Cianciolo. Copyright © 2004 Sage Publications, Inc. Reproduced with permission of Sage Publications Inc., via the Copyright Clearance Center.

"The Alchemy of Leadership" is reprinted by permission of Harvard Business Press from *Geeks & Geezers: How Era, Values, and Defining Moments Shape Leaders,* by Warren G. Bennis and Robert J. Thomas. Copyright © 2002 Accenture LLP. Published by Harvard Business Publishing Corporation; all rights reserved.

"Epilogue to *On Becoming a Leader*" is from the 2009 edition of *On Becoming a Leader,* by Warren Bennis. Copyright © 2009 by Warren Bennis, Inc. Reprinted by permission of Basic Books, a member of Perseus Books Group.